MOVING PICTURES

Moving Pictures

A New Theory of Film
Genres, Feelings,
and Cognition

TORBEN GRODAL

CLARENDON PRESS · OXFORD

Oxford University Press, Great Clarendon Street, Oxford OX2 6DP

Oxford New York

Athens Auckland Bangkok Bogotá Buenos Aires Calcutta
Cape Town Chennai Dar es Salaam Delhi Florence Hong Kong Istanbul
Karachi Kuala Lumpur Madrid Melbourne Mexico City Mumbai
Nairobi Paris São Paulo Singapore Taipei Tokyo Toronto Warsaw

and associated companies in
Berlin Ibadan

Oxford is a registered trade mark of Oxford University Press

Published in the United States by
Oxford University Press Inc., New York

© Torben Grodal 1997

First published 1997
First published in paperback 1999

British Library Cataloguing in Publication Data
Data available

Library of Congress Cataloging in Publication Data
Data available
ISBN 0-19-815983-8

1 3 5 7 9 10 8 6 4 2

Typeset by Hope Services (Abingdon) Ltd.
Printed in Great Britain
on acid-free paper by
Bookcraft Ltd.,
Midsomer Norton, Somerset

Acknowledgements

The present book (and its embryonic form, the prepublication *Cognition, Emotion and Visual Fiction*, Copenhagen 1994) has been in preparation for several years, and I would like to express my gratitude to the people who have rendered assistance and inspiration. Carol Clover was among my first audience at UC Berkeley when the work was still in embryonic form, while a number of people at UCLA, and especially Nick Browne, provided me with hospitality when the manuscript had its final revision before publication. Peter Madsen and Martin Zerlang made valuable comments on the first draft. My colleagues at the University of Copenhagen Department of Film and Media Studies have provided a stimulating environment, and Peter Schepelern has helped to eliminate factual errors. Christian Metz, David Bordwell, Noël Carroll, and Paul Messaris have provided inspiration, comments, and stimulating counter-arguments. Edvard Branigan, Murray Smith, and especially Peter Larsen have made very constructive in-depth criticisms of the manuscript, for which I am greatly indebted. Marion Fewell has provided invaluable help by meticulously correcting my English text word by word, and often her linguistic revision has led to a clarification of content. I furthermore wish to thank the editors at Oxford University Press, Andrew Lockett and Michael Belson, for their helpfulness; the copy-editor, Christina Malkowska Zaba, for rigorous copy-editing; and the Faculty of the Humanities at the University of Copenhagen, for financial support in the linguistic revision of the book. Last but not least, Birgit Grodal has shown me the beauty of scientific perseverance and cognition, and has given me emotional support on my journey through moving pictures.

Contents

Introduction

To picture emotions must be the central aim of the photoplay.

Hugo Münsterberg[1]

The purpose of this book is to describe the experience of viewing visual fiction and the way in which this experience is created by the interaction between fiction and viewer. The word 'experience' is used to indicate a 'holistic' approach to the ways in which we view visual fiction. The film experience is made up of many activities: our eyes and ears pick up and analyze image and sound, our minds apprehend the story, which resonates in our memory; furthermore, our stomach, heart, and skin are activated in empathy with the story situations and the protagonists' ability to cope. Different fictions activate and foreground different aspects of the psychosomatic processes in our embodied minds. A change in some aspects, of a given visual fiction will influence the experience of other aspects and the framework for this interaction is the way in which our embodied mind works. It is a central aim of this book to describe the relations between the cognitive and the emotional aspects of this experience.

My hypothesis is therefore that cognitive and perceptual processes are intimately linked with emotional processes within a functionally unified psychosomatic whole. Because visual fictions are experienced in time, a description of the interaction between cognition and emotion will be concerned with temporal flow. The theories and models for describing the flow of experiences must be brought together from several disciplines: film theory, first and foremost; and general aesthetics, narrative theory, neuroscience, physiology, and cognitive science.

The film scholar David Bordwell has stated: 'I am assuming that a spectator's comprehension of the film's narrative is theoretically separable from his or her emotional responses. (I suspect that psychoanalytic models may be well suited for explaining emotional aspects of film viewing)' (1986: 30). To separate comprehension and emotional response, however is not easily achieved. If a person watches Dreyer's *La Passion de Jeanne d'Arc* and enjoys Jeanne's torture, has this viewer then comprehended the film but made a problematic emotional response? Is it possible to 'comprehend' the narrative in *Casablanca* or *Psycho* without any idea of the types of emotions cued in the films and their relative strength? The answer seems to be no: the emotional response is just as much a part of the narrative as are the 'cognitive'

[1] Münsterberg (1970: 48).

inferences for our understanding of the intradiegetic relations, as well as for our understanding of the cued type of 'distance' to the diegetic world. If Godard uses 'self-conscious' devices in *Pierrot le Fou,* this has implications for the type of emotional response we are supposed to feel when watching love-scenes or killings. Emotions 'take place' in the 'body–mind' interior of the viewer; but so do cognitions, and both represent reactions to states and sequences of acts in the film. There is no reason to believe that it is easier to predict the viewer's cognitive reactions to the film than his emotional ones.

EMOTIONS, EMOTIONAL MODALITIES, AND GENRES OF VISUAL FICTION

A holistic framework for describing cognition and emotions in visual fiction necessitates descriptions on several levels. The description encompasses a physiological level (heartbeat, sweat, and so forth), a human being's mental state, and usually also a scenario, a story-situation that defines cognition and the emotions. Some feelings may be generated from interior sources, but in visual fiction even feelings with interior sources, like memory, have to be cued by some exterior means. The superior anthropomorph level of scenes and story is the primary format for the interaction of body, emotions, and cognitions. The holistic approach therefore expands a structural and a cognitive narrative analysis in order to describe the way in which cognitions, emotions, and feelings interact in the narrative flow. Important aspects of such an analysis are the way in which situations relate to the intentions and abilities of the protagonists, as the interpretation of such phenomena has a strong influence on the experience (for example, whether a situation is being felt as fatalistic, tragic, or as expressing will and empowerment).

Feelings and emotions are motivational forces, but they also represent a set of 'experienced tones' characterizing different holistic body-mind configurations in our experience of everyday life and of visual fiction. Fictions are experienced as, for example, sad, funny, romantic, or melancholic. They are also experienced with some *modal* qualities: tense, intense, saturated; whereas terms like 'lyrical' or 'sublime' may be conceived as lying somewhere between valorized feelings like 'sadness' and modal qualities like 'saturated'. The emotional 'toning' of experience is not a bounded phenomenon like the motivational aspect, which takes place only in connection with a given agent, time, situation, and preference-and-goal structure, but is a continuous temporal phenomenon, although tones and modal qualities fluctuate.

The affective toning is an essential feature of consciousness, but has an extra prominence in temporal arts, probably because the mental processes cued in viewers possess a salience and vividness 'larger than life', in the sense that cognitions, emotions, memories, and acts are constructed there in a more concentrated and characteristic way than is typical in everyday life. The emotions and the emotional toning play a very important role in our preferences for visual fiction. A given viewer at a given time will often want to see something funny, lyrical, tense, thrilling, sublime, or tear-jerking. One prominent way (among several others) of categorizing visual fiction in relation to consumer information is by emotion evoked: horror, comedy, melodrama, or thriller.

A central purpose of this book is to investigate the way in which emotional tone and modal qualities vary in relation to narrative structure and to the mental processes activated. Different types of film emphasize different types of mental processes. In an 'action film' there is a close relation between perceptions, emotions, and acts; in a 'lyrical film' perceptions, emotions, and memories are often cued without strong explicit connections to acts. Horror films present perceptions and emotions in relation to passive protagonists and an aversive excitement; melodramas of passion also present perceptions and emotions in connection with passive agents, but linked with a more 'symbiotic' excitement. In Chapter 2 I shall also describe a system of modalization using four main terms: 'intensities', 'saturations', 'tensities', and 'emotivities', connected with the ways in which the brain-mind processes audiovisual phenomena.

My hypothesis is, then, that there is a systematic relation between the embodied mental processes and configurations activated in a given type of visual fiction and the emotional 'tone' and 'modal qualities' of the experienced affects, emotions, and feelings in the viewer. Prototypical genres of visual fiction will evoke typical tones and modalities, as analyzed in the following chapters.

There is a traditional objection to dealing extensively with the emotions of an artwork by describing its impact on an addressee: if the emotions are closely related to other structural features of the visual fiction, why describe the emotional impact on the viewer, instead of just describing the emotional structure of the artwork? The emotions, it might be said, should be implied in the structures and meanings of the artwork itself. This was the position taken by new criticism, as explicitly stated by Wimsatt (1954; cf. also Culler 1983: 35 f.). The premise for this position was that artwork was supposed to be autonomous and describable without any consideration of addresser or addressee. A simple argument against this position is that feelings and emotions are states and processes in humans, not in texts. Although it may be feasible to describe features in an artwork without reference to the way in which it is processed and experienced in the mind, many aesthetic discussions become unnecessarily complicated by this procedure. Hermeneutically and phenomenologically inspired reception analysis, such as that carried out by Jauss (1982) and Iser (1978), for example, and cognitive reception analysis as

Bordwell, have convincingly demonstrated the validity and necessity of describing the reception process as one taking place both in time and in an addressee.

Meanwhile, these approaches are mostly directed at explaining the cognitive aspects of reception, not the close interrelation between cognition and emotion in fiction. Fictions are not only about constructing a product, or 'meanings', out of perceptions. Sensuousness and emotionality can only be described according to theoretical ideas about the ways in which cognitions are related to other psychophysical processes. The reason that 'problem-solving' in chess is different from problem-solving in, for example, crime fiction is because of different types of links between cognitive and emotional functions.

In emotion research there are two extreme theoretical positions employed in describing emotions, together with a number of different positions that fall somewhere between these two poles (see Gross 1987: 431 ff.). One school, following James and Lange's theory of emotions, asserts that emotions *are* identical with the bodily reactions in a given situation. Another claims that emotions are mental-cognitive states, following, for example, Cannon's (1970) assertion that emotions rely on subcortical structures. Yet others prefer different mediations, following Schachter (1971: chs. 1, 4), for instance, in holding that while a cognitive evaluation of situations is very important for emotions, 'full-flavoured' emotions need the resonance of bodily reactions. The present book steers a middle course, asserting that the emotions cued by visual fictions rely heavily on cognitive evaluations, but that the strength of the experience also relies on the body activation. Ortony, Clore, and Collins, among others, have proposed a purely cognitive approach to emotions, defining them as 'valenced reactions to events, agents, or objects, with their particular nature being determined by the way in which the eliciting situation is construed'(1990: 13). This definition does not hint at the bodily basis of emotions, but defines it in exclusively cognitive terms.

The word 'emotion' is used in this book as the prototypical term within a broader category of phenomena along with other prominent members, such as feelings, affects, and drives. Efforts to make strict definitions of emotion-words have as yet failed. Sometimes the distinction between the terms is one of intensity: emotions are stronger than feelings. Sometimes the terms are used to distinguish between object-directed and non-object-directed qualities. Feelings are often non-object-directed (I feel sad, happy, and so on), whereas emotions often have an object-directed quality; strong emotions like love, hate, or jealousy are often object-directed, but romantic feelings are often non-object-directed. Following for the most part Izard's definitions (1991: 54) as a guideline, one might say that drives are motivational states brought about by tissue change or tissue deficit and having a strong innate, 'instinctual' component (such as hunger, or thirst). Emotions are complex phenomena having neural, motor-expressive, and experiential components, and they may also have an innate component. A phenomenon like sex has drive aspects as well as emotional aspects. Affect is a general non-specific term for emotions and drives. Feelings are an aspectualization of emotions, and tend to be linked to interior states rather than being related to objects.

EMOTIONS AND PREVIOUS FILM STUDIES

For the last thirty years the dominant framework for understanding emotions and affects within film and media studies has been psychoanalysis; for film-makers, the use of psychoanalytic explanations in films started as early as sixty years ago. Mainstream psychology, whether based on physiology or cognition, has had very little impact on humanistic film and media studies, except in descriptions of visual perception. It is not the purpose of this book to give a general assessment of the achievements and shortcomings of psychoanalysis, such as its many valuable contributions to the understanding of the importance of childhood in emotional development, although I shall comment on specific uses of psychoanalysis in explaining visual fiction. But psychoanalytic theories describe desires and emotions in relation to cognitive functions within a romantic, dualist model incompatible with a theory that describes cognition and emotion as aspects of a functionally unified psychosomatic whole. According to psychoanalytic theory, man is torn between id and superego, between principles of pleasure and principles of reality. As a consequence of this, visual fictions are often described as if they were battlefields: some aspects of fictions are expressions of feelings, desires, or the body, and they confront the rational order, the law, the phallus, or the centred bourgeois or Cartesian subject. Emotions become alternative 'cognitions'. Reason, the reality principle, or the secondary processes demand that two plus two equals four; desire, emotions, or primary processes say that the sum might be any given number. The Cartesian subject tries to establish his priorities; the alternative subject enjoys living in an eternal flux.

Dualistic theories are problematic for many reasons, of which I shall present only the ecological/evolutionary one. The cognitive skills of humans have not been developed in opposition to their emotions and their bodies; on the contrary, they have been developed to carry out the preferences of the body-mind totality. The evolution of cognitive skills has pragmatic origins: it is easier to obtain food and avoid danger if we have precise cognitive maps of the world than it is if the world is just an eternal deconstructed flux. The emotional ties among humans have developed because such affective bonding has had a positive ecological value. The cognitive processes, which Freud and others call 'secondary' processes, are, from the point of view of evolution, the primary ones, which we share with the rest of the animal kingdom because we want to perceive and represent the world in such a way that by actions we can implement our body-brain preferences in an optimal way. It is not because fathers want their small sons to stop wishing for sex with their mothers that we can distinguish a tiger from a cat, and that we fear the first and stroke the second, but because, without this distinction, we will probably die. The processes which lead to some unambiguity in representations are not caused by 'reality principles' linked to 'patriarchal' procedures, but by the ecological advantage for women and men of avoiding tigers or cats. I therefore remain unconvinced when psychoanalytic film theoreticians like Metz (1982: 56 *passim*) describe the consciously experienced story-world as a secondary aspect of the cinematic experience, or when identifications with characters are called a secondary identification. The primary film experience should be linked to the way in which the spectator relates to the film-image *per se* as a mirror-image of himself. The film-image should be imaginary, an image of something absent, although the viewer denies this (analogous to a fetishist denial of castration). Imagination is here platonically understood as something that has no function in ordinary life except as a cause of illusion. However, as I shall discuss more extensively later, imagination and 'mental models' are indispensable tools for higher mental life and for a sophisticated representation of and interaction with the world.

To emphasize that our embodied brain is a product of evolution is not an argument for a normative 'ecological' aesthetic, in which evolution has dictated some optimal ways of representation; for example, film-makers or viewers will often (and for good reason) prefer ambiguous representations to unambiguous ones. There is, however, an argument for taking our point of departure in consciousness and in the 'mimetic' story-world when we describe cognition and emotion in visual fiction. Visual fiction is viewed in a conscious state, and is mostly about human beings perceiving, acting, and feeling in, or in relation to, a visible and audible world. The viewer's experience and the phenomena experienced often demand explanations that imply non-conscious activities; but the emotions and cognitions must be explained in relation to conscious mental states and processes. For evolutionary reasons, it is improbable that the way phenomena appear in consciousness is just an illusion caused by certain quite different non-conscious agents and mechanisms. The consciously felt experience during film-viewing has to be described, explained, and analyzed. In using this formulation I partially adopt the phenomenology of, for instance, Merleau-Ponty (1962), that perception and consciousness have a 'facticity' which is our point of departure in understanding reality, although I do not accept the phenomenological separation of description and analysis.[2] One important aspect of visual fiction is the anthropomorph world

[2] Phenomenology overrates the possibilities of unmediated introspection and perception; cf. P. M. Churchland's emphasis on the 'Theory-Ladenness of All Perception' (1988: 79 f.). To

in which characters have intentions, plans, and will, and in which they act in a symbolically real time-space, have tender feelings, and are moved by emotions. The 'naïve' notions of what a 'film is about' cannot be explained away as merely illusory surface phenomena or as formal features of film art.

Many film theoreticians, however, using different, 'formalist' arguments, describe the film experience as being out of context both with the experienced world in general and with its connection to the experiencing viewer. The different features of films are described as 'devices' and 'style' (Russian formalism), 'narrative logic' (French structuralism), and 'style schemata' (Bordwell's and Thompson's neoformalist constructivism). A formalist description frequently adopts a two-step approach. The first step describes some salient features of a given set of artworks, and demonstrates the way in which they represent a formal pattern. The second step takes this formalism as an argument for a culturalist position (as these phenomena are formal patterns, they are historically specific aesthetic formulas or ideological constructs). The second step is polemically directed at those theoreticians like Bazin (1967, 1972) and Kracauer (1961) who advocate mimetic theories, for which some representations are more 'like reality' than others.

The first step is unproblematic: formal analysis has immensely increased our understanding of artworks, particularly those of visual fiction. The second step is, however, more difficult, because the formal patterns may be representations of prototypical ways in which our embodied minds relate to the world, and thus may be motivated in a stronger sense than by mere ideological motivation (Barthes) or by representing a historical style (Bordwell). The problems with a formalist description can be exemplified by Bordwell's description of classical Hollywood narration (1986). The description claims to overcome mimetic theories (no need to describe classical narration as 'transparent' (156)) as well as modernist theories (no need to describe classical narration as 'concealment of production' or '*discours* posing as *histoire*' (156)). Bordwell's main points about the classical style are that classical narration uses a limited set of film techniques as means to tell the story, which takes place in a coherent, consistent time and space (e.g. 162 f.). Because the films are made according to certain paradigms, he argues that 'this paradigmatic aspect makes the classical style, for all its "rules", not a timeless formula or recipe but a historically constrained set of more or less likely options' (164), in many respects a rephrasing of a modernist perspective on classical mimesis.

The classical style might, however, be a 'timeless formula' based on certain prototypical ways of making mental models of reality, and yet still be one

oppose an explanatory and objective research attitude (structuralism/semiotics) to a descriptive and immersed (experimental) research attitude (phenomenology) as undertaken by Andrew (1985: 627) is an unnecessary isolation of phenomenology; the phenomenological approach should have its strength in the effort to *describe and analyze* the phenomena of consciousness.

artistic option among several. If the way in which we cognitively process inter-subjective relations among humans is by making mental models of act-schemata and motive-schemata that are similar to those of a classical and a canonical narrative, and by making mental models of a coherent and consistent time and space, then classical Hollywood narration is not 'just' style, but is motivated by fundamental aspects of the mental architecture of humans.[3] Other types of representation (other 'styles') are evidently also compatible with this 'architecture'; many people appreciate avant-garde films in which there is no way of making unambiguous models of time, space, agents, acts, and motives. If these representations are intended to cue types of experience other than classical Hollywood narrative, there need be no problems in working with many different 'timeless formulas' serving different purposes, which nevertheless are produced for the first time at a certain point in history. When Bordwell treats different 'formulas' in connection with their historical first or most significant appearance, for example expressive or conative functions in connection with 'Historical-Materialist Narration' or representations of such matters as subjectivity in connection with 'Art-Cinema Narration', this does not exclude the possibility that their key representational devices are not just historical styles, but relate to fundamental formulas of consciousness. There is an obvious technical aspect to moving from a passive experience to an active communication of the experience in an intersubjective representation; but this does not exclude the historical significance of given sets of features having prominence at given periods.

The description of these 'formulas' as 'style' has possible implicit normative aspects, because 'style' is often understood to indicate certain formal, meaningless features, especially connected with purely visual perception. To make the modes of representations into 'styles', and to make perceptual features the essential features of film style, has implications for the role of emotions in visual fiction. Emotions will be made into a marginal element of the 'essential' stylistic aspects of the experience of film-art, to the extent that emotions are linked to certain narrative patterns and to certain anthropomorphic and mimetic features of the representation. In this book I shall show the close links between narrative and cognitive-emotional activation.

The description of narrative as something not essentially belonging to film is a position that is adopted implicitly by some realists. Kracauer describes the way in which many genres are popular 'for reasons which do not involve questions of aesthetic legitimacy' (1961: 38). For Kracauer, cinematic merits are linked to visual perception of the exterior world; the role of film is to 'document' the physical reality, including motion; and, although in principle he is for narrative film, this is not primarily in order to participate in the recon-

---

[3] The fundamental role of story-schemata as mental models has been described, for example, by Schank (1990).

struction of the associations and subjective experiences of inner life. Reality, 'nature', is something 'out there', to be perceived, documented, and worshipped. Brecht (1963: 22 ff.) fought against an 'Aristotelian' theatre which evokes emotions by its 'illusionistic' story. Although he advocated an 'epic' theatre, his use of the word 'epic' excluded many of the aspects traditionally associated with narrative, and influenced many film-makers and theoreticians into developing a negative relation to central narrative devices.

For many critics an ambivalence in relation to narrative goes hand-in-hand with a problematic relation to film as a temporal art. For some critics— Barthes (1981), among others—the transience of moving pictures even makes photography and stills more appealing than film, in which the viewers' perceptual and fantasmatic symbiosis with the images is continuously disrupted. Metz states (1974a: 21 f.) that presence of space and time is what is supposed in 'reality', and, as soon as it is 'narrated' or when two images are put together in succession, the presentic qualities disappear and images become language. Language is the model for temporal sequences of events, and this indicates the invented and constructed aspects of film. Language, the invented, is not fully real, although it may be perceived as real, and although narrative film is the central film form (cf. Metz 1974b: 96).[4]

Many film theories are implicitly or explicitly normative. It is, however, mandatory that the fictions are described without interference from normative criteria of dictating the way in which film, the world, or the human subject should ideally be. A theory of visual fiction or 'film as art' should describe all the different types of visual fiction, just as the different structural principles and effects in the viewer should be accounted for and explained. The perceptual, the cognitive, and the emotional, and the temporal as well as the spatial aspects, are *a priori* equally important aspects of the viewing experience. Many normative discussions of film are implicitly futile discussions about hierarchies of mental functions: some prefer 'perceptual' films; others prefer associative-memory-activating films; yet others like mental problem-solving. Film and television cue mental and bodily states in the viewer by means of representations that have some relation to their experience of a world beyond the media. Although the viewer is accessed by hearing and vision, this does not *per se* give these senses a privileged role in understanding what visual fiction is about, as they are intimately integrated with other types of experience. The function of perception by remote senses is to provide information analyzed cognitively and evaluated emotionally by means of

---

[4] For Mitry (1990: 78 *passim*; cf. also Andrew 1976: 191), film can be perceived as a framed image, as form and transcendence, as a window to a reality, and to the object as immanence. However, both ways of understanding the filmic image are based on an atemporal 'now'. Mitry extensively treats rhythm, *sujet*, and narration, and claims that, in film, space becomes subordinated to time (1990: 473); but his models of time, like 'rhythm', 'motion', and an equilibrium of orders, do not describe time as change, but time as '*durée*', just as the '*sujet*' ends up being meaning and image, not process and intentionality.

memory and cognition; and this will be the basis on which possible acts will be planned or executed. Although we receive our information by sight or sound, this activates many other mental processes, and it is not really possible to isolate perception from cognition, memory, emotion, and action, and our perception of 'space' is not independent of our concepts of active motion; our perception of objects is not independent of memories and emotional relations. A given percept, a given scene, exists as a phenomenon within a complex set of mental processes, and our understanding of 'reality' further depends on complex mental models.

The prototypical narrative film worships what Durgnat (1967) has called 'the mongrel muse', a fusion of many different phenomena from the other arts, and also from many different cultural, social, and psychological domains. Although some very specific cinematic conventions exist, large parts of our comprehension are, as pointed out by Bordwell (1989b: ch. 6), based on the heuristics of daily life. The exterior world and its representation in consciousness is a concrete interaction and fusion of many different phenomena, each having its own relative autonomy. The fiction film cues mental processes, in which perceptions, memories, emotions, and acts constantly interact. There is, however, a framework within which they interact: that of the narrative structure. Narrative structure specifies some basic relations between perceptions, emotions, and acts, and connects to fundamental ways in which we experience the world.

The name 'narrative', or its popular equivalent, 'story', might lead us to understand narrative as something verbal and something connected with speaking ('enunciation'). The reason for this is that, until the invention of audiovisual media, language was the prime intersubjective medium for narrative structures. But, as pointed out by the Russian formalists and by Jakobson (1960), a narrative can be represented in many different ways, such as ballet, opera, film, novel, and cartoon. This is because a narrative structure is a basic mental model that directly relates to the way in which humans make models of the relations between certain types of perceptions, memories, emotions, goals, and acts. These models need not be verbalized: a silent film can tell a story by showing protagonists perceiving objects and displaying emotional reactions, possibly followed by physical acts; and, in dreams, visual perceptions, emotions, and acts will often be linked without any verbalization. Furthermore, these models need not be 'representations', but functional relations. Mark Johnson (1987) has clearly shown the way in which images directly serve as the basis for establishing a cognitive relation between man and world. The images are not of something else, but a kind of 'software' which establishes and grounds our knowledge *in* the world. For this very reason, *film does not possess a semblance of reality;* it is not an illusion, as has been claimed by numerous film scholars and critics; on the contrary, *film is part of reality*, its experienced power connected to the way in which it cues experiences of central processes in the mind–body–world interaction. From this point of view, narrative structures or schemata are not in principle imposed from without, for instance on images, emotions, or memories, but are related to the synthetic-functional processes by which our different mental faculties and different aspects of the world are connected. This point of view need not conflict with Kant's (1790) famous definition of art as purposeless purposiveness, *Zweckmäßigkeit ohne Zweck*. Imagination, consisting of hypothetical simulations of possible relations and processes, is a central aspect of everyday life; the difference between art and everyday imagination is not one of kind but of degree, of direct 'interestedness', and of 'art' understood as superior know-how.

REDUCTIONISM, UNIVERSALISM, AND CULTURALISM

The present book includes neuropsychological and physiological as well as cultural backgrounds in its explanatory framework of visual fiction, and may provoke an objection that it is reductionist. Reductionism is mostly used as a pejorative term, to describe analytic procedures that supposedly 'reduce' complex mental phenomena to something more simple. The pejorative use of 'reductionism' is often caused by a problematic understanding of the relation between aesthetic experience and scientific explanation. The qualities of consciousness 'as such' are phenomenological facts, and if we want to 'experience' a given work of art, the only way to do so is to 'experience it', to expose ourselves to the work of art and to let it be (re)produced in our consciousness in all its complexity and specificity. The sensuous *qualia,* the 'experienced greenness' or the 'experienced pain', can be described and explained as a configuration of neurons firing in a certain way, caused by certain phenomena in the exterior world (for example, electromagnetic waves); but the descriptions do not evoke the experience of 'greenness' or that of 'pain'. To create aesthetic experience *per se* is an expert job for art and artists, not for science or scholarly studies of aesthetic phenomena. A scientific explanation is not a reproduction of, or simulation of, a given phenomenon, but a reduction of complex phenomena by means of less complex models, theories, and descriptions (although the result of the 'reduction' often leads to an insight into the complexity of what seem to be simple phenomena). To oppose 'reductionism' as such is to oppose scientific research as such. The purpose of scholarly studies of aesthetic phenomena is not to evoke the 'sensuous *qualia*' of consciousness, but to describe and explain them; and this is where my approach differs from phenomenology. The scientific explanations have not 'reduced' the phenomena, but, on the contrary, have enriched the phenomenologically 'felt' qualities with cognitive descriptions of the mechanisms that make these qualities possible.

Some would argue that the phenomenon of film is a specific one, so that film research should study this specificity, this *filmnost*, without reducing it to other areas of scientific research, such as psychology or sociology. The idea that each aesthetic field has its own exclusive object of analysis and its own methods was especially popular in the 1950s and the early 1960s. But such a conception of specificity leads to a much larger 'reduction'; a narrow definition would leave out most of the viewer's film experience. The experience does not take place in a vacuum; it is connected to broad cultural and social types of practices, and to psychosomatic phenomena. Therefore, the experience of visual fiction is not an 'exclusive' essence, but an 'inclusive' specificity: although almost all its constituent parts evolve from different spheres of human life, the sum of these elements results in some specific configurations, and many different methods are needed to understand the full complexity of the phenomenon, although some theoretical frameworks will be more central than others: the psychology of perception, narrative theory, and cultural history will be far more central than quantum physics (see Bordwell 1989*b*: 272). The need for and benefit of close interdisciplinary cooperation in the humanities has been acknowledged increasingly in the last fifteen years by the two expanding paradigms of research, those of cognitive science and cultural history.

A special problem connected to 'reductionism' is the opposition between universalist explanations and those emphasizing specificity. In the 1950s, universalist explanations were prominent in the humanities: Cassirer's (1944, 1953/7) writings were widely read; Frye's (1957) universalist genre theory was popular, and Jung's psychological theory of archetypes also. The early structuralism of Lévi-Strauss (1958) presupposed universal mental structures and themes. The structuralism of the 1960s was more ambivalent as to universals. The emphasis on the 'arbitrariness' of all social phenomena meant that, although a few structural features such as sign, paradigm, and syntagm seemed to be universals, no special architecture of the brain was presupposed. Chomsky's idea of the innateness of central preconditions for language competence contrasted with many aspects of structuralist thinking. In the same way, the psychoanalysis of the 1960s was an ambivalent mixture of culturalism and universalism. Freud was mainly interpreted as a spokesman for total culturalism; there existed no innate mental architecture, only some prototypical patterns of socialization. This interpretation was part of an emancipatory perspective: alienated contemporary psyches were mainly products of special social, political, and gendered historical forms which one hoped could soon be transgressed. The poststructuralism of the 1970s, as well as aspects of Marx-inspired historicism, put further emphasis on 'specificity', either a historical specificity or just 'difference' or 'otherness'.

A more nuanced point of view may be desirable. It is hardly credible to speak about human nature with the confidence of enlightenment. Some phenomena are ruled by structures developed in time-spans of hundreds of thousands of years; other phenomena are ruled by structures changing within very short time-spans. The general structure of human emotions is not among the phenomena that have changed radically in the last thousand years, although these emotions have been modified by being related to new contexts.

COGNITIVISM AND ITS RELATIONS TO OTHER THEORETICAL SCHOOLS

Film studies and humanistic studies in mass communication do not possess a broad common paradigm of research. Research is carried out within more local paradigms, 'schools'; and, compared with the natural sciences and even with the social sciences, it sometimes seems as if these individual schools have been more interested (perhaps for marketing reasons) in emphasizing differences than in analyzing common assumptions and finding out whether differences in terminology correspond to differences in concepts. The last thirty-five years have seen many different schools: phenomenology, hermeneutics, structuralism, semiotics, Russian formalism, critical theory, Marxism, psychoanalysis (Freudian and Lacanian), poststructuralism/deconstructionism, reception analysis, and cognitivism. Although some of these have existed simultaneously, there has also been a tendency to shift to a new dominant school in a fashion-like search for novelty.

An important paradigm of research in this book is cognitivism and structural, semiotic text-analysis. But, in order not to add to the Babylonic confusion of terminologies and schools, I shall try to outline the way in which cognitive science is compatible with, or has roots in, different, earlier theoretical schools in the humanities, and their special variants within film and media studies.

Cognitive science is based on a non-behaviouristic, psychological framework of research. To understand language, visual phenomena, or behaviour, we need to understand the mechanisms and structures by which these activities are processed by the human mind-brain (including the perceptual systems). Aspects of cognitive psychology and cognitive linguistics clearly have their roots in gestalt psychology and phenomenology. Unlike behaviourism, these schools have tried to describe the way in which perception and meaning are structured by human mental structures and mechanisms. Terms like 'gestalt' are closely related to cognitive terms like 'pattern' and more loosely related to cognitive terms like 'schema'. George Lakoff's cognitive semantics represents a systematic research into the mental models that structure the human phenomenological world, and, although the precision of his theories and analytical examples of images and metaphors as mental models is new, his way of thinking is very similar to that of phenomenological analysis of aesthetic phenomena carried out in the 1950s and early 1960s.[5] Furthermore, some mental models made by Johnson-Lairds and others analyze intentions and other mental mechanisms central to phenomenology.

Secondly, many aspects of cognitive science are genetically closely related to structural linguistics (and to theories of information from Shannon/Weaver onwards), and freely share terms like 'code', just as the symbiosis of computer science and structural linguistics has made terms like 'syntax' household words in cognitive science. The cognitive study of stories and scripts, as carried out by Mandler and Schank/Abelson, has roots in the structural studies of narratives from Propp onwards. Structural and semiotic text-analysis (Jakobson, Barthes, Todorov, Greimas, *et al.*) also has strong roots in Russian formalism, so that claims made by some critics for a formalist approach totally different from structuralism and semiotics do not seem warranted.

But there are important differences between structuralism and cognitive science, and one of these is that structuralism is object-oriented and 'static'; structuralists describe objective structures in texts, not the mental principles and the processes in the human mind that generate the structures. The concept of language as a fixed social system, and the idea of the fixed relation between signifier and signified, is not a good basis for understanding the functioning and processing of information in the individual mind. The concept of the arbitrariness and the exclusively social nature of meaning, connected with ideas of the way in which language controls perceptions and meanings, made language the sole model of meaning and consciousness; but this is detrimental to understanding, for instance, the way in which vision works according to non-linguistic principles and the types of mental phenomena processed by non-linguistic means and often by non-arbitrary, innate mechanisms. 'Linguistic hegemony' is problematic, especially for the use of structuralism in the analysis of visual communication, because many visual phenomena are structured and processed by means of mechanisms quite different from linguistic structures; although other structures, like narrative ones, have a linear structure similar to language.

Perhaps the strongest difference of approach is found between cognitivism and most aspects of 'poststructuralism' and 'deconstructivism'. The constructivism and functionalism of a cognitive approach are quite different from the predominantly hermeneutic approach of deconstructivism. Communication is understood as a part of broader cognitive and social activities, in which social negotiations and social functions construct intersubjective representations that are neither floating signifiers nor metaphysical essences.

---

[5] Inspired by Merleau-Ponty (1962) and the works of Gaston Bachelard.

OUTLINE OF THE BOOK

The book is structured in four parts. Part I, Visual Fiction as Embodied Mental Flow, Chapters 1, 2, and 3, deals with descriptions of basic problems in the psychosomatic activation caused by film, and shows that we mentally simulate fictitious worlds; that this is a result of certain brain processes, whether associative or sequential, which determine our cognitive and emotional experience; and that our experience is moulded by an attentional hierarchy. Chapter 1 notes that our symbolic simulations to some extent rely on ecological conventions; that a given type of reality is represented by an emotional tone; and that the evaluation of reality-status is a special mental function. Chapter 2 describes the ways in which basic forms of aesthetic experience are related to perceptual, associational, and sequential structures and to innate autonomic emotional reactions. It provides models of the experiential flow, based on the mental flow from perception via emotional evaluation and cognitions to enaction; and it shows that experienced modal qualities of the flow (intense, saturated, tense, and autonomic experiences) are effects of the mental flow as cued by narratives. Chapter 3 proposes a model for understanding the reception of fiction as an attentional hierarchy (in which focus of attention is opposed to associational patterns with a lower degree of activation), and describes the importance of visual thinking in understanding visual fiction.

Part II, Narratives as Basic Mental Models, Chapters, 4, 5, and 6, deals with the way in which fictions are about, and are moulded by, basic anthropomorph mental 'structures', such as models of humanness, processes of empathy and identification, models of intentions and of goal-directed acts, and models of time. I argue that canonical narratives are base models that link perceptions, evaluations/emotions, cognitions, and acts. I also consider ways in which one can make subjective representations by putting constraints on some parameters of the basic models.

Chapter 4 discusses cognitive labelling of emotions and describes two types of narrative mechanisms, *telic* (goal-oriented) and *paratelic* (process-oriented), which provide an alternative to the problematic theories of 'narrative desire'. Chapter 5 describes the importance of will and voluntary, intentional phenomena, and the contrast of this with autonomic phenomena in the viewer's experience of visual fiction. It further compares Lacanian theories of mirror-identification with cognitive theories of mental models. Chapter 6 shows that subjective, 'proximal' experiences may be cued, that temporal experience may be an emotional tone, and that the different kinds of temporal experience are cued by different mental models of acts and processes.

Part III, A Typology of Genres and Emotions, Chapter 7, summarizes some of the characteristic dimensions that produce emotions in visual fiction, and

I use these dimensions to formulate a typology of prototypical emotion-producing genres. The eight prototypical genre-patterns in visual fiction, based on their emotional effect on the viewer, are: Lyricism, Canonical Narratives, Obsessional Fictions, Melodramas, Horror Fictions, Schizoid Fictions, Comic Fictions, and Metafictions.

Part IV, Laughter, Distance, Horror, and Tears, Chapters, 8, 9, 10, and 11, takes up some of the generic prototypes: comic fictions, metafiction, canonical crime fiction, horror fiction, and lyrical and melodramatic fictions, for a more fine-grained analysis.

Chapter 8 provides new descriptions of central dimensions in comic fictions. I discuss comic fictions as hypotheses of reality-status and show that the perception of humour is an illocutionary mental act, related to an autonomic response, laughter, at a high level of arousal and mental overload. I discuss the relations between the comic and pleasure, and the role of empathy and voluntary acts as exemplified in our relations to clowns. I discuss the role of the comic in narrative sequences, especially the way in which, as a parasympathetic reaction, it supports 'fusion' and incorporation. Chapter 9 characterizes the way in which metafiction filters emotions, and contrasts formalist and Brechtian concepts of distanciation. I demonstrate that 'self-conscious' devices serve a lyrical function in some modernist films, and discuss emotional problems in frames like naturalism and realism. I further show that 'game' and 'role' may serve as brackets enabling the sophisticated viewer to accept narrative or social stereotypes in order to receive a controlled autonomic experience. Chapter 10 considers the way in which crime fiction relates to canonical narratives, metanarratives, and horror fiction, the means by which it modifies empathic relations, and that by which thrillers and horror fiction furthermore rely on cognitive dissonance for creating effect. Chapter 11 illustrates lyrical and melodramatic patterns in *Gone With the Wind* and *Vertigo,* with emphasis on the relations between temporal rearrangements and passive, lyrical, or melodramatic-autonomic mechanism, and on the mechanisms of relabelling arousal; and the main findings of the book are recapitulated in a final chapter.

Part I

Visual Fiction as
Embodied Mental Flow

Fiction, Symbolic Simulation, and Reality

A recurrent problem in aesthetics and theories of fiction and representation in art (whether literature, art, or film) is the status and validity of representation itself. Are representations true or false? Are fictions lies? Are images illusionistic in a pejorative sense if they try to convey a three-dimensional effect on a two-dimensional screen or canvas? What are the relations between metaphors and literal meaning? Are films just imaginary signifiers, as argued by Metz? In this chapter I shall show that many of these intricate problems are easy to understand in the context of our mental makeup. I shall deal, in particular, with the ecological conventions moulding our visual experience; and I shall further discuss the way in which fiction is symbolic simulation, and the way in which evaluations of the reality-status of given phenomena are often represented as emotional tones.

FORMALISM, REALISM, AND ECOLOGICAL CONVENTIONS

'Realism' and 'formalism' have been the two main theories of representation upheld by artists and theoreticians. The realist position has been that there exist true and unmediated representations, and that one can therefore assess the degree of realism in any given representation. The formalist position has been that all systems of representations, even visual ones, are conventions, often thought of as learned in the same way as languages.

Realist film theory (Kracauer (1961) and Bazin (1967, 1972)) has had few adherents in the last decades: formalism appears to have become the dominant paradigm. Nevertheless, implicit in many 'formal' experiments are realist ideas: painters and film-makers have tried to make two-dimensional paintings and films because they are more 'true' to the two-dimensionality of the canvas or screen (cf. Peterson 1994: 85 ff. *passim*). Realism is an objectivist theory of representation in the sense described and criticized by the philosopher and linguist, Mark Johnson (1987) and by Winograd and Flores (1986). Objectivist theories of representations presuppose that there is a 'God's-Eye' point of view, from which one should be able to make the 'true' representation of the world. But the use of words like 'true' or 'false' is, outside axiomatic systems, misleading. Human intelligence works 'inside the world', and makes theories, models, and representations of phenomena in the world; and these can only be judged according to temporary 'functionalist' criteria, such as 'best available model for the time being for solving a given problem'.

Realism might be said to imply a bottom-up, data-driven approach to the way in which we receive representations: a given film will, via innate mechanisms, be reconstructed in the viewer. In contrast to this, formalism will typically imply a top-down, constructivist approach to reception: a given reception of a film relies on culturally acquired skills, procedures, and information, which will be used to access the film text; in other words, the reception of a film will take place from 'top' (our knowledge and skills) to 'bottom' (the film text).

Formalism has been in accord with prominent trends in film-making. Modernist film-makers, like Bergman in *Persona,* were anxious to prove that the screen image was man-made by showing projection machines and trying to give the audience a feeling of the film stock, while, for example, Antonioni's *Blow-Up* focuses on the graininess of the stock and thus the limits of representation (but the 'grains' in the retina, the limited number of rods and cones, also put a limit on representation). Impressionism tried to short-circuit the contour-mechanisms[1] by which the eye–brain normally makes object-representations; many visual experiments of the twentieth century have been centred on breaking with the central perspective as a western or bourgeois prejudice or ideology. Linear narratives were suspicious, because they were thought to be experienced in an alluringly 'realistic' but occidental–logical way, whereas complicated and often 'self-reflexive' types of narration showed the relativity of representation. To 'lay bare the devices' and to show 'self-reflexivity' by pointing to such matters as the processes of enunciation have acquired moral overtones of destroying false icons of God.

Whereas the formalists were mostly concerned with the cognitive aspect of representation, psychoanalytic film theories, which gained prominence from the middle of the 1970s onwards, described the film image as a fascinating but illusory and false 'realism'. Psychoanalytic film-theory thus had emotions as its focus of attention. Its 'formalism' does not fully presuppose non-arbitrary systems of representation, because most representations and viewers will be caught up in the same 'realist' illusions. Seminal were Metz's Freud- and Lacan-inspired book (1982) and articles by Baudry (1988). Metz provides two main reasons for the 'alluring' attractiveness of film. The first is that the spectator's identification with the film-screen enacts a 'pre-oedipal', narcissistic repression of lack and castration: the film-screen is like a mirror image in sug-

---

[1] The contour mechanisms ('zero-crossings') have been described in Marr (1982: 54 ff.). For a description of the connection between visual processing and artistic systems of representation, see Willats (1990).

gesting an imaginary wholeness. The second reason is that the filmic experience, although different from a dream, activates similar mechanisms. Metz compares film-viewing with such states as somnambulism, hallucination, and day-dreaming. He claims that the impression of reality is related to the illusion of reality.[2] The psychoanalytic description of the film experience has been criticized vehemently, especially by Carroll (1988), and also by Eitzen (1994) and Plantinga (1994). Some key concepts of psychoanalysis used in film theory, such as its description of dreams, have been strongly contested, for instance by Hobson (1988) and Cavallero and Foulkes (1993).

The cognitive and neurological research of the last twenty-five years has provided evidence for a third, mediating position between realism and formalism that I will call 'ecological conventionalism', and which also provides explanations for the links between representations and emotions. This research has made a good case for some realist assumptions: basic mechanisms for many types of representations are innate and a product of evolution, and are therefore to be understood transculturally, although of course visual perception, for example the representation of lightwaves as 'colours' in our minds, results from a set of biological conventions, not transcendental 'truths', as some realists believe. The more specific contents and competencies are, however, products of culture and learned skills. Furthermore, even a bottom-up reception often implies sophisticated processes of construction, filtering, and feedback from stored memories (see Kosslyn 1994).

There are a number of reasons why a strong version of the formalist and culturalist position seems improbable. If we follow the description of visual perception in Marr's influential models for visual processing (1982) and combine this with the neurobiologist Zeki's descriptions (1993) of the functioning of the visual cortex, we end up with something like this: many visual processes take place by means of innate modules, which, furthermore, are sealed, so that we cannot consciously or unconsciously modify their working. Zeki's central example of visual perception/cognition is colour vision: colour is analyzed and 'created' in the part of the brain called visual cortex area 4, with input from visual areas 1 and 2. A person working professionally with colour might 'sensitize' his colour vision, and thus become more skilled in perceiving colour and colour differences, but he would not be able to modify the structure of colours. If the module is damaged, one's ability even to imagine colour disappears. The same applies to basic aspects of the perception of objects, space, and motion. Messaris (1994) has further argued that we use the same competencies for viewing visual communication as we use in everyday life, and has shown that many of these are transcultural.

The modularity of brain functions, and the fact that many procedures take

[2] A similar occupation with the 'passivity' of the spectator is found in Morin (1985: 100 ff.).

place by bottom-up processes, do not preclude other processes from occurring as a result of constructivist top-down procedures.[3] Kosslyn (1994) has shown how visual imagination takes place, activating visual modules by means of memory- and higher-level functions that correspond to the role played by memorized templates (cf. Bordwell 1986: 34 f.) in disambiguating a low-quality input. This happens, for example, when we see something in the fog and 'project' memorized images onto the perceived in order to see whether they match or not; or when, like Scottie in *Vertigo*, we perpetually and mistakenly think we see a sought-for person because we 'project' our expectations onto our perceptions. But the modularity of the mind indicates some constraints on what can be constructed, and how.

We may then add the information provided by research undertaken by Antonio and Hanna Damasio (1993). Their theory specifies the relation between analogue 'perceptual' representation and 'natural language'. One of their important findings is that the natural languages are signifier systems which rely heavily for their semantic components on perceptual and motor modules. The signifier part of a word serves as an activator-component for the perceptual modules, and activation of these and connected association areas provides the semantic component of language. Different categories and meanings are thus located in different parts of the brain. If we say 'blue', the signifier activates the visual cortex and association areas. If we say 'coffee cup' we may evoke visual and tactile representations of its shape, colour, texture, and warmth, along with the smell and taste of the coffee, or the path that the hand and the arm take to bring the cup from the table to the lips and the motor sensations linked to this movement. All these representations are re-created in separate brain regions, but their reconstruction occurs almost simultaneously. When we see coffee-drinking on the screen, we may therefore mentally simulate taste, heat, and motor sensations, as well as the visual appearance of the cup.

Thus, the semantic components of natural languages rely heavily on the non-arbitrary sensory–motor component of the mind. Visual communication is a direct-analogue activation of the perceptuo-motor processes that ground our experience of meaning and meaningfulness. Fig. 1.1 shows in schematic form that audiovisual communication is only the last step (until now) in a process which has enabled living organisms to rerun perceptual phenomena: any type of memory-based activation of perceptual–motor phenomena prepares for the break between sensory-motor activation and online 'real' stimuli.[4]

---

[3] For an overview of cognitive constructivism, see Bordwell (1989a). A proto-constructivist approach is given in Arnheim (1957).

[4] The close link between intelligent processes (meaning-processes) and sensory-motor processes is in accord with the fact that very many intelligent processes are carried out by animals. Although, for example, primates do not have language, they can perform many intelligent activities. When humanity developed language some 100,000–200,000 years ago we may hypothesize that it developed as a 'superstructure' on top of the basic intelligent sensory-motor

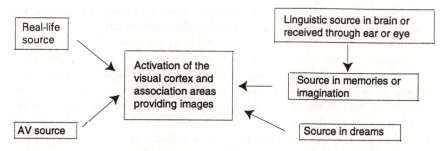

Fig. 1.1 Part of the mental activation is the same whether a given visual experience is caused by a 'real' experience, or by a memory of an experience, possibly activated by means of language, or caused by seeing a film or other audiovisual sequence.

The relative autonomy of vision *vis-à-vis* representational systems has been confirmed by Rosch's research into colour categories among the Dani people (quoted in Lakoff 1987: 40 f.); she examines the precept that linguistic categories decide or mirror the way that people conceive the world, as claimed by Whorf. In Dani there are only two conceptual categories of colour. Rosch carried out an experiment in which one Dani group learned arbitrary names for non-focal colours, while another learned arbitrary names for focal colour.[5] The experiment showed that the focal-colour names were learned more quickly than the non-focal, implying that, although the Dani did not have verbal representations for focal colour, these categories existed in their visual processing of the world. Representational systems and categories may give increased salience to visual phenomena. A highly developed verbal system of names for shades of colour might well enhance attention to these shades; and Impressionism has enhanced attention to local colour and to the 'intensity array quality' of vision, as opposed to the visual field composed of clearly

processes. Language added some more advanced functions to the sensory-motor categorizations and schematizations. Human language may be said to *stabilize,* to *compress and abstract,* to *retrieve,* and to *communicate* sensory-motor phenomena. Language stabilizes percepts, because to provide a 'name' for a given concept virtually worked out by, for instance, visual categorization stabilizes this categorization. If we have the word 'red' it stabilizes our perception of this colour category. Corballis (1991) believes that language may have been important for 'supplying' a Gibson-style holistic perception (1986) with types of perception that rely more heavily on discrete units. Language compresses percepts (P. S. Churchland 1986), because it can make categories on a level higher than analogical perception: all the subcategories made up of different percepts of animals can be compressed into one term: 'animal'. Language is thus essential for making 'abstract', higher-order concepts; it may directly express negative statements; it serves as labels which make it more easy to retrieve percepts and motor schemata; and it makes it possible to communicate 'interior' perceptions and perceptual phenomena to other humans.

[5] Focal colours are, according to Berlin and Kay, red, green, yellow and blue, orange, pink, and purple; and the three acromatic terms are black, white and grey: see Lakoff (1987: 24 ff.), and cf. Davidoff (1991: 150 ff.).

defined objects and grounds.[6] Representations using 'Renaissance' perspective may enhance the salience of these features when seen in daily life, and influence the choice of 'type of preferred visual representation'. Systems of visual (or linguistic) representations are, however, made against the background of an innate perceptual architecture. A critique of the Renaissance perspectival system as a wholly cultural and 'ideological' product of 'western linear thought' disregards the neuropsychological foundation for this as well as for an object-centred representation.[7] For the same reasons, it is problematic to infer that the fragmented visual world of a music video directly mimics the way in which producers or viewers 'see' the world. The modes of representation in film and art are different cultural constructs produced against a background of innate perceptual-cognitive structures, and the constructs will highlight different aspects of the complex totality of procedures by which we construct reality.

From a given visual representation in art or film we cannot infer the way in which producers or receivers of visual representations typically see the world. It has sometimes been argued that, when people in the Middle Ages made non-perspectival representations in pictures, this also meant that they saw the world in a less perspectival way. But that medieval artists chose more object-centred systems of representation only shows that they based their representations on an object-centred level of processing, choosing a canonical view of the individual object, and painted 'additively', by making collections of object representations. It may be a significant cultural choice to select one or several steps in the visual process as a basis for representation, but it is not an indication of the way in which people in the Middle Ages perceived the world.[8] When Heath (1981: 27 ff.) described the advent of Renaissance perspective and its relation to the photographic image and cinema, he implied that central perspective has ideological implications connected with a 'central master-spectator'. He further argued against comparing the camera with the eye, by pointing to the saccadic movements of the eyes; and he implicitly linked this to something characterized by 'process and practice' as opposed to the 'central master-spectator', but forgot to add that these movements are only input to a pre-programmed process making relatively stable images.

---

[6] Davidoff (1991: 153 ff.) discusses research into the relation between linguistic coding and colour perception, and concludes that a Whorf-type claim of a strong connection between linguistic categorization and colour perception is unwarranted; the linguistic categorizations have some influence, but do not in any way determine colour perception.

[7] Goodman argues for the 'cultural' aspects of central perspective (1969: 10 ff.) indicating problems of exact representation caused by scaling and viewer position, just as Arnheim (1974: 283 ff.) notes problems in the representation of vertical lines and assumed viewer position, for example. This is, however, only an argument for the problems of representations of (especially large) three-dimensional spaces on a two-dimensional surface.

[8] Cf. the discussion of whether perception of depth is innate or based on experience, in Spelke (1990); the main conclusion is that many features of depth-perception are innate.

Fortunately we do not consciously see the saccadic movements, otherwise erratic vision would have resulted in the extinction of *homo sapiens* long ago.

HYPOTHETICAL ACTS, THOUGHTS, AND OTHER TYPES OF SYMBOLIC SIMULATION

To describe art representations and fiction as the opposite of ordinary reality by using terms like 'illusion', 'lie', 'hallucination', or 'dream' is problematic because it presupposes 'true', unmediated forms of representation. As pointed out by William James, the question of reality has to be reformulated so that reality is not something absolute, transcendental, but something characterizing certain feelings and cognitive evaluations that are applied to certain experienced phenomena in contradistinction to other experienced phenomena. Similarly, the philosopher Brentano distinguished between perceptions and the reality-status we give to the perceived.[9]

The belief that there is no difference between the way that we receive fiction and the way that we receive non-fiction has been upheld by Carroll (1990: 74 f.) and states, for example, that whereas children have a clear awareness that they are playing a game of make-believe when they make mud-pies or pretend to be cowboys, there is no such awareness of playing a game when consuming fiction: 'I read historical nonfiction and I watch documentary films, and I see no discernible difference in the way that I read and watch these from the way in which I read and watch fictions.' However, to watch fiction must be different in some respects from watching documentary films, because the viewer knows or guesses at whether a given sequence is 'true', a documentary, or not. If he did not do this he would be in trouble if, for example, having seen *Escape from New York,* he refused to go to New York as a result of the information given in the fiction film.[10] The mass panic caused by Orson Welles' radio dramatization of H. G. Wells' *The War of the Worlds* shows what happens when the clues for a fictional as opposed to a fact-based construction of the message are not placed or not understood by the audience. When, therefore, we look at fictions there are some aspects of the information provided which we process in the same way as playing a game.

The trouble that many people have with the word 'fiction' comes from a hard-boiled opposition between 'reality' and 'fiction'. To overcome the problem, we must look more closely at the family of phenomena to which fiction

---

[9] Cf. Goffman (1986), who describes the development from William James and phenomenology to Alfred Schutz in understanding 'reality' as types of experience.

[10] In another context (Carroll 1988: 101 ff. *passim*) he in fact criticizes illusionist theories of visual fiction. This raises the question of how fiction can exist in the brain in the same way as non-fiction and yet not cause illusions.

belongs. Prominent members are hypothesis-formation, imagining, playing, acting-pretending, and simulating (in the natural-science sense). The basis of all these phenomena is that a given behaviour, a given cognitive process, or a given arrangement of the exterior world is carried out under circumstances which put specifications on their relation to 'real-life' processes. A simple and 'old' example of this is the hypothetical use of a behaviour with a communicative intent: a dog activates part of an attack-behaviour by exposing its teeth and showing a posture marked by muscular tension in order to intimidate another dog. The communicative pattern of behaviour is similar to aspects of an actual attack-behaviour, but it is made conditional. An equally 'old' type of behaviour is 'playing', as, for example, when puppies play out fighting and attack-behaviour with each other as opponents, or with inanimate objects as 'fictitious' prey. The simulation of the attack-behaviour trains the puppies for the real thing. Higher animals can perform a given behaviour in at least two modes, 'actual' and 'hypothetical-playful',[11] and they are usually quite well-separated mentally; puppies normally do not hurt or kill each other during fighting, and considerable intra-species communication of hostile behaviour and claims of dominance do not lead to a full-scale fight (just as not all communication of mating-related behaviour leads to an actual mating). However, the fights between Inspector Clouseau and his servant in the *Pink Panther* series exemplify the way in which the marks of playfulness may disappear and trigger non-play. Humans have expanded the 'hypothetical-playful' mode by not only performing in direct communication with other humans, but also performing for the benefit of third parties, spectators to the hypothetical-playful behaviour. Fiction is therefore not an alternative, 'unreal' activity, but is closely related to our ability to construct reality.[12] Fictions allow us to try out behaviours and to imagine prototypical behaviours and settings as well as alternative equivalents.

That symbolic acts are often part of our coping procedures has also been pointed out by some psychoanalysts: for instance, Winnicott (1971) has emphasized that symbolic action is important. He describes the way in which children try to overcome their passive position, their being emotionally dependent on the nursing person (mother, father, or other), by creating what he calls *transitional* objects, things like toys which, on the one hand, have a symbolic connection with the child itself or the nursing person, but which, on the other hand, the child can manipulate. Winnicott regards this active role by symbolic manipulation as the nucleus of the development of play, art, and fiction. A famous case study by Freud (1920; 1955 edn., 11 ff.), his observa-

---

[11] Cf. MacLean (1986: 62): 'The evolution from reptiles to mammals has involved the acquisition of three distinguishing forms of behaviour recognized as (1) nursing, in conjunction with maternal care, (2) audiovocal communication for maintaining maternal-offspring contact, and (3) playful behaviour.'

[12] Bateson (1985) has pointed to the adaptive advantages of 'play'; cf. also Goffman (1986: 40 ff.).

tion of his grandchild playing *Fort/Da* ('not present/present') symbolically and actively trying to control the disappearance and reappearance of his mother, likewise supports the close connection between some types of fiction and mental-symbolic models of acts. By playing with transitional objects and toys, children make mental models of the world and construct possible story-like schemata of sequences of actions. However, Freud did not deal extensively with symbolic and hypothetical acts from a 'positive' point of view, i.e., focusing on the way in which such acts are essential for creating and coping; instead he emphasized the negative aspects, i.e., the possible pathological compensatory illusions (the little boy does not really control his mother) and relation to 'death drives'. Metz and many others adopt Freud's sinister view of life by seeing symbolic phenomena as illusions and compensations for infantile traumas, not as symbolic software for active coping.

The previous examples of symbolic hypotheses have been taken from the realm of motor behaviour, but, within perception and central processing, 'simulation' also plays a crucial role, at least in humans and probably in higher animals too. Memory and 'imagination' are based on simulation. Memories are stored perceptions of the exterior or interior world, and to remember means mentally to retrieve, reactivate, and 'run' features of the original, memorized set of perceptions; to imagine means to make a recombination of memorized perceptions, for example by creating 'unicorns' or a Pegasus out of features of different memorized perceptions. Merely planning to go to the supermarket implies a series of hypothetical thoughts, in the sense that the imagined has not yet any equivalent in reality. A memory or a plan for future acts and goals is 'fictitious', in the sense that there is not actually a perceptual equivalent to the imagined.

To 'recycle' previous percepts obviously has enormous cognitive advantages, but also demands systems for keeping track of the reality-status of a given mental state. A given segment of a conscious state must therefore be marked according to its reality-status, or people would confuse perceptions with memories and imaginations, as in the malfunction of the reality-evaluating system known as hallucination. It would be simple if this system were based only on formal principles, for example by distinguishing a 'real percept' with a simultaneous exterior source from an act of imagination by, say, salience and resolution of the mental event (memories having less vividness, less detail, than instant perception). But, as Jackendoff has argued (1987: 303 f.), this is not very likely, as the quality of our percepts is quite variable: objects seen dimly through a fog have quite another salience than objects seen in broad daylight. The perceptual process as such is non-conscious, the processes from retina to cortex are inaccessible for conscious introspection, and, furthermore, perception and imagination partly use the same central brain circuits. To distinguish 'real' from 'imagined' we therefore need two things: systems for a cognitive evaluation of the reality-status of the 'mental event' by means of cues of context or internal features, and a system for mentally representing the difference between percepts and images. Jackendoff argues, in connection with the latter requirement, that the difference is mentally represented by a system of feelings and affects, and I shall return to this problem later. The first requirement implies that cognitive systems evaluating the reality-status of a given mental event are crucial for the functioning of higher mental life. An important aspect of the production and viewing of visual fiction is therefore to analyze the cued reality-status of a given sequence (memory, hallucination, online perception, plan, or fiction), and, according to Jackendoff, the cognitive evaluation will be partially represented by an emotional tone. As the cognitive evaluation of reality-status is partly represented by 'feelings', manipulation of reality-status can be used for evoking emotions and feelings.

The question of reality-status and simulation is also pertinent to the world of real percepts. A visual percept, a mirror image, a photograph, or a film might, under certain circumstances, be quite indistinguishable from a percept caused by the real thing. Whether a given behaviour is an act, a play, or the real thing requires analysis on the part of participants or spectators (and, possibly, cannot be solved). The greater the abilities of animals or humans to simulate behaviours, the greater the abilities of interpretation needed for other animals or other humans. Many poets and film-makers have shown an enormous interest in mirrors and the phenomena of 'acting', that is, the ability to simulate some aspects of a perceptual situation (for example, the visual components), with other components of normal reality being absent. Mirror-images or film images do not have physical bodies; acted behaviour lacks some real-life components of intent and implementation. Their interest is often driven by the fact that we can make mistakes; that we can believe that a mirror-image is a person with a tangible body, or that voluntary and communicative behaviour which expresses rather than 'feels' anger is the real thing, or we can mistake a dream for a real experience. Confronted with the constructivist basis of consciousness, many artists conclude that world or consciousness is illusionistic. But the mistakes must be viewed against the background of a normal ability to distinguish between simulations and reality, although new behaviour and new technologies demand new abilities to analyze the perceptual input.

'Reality' is a special mental and emotional construction. Seen from a distance, a stone has no weight, it provides no tactile qualities and, even if quite large, it produces a very small retinal image. If we experience something like weight, hardness, and considerable size when we look at the stone, it is because we infer these qualities from previous experiences of close contact with stones and our experiences of scaling in relation to distance (Gombrich 1968, Hochberg 1978: 70 ff.). We use exactly the same constructive procedures when watching films or television that we use in constructing reality out of our real-life perceptions. A given object is seen under varying light conditions and from varying distances and angles, and the eye itself moves continuously, for example by saccadic movements. A given object will therefore make millions of different retina stimulations, and if our perceptual system did not undertake continuous 'calculations' and constructions we would not be able to construct the object as a singular phenomenon, but would be left with an infinite sequence of different retina stimulations. Compared with the problems of perceiving objects based on retina input, the transformations needed to simulate reality out of audiovisual sources are minor.

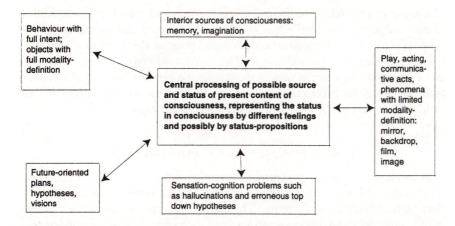

Fig. 1.2 The construction of reality as a sequence of cognitive procedures in the mind, indicated in bold. The surrounding text-blocks represent possible reality-options of the experienced. Fiction frequently manipulates these different reality-status options, often in order to create effect by short-circuiting the evaluation process.

Figure 1.2 shows some dimensions of the construction and evaluation of reality-status. It highlights the holistic and 'felt' in the experience of 'reality'. If a film with sound-producing activities suddenly removes the sound from a dramatic scene, this is often done to produce an 'unreal', 'subjective' effect, and a way of describing this is to see it as an aesthetic device. It also shows negatively the way in which the two modalities, hearing and vision, fuse into a holistic experience that is not only represented as what is seen and heard but also includes an additional 'tonality' of reality representing the non-conscious cognitive evaluation in consciousness. When, therefore, film and other arts are 'laying bare the devices of art' there is also a 'laying bare' of the devices by which the brain constructs holistic experiences out of different perceptual sources and different elements within these sources. An experimental 'reflexivity' in visual fiction and other arts certainly has elements which point to very specific cultural conventions of 'representation'; but to focus exclusively on the cultural conventions, and to tone down the extent to which 'reflexivity' is about the foundation of human experience as such, is to let art play too modest a role (and further, perhaps, too vicious a role as perverting the naïve).

The experience of status of reality is determined by many parameters, and I would just like to mention a few of the fundamental parameters of reality-experience:

It has a temporal parameter

Present states are felt as more 'real' than previous or future states, and future states ordinarily less 'real' than previous states. Past and future are, in a double sense, mental constructions, constructions of the 'presentic material' (memories, pictures, descriptions, and so forth), and constructions of temporal dimensions. In a media society the distinction between 'live' and 'non-live' sources of a given perceptual input has to be constructed and represented as a felt dimension in the mental representation of the event.

It has a 'perception-source' space parameter

Conscious states with a perceptual source in exterior space are more 'real' than states with an interior source, whether they are memories or mental constructions, like plans or fantasies. The exterior perceptions are further subdivided into full-modality perceptions and perceptions like mirror-images, backdrops, and film images with, for instance, only a visual existence.

It has a parameter related to evaluating correspondence with/deviation from 'normal perception'

An example might be blurred images motivated as subjective.

It has a parameter related to behaviour and intent

Behaviours with a non-communicative intent are felt as more 'real' than those with a communicative intent, whereas there is no clear pattern in whether behaviours that communicate directly with the addressee are felt as more real than behaviours like play-acting, which also communicate indirectly with the spectator-addressee. The distinction between communicative and non-communicative phenomena also comprises 'products of behaviours', as in the difference between a full-scale model of the 'home of the future' at an exhibition, or a full-scale model of a frontier town made as a set for a film, and full-scale phenomena made as a part of ordinary life. As all phenomena concerning 'intent' are mental constructions (of the type, Is he really angry or is he only pretending? Is the house really built as a house or is the house, for example, Xanadu in *Citizen Kane*, only built to communicate the owner's grandiose ego?, the evaluations are uncertain and relative to a given level of interpretation.

It has a parameter related to 'abstraction' as against 'concretion'

A given image or a given act can be perceived as an abstract 'structural' description of many concrete objects and many concrete events, or it can be perceived as a concrete, unique phenomenon, often with a complex and salient texture. Structural 'descriptions' will often be felt as 'human' and 'mental' phenomena, as the working of the mind will often 'abstract', process, and store structural descriptions, or prototypes, based on a complex perceptual input. Abstraction and concretion have each their own intensity and salience. The family of phenomena, like fiction, a game, playing, scientific models, or artistic representations, are 'abstractions' in this sense; they are 'structural descriptions', 'prototypes', and 'schemata'. Although different types of fictions can be made with different degrees of concreteness and with different degrees of textural complexity, for example, their relation to reality will be that of being models of the world (whether they are models of existing or possible processes and states of the world and mind).

It has a parameter related to modality synthesis and perceptual intensity

Normally hearing and vision (and possibly touch) co-operate to provide a holistic experience. A splitting-up of modality-synthesis—such as sound without image, whether motivated by darkness or unmotivated; image without sound; represented acts in which 'solid' phenomena lack their tactile qualities (such as ghosts, and mirror-images); lack of synchronization, and so forth—may lead to a loss of reality. An aspect of modality-synthesis is whether something cannot only be perceived, but also acted upon (and thus possibly possess tactile, or gustatory qualities). Seen from this point of view, the reality-status of mental phenomena is linked to modality-synthesis. Furthermore, film-makers will often use modality-dissociation to represent mental phenomena, with mirror-images and ghosts as prime examples of dissociation of different perceptual and motor qualities.

It has a parameter connected to emotional response

There are some standard expectations as to emotional response. Responses felt as weird, psychotic, cold, or similar will influence reality-evaluation.

When the presence of a corpse in a scene from Godard's *Pierrot le Fou* initially has no affect on daily life, the scene is felt as 'unreal'. Emotional dissociation is a central phenomenon in many thrillers and horror films.

Besides these parameters, all standard schemata of 'reality' may be used for creating reality effects. The above-mentioned parameters, however, have special links to central dimensions in our perceptual, cognitive, and emotional processing of the world and probably for that reason are also central to reality-construction in visual fiction, as they can draw on near-universal mental processes of reality-construction.

ATTENTION, SALIENCE, AND REALITY-STATUS

In many 'illusionistic' accounts of visual fiction, the experience of activation-strength and that of reality-status are described as the same thing. *There is, however, no simple correlation between the strength of a given experience and the reality-status of the object of the experience.* An extreme example of the way in which film percepts activate, irrespective of their reality-status, is a phenomenon like 'perceptual shock' during film-viewing. If we suddenly see or hear something, we may experience a shock although we may find out after a short analysis that there is no reason to be alarmed, as when the protagonist in Kieslowski's *Blue* swims out of sight and suddenly surfaces with splashing noises into the film frame from below. The perceptual impact is caused by inferior, automated, and non-conscious processes that register strong changes of stimuli, whereas the evaluation of reality-status is performed later and at a superior level. To evaluate the shock in terms like 'illusion' or 'willing suspension of disbelief' is not relevant, because a reality-status is not defined for the automated processes that set off the shock reaction.[13] To propose a different case: we may be so occupied with thinking about the riddles in *Vertigo* that this uses all our conscious capacity, leaving no conscious attentional capacity for thinking about it as a film. This is no different from other mental activities, for example when we are fully occupied in thinking about chess problems or aspects of nuclear particles without considering whether chess moves or quarks are 'real'. Evaluation of reality-status is a meta-activity that presupposes that part of our limited capacity for conscious attention is used for that activity (see Baars 1988: 321 *passim*; Eysenck and Keane 1990: 97 ff.; Eitzen 1994). To establish hypothetical frameworks demands concentration and would compete with 'real life' frameworks for a limited atten-

---

[13] Cf. Lazarus (1991: 53 f.) which discusses 'pre-emotions' and cites an experiment carried out by Ekman *et al.*, showing that anticipation of a gunshot had limited effect on bodily and facial reaction.

tional capacity.[14] Emotional arousal is often activated during film-viewing, and it may help to focus our attention (Norman 1976: 63 ff.). Because fiction film often deals with basic human situations and correlated emotions, it will possess situations which will be experienced as strongly *motivated*. Fiction films will therefore often evoke intense experiences (Carroll 1988: 102 f.).

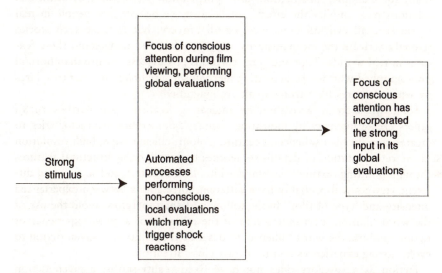

Fig. 1.3 During film-viewing the consciousness reacts to a strong stimulus, and the local evalua-tors of stimuli function automatically and activate a shock reaction while the focus of conscious attention is elsewhere. Later the local reaction becomes embedded in a global evaluation, which might, for example, analyze the stimulus and evaluate the reason for its being quite harmless. Thus activation may happen at the periphery as well as at the centre of conscious attention.

We may distinguish between *local* and *global* 'reality' and activation. Any per-cept or schema has the same 'local reality' as existing in the mind, whether it is part of a fictitious or a real event, and as such it has an activating impact on the mind. The cognitive evaluation of reality-status takes place on a global level as an operation, a labelling of the local phenomena. It is improbable that hypothetical and symbolic phenomena locally exist in a different way than 'real' ones. Salient features may activate locally irrespective of global reality-status. We may be haunted or aroused by quite salient sensations irrespective of their reality-status; the perceptual impact of Imax projections may be very strong, although we know perfectly well that sound and image are simulations. The flourishing pornographic industry is based on the 'local' acti-vation of perceptual cues. The salience and vividness of analogue-iconic

[14] Carroll argues (1988: 23 f.) that attention to films is independent of other motor activities, such as walking: this would, however, only be the case if the motor activity were simple and highly automated. Generally, fiction demands much attentional capacity which would have to compete with other activities for a limited attentional capacity.

presentations may thus be caused by their ability to activate at complex local levels,[15] and the reason for this can only be explained at the level of perceptual-mental processing.

The activation of normally subordinate parameters and features will surface if we isolate and amplify some of these features. As we know from fairy tales, for example, 'abstraction' and 'purification' of features or structural relations may amplify the effect, not because we believe that people in real worlds are all evil, all innocence, or all bravery, but because such stories strongly activate the mechanism by which we feel and understand these features in real worlds. Tom and Jerry cartoons possess less texture than normal photographed worlds: the activating mechanisms are linked to the procedures by which features like strong/weak are magnified.

Some films create activation by indicating 'realism' (see Barthes 1978); others create intensity by indicating 'fantasy'. Sometimes a director tries to create intensity by a salience of texture (colour, cinemascope, high resolution in the representation of detail), sometimes by highlighting structural features through omitting texture (black-and-white, lack of detail, and so on), and different viewers will probably have different correlations between experienced intensity and 'type of film'. In the following I shall therefore avoid the use of the word 'illusion' as a description of the intensity of a given experience of fiction, and use the word 'salience' to describe the ability of a given fiction to evoke strong experiences and to attract close attention.

Fiction as a category does not have fixed reality-status; a given fiction hypothesis or a given segment or frame or a part of a frame will have a reality-status of its own. An episode can be quasi-documentary, pure fantasy, or based on 'a true story'; the narrative can be fictitious but made on location in New York and using 'real police vehicles', or made with backdrops in a studio, or whatever. The 'realist' living-room might have a fantasy creature sitting on the couch, or an everyday conversation could be enacted in a space bereft of any decor. A film, a sequence, and a single frame will thus be composites of many different schemata, each of which may have a reality-status of its own, and the schemata will interact and possibly create a dominant local and/or global reality-status. The often complex levels of reality in the aspects and segments of fiction are continuously analyzed by the viewer, and the cognitive evaluations of its reality-status will also be mentally represented in shorthand as feelings.

Different hypothetical systems of representation can interact with each other, just as hypothetical systems can interact with thematizations of the 'real'

---

[15] S. T. Fiske and Taylor (1991) discuss vividness, and express doubt of any special vividness-effect enhancing a persuasive effect, although they point out that, for example, a story format illustrated with a photograph is more convincing than an abstract, non-vivid description, and that vivid information is more 'entertaining' (i.e. more activating) than non-vivid information.

viewing situation. A film with a medieval setting might suddenly contain cars and television sets, and 'The Flintstones' was made in order to enjoy anachronism. A spatial hypothesis may collapse if a polar explorer steps out of an igloo and sees palm trees and sunny beaches; Wender's *Wings of Desire* confronts natural and supernatural systems of representation, and a description of a hypothetical universe may be interrupted by a representation of the viewing situation. Interference between different systems of representation and between different systems of reality may create surprise and a need for a reorientation and reshuffling of the hypotheses of viewing. Such interactions are often described as 'breaks of illusion', a term that, for the reasons given above, is misleading. A shift of hypothesis and system of representation will often lead to a shift in the kind of salience activated. If the salience of a tense narrative is interrupted by anachronisms or metafictional elements, the viewer's processing will be reoriented, for instance, to a not less salient change of focus of attention, and an intense reshuffling of hypotheses and systems of representation. The change of focus of attention may highlight the systems of reality-representation, but that does not mean that the previous mode of attention implied an 'illusion'.

REALITY INDICATIONS IN VISUAL COMMUNICATION

There are various systems for indicating the reality-status of a given phenomenon. Many languages have constructed distinct representational forms, like tense and several types of case, for instance, to represent differences between hypothetical and actual phenomena and differences between present, past, and future phenomena. This is also the case in audiovisual communication. In the early days of film production, marks were given for the reality-status of a given film sequence, with marks indicating the reality-status of a given sub-sequence within a whole as well as of the sequence as a whole. In the first subgroup we have marks like wipes as indicators of time jumps, and close-ups, followed by blurred images as indicators of dreams and similar subjective states.[16] In the second category we have, for example, marks of a fictional sequence indicated by a credit sequence stating director, cast, and so on, or marks indicating a 'semi-fictional' sequence by written statements such as 'based on a true story', or that this is a newsreel or a commercial.

But explicit marks of reality-status are only possible options. Modern cinematic narrative often dispenses with explicit, conventional marks of the reality-status of a given sub-sequence. We have to infer whether a given sub-sequence is, for example, a dream, or a past event by many different

---

[16] Metz has pointed out (1986: 111 ff.) that these phenomena do not correspond to punctuations in language. They often serve as indicators of a type of mental state, as temporal indicators or as directors of attention.

cognitive procedures, like logical consistency, clues indicating 'marks of age of protagonist', use of competence for evaluating differences between dream-world and reality, or use of competence for evaluating historical, political, and geographical phenomena. In the same way, a given sequence need not be marked as to its reality-status right away. Many fiction films begin *in medias res*, and conventional markers, such as a credit sequence, are placed later in the film (although company indications still precede the beginning of the fic-tional sequence). Secondary signs, such as degree of dramatic structure, must take over the role of indicators of fictitiousness.

Leaving out explicit, conventionalized marks of the reality-status of an audiovisual sequence or sub-sequence is not necessarily a sign of a blurring of the distinction between different types of reality-status (as many Baudrillard-inspired critics seem to think[17]). Seen in a historical perspective, the leaving-out of explicit, conventionalized marks of reality-status has been made possible by relying on viewer competence in constructing the reality-status by means of inference from implicit indications (Messaris 1994). An experienced 'zapper' needs very few seconds to find out whether a given audiovisual sequence is a fiction film or a non-fiction programme, and very few minutes to detect such matters as genre. Television has increased the possible formats of reality-status in audiovisual representations. Those formats have produced the distinction within the temporal mode of the representations between 'direct' transmission and taped representations, and have thereby made the 'taped' qualities of fiction films and their various schemata more visible. The massive reproduction of non-fictive audiovisual material, by increasing the viewers' visual knowledge of the world, has enhanced their competence to judge the reality-status of a given audiovisual phenomenon.

The evaluation of reality-status is closely linked to *the types of acts it makes possible,* although most of these acts are virtual and/or mental-symbolic. News, which is received more or less as it takes place, creates a virtual and undetermined time-space of acts in which the viewer can interfere and/or which can interfere with the viewer. Although viewers almost exclusively interact with the phenomena by a pure cognitive and emotional processing of information, online information activates in a different way from transmis-sions of phenomena, which already represent history and are thereby 'closed', and in yet another way when confronted with fictive-hypothetical phenom-ena, in which the relation to everyday reality is schematic-symbolic and thus cues hypothetical acts and thoughts. Virtual real-life interactions are felt dif-ferently from symbolic acts. The effect of a television programme like *Rescue-*

---

[17] I disagree with the description of the destruction of 'reality' in modern societies by the media as put forward, for example, in Baudrillard (1981); his use of the term 'simulation', for instance, makes a problematic distinction between what is 'real' and the communicative use of behaviours and representations. Cf. Grodal (1992).

911 is linked to the ability of the viewers to construct the seen as real, and thereby to activate an emotional response that is different from an overtly fictitious narrative. Processing given information into complex patterns of 'type of virtual mode of interaction' plus 'type of correlated emotional activation' is a sophistication of the skills necessary to keep track of the reality-status of phenomena of consciousness according to such factors as intent, temporal status, and modal definition, crucial even in a pre-media society.

As 'reality' is determined by several relatively independent parameters, the experience of reality also comes in different forms. Some fantasy films have a 'narrative realism'—the agents act in time-spaces, and have motivations and intentions similar to those in everyday life—combined with a thematic irrealism (talking plants and weird décor, for instance); other films may have a perfect naturalistic setting, but with a temporal structure quite dissimilar to everyday experiences of linear time. The feeling of reality is thus created using a large set of standard assumptions about the world, assumptions which are checked during viewing.

The development of modern audiovisual communication has immensely enhanced the possibilities of producing sound and images, and has therefore reduced the former role of perceptions of audiovisual stimuli as natural indicators of reality, in which echoes and mirror-images were among the few examples of high-definition 'unreal' perceptions. Other indicators have gained more prominent positions as input for the reality-evaluating processes. But, contrary to that which is implicit in a Baudrillard-type understanding of 'reality', any behaviour and representation, even among lower animals, needs cognitive analysis and interpretation. The use of language in humans has massively increased the number of representable phenomena, and written language has eventually removed the physical bonds of time and place between addresser and addressee; the increase in the number of representable phenomena has demanded a corresponding sophistication in the evaluation of the reality-status of the represented. Until quite recently, it has been much cheaper to lie with words than with images, just as the possibility of 'montage' and 'zapping' with words has been immensely greater than with images.[18] Compared to the leaps in the demands of evaluating reality-status caused by the development of language, writing, and print, the development of audiovisual communication seems to demand sophistication in existing cognitive skills rather than radical new ones.

The history of mentality, and especially studies on the transition from orality to literacy, has been concerned with the cognitive consequences of the different linguistic media (see Loewe 1982). A focus of research has been the

---

[18] Part of Eisenstein's motivation for advocating montage was to provide the same ability to connect heterogeneous phenomena as exists in language; cf. his description of the haiku poem as a montage (1949: 28–45).

intellectual and emotional effects produced by writing and by the printed book as special systems of signifiers. Ong (1982) has pointed out that the reading of the printed book leads to a visual representation 'out there', i.e. on the pages of the book, of the body-perceptions of touch and hearing. It has been claimed that this leads to a visual objectivism, as meanings increasingly acquire an existence in the writing 'out there' independent of their mental realizations and, for example, their tactile or olfactory life-world contexts. Havelock (1963) has analyzed the way in which the development of writing in ancient Greece meant that words and their meanings became isolated from the life-world context. In a pre-literate society, oral signifiers had no existence independent of the situations and phenomena signified or the person signifying; they disappeared when spoken, whereas written words have an existence that transcends the immediate time-place-context-addresser-addressee. The meanings have become properties of the words not the world. As an analogy, one might argue that the development of audiovisual representations means that the visual aspects of the world and society have now acquired representations that exist relatively independently of the immediate context in time and place of the addressers and addressees in which they have been filmed (which in itself may be staged), and that they therefore induce the impression that meanings become aspects of the audiovisual representations, not of man, world, or specific historical conditions. If I switch on a multi-channel television set I will be flooded with audiovisual sequences from all over the world, some as old as the turn of the century. In bookshops and libraries it is possible to find texts written several thousand years ago.

It has become impossible to fully receive audiovisual or written text according to something that would be the equivalent of fusion of the different perceptual, cognitive, and emotional dimensions of experience and life-world in oral societies. The experienced viewer watching *The Battleship Potemkin* may have some rough ideas about the Soviet Union in the 1920s and about Czarist Russia, or about Eisenstein and his aesthetic and political ideas, but has normally to rely on general knowledge and a relatively small set of interpretation procedures and assumptions. The abstraction characteristic of fiction reception in media societies changes the experienced emotional tone. For most people, however, this does not lead to feelings of unreality but to types of experience in which the conscious, cognitive aspects of the experience have a more prominent role.

2

Cognition, Emotion, Brain-Processes, and Narration

In this chapter I shall present a general outline of the way in which the brain processes information and the connections between this processing and the basic structures of visual fiction.

Many different methods of reception analysis of fiction exist, but there are two main approaches. The first deals with media reception from a sociological and behaviouristic point of view, in order to understand the 'permanent' impact of media reception on viewers. The second approach describes reception as a process in time realized by a viewer. Important theoretical contributions to this area have been made in German reception studies (see Iser 1978 and Holub 1984), and in the cognitive constructivist approach as developed by Bordwell (1986), related to an approach based on processes of perception as propounded by Arnheim (1974). These approaches make it clear that an audiovisual event consists of a continuous interaction between viewer and viewed. It is therefore dificult to give an autonomous description of the media event irrespective of the viewer. An 'objective' description of what takes place in a fiction film is not identical with the process of viewing.

My purpose in this chapter is to expand the cognitive-constructivist point of view by integrating the perceptual and cognitive with the psychosomatic processes connected with emotions and motivation. Media reception can be seen as a sequence of psychosomatic processes caused by the audiovisual input, but taking place in the viewer's nervous system. One way of describing the reception of the audiovisual flow is therefore to make an exhaustive description of the neurological flow as it takes place in the viewer. Given the present state of psychological knowledge this represents utopia, of course, especially for a non-specialist. However, it is possible to outline certain functions and dimensions of the internal processing.

The need for description of the internal processing is especially strong if we are to describe the subjective aspects of a narrative flow, such as feelings, emotions, and aesthetic effects. It is relatively easy to analyze phenomena belonging to the exterior world, and to come to an inter-subjective agreement about what is taking place: if one person shoots another, the action is there in front of our eyes. Furthermore, classical narrative theory (as put forward by Propp, Bremond, Greimas, and others) is a theory of visible behaviour as represented in visual and linguistic media, sometimes combined with a small set of motives, i.e. mental causes for action. When we analyze the story of a given narrative, we construct a chain of acts and consequences progressing in time and space. Feelings, emotions, and aesthetic perceptions 'take place' in the invisible body/mind interior, and are only parts of the narrative proper if they become the motives for actions or the permanent mental states of the protagonists. It seems as if actions and motives for actions somehow legitimately 'belong' to the screen, to the objective narrative 'out there', whereas aesthetic experiences and emotions belong rather to the subjectivity of the viewer. Alternatively, the subjective and aesthetic phenomena belong to the addresser as a feature of enunciation (see Metz 1991). But, as Bordwell has pointed out (1986: 27–62), the story, or 'fabula', as he calls it, is not something which the viewer receives passively but which he or she has to construct by a series of cognitive acts. Subjective and objective aspects of visual fiction are different mental constructions which both represent 'objective' neurological phenomena. From that perspective, feelings and emotions are just as much 'objective' aspects of the internal constructions of the fabula as cognitions are.

NEURAL STRUCTURES AND MEDIA RECEPTION

A closer examination of the general features of the nervous system will make the reception process clearer, and is essential for understanding the relation between cognitions and emotions. The basic structure of the nervous system is constructed as an input-output machine. The input is fed into the system through the senses, mainly through the tactile, gustatory, and olfactory body senses, and through the remote senses of hearing and vision. The output leaves by the motor-system, that is, by means of the striated muscles which are under voluntary control from the central nervous system. In primitive animals the connection between input and output is more or less hardwired: a stimulus of the senses will cause a reflex, a pre-programmed output, as we know from the knee-jerk reflex and some other stimuli of the body senses.

But in higher animals, and especially in man, the relation between input and output is much more complicated. This complication is, to a large extent, caused by the potential and the problems associated with the remote senses, especially vision, and by our advanced cognitive capabilities. Vision provides a relatively 'objective' representation of the exterior world, which is only possible if this representation of exterior space and its objects is partly separated from the interests and preferences of the body, or from a reflex-like combination of sensation and subjective evaluation of the body-sense type.[1] Vision

---

[1] In connection with the phylogenetic development from primitive organisms to lower mammals, R. G. Heath (1986: 5) says, 'And with this evolution of the central nervous system, emotion appears in intricate relationship with an elaborate sensory system capable of perceiving from

is used for a continuous and partly 'disinterested', but interest-driven, mapping of the environment, which continues for as long as man is awake. The subjective interests now receive their own representations in the emotions and desires, as represented in the memory, in the autonomic nervous system, and in part of the hormonal system.

Many psychoanalytical theories describe the desire to see, the 'scopophilic drive', in Freud's terminology. These theories explain the desire to look, including the desire to watch films and other visual fictions, as having sexual causes, such as being consequences of the castration complex. This is not plausible as a general explanation: vision is a 'built-in' tendency in animals and humans activated throughout their waking hours, and their interest or lack of interest in specific visual objects (whether erotic, life-preserving, life-threatening, or whatever) takes place 'on top' of this continuous visual activity. Freud's conception of 'sublimation' and of the 'superego' presupposes that the mental division between vision and body senses, for example, like the erotically important sense of touch, is mainly culturally reproduced. But the feelings and emotions connected with 'touch' presuppose in evolutionary history that other perceptions work relatively independently of specific feelings and emotions (that vision, for example, makes relatively objective representations). Feelings and emotions are unnecessary in hardwired robots: their motivation for performing actions is that of the humans who build them. But in man (and other higher animals) the remote senses, especially vision, depend partly on motivation produced by the body senses, so that the subject must perform certain operations to 'bridge' the gap between subjective interests, as imprinted in the body and memory, and the object world, as represented by cognition and vision. Experience enables humans to make new links between objects and their general emotional motivation.

In this more complicated system, the input-output axis of sensation–motor output has been supplemented with an intersecting axis of representation against affect-motivation. This makes possible far more sophisticated and flexible mental systems than if we had hardwired stimulus-response patterns (we need not wait for a change in gene codes in order to respond to road signs) but, of course, it also makes the 'mediation' of the different inputs more complicated. Emotions are therefore intimately linked to the large cognitive-emotional 'buffer' between stimulus and response. Frijda (1986: 71) characterizes emotions as 'modes of relational action readiness, either in the form of tendencies to establish, maintain, or disrupt a relationship with the environment or in the form of mode of relational readiness as such'. If Indiana Jones sees a poisonous snake, his emotional arousal may be felt as anger if he intends to attack it, fear if he tries to evade it, despair if he gives up coping.

a distance. Specific patterns of arousal consequent to detection of signals from a distance are now possible. Memory patterns become progressively more complex.'

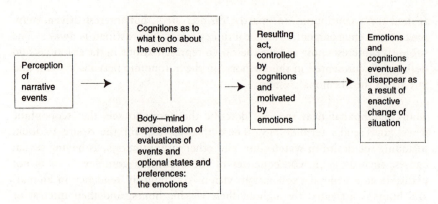

Fig. 2.1. Model of the mental/narrative flow in a viewer's evaluations of protagonist experiences, by which cognitions and emotions build up and cooperate in order to cope with situations, and are possibly followed by deactivation.

In this way cognitions about situations determine the type of emotions felt, and the emotions motivate the cognitions and acts.

EMOTIONS AND THE AUTONOMIC NERVOUS SYSTEM

Our vision and our ability to act through the motor system are experienced as being under the control of our will. An important part of the experience of emotions, however, relates to involuntary body reactions, and 'physical' films try to cue and activate such response. These involuntary reactions are controlled by the autonomic nervous and endocrine systems which regulate the viscera, the heart, stomach, lungs, liver, and skin, and which play a major role in the constitution of emotions. The connection between 'viscera states' and emotions has been known for centuries, because everybody experiences strong changes in the viscera when excited: tears, salivation, change of respiration, butterflies in the stomach, a pounding heart, blushing and sweating. The regulation partly takes place via nerve cells, partly via chemical transmitters such as hormones like adrenalin, and steroids.

The autonomic nervous system is divided into two subsystems. The first is the sympathetic branch, which serves as support for the striated, voluntary motor system when it needs more energy. The sympathetic nervous system is therefore based on support for 'negative' and aversive feelings like anger and fear, connected typically with fight or flight. These reactions are based on subject-object disjunction, such as expelling and rejecting, and therefore the sympathetic nervous reactions support our narrative constructions which are themselves based on subject-object disjunctions. As soon as we start to think about complicated problems in a narration, not only will motor tension build up, but our hearts will also start to beat faster and more adrenalin will be poured into the bloodstream.

The second subsystem is the parasympathetic branch, which is based on restorative activities and is closely related to mostly positive, pleasurable emotions such as serenity and elation. These parasympathetic reactions are based on integration and incorporation. Hunting is therefore supported by sympathetic functions, for instance by a strong pulse and vasoconstriction, so that blood goes to the muscles, whereas the eating of the prey is supported by parasympathetic functions with a lower pulse and vasodilation and blood returning to the stomach; erections in men are parasympathetic reactions, whereas ejaculation is a sympathetic reaction.

Negative situations in which coping action is (or is perceived as) impossible, and which result in reactions like crying and severe stomach upset, are also based on parasympathetic response (see Frijda 1986: 160). Depression is a negative emotion based on loss of control and on subordination; it is based on parasympathetic reactions that are normally connected with positive emotions. Furthermore, depression is characterized by an increase in the secretion of the morphine-like neuromodulator endorphine (Henry 1986: 43). This might partly explain something which intuitively seems problematic: namely the reception interest in depressive, melancholy fictions such as those offered by a number of melodramas and many music videos. The affective response to loss of object or loss of enactive control is not *only* negative: there is a built-in 'pleasure-producing' aspect of loss and heteronomy in the combination of high arousal and lack of motor tension.

The main division between sympathetic and parasympathetic reactions seems to be whether these reactions support active-aversive-controlling or passive-accepting situations irrespective of hedonic tone; in other words , whether the situation is positive or negative. Although we do not have the same kind of instant, voluntary control of our autonomic as of our voluntary nervous system, the autonomic nervous system none the less reflects the situation and the evaluations made 'higher up' at the voluntary-conscious level. When a viewer chooses to watch a film, he thereby chooses to be cued into having constant fluctuations of heartbeat, perspiration, adrenalin-secretion, and so on. These reactions not only passively trail film input, but also have voluntary elements such as empathic, vicarious evaluations of situations and of hypothetical options for the protagonists.

The emotions are generally divided into four to eight basic categories. Plutchik (1980), for example, propounds eight basic emotions: Fear, Anger, Joy, Sadness, Acceptance, Disgust, Expectation, and Surprise.[2] But these may all be seen as complications of the fundamental division between positive and

---

[2] Ortony, Clore, and Collins (1990: 27) compare the 'basic' emotions identified by fifteen leading researchers and find discrepancies.

aversive emotions, or of an approach, a fight-flight, and a behavioural inhibition reaction (Gray 1994).

In relation to our general input-output model there are three different ways of looking at emotions and the autonomic nervous system.

1. Emotions are output-delays

Instead of instant motor output, motivational states are produced in order to be subjective vectors on which the cognitive decision can take place (see Scherer 1994, Damasio 1994). The reason for this is the previously mentioned division between representation, cognition, and the subjective evaluation made possible by the development of the remote senses. The emotional activations are very closely related to memory because, among other reasons, memory has to provide the perceptions from the remote senses with stored information about previous consequences for body senses of given remote-sense percepts. The emotions evoked by memory motivate future acts (see 3 below) and keep the motivation active during possible delays to allow 'deliberation'. The representation of reality-status by feelings is linked to the function of feelings and emotions as 'advisers' for acts.

As output-delays, emotions are closely connected with cognition, which is the reverse side of the output-delay; emotions are not irrational forces, but necessary motivators for cognition and the possible resulting actions. Cognition can be seen as a sequence of hypothetical mental test acts. From this point of view, media reception is also a series of mental test acts. Related to 'delay' is the communicative use of emotions as 'acts' which influence the addressee. Expressions of 'anger' and 'love', for example, may delay physical communication in order to induce a change of behaviour.

2. Emotions represent auto-modifications

These replace voluntary object-directed motor output, and therefore emotions represent safety-valves as well as permitting subjective excitation coupled with release mechanisms that are independent of enactive object relations.

3. Emotions form part of the mechanisms which create body-states that support and facilitate acts or body restoration

Emotions like anger and rage, which motivate actions, are linked to autonomic reactions which, for instance, increase the blood flow to the muscles; whereas peaceful mental states decrease blood-flow to the muscles and increase it to skin and stomach.

In the processing of the audiovisual flow these aspects work together.

Output can be delayed by inducing conflicting motivation which must be resolved, for instance, by a choice between rescuing a lady in distress or running away from tigers or snakes, or it can be delayed by a slowing down of opportunities for enactive outlet. Autonomic outlet in the form of, say, tears, laughter, or depression can be cued by many means. As a series of mental test acts, fiction builds up and maintains brain and body routines in hypothetical situations that are partly transferable to non-fictive life.

The expression 'autonomic nervous system' indicates that it consists of biological mechanisms that operate without voluntary or cognitive control. However, as mentioned above, it is mostly the cognitively and voluntarily accessible situations that evoke the autonomic reactions, and thus the strong distinction between emotion and cognition seems to disappear. One cognitive theory of emotions which emphasizes this interrelation is the acclaimed (but also much-criticized) so-called cognitive labelling theory formulated by Schachter, who has tried to demonstrate that different interpretations can be made of autonomic arousal; depending on context, different labels can be provided for the same state of body arousal (see Chapter 4 below). Another approach is that of Averill (1980). He describes the way in which emotions are constructed as transitory social roles, characterized by reactions to phenomena that are interpreted as being beyond self-control. Crying provides an outlet, but it also solicits support from the environment and understanding of an inability to cope; anger is not only a reaction, but also a message. Emotions in this context are not primarily reactions, but means of communication. Between loss of self-control and full control of emotions lies a spectrum of mediating states, in which emotions serve as voluntarily induced enforcers and legitimators of 'autonomic' roles and attitudes.

LYRICAL PERCEPTION, ASSOCIATION, AND NARRATIVE ENACTION

In order to describe the flow from perception to motor enaction and its influence on the emotional toning of experiences we have first to describe fundamental dimensions in the way we exist in and comprehend the world: space, field, synchrony and time, line, diachrony. The film image and the world exist as space, just as our eyes are able to analyze space and our visual cortex is able to make maps which possess some of the same spatial features as the space seen. Our response exists in a linear, sequential time, just as we perceive films as sequences of processes and acts taking place in *time*-space. Visual fiction exists as a positive presence, as picture-sound with a perceptual relation between viewer and the presence of the fictive phenomena. But this presence is a point in a temporal sequence of past and future perceptions of the phenomena of fiction. The difference in affective tone between these two dimensions is visible when we stop a video recorder and change the status of a frame from that of an element in a spatio-temporal sequence to that of a spatial entity to be perceived. Time has stopped 'out there' and continues only in the spectator. This difference between a still frame and frames in motion is analogous to the difference between a photograph (or a painting) and motion pictures, or between a lyrical poem and a narrative. A still or a photograph is 'dead' and 'lifeless', yet saturated with special emotions. It is present in front of our eyes, but also 'absent' in the sense that it clearly shows itself to be a trace of something else, a past, an elsewhere which only reaches the spectator via the shadows of the electronic or photographic record. It has lost its sequential, open, and undecided meaning.

Part of the salience of motion is generated from basic motion-detecting and motion-representation systems; but part of the live salience is also created by 'higher' mental models of enaction, of enactive meaning and enactive interaction between subject and object. First, the basic visual experience of motion: the visual system has three prominent subsystems, one concerned with the analysis of dynamic form (for example, bodies dancing), one concerned with colour and form-with-colour, and one devoted to analyzing signals about motion (see Zeki 1993 and Movshon 1990). Motion is therefore normally not only perceived as a succession of 'frames', like a succession of isolated film frames, but, as a result of a space-time system that has its own intensities, it is felt in the 'live' quality of motion pictures (unless they reproduce a freeze-frame). From an evolutionary point of view, the motion-detecting system is older than shape perception, and the edge of the retina is only sensitive to motion. People with a damaged motion-detection system experience problems with the mental construction of motion as such, including the 'feeling' of motion and its intensity. A patient with a damaged motion-perception system, for example, complained that when he poured tea into a cup, the tea appeared frozen 'like a glacier' (Humphreys and Bruce 1989: 110): the means of representing motion was absent. Therefore the 'live' quality of film and television is no more an illusion than object-recognition by means of a picture; the live quality is the (strongly) felt aspect of an activation of functions necessary for constructing motion in the world as well as on film.[3]

Part of the 'live' salience is, however, also linked to activation of 'higher' narrative expectations and correlated autonomic activation cued by the steady stream of emotion-evoking situations. In a real-world situation, a person has two simultaneous means of connection to 'reality': he has perceptual access

---

[3] The gestalt psychologists were very interested in what they called the 'phi phenomenon', seen when two sources of light located close to each other in a dark room are switched on and off: this is perceived as a continuous movement of light between the points at which the sources of light are located. They thought that an electrical charge in the brain swept across the visual projection area and filled the gap. Gregory (1990: 120 f.) criticizes the gestalt-psychology explanation of the 'phi phenomenon', but replaces it with an explanation that also emphasizes the continuity-persistence problem: the brain is preset for filling minor lacunae in retina input. This does not however, explain the experience of motion as such.

and enactive access. When he sees or hears something with his remote senses, he can decide to perform acts related to these perceptions. He can perhaps decide to avoid the seen by looking away, or he can walk toward it, taste or touch it, transform it, have a closer look, or whatever. Perceptions will activate emotions, which will cue actualized or optional acts. Time as future is linked to the ability to act and, in a voluntarily and enactive way, to change the perceptual setting. What we see with our eyes could at some future point be touched by and modified by our hands.

Most narrative fictions will simulate reality because emotions aroused can be symbolically and vicariously gratified by fictitious acts. In standard fictions, as in real life, the future has not yet taken place, therefore it activates the wish for or an option of future mediation between the different registers of sensation. For someone looking at a painting, a still, or a photograph of an aversive or attractive phenomenon, the distance is absolute, beyond mediation in the non-existent future, despite the perceptual presence; whereas a spectator seeing aversive or attractive phenomena in visual fiction is promised possible future mediations with its objects of desire or aversion, by identifying with a protagonist and his mediating acts. To participate at this level of meaning when consuming fiction, the viewer or reader must identify with some protagonists' capabilities for subjectivity and action within the fictive world of the screen.

In visual fiction it is very easy to demonstrate the enactive participation and projection into the fictive sequence, and the resulting creation of a 'deep' fictional time-space, by showing what happens when action and motion are removed. If a film or videotape is played in slow motion it becomes more 'shallow', 'lyrical', 'timeless', 'saturated' (cf. the prototypical use of slow motion in Antonioni's *Zabriskie Point*). We can no longer have full enactive identification with the fictive phenomena. The acts and characters become objects controlled by an invisible subject. It is not only because slow motion, for instance in sports coverage, is often used in replay that the future aspect of the fiction is transformed into a mood of pastness, memory, or abstraction, but also because the very definition of a present as possible future implies enactive identification on a human scale. The sensations projected by enaction into the deep space of action and object gratification now surface in slow motion, transformed into a more metaphoric-saturated form. The same difference exists between the saturated experience of poems compared to the tense experiences of a story. The analytic use of slow motion in sports coverage or fiction shows the connection between the 'abstract' and the 'mental'. The transformation of enactive tensity into intensity and saturation by using slow-motion is at work even when slow-motion is used with the narrative purpose of increasing tense expectations to create emphasis: de Palma often uses 'emphatic' slow motion in dramatic situations, for example, in *Carrie* and *The Untouchables,* which results in a saturated effect for the viewer.

In a video game, the connection between the screen and the viewer is established both as the visual perception of what is taking place and as a capacity to influence the action by intellectually controlled motor response via the joystick. The viewer of visual fiction has only perceptual access to the screen world. Nevertheless, cognitive and 'subliminal' motor simulations of motor schemata exist as underlying, but suppressed and projected, patterns in the viewing situation, similar to the way in which children learn to read silently, even learning to suppress the movements of their lips. In moments of peak tension during an action-suspense fiction, this muscular pattern will surface as a barely suppressed muscular tension in the viewer aiming at release in physical action. Adopting the terminology of the psychologists Bruner and Horowitz (Horowitz 1970: 80), I shall call this pattern of signification or meaning 'enactive', a level of 'motor meaning', i.e., motor schemata (procedural schemata) which anchor the structuration of the relations of a subject to objects. This enactive meaning is somehow fused with visual and verbal levels of meaning, and is especially connected with meaning's vectorization, its directedness, the telic, sequential schemata diminishing arousal. (In contradistinction to meaning as perception and differential sets of perception creating clusters of associations, as in the connectedness of memory and nonnarrative 'fiction', see the description of associative networks in Chapter 3.)

Active control of the world, as modelled in fairy tales and in play, is only one of two basic ways of relating to it. The second way is the passive one. Human beings, and especially small children, are often passively bombarded with aversive or pleasant stimuli without being able to control the situation and react. In the passive position the perceptual and associational activation cannot be transformed into a voluntary enactive response. The only way that a person can 'control his condition', the perceptions and excitations he receives passively from without or within, is by motor outlet: by autonomic motor response (shivering, crying, blushing, and so on) in active motor modification of the environment, or by mental acts. The common-sense conception of a subject is closely connected with the ability to act, to modify a situation by motor outlet. Nevertheless, many incoming stimuli are beyond enactive control, and will cause interior modifications (for example, fear, and sorrow).

NARRATIVE AND LYRICAL FUNCTIONS AS INDICATED BY BRAIN ARCHITECTURE

In the paragraph above, I noted some aspects of perception-enaction, space-time, the lyrical, and the epical; and we may now expand the description of fundamental mental functions related to visual fictions. The first set of functions relate to the distinction between voluntary-goal-directed and involuntary, and possibly repetitive-rhythmic, acts. These two types of reaction represent two stages in evolutionary development, and support different narrative forms as well as different emotional types. The second set of functions relates to the relation between linear and associative field functions.

The mental system may be divided into two types of functions: one type, located in the rear of the brain, in man normally dominant in the right hemisphere, is predominantly occupied with input processing (often by means of analogue and parallel processing of, for instance, space-perception) and with automatic, repetitive output processing. Another type, located in the front of the brain, normally dominant in the left hemisphere, is predominantly occupied with voluntary motor output, and with cognitive processes of the sequential and logical-propositional type.

Cognitive psychologists have studied the effect on linguistic performance of damage to the left hemisphere of the brain (Ellis and Young 1988: 251–8). These studies indicate that the ability to sing, to recite lyrics, to repeat cliché phrases, and to use tone of voice in order to express affective emphasis often remain unharmed; these patients are able to sing, but unable to speak propositional sentences. Persons with certain types of left-hemisphere damage are unable to perform fictitious 'hypothetical' acts, such as drinking an imaginary glass of water, but are able to drink a real glass of water (see Woody 1982: 297).

Patients with damage to the right hemisphere of the brain often have problems in understanding metaphorical sentences, in understanding humour, giving a résumé of a story, and comprehending emotions attributed to characters in a tale; furthermore, they have problems with tasks involving visual imagination. In the language of structural semiotics, it appears that the functions dominant in the right hemisphere are necessary for paradigmatic-synchronic and achronic phenomena, whereas the functions dominant in the left hemisphere are necessary for syntagmatic-diachronic phenomena, if we understand achrony-synchrony as including repetition (see Jakobson 1956).

It is not particularly interesting in itself for non-neurologists to know that a given phenomenon takes place or presupposes a given brain hemisphere or brain localization, because most people have a complete brain. What is interesting is that the synchronic and repetitive phenomena are based on functions that are different from certain types of diachronic phenomena. That patients with left-hemisphere lesions may maintain the ability to sing and to produce 'automatic', non-propositional sentences indicates that the brain has two types of dynamic function, a lyrical and a narrative, so to speak.

I shall examine the propositional-narrative function first. The key structural basis for this function is literally or figuratively a voluntary motor relation directed from a subject and toward an object, for example: James grasps the apple, or: James is working hard on the problem. The ability to perform voluntary and sequential real or mental acts seems to be connected with the ability to combine motor-act simulations with imagined object-targets for these acts. The imagined objects are fetched from memory, from the past, and transported ahead in time as objects of these acts. As mentioned earlier, a person with a dominant hemisphere lesion is not able to perform fictive acts, but can perform acts that are triggered by real stimuli in a way similar to a reflex. As Woody (1982: 297) notes: 'Ideational apraxia is the inability to perform conceptualized motor acts . . . It is not the movement that is lost, but the ability to perform it as an imagined proposition. This disorder is seen with lesions of the dominant parietal lobe.' He describes two image types in the brain: The primary image is processed in the non-dominant hemisphere and is based on sensory input, and it is this image which is the 'raw material' for a possible construction of an extended image[4] by the dominant hemisphere.

In the context of narrative reception this implies that, if the input activates the sequential functions, for example by sympathetic reconstructions of mental or physical acts, this will cause a processing of the primary image into an extended, conceptualized one. *The narrative constructions will be long chains of simulated acts directed toward conceptualized images of objects or situations which serve as goals for the acts.* This activity can be seen as 'just' cognition and simulation of action, but it is also a particular type of gratification, characterized by tensity followed by relaxation. Furthermore, this vectorized, sequential meaning is not only object-related: it is also a subjective attitude, and we can construct narratives that activate meaning-vectors, meaning-functions without any clear meaning-objects.

Directedness, the voluntary acts/simulated acts directed toward imaginary concrete or abstract objects, constitutes time as going toward the future and also constitutes intention, two key structures in producing narratives. Fiction, scientific hypothesis-formation, and the everyday intentional construction of a future as the goal for day-to-day actions are three closely connected activities. The problem of understanding the 'free, teleological will' consists in comprehending the way in which mental constructions, fictive scenarios of the future, can function as causes for acts.

One mark of full consciousness and intentionality is the ability to construct present or future objects and to establish teleological relations. People suffering from spasmodic cramps, lower animals, or robots are normally perceived as ruled by causal and unintentional mechanisms. Much fiction is, as I shall discuss in detail in Chapter 8, centred on the reaction to such causal behaviour as laughter-reactions evoked by comic automatism, fascination evoked by

---

[4] The 'term, which was developed by Bergson . . . implies some inference drawn from perception. It is an image of an image. The construction itself may or may not correspond to physical reality. . . . According to Kant, the world causes only the matter of sensation . . . ; it is our own mental apparatus, that is, the CNS [central nervous system], that orders this matter in space and time and supplies the concepts by means of which we understand experience. It does this by extended imagery.' Woody (1982: 309).

rhythmic movements, or fear evoked by 'hostile' automatism in robots or in reptiles and other lower animals.

Damasio (1994) has described as a hypothesis the way in which the brain in the right somato-sensory area produces an image of the present state of the body. This is then passed on to pre-frontal regions, which will normally cognitively and affectively assess present or hypothetical situations involving the person. If these brain structures are damaged, a person will be incapable of emotionally evaluating situations and will therefore not be able to act 'rationally' either, because of lack of proper motivation. Without the priorities of emotions, the brain does not have guidelines for functioning and for goal-setting.

It is not only the brain that participates in the directedness toward a goal. Experiments have shown that activities involving sequentiality and goal-directedness activate the motor system and create muscular tension (see Malmo 1975: 34 ff. *passim*). This has been demonstrated by measuring electrical activity in the nerves of the motor system through electromyography or EMG. At the beginning of a directed, sequential act, tension as measured by EMG gradients starts to rise until the task is completed and the tension drops. Tension has, for instance, been measured in forehead muscles; this tension rises continuously in people listening to detective stories and then drops at the end of the story. The same rise and fall take place during intense intellectual operations, like solving mathematical problems. To express intellectual activity in muscular terms like tension and relaxation is therefore not merely to use metaphorical expressions. These curves of tension followed by relaxation constitute the basis for the 'closed', non-cyclic aspects of narration. According to Malmo (1975: 57), 'A prompt, large EMG drop generally coincides with successful completion of a task, giving the person a "feeling of closure"'. When Eco, Barthes, and others argue against *la clôture du texte*, they are not arguing against something that is *per se* an ideological construction.[5] Closure is part of the neurologically built-in schemata by which we comprehend the world as acts or series of acts in which tension is followed by relaxation. If motoneuronal activity is blocked, for example with curare-type drugs, the result, according to Malmo, is probably an unfocused stream of consciousness, correlated with the heterogeneous and synchronous associative fields of the world as sensory input. Furthermore, the tension-relaxation pattern is not

[5] Although Eco (1989; 1962) tries not to be normative when discussing 'openness', this is nevertheless associated with freedom of choice and options and with life as characterized by chance and random phenomena, because his point of view is 'perceptual', not 'enactive'. When Eco (1989: 105–22) discusses television aesthetics and Antonioni's *L'Avventura*, for example, the 'openness' is connected to the unplannedness of the totality of reality as exemplified in live television, whereas he indirectly presupposes the 'intentional closure' connected to the planning of the experienced 'open' work *L'Avventura*. Barthes (1972b: 7) speaks about 'the closure of western discourse', implying that closure must be a special 'western' mechanism.

necessarily erotic, and *narrative tension is therefore not identical with 'posi-tive' narrative desire as is often implied in narrative theory and film theory.* Tension could, for example, be motivated by aversion.

Let us now return to some aspects typical of the right hemisphere (or, more correctly, the non-dominant hemisphere). Three important functions of the right hemisphere can be singled out. The first is the coordination of primary image-processing; the second concerns the regulations based on affective structures of repetitions and redundancies; the third is the assembling of an image of the body state that provides support for emotionally evaluating present and hypothetical situations.

The retina has millions of rod and cone cells. The activation of these cells does not in itself provide what we understand by the word 'image', but it does provide an array of intensity values (comparable to the result produced if we imagine our visual input as consisting of a vast number of discrete pixels without any structure). Marr has produced a model showing the way in which these intensity values are processed (1982: 37, for example). According to this model, the main steps are as follows.

The intensity values registered from rod-and-cone input are processed by filtering so that significant changes in light intensity are registered. Significant changes in light intensity will often correspond to significant changes in the visual world, such as the border of an object or a major local change in the form of an object. A face will have significant changes in light intensity where hair borders air or borders the temple. By this filtering of the major changes in the fluctuation of light intensity of a two-dimensional array, the visual input is transformed into a structure of outlines of objects, *the primal sketch,* similar to an artist's drawing. The type of analysis which an artist makes when drawing is closely related to that which the visual system performs automatically by a bottom-up process. The next step consists of providing a third dimension to the primal sketch. This is done by various means, from stereopsis, in which the input from the two eyes is compared, to evaluations of other clues, such as texture gradients, clues of shadows in relation to hypothesis of direction of light, etc. This leads to what Marr calls the 2½-D sketch, meaning that the image is seen from a given point, therefore the objects are seen from a given angle, and so the 2½-D sketch corresponds to what is ordinarily called a three-dimensional representation, and which Marr would call 'a viewer-centred' description.

Marr reserves the term 3-D for the result of a further processing, the making of an abstract model of a given object that represents its essential three-dimensional features irrespective of the given point of view. The 3-D model serves as a reference model for computing that a given 2½-D sketch is a specific view of a given 3-D object, because a given 3-D object can be seen from many different viewpoints and therefore gives rise to many different 2½-D sketches. The 3-D representation is an 'object-centred' representation. The need for a 3-D model has been disputed: it has been argued that the memory stores some 'canonical views' of objects (say, a horse seen from the side where its outline provides optimal information), and these canonical views are used as reference models for calculating identity when objects are seen from 'untraditional' points of view, for example, a horse seen from above or from the back, or a face seen from above (see Humphreys and Bruce 1989: 78 ff., Kosslyn 1994: 127–45).

Marr's model of vision is a bottom-up, data-driven one. The visual input is automatically processed step by step without any interference from top-down, concept-driven procedures. It has been argued that some top-down elements in the processing of visual data cannot be avoided, that, for example, a phenomenon like figure-ground organization presupposes a top-down function (see Weisstein and Wong 1987, Kosslyn 1994).

Primary image processing is characterized by parallel processing. Based, for instance, on excitation from more than 100 million rods and cones and on memory-stored schemata, the brain constructs gestalts and holistic fields of intensities (see Arnheim 1974, Gregory 1990; 1970). These may be fields of texture, as in the processing of areas of colour- and light-intensities, geometrical figures, and complex visual patterns. The excitation created by this process of primary input-processing and by these asynchronous fields is often connected with visual aesthetics proper, and this excitation is perhaps one half of what Barthes (1970a) speaks of when he uses the term 'third meaning'.[6] Such field excitation cannot be fully transformed into propositional form or into sequential processes of the motor-output type.

Many modern modes of representation in art, and to some extent in film and video art, could be considered as ways of seeing 'upstream', 'against the grain' of the processes of vision, and are therefore often an attempt to move from systems of 'meanings' to those of 'intensities'. One way of looking at meaning is to see it as defined in relation to 'mental models of a mid-sized world'. This implies that the prototypical level of meaning is one at which we have objects, and agents, and acts and preferences relating agents to objects. The sentence 'The cat was hungry and ate a mouse', or a visual representation of agents and objects, has a prototypical and self-evident 'meaningfulness'; whereas a distinctive feature in language or a pixel element in vision is meaningful not in itself but only as part of a signifier producing significant entities in the 'mid-sized', 'human-sized' world of subjects, objects, and their properties. In the same way, we have to 'scale down' cosmic dimensions for them to 'make sense'.

[6] The 'second half' of Barthes' 'third meaning' may be the non-conscious priming effect of saturated private and public networks of associations; cf. the paragraph on 'Networks of associations' in Ch. 3.

The visual system is preset to transform local intensity-values into a primal sketch (of objects and major features of objects), and, further, to produce a 2½-D sketch; and the directedness of these processes is mentally *felt* as a search for 'meaningfulness', for what it 'looks like'. This meaningfulness represents the way in which the embodied human consciousness is constructed as a 'holistic' coordinating mechanism for survival in the 'midsized world' of acts and objects. Consciousness has no direct access to the pixel level of vision or the level of the singular muscle innervation: it has its focus of attention on the superior level (indicated by primal sketch and 2½-D sketch) at which the holistic cognitive coordination of the total organism enhances survival by mapping and acting on objects in space. Thus when Derrida and others are surprised to discover meaninglessness when they go to an 'atom', 'distinctive feature', or 'pixel' level of 'difference', it is because they have assumed the wrong hypothesis, that meaning can be defined at all levels, instead of seeing meaning as a relatively high-level phenomenon.

The processing of the visual input can be 'short-circuited' by making representations that, to a greater or lesser extent, resist processing. Op-art pictures have an outlay which short-circuits the function of feature detectors or filtering processes (see Blakemore 1990). Some abstract expressionists paint pictures that cannot be turned into a primal sketch, but resemble texture without any definite 'structure'. Although the works of impressionists can provide the basis for a primal sketch, they still highlight phenomena of local intensities. Film experiments, in which the images are made 'grainy', are comments on the cinematic mediation, but the grains representing the film stock are as discrete as an individual retina cone and produce a highlighting of the local qualities of vision *vis-à-vis* the global qualities; out-of-focus sequences blur the delimitation of objects and put emphasis on fluctuations of intensities. 'Non-figurative' experiments are mostly to be found in experimental film, but often mainstream narrative films will also briefly insert images which short-circuit the visual processing by contextual masking or close-ups, or which in other ways evoke 'upstream' steps in visual processing.

One of the effects of 'short-circuiting' the preset processing of visual input is to give salience to pre-meaning intensities. In the last 100 years there has been a tendency to identify 'aesthetics proper' with pre-meaning intensities, whether these intensities are caused by a return to a more non-figurative, texture-dominated level or by 'short-circuiting' high-level narrative structures of meaning. The many 'mimetic' schools and trends during the same time-span have been seen as intending a 'meaning-effect', not an aesthetic effect. However, other periods have had other criteria for the 'aesthetic proper', for example definitions closely related to 2½-D representations of discrete objects in a viewer-centred space, or representations of directly 'meaningful' narratives. The 'third meaning' or 'excess' does not represent more genuine artistic phenomena than 'first' or 'second' meanings, just as mimesis *per se* is as 'artistic' as anti-mimesis *per se*. (None the less, to tell a story or to make mimetic representations is not felt in the twentieth century to be quite the central 'aesthetic' endeavour that working with basic perceptual phenomena is.)

As noted earlier, it seems that the right hemisphere is governed more by causality and repetition than by teleology, goal-directedness, and will. To sing or to recite poems are acts that repeat previously learned patterns, and the acts therefore possess involuntary aspects. Furthermore, singing or the reciting of poems are often expressive acts; that is, they are not object-directed, teleological acts. Rhythm has traditionally been one of the most characteristic features of songs and poems, and is, furthermore, characteristic of the function of many processes regulated by the autonomic nervous system, like pulse and breathing.

Pribram (1982) has described the way in which repetition and redundancy are fundamental for habituation and positive feelings of familiarity, and has stated that structures in the autonomic nervous system 'amygdala' play an important role in the affective aspects of repetition. Damage to these structures leads to a syndrome of *déjà vu* or *jamais vu*, an inappropriate feeling of familiarity or unfamiliarity. Pribram summarizes some of his points as follows:

Repetition results in habituation and recognition. Variations on a repetitive pattern (novelties) evoke dishabituation (orienting) which is felt, and the feeling is generated independently of the recognition of the variation. . . . while the aesthetics of music is a function of the recognition of variations, musical meaning results from the generation of feelings produced by these same variations or patterns of repetition. (1982: 27)

And, later, he states that aesthetics is concerned with recognition of invariances, processed hierarchically, whereas meaning (which in this context is connected with feelings) is processed in a more web-like 'associative' organization. Style may be a type of organization of patterns of repetition that mediate aesthetics and associative meaning, and which combine fields of space with repetitive fields in time.

Thus Pribram describes a polarity between, on one side, a mental function (placed at the rear of the brain) which makes a cognitive and hierarchical analysis of a work of art by isolating the invariant features, and, on the other side, a more affectively oriented mental function (placed in the limbic structures at the front of the brain), which retains repetitions and redundancies and connects them by an associative network, for example via feeling. These associative structures Pribram calls 'meaning' as opposed to semantic reference, and they are objective structures consisting of the network and its feelings.[7] This means that meaning is a function of the history of the subject (in a broad

---

[7] Reference is therefore the directed link by which a signifier points to a phenomenon: 'cow' refers to a four-legged animal, whereas the meaning of cow is a network of associations, of which the signified in a structuralist sense would be one subset, and activated connotations another.

sense of history which includes the minor history of the given reception of a work of art/piece of communication that creates local redundancies and associations, as well as the more comprehensive networks made during longer periods in the history of the individual). Dreams may be formed by such cobweb-like, associative patterns of images, which become activated by processes more of the causal-repetitive than the sequential-teleological type, not least because of the total motor block during REM sleep (see Hobson 1988). But at the same time the dream-situation activates strong narrative schemata for meaning-production.

Rhythm and repetition create habituation, and that means that these processes create an accordance between the perceptual input-world and the interior processing. Rhythm and repetition synchronize the world as input, with the brain and its rhythmic patterns of self-activation. However, this could also mean that the voluntary cognitive and motor-based sequential functions become suspended. The power of the cliché, the musical pattern, or the dance, and their capability to evoke emotion, is a well-known effect of the suspension of voluntary control and voluntary output by repetitive non-object-directed patterns. Overload might further result in autonomic outlet, for instance crying, sobbing, or laughter.

Emotions are—not surprisingly—connected with input-processing. We speak of passion as something which exists in opposition to action: passion expresses heteronomy, dependence either on world-input or body-input. And we describe the way in which we become 'touched' and 'moved', words that describe our perceptions as passive input, not as possible targets for output. From a narrative point of view, this means that, in order to simulate certain emotions and feelings, the input-output processing in the viewer must be delayed or blocked, possibly by identification with the protagonist. Melodrama, for instance, uses a series of devices to block voluntary action, such as simply removing the possible objects (for example, by allowing the beloved to die or disappear) and thus making action impossible. Not only sensations but also memories and images of mental states are characterized by suspension of a motor attitude. This suspension leads to an affective charge of the images and perceptions that I shall call *saturation,* and which, in some respects, corresponds to the feeling-aspect of what Pribram calls meaning, while also comprehending more specific emotional values. By reception of fiction and other media products, saturations are the results of emotionally toned and memorized perceptions which have not been transformed into 'motor' tension, and therefore sensation, input-processing, and memory-functions become visible as distinct phenomena. In memories this saturation is a trace of not-enacted excitation that is cut off from its original context of enaction, but that also serves as an emotional marker of future events.

Above I have characterized several different modes or tones that relate to the types of mental processes experienced. If the mental focus is linked to non-figurative perceptual processes, the experience will be *intense;* if the mental focus is on a figurative associative web, it will be *saturated;* if the focus is on goal-directed mental or motor acts, it will be *tense;* if the mental focus is on autonomic-rhythmic processes, it will be *emotive.* Films cue and amplify such mental experiences, and may switch focus between the different mental functions and correlated emotional tones.

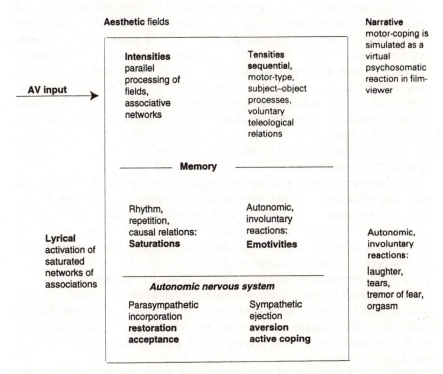

Fig. 2.2. The relation between mental function and emotional tone: perceptual processes are felt as (aesthetic) intensities; memory functions and/or dynamic repetitions are often linked to feelings of saturated emotions; 'muscular' coping is linked to feelings of tense emotions; autonomic response provides strong, characteristic emotivity tones.

AESTHETIC DIMENSIONS AND A MODEL OF THE NARRATIVE FLOW

In Fig. 2.2 I have constructed a very simplified model of the dimensions of the flow seen from the point of view of the processing of the audiovisual flow. The model brings together many of the above-mentioned functions. The flow from left to right suggests the movement from input to output, from sensation and perception to sequential cognition and action. Before the left- and after the right-hand side of the model is the 'world', the *Umwelt*. But although it is the 'same' world, the model indicates that this world exists in two roles, as addresser of sense impressions and as object of cognition and action, although they are linked together as acts that, while modifying the world, will modify sense-impressions (like painting a wall). But the world might well look different as addresser of sensation than it does as object of action and cognition.

The movement from left to right also represents the time axis: sensation and memory (re)construct present and past, whereas action, fiction, and hypothetical thought construct the not-yet-existing, the future, which, of course, will always be a hypothetical, fictive construction based on a processing of present and past, although, paradoxically, these 'forward-directed' and act-oriented constructions are felt to be more 'real'. To a certain degree the movement from left to right furthermore corresponds to the movement from 'inward-mental' to 'outward-objective'. We have access to inner and outer reality only through mental constructions and modelling based on sensation, and therefore the distinction between the inner and the outer reality is a one between the mental principles of construction used.

The dimension from top to bottom suggests the polarity or axis between body and representation and calculation of environment. The aspects that make a more 'passive' representation of the world, sensation, are shown in the top-left-hand corner, and the 'active' representation of the world in the top-right-hand corner. At the bottom are the aspects that represent body preferences, either innate-autonomic preferences, such as heartbeat, or those obtained by the programming of memory through socialization.

Whereas the horizontal dimension seems to advocate a modified stimulus-response point of view, the vertical dimension emphasizes the point that the subject is, to some degree, self-activated and self-motivated within the framework constructed by the bio-history of the gene-codes and the history of socialization of memory.

At four of the corners of the upper square, characteristic functions (aesthetic, narrative, lyrical, and autonomic) are indicated, corresponding to four modes of affects: intensities, tensities, saturation, and emotivities. The fourth corner could be provided with the indication 'melodramatic/comic functions', here labelled *emotivities* as a term for the dynamic-autonomic form of saturations that, in their extreme form, find an outlet by autonomic expressions like laughter and tears.[8]

My intention has been to provide tools for understanding and analyzing the dynamic and process-oriented nature of reception using this psychological description. Reception is not a continuous labelling of discrete and autonomic

---

[8] Branigan has suggested that I should call autonomic reactions 'autotelic'. This terminology is useful if we remember that autonomic, autotelic reactions like tears might be used as means of influencing other people.

aspects of the flow. Perceptual, emotional, and cognitive aspects are functionally related and represent interacting neural processes in the brain-body totality. Most of the neural processes are not conscious: much of the constructive work in image-formation, and much of the implementation or simulation of motor programmes, takes place at a non-conscious level, but many processes will be felt, for instance, as intensities, saturations (emotivities), and tensities.

The viewer's processing of fiction can be described in a flow diagram with four main steps, shown in Fig. 2.3. Of course, such a diagram represents a great simplification; it does not describe all possible feedback processes and top-down hypotheses, and does not reflect the fact that all the processes of the different steps might take place simultaneously. Nevertheless, this kind of 'linear' diagram serves as an illustration of the importance of flow direction.

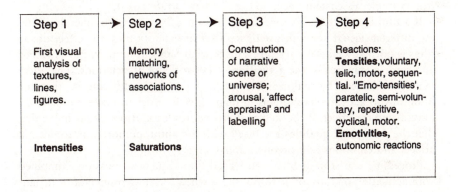

Fig 2.3 Four steps in the processing of the audiovisual input.

The first step consists of basic perception. Rays of light enter the eye and activate the millions of rods and cones there. The brain makes its first analysis of input. It will try to analyze colour, contrast, and so forth, and find figures, ground, and spatial dimensions. This process creates perceptual intensities without any meaning in the ordinary sense of the word. Many abstract paintings and many experimental films try to produce an input that can only be processed at a Step 1 level. Modern ideas of 'pure aesthetics' often equate aesthetics with Step 1 processes, as in Pollock's paintings and Brakhage's film, although this is a limited definition of aesthetics, systematically as well as from the point of view of the history of aesthetics. Arousal may be generated in relation to surprise and orienting activities.

The second step consists of memory-matching. If Step 1 has produced, say, an animal-like figure, the brain runs through its memory-files of animal shapes in order to match it and determine its identity. (For the sake of simplicity, I am omitting the feedback loops of top-down procedures, and pretending that all this takes place in a bottom-up fashion.)

So the brain searches its memory-files for possible matches, aided by feelings of familiarity or unfamiliarity. The items in the memory-files are not only stored by, say, visual structures, but also with affective values, affective labels. If the match of the figure is 'snake', then the item will surface in consciousness with its visual features and with its affective value, fear. To be conscious of snakes implies weaker or stronger simulation of an affect or emotion: fear, say. If the match is 'Marilyn' or 'teddy bear', the match will evoke erotic or tender feelings. If the figure input is complex, say snake + grizzly bear + Marilyn + teddy bear, the match-activation of the memory-files will, of course, evoke complex, mixed feelings. This accords with Eisenstein's description of the way in which emotions are represented and evoked by montage (for example, Eisenstein 1949: 30 f. and Metz 1974b: 204 ff.).

If a film concentrates its representations on a Step 2 level by merely showing different visual items that activate a set of memory files, the effect of the films is normally labelled 'lyrical'. This is what happens in many music videos and some commercials: the activation of networks of associations. The effect may be enhanced by making the matching procedure difficult, so that the brain has to activate many items in many files in order to make the match. I have called the effect of the step two procedures 'saturations', thus indicating that the perceptual qualities are fused with the anthropomorph or zoomorph affects and emotions in a preoperational state.

Processing can stop at Step 2 in lyrical film sequences, possibly combined with activation of autonomic response, as when certain sentimental or melancholic associations evoke tears. But in most narrative films, Step 2 processing immediately leads to Step 3, which consists of relating and contextualizing the items seen and determined in Steps 1 and 2 to a living being (a human being or an animal, like the mice, ants, and dogs in cartoons) and a scene.

We can call Step 3 the cognitive-emotional appraisal and motivation phase. 'Snake' or 'Marilyn' are now put into the framework of a hypothetical narrative scenario. Snake represents 'possibly lethal danger' for a specific creature NN, and the viewer experiences strong arousal, while the body-mind is put onto red alert with heartbeats, sweat, adrenalin secretion, and so forth. In order to produce and label the arousal, the viewer has to identify with one of the agents: say, identify with the little girl and not identify with the poisonous snake approaching her. Then the arousal can be labelled fear. The same goes for Marilyn in Step 3: she is not just 'pretty woman' but a possible mating partner for NN. The viewer experiences strong arousal and labels it 'love' or 'desire'. State 3 is not a stable state: strong arousal needs an outlet, because arousal states normally activate telic arousal-reduction procedures (otherwise paratelic evaluation is activated: see Chapter 4). If no cognitive, voluntary, or autonomic outlet is found for the scenario, it will 'regress' to a Step 2 mode.

Therefore, Step 3 leads to Step 4: reactions at a high level of arousal. There are three main types of Step 4 reactions. I shall mention them only briefly here, and give a more detailed description in the following chapters.

1. *The first type*: These are reactions corresponding to canonical narrative schemata, implying hypothetical or actual voluntary and teleological response, which I shall abbreviate to 'voluntary telic response'.

2. *The second type*: This consists of hypothetical or actual semi-voluntary paratelic response. By paratelic response, I mean a semi-voluntary response which is not goal-directed but repetitious (cf. the 'module' difference noted above between telic and paratelic activities, underlined by the fact that people with certain brain damage are able to sing but not to perform telic activities). Dancing and singing are paratelic activities. Long sequences in musicals are often paratelic: people in musicals sing about love without doing anything about it. Modernist or 'postmodernist' metafiction also uses paratelic patterns, for example many *Nouvelle vague* films (Deleuze 1991: 9), McLaine's *The End*, or Wenders's *Paris-Texas*.

3. *The third type*: In this type we have an autonomic response, such as crying, laughing, shivering, or making involuntary body movements.

I shall return to a more detailed analysis of the relations between emotional types and genre prototypes in the following chapters.

3

Associative Networks, Focus of Attention, and Analogue Communication

This chapter will demonstrate the means by which visual communication relies on attention hierarchies structured as associative networks. I shall discuss the ways in which central mental models rely on visuo-motor categorization and analogous forms of representation relate to language.

ATTENTION

When our consciousness and senses are active, some phenomena are, at a given time, more central or 'superior' than others, because of capacity limitations in our brain. We describe this ability to make mental 'centres' and 'hierarchies' as an ability to 'pay attention' and to 'focus' our consciousness. Some aspects of the problems are dealt with in narrative theory as point of view, focalization, filtering, and so on.

The basic mental models (and procedures) for depicting attention are based on sight: our eyes have at a given time a point of origin, a direction, and a focalization that highlight some phenomena and exclude others. The attention works like a spotlight beam that can be focused (see Eysenck and Keane 1990). This part of human attention is mimicked by a camera, which also controls what can be visually attended to by a location, a direction, and a lens configuration. I shall call the situatedness of a camera in a point of origin and a direction the 'vector'. We can furthermore 'filter' the seen, for example, by looking for something special: we are somehow able mentally to give some phenomena a higher priority than others when we actively look for these phenomena. The makeup of our eyes with the high resolution in the fovea area and lower resolution at the periphery of the eyes is part of this ability to centre and filter. Other types of special attention, too, rely on some kind of mental filtering. Non-optically controlled attention in films will be cued by the previous forms and contents. In *Notorious*, Hitchcock decided to represent the focal attention to be given to a key by a zoom-in leading to an optical enlargement in a close-up; but he might alternatively have relied on a 'mental enlargement' in the mind of the viewers cued by the narrative context.

Format and vector of the film image will, to some extent, cue attention so that there is a kind of homology between our film-experience flow and a real-life perceptual flow. If, however, we have a surplus capacity such that we can scan a given film-screen situation as if it were a photograph, our attention will become separated from the screen cues, which will be perceived as objects for the attention or as the secondary focus of a dual focus of attention. Terms like 'motion pictures' suggest that, in order to understand what film is, we can start by analyzing an image—a 'picture'—and then describe motion 'pictures' as a special extension of the use of 'stills'.[1] However, the task ought in fact to be carried out in the opposite direction: visual input is primarily given as 'visual cues for constructing a dynamic time-space', and 'stills' and 'pictures' are special ways of representing undynamic aspects of space-time (see Gibson 1986: 294). As our field of vision is limited and fades toward the periphery, we do not necessarily need to be aware of the image frame, because if we focus our eyes on the centre of the screen our vision will fade before it reaches the frame.

The visual cues are not used to make a copy of what is in the field of vision—an image—but to make mental models of space, objects, motion, and so on. Space is not imagined as 'stopping' at some point during fading. Objects are not necessarily perceived as cut by the field of vision: we may only see part of a wall or part of a tree, but the way we represent this is not primarily as 'fragment of tree', but as 'tree' acquiring its meaning by being an aspect of a 'tree concept', of which the aspects seen with a certain resolution have higher salience than the areas at which the fading occurs; whatever lies 'beyond the fade-out' at the limit of the field of vision is normally not given any attention, although it exists as a number of general non-conscious pre-suppositions. Normal viewing of films and television is also based on the making of models constructed within an open space. The frame is not a limit, but a support for focus of attention. Reframing serves to refocus and redirect attention. Space and objects will phenomenologically continue outside the frame that masks the represented, in the sense given to masking in phenomena like windows, as well as in the sense that a certain focal length of a lens may mask some phenomena and focus the visual attention on others. The film-makers can activate the 'frame', the boundedness, in many ways to produce specific effects. The typical boundedness of film and television is not

---

[1] Arnheim, Kracauer *et al.* tend to understand visual fiction as based on photography. Burch's (1981) description of the spatial dimensions of film is three-dimensional and describes the different types of 'off-space' and ways in which they can be activated. The description in itself is unproblematic, as it points to possible uses for the boundedness of what is seen. Nevertheless, a purely spatial description of film space easily becomes an objectivist understanding of space. Local areas of space might be understood as existing in an achronous contiguity. But a typical mental model of space would include time: what is masked 'in space' is just as much masked 'in time', as a focus of attention can only grasp a limited amount of space from special angles.

spatial, however, but temporal: the boundary is not 'what is outside the spatial frame?' but 'what is beyond the temporal now?'

In Chapter 2 I mentioned that the meanings of a given phenomenon depended on its relations to a 'web-like' structure of associations. 'Association' is a fundamental mental phenomenon implying that phenomenon A is somehow linked with phenomenon B, so that an activation of A is related to an activation of B.

Many associations are not meaningful in the ordinary sense of the word. Basic aesthetic phenomena, such as rhythm or melody in music, group-structure in visual art, or alliteration in literature, represent mental associations in the addressee, but need not have any strict meaning. A classic 'gestalt' problem, 'grouping', means that we can 'chunk' phenomena by associating subgroups of the phenomena, and perceive the 'chunked' result by means of some kind of second-order schema. The following dots will be 'chunked' into groups of significant proximity. Instead of seeing sixteen dots, we see four groups of four dots.

•••• •••• •••• ••••

Although the 'chunked' perception of the dots in four groups has no 'meaning', it certainly has a 'salience' or a felt significance that is 'higher' than would ordinarily be felt if the dots were distributed on the page at random or if they were printed without intervals, so that they could only be perceived as a 'line made up of dots', instead of, as now, a 'line made up of groups of lines made up of four dots'. The verbal description of the result is *ad hoc*, but many phenomena of low-order grouping acquire a permanent name like *symmetry*.

At the other end of the spectrum of associations, we have fully 'meaningful associations', as when 'wall', 'roof', 'window', 'door', and 'chimney' are chunked together and produce the conventional word for the 'associated group': 'house'. But the mechanism of association may be the same in both cases, and the feelings of intensities concomitant with the activation of associations will often be graduations of the 'same' type of feeling of 'significance', whether the associations are 'purely perceptual', as in many types of 'aesthetic' associations, or are made between propositional elements. Jackendoff (1987: 306) says of language that the affect *meaningful* and the phonological structure are present to our awareness, but the conceptual structure is not. A series of characteristic and similar shots in a film might, for example, be associated by the viewer, and this will create an intensity of association similar to that of 'meaningful associations'; in addition, the intensity will possibly trigger an effort to interpret in order to convey a full meaning to the associations (see Bordwell and Thompson 1990: 119–27; Bordwell 1989*b*). Seen as a mental process, the mechanisms of association have three aspects: establishing connections; 'chunking', i.e. grouping (making gestalts, structures, and so on); and 'labelling'.

In gestaltist language, grouping means that the 'whole' is more than the sum of its parts. 'The whole' is a description of the result of the interaction of the parts: it does not imply a mysterious 'essence' (Minsky 1988: 28). Another way of expressing this is to say that we establish a phenomenon, a concept, or a schema, for which the associated features and aspects are determiners. When we see a robin, we normally perceive a structured group of associations, in which beak, wings, eyes, and other elements are features specifying the concept 'robin'. When we see a parade, we perceive the individual soldiers and their movements as features specifying the schema 'march'. A given format and a given focus of attention will prefer a given concept or a given schema, but the 'concept-centripetal' associations do not rule out those between features organized in a different concept or those between concepts leading to new, more comprehensive groupings. In *Psycho,* the eyes of the stuffed birds are a feature that, with other features like feathers and beak, specify the schema 'bird'. At the same time the birds' eyes are metaphorically associated with those of Norman Bates.

That the focus of attention at a given moment is directed toward a certain concept- or schema-level does not mean that the features constituting the concept or the schema have disappeared from consciousness. They are activated, but their 'determination' of the concept or schema does not have conscious salience. We can give conscious salience to the 'determiners', for example, by asking what is understood by a given concept, or by trying to reveal the underlying network of associations. Psychologists have investigated the activation of networks of associations by investigating associative *priming,* that is, the way in which one phenomenon activates an associative network and by that facilitates mental operations on the items in the activated network (see for instance, Anderson 1990*a*: 160 ff.). An example of these experiments is the ability of subjects to judge whether a given word is real or meaningless; the subjects were faster in answering when the words were related, like bread and butter, than when they were unrelated, like nurse and butter. Such findings make it probable that a given phenomenon with varying intensity activates a large network of associations below the threshold of consciousness. It would be a mistake to equate this activation, however, with 'connotation': bread does not 'connote' butter, butter is an item in the network of associations surrounding bread and providing it with meaning. Some associations, such as the features constituting the propositional structure of a concept, will be more central than others, and terminology describing the centrality-*vs.*-non-centrality of a feature is more adequate than terminology describing denotation-*vs.*-connotation. The dichotomy of 'central' and 'peripheral' suggests a gradation, whereas denotation suggests a water-tight set of features defining denotation, and denotation is often understood as implying objective features and existence as opposed to subjective features expressed in connotations.

When viewing a film we will therefore perceive it at a certain conceptual level as directed by viewer and/or addresser, programming, for example by means of narrative schemata, framing, zooming, and other indexical procedures indicating formats of attention (see Reisz and Millar 1968: 213 ff., Carroll 1988: 199 ff.); and, at the same time, the viewing will activate networks of associations below the threshold of consciousness, and activate superior, 'propositional/abstract' frames and themes. Most films cue an anthropomorph-narrative 'mid-focus'. But viewers of films like Griffith's *Intolerance* are supposed to focus directly at the high, propositional level of 'intolerance', and this may cause some problems, because the main focus is supposed to be at a level that is not visually existent. The activated network below the threshold of consciousness does not usually imply Freudian repression: the consciousness has a very limited capacity compared with the capacity of the whole nervous system, and therefore it has to continuously choose a certain level or a certain aspect as central for the processes of allocation of consciousness. The selection of level and focus of attention will often imply a 'discriminatory' choice between options, and some of these choices are certainly of a 'Freudian' type. However, when something is out of the focus of attention, it is not just the result of 'resistance' and 'repression' but often simply because something else is more interesting for the time being, just as it is easy to take oblivion for repression. Although the levels and aspects of a film that have fully conscious salience are only the top of the 'iceberg', with most of the activation going on below the threshold of consciousness, there is nothing mysterious about the associations and features 'below the surface' except the complexity of the networks of associations (or the 'paradigms', to draw on a structuralist vocabulary). A single film will contain myriads of pieces of information at many levels; at a given moment of viewing most of the previous pieces will be activated, although not as the focus of conscious attention.

A description or an interpretation of a film will often consist of a deviation from a given film's primarily cued level of focus of attention. This descriptive deviation may either come about by choosing a 'higher level', as when the salient elements in a Western are 'chunked' into more comprehensive schemata (for example, the film is about the conflict between good and evil or the opposition between nature and culture), or by choosing a 'lower level of attention', when the analyst highlights some features that the enunciatory strategies of the film have put below the level of conscious focus. The dangers involved in making idiosyncratic and far-fetched interpretations have been excellently criticized in Bordwell (1989*b*), but, for now, close analysis

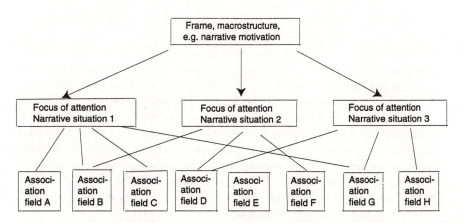

Fig. 3.1 Attention and mental processing as a hierarchy. A to H depicts association-fields below the focus of attention and activation, existing as background and non-conscious activation. The frame, theme, and setting will frequently exert its influence without being at the centre of consciousness.

and viewer interviews are the only available tools for analyzing the networks of associations activated during viewing.

My description above of the activation of networks has mainly emphasized the asynchronous, non-narrative aspects. But the activation can also be linked to narrative expectations. In an article 'Mental Models in Narrative Comprehension', Bower and Morrow (1990) describe the way in which they tested priming in readers of narratives. The test readers learned the spatial layout of two buildings that would later provide the settings for narratives. The test showed that the readers answered questions about objects in the room in which a major character was located more quickly than questions about objects in the room in which minor characters were located. The readers furthermore constructed the goals and intentions of the main characters, so that when, for example, a character in the narration intended to move from room A to room B, this activated the items in room B in such a way that the readers answered questions about the goal room more quickly than questions about the room in which the characters were actually located. Compared to normal viewing or reading conditions, the test was atypical because the readers were allowed to memorize a well-structured layout of locations, and most viewers do not have such specific mental models of, for example, the phenomena specifying the possible goals of a given fiction character. However, the main point is that reading and viewing depend on the addressee's reconstruction of the goals and intentions of the main characters, while the direction of character-intentions activates associative networks even when the goals are invisible.

PRIMING, SEQUENCING, FRAMING, AND FOCUS OF ATTENTION

The processing of information in visual fiction has a certain timing in a certain sequential order. A given perceived phenomenon will normally represent a set of features that can be perceived in several or many different ways, depending on the 'context' or the 'frame' (Goffman 1986), the 'dominant' (Eisenstein 1949: 64 ff.) or the 'macropropositions-macrostructure' (van Dijk 1980; van Dijk and Kintsch 1983) of the given phenomenon. The way in which we structure 'context' is not independent of sequencing a string of phenomena: the first item presented will determine the field of expectations so that it will 'prime' the expectations for the succeeding items. An example (from Mayer 1983: 67) of the way in which categorization is primed by sequencing is shown in the following ordering of the same words:

> Skyscraper, cathedral, temple, prayer
> Cathedral, temple, prayer, skyscraper

In the first sequence, 'skyscraper' primes the categorization 'building' (and also possibly 'high') but has no religious purpose, so that the feature 'something connected with religion' does not surface when we proceed to 'cathedral'. It does, however, strengthen the category 'building' and finds further strength in 'temple', and so 'prayer' seems to fall out of the pattern of categories of perception. The first three items are chunked. In the second sequence, however, it is 'cathedral' which initiates the priming process, and therefore the religious feature of building primes the perception of 'temple' and 'prayer', so that they can be perceived as having a common denominator, whereas 'skyscraper' falls out. This is in accordance with van Dijk's and Kintsch's 'leading-edge' strategy for text-comprehension: the reader keeps active the most recent proposition processed and propositions that are superior to it in a hierarchical representation of the text. But, in order to understand the specificity of the words, the features of the words that are not selected as 'common denominators' must still be active: the 'chunking' of 'skyscraper', 'cathedral', and 'temple' as 'buildings' will still keep 'Christian building' and 'heathen building' active at a lower level, otherwise the words would be synonymous; the chunking of 'cathedral', 'temple', and 'prayer' as 'religious phenomena' would still keep some features like 'building' (temple, cathedral) and 'activity' (prayer) active, although in a non-focused way. By this we can see that a given sequence will select a certain level and system of high-focus attention, and that this level will be anchored in many associational fields with a lower focus of attention and lower activation.

Priming and direction of attention as 'misdirection' represent one of the main tools for producers of fiction. As I shall describe in more detail in Chapter 10, the 'manipulation' of attention and the construction of special macrostructural frames play a very prominent role in crime fiction. As already noted, the contextual-framed aspect of 'focus of attention' and 'chunking', 'categorization', and so on has been connected by Freudian critics with sublimation and 'secondary elaboration'; but, as can be seen from the example of the sequencing of four words, the mechanism for selecting a specific level of attention is a very general one necessary for structuring vast data in a short-term memory, STM, of limited capacity (the famous capacity of seven items in the STM plus or minus two (outlined in Miller 1956). The relation between 'secondary elaboration' and 'framed focus of attention' can be illustrated by an episode from Brian de Palma's *Dressed to Kill*.

During one episode in the film the 'detective', a very young man, Peter, who is trying to investigate the murder of his mother, receives help from a prostitute. They think that the murderer must have been a client of Peter's mother's psychoanalyst, and, in order to find out the name of the client, the prostitute enters the psychoanalyst's consultation room, begins to talk about her sexual problems (including recounting a pornographic situation), uses sexual language, and tries to seduce the psychoanalyst verbally and by taking off her clothes and showing her 'whorish' black underwear. Then she pretends to go and powder her nose, but instead looks through the psychoanalyst's file, and finds the name of the client; when she returns she is nearly killed by the psychoanalyst, who is the real killer, but is saved. During the whole episode, Peter is a 'voyeur' outside the consultation, trying to see what is going on inside, and the scene is further complicated by a policewoman disguised as and mistaken for the killer.

Because of the narrative motivation, the situation has a macrostructure: that of obtaining information from the psychoanalyst. From our point of view and that of the prostitute, the situation is not primarily a sexual one: her language and body exhibition are means used to achieve the goal 'information', leading to 'justice', just as Peter is concerned with the same problem. The global expectations are therefore focused tensely on the achievement of this goal (and on the possible dangers associated with the murderer). Further, the prostitute is performing in a professional capacity: her story and exhibition are 'framed' as professional techniques and, by being transtextually motivated (see Thompson 1988; Bordwell 1986: 36), as 'a pornographic discourse'. But this does not mean that the viewer is supposed to overlook the sexual language and imagery: quite the contrary. De Palma calculates the frame in such a way that the viewer activates sexually charged fields of associations, *but they will be activated as a background in a saturated mode*. A tense activation of sexuality would presuppose a liquidation of the frame-goal of 'getting information' and the creation of a new motivation of 'getting sexual pleasure' (and a viewer-acceptance of the social-stereotype models of sexuality, in which individuality is negated by social-icon/social-role features like 'doctor–patient', 'prostitute–customer', and 'uniforms of consent = black underwear').

From a psychoanalytic perspective one could assert that the scene is a 'secondary elaboration', made in order to fool the superego, and a sublimation, made in order to adjust to the demands of the principle of reality.[2] But this is by no means the most convincing description. The construction of the scene enhances the level of arousal by combining several different sources of excitement: excitement caused by the wish to elicit information; excitement caused by threats to life and safety; excitement caused by sexual activation. If de Palma had re-centred the story and put the primary narrative focus on the sexual elements, the type of excitement might have been different: the same elements could be made into an explicitly pornographic narrative, in which 'getting information as detective' is an element within a pornographic macroframe as primary focus of attention. De Palma has clearly made the film within a cultural context in which Freudian and Lacanian concepts of voyeurism, castration, and so forth are prominent beliefs, but also within a cultural context in which neither the director nor his audience represses sexuality from consciousness. The framed focus of attention may be seen as part of a relatively explicit social negotiation: pure pornography is not acceptable as a mainstream film-genre. But the focus can also be seen from a point of view of emotion-engineering, enhancing emotions using combinations of different registers of behaviour.

Sequencing is a tool for controlling those meanings that should be 'foregrounded' and which should function as 'background' in a given text, and it is thereby also a tool for making complex configurations (but, as indicated in the metaphor 'background' and the implied 'foreground', there are other, nonsequential ways of creating an attentional hierarchy in visual fiction). Therefore, in order to describe a given narrative sequence, we may describe several levels of activation. The primary level is often the level of tension, whereas the others are levels of saturation.

IMAGES, VISUAL THINKING, AND VISUO-MOTOR SCHEMATA

The question of 'visual thinking' holds an obvious interest for cultural politics: a hot issue for public debate has been the possibly detrimental intellectual effects of increasing (audio)visual communication. However, for cinema and media studies proper it has further significance. If the brain could only think and remember in a propositional-linguistic form, it would imply that

---

[2] The Freudian opposition between the principle of pleasure and that of reality suffers from some logical flaws. If we refrain from doing something pleasant because we are afraid of punishment, we might say that this was done in the service of the negative formulation of the 'pleasure principle': avoidance of pain. We evaluate a given situation and find solutions in accordance with preferences. Preferences can be conflicting and demand a choice, for example giving up a pleasure in order to avoid a pain. But both preferences are defined in accordance with their subjective hedonic value (pleasure/pain) and are equally real.

the 'non-meaning' level of film and television only existed in the very process of perception and then was either thrown away or transformed into a propositional form; during viewing the viewer would only be able to establish connections to the previous parts of the film via the propositional form. Bordwell (1986: 36) describes the way in which the viewer uses the film as a series of cues to construct the narrative, whereas stylistic information tends to be thrown away and may be difficult to retrieve. On the other hand, we have an almost unlimited capacity for storing and recognizing images.

The problem has an affective side, too, which can be illustrated by the affective difference between perceiving meaning by language (an arbitrary system of signification) and perceiving it by visual representation. An arbitrary system of signification consists of three elements, a signifier, an associative 'pointing' relation, and a signified (signifier → signified). A signifier will activate a search process leading to a possible activation of the signified. The signified could very well be an image-concept, as when the signifier 'tree' activates a set of propositions or an 'image' constituting the concept. But by an analogical representation of a tree, there is no pointing function: identification of the 'signifier' will instantaneously provide the signified, although construction of images and the associations determining them is in itself a very complicated mental process. The 'pointing', 'signifying' function is 'felt' as meaningful, so that even if a novel and a film express the same 'concepts', the novel would be felt as more 'meaningful' because of the additional tensity created by the pointing-function of the arbitrary system of signification as opposed to the greater intensity of the visual representation combined with the familiarity/unfamiliarity feelings characteristic of visual object recognition (see Pribram 1982 and Jackendoff 1987: 306). To deny any meaningful, intelligent qualities to a purely visual medium may be a more affective than an analytical attitude.

As noted earlier in connection with Marr's model of vision, the feeling of meaning and meaningfulness has its centre at a certain level of representation (with a centre in mental schemata, such as objects, properties, acts, goals, and so on) and at a certain stage in the information-processing. Language is modelled at this level of 'meaningfulness', each schema having its own discrete representation; even *qualia* like colour are represented as categorical entities, whereas the schemata are fused in vision; 'greenness' and 'cubeness' are fused when seeing a 'green cube', and 'on' has no discrete representation when seeing 'a book on a table'. Sometimes the 'analytical discreteness' of language carries more information than images, but often the ability of images to carry much information (for example, spatial information) that can be picked up instantaneously is not 'felt', because of the ease by which we pick up complex visual information without tense indexical effort. A verbal description of even a simple shot would take many sentences, and yet would still not reproduce all the available visual information.

Often visualization and the work of association are regarded as primitive and closely connected to alogical and unconscious processes, whereas language and logic are connected with the world of consciousness. Recent research into the cognitive function of vision does not seem to confirm such conceptions. Visualization (for instance, by means of visual mental models) plays an important role in many different types of problem-solving, ranging from those that arise from everyday life (like deciding the relative size of objects) to the solving of complex mathematical problems (see for example, Kaufmann 1990; Kosslyn 1980; and Arnheim 1969). Linguistic representations are often more economical formal tools for some types of problem-solving, but new or complex problems frequently demand visual thinking. Furthermore, many linguistic functions are related to emotions; many theories of the origin of language have even seen the roots of language in communicative expressions of emotions (see Cassirer 1962: 114 ff.). Visuo-motor memories, models, and schemata are fundamental mental phenomena which participate in nearly all mental activities. The analogue, 'iconic' functions are, as discussed in Chapter 1, not only perceptual phenomena but characteristic of some semantic components of natural languages. Although the natural languages have very different systems of signifiers, the systems of signifieds show much less variation (see Holenstein 1995), and this makes sense if essential semantic components consist of activating visuo/sensory-motor categories.

Interest in research into images reached a low point during the heyday of behaviourism, when it was regarded as obscure mentalism. But since the 1960s an increasing amount of research into image-processing has been carried out, especially by Paivio (1966), Kosslyn (1980; 1983; 1994), and Arnheim (1969). A major finding is that the brain has the ability to process images in an analogue fashion. It is able to imagine three-dimensional objects and 'rotate' them, and it is able to 'recall' an image and scan it, that is, move the focus of attention from one area to another. The mind has the ability to choose a given scale of representation, and if we imagine an elephant with a mouse, the scale of representation will be different from that chosen if we imagine a mouse with a fly; the elephant-mouse representation would represent the mouse with a lower resolution, making it more difficult for us to be aware of details than would be the case were the mouse imagined with a fly. The opportunities of cinema and television are closely related to these abilities to process images: if the brain worked only by the simple matching of images stored on a certain scale and from a certain point of view, the constant rescaling and changes of perspectives in the images of film and television would make reception almost impossible. Natural perception and visual imagination, however, presuppose the ability to rescale perceptual systems of reference rapidly, and to match with prototypes.

Visual representation and processing are closely related to spatial representation. Vision and space representation are furthermore intimately connected with another modality, motoricity, and its main activities, body motion and object manipulation. Lakoff and Johnson have described basic mental schemata, making up a sort of mental software package used in the mind as a central instrument for thought. There are many similarities between this approach and Greimas's semantic analysis, and they both bear some relation to Lévi-Strauss's idea of using percepts as tools for the mythical thought. Johnson's list of some of the most important schemata is as follows: Container, blockage, enablement, path, cycle, part-whole, full-empty, iteration, surface, balance, counterforce, attraction, link, near-far, merging, matching, contact, object, compulsion, restraint removal, mass-count, centre-periphery, scale, splitting, superimposition, process, and collection (Johnson 1987).

The schemata have been found by linguistic analysis, but they are mostly visuo-motor, indicating that the central mental models have their basis in visual and motor schemata. The central mental models exist on the level at which enaction in a 'natural' world takes place, and on which central narrative structures develop. Indiana Jones will assess whether he is in a container (for example, a cave or a room), which may or may not block his path, regulate his movements and ability to touch, and so forth. His (and our) attention may not be focused on the texture of, for instance, the snake-pit, but rather we will try to find a 'door', an 'exit' from the container, and thus our attention and categorization will be cued by the downstream processes from perception to action, not the 'upstream' meta-attention to the perceived *per se*.

For this reason, the perceptual categorization and its level of abstraction are typically linked to its use in the motor interaction with space, objects, and animate beings. This is compatible with Bordwell's above-mentioned observation that stylistic information is often thrown away, and that films cue the reconstruction of fabula, with the modification that perception and memory also strongly support 'passive' recognition. The visual information is not thrown away, as our visual memory is almost unlimited: it exists as a passive potential for recognition and as an intense or saturated associative background.

The analysis of visuo-motor schemata provides a tool for avoiding some of the manifold problems caused by having language and 'narration' as sole models for sequences in visual fiction. A linguistic representation of a story of visuo-motor schemata, such as 'Indy leaped across the gap and grabbed some plants', is not its essential form: the verbal story represents mental schemata that exist in connection with the cognitive and affective processing of visual and motor phenomena. A sequence, say, of images, or acts is thus not a 'narration', in the sense of a manifestation of a 'story' unfolding 'as if it were told': on the contrary, the sequence relates to holistic sensory-motor mental models of which verbal stories are 'representations'. The reason that so many film theoreticians have felt forced to use 'narration' as a model has been because the general schemata ruling exterior behaviour and perception seemed only to have stories and 'telling', as mental equivalents to a diegetic process understood as an active intentional and cognitive procedure. However, silent narrative films show that the intentional and sensory-motor narrative schemata can be communicated without language.

AUDIOVISUAL COMMUNICATION: SIGNS OR PROCESSES OF PERCEPTION AND COGNITION

In the analysis of audiovisual communication inspired by structuralism and semiotics, it is often tacitly assumed or explicitly claimed that the way in which we receive audiovisual fiction as a whole is analogous with, or identical to, the way in which we process natural languages. The use of the metaphor 'film.language' goes back to early cinema studies, but, with the coming of structuralism, it seemed that language became the only model for the analysis of visual communication. Central to such a linguistic-semiotic point of view was Eco. Gombrich's constructivist approach to art analysis seemed to strengthen the case for a total relativist, conventionalist conception of the analogical elements in images, although in 1982 he distanced himself from such an understanding of his work.

In a widely used handbook like Fiske (1990), semiotics is employed as the methodological foundation for the analysis of all types of communication, including visual communication. The introduction tacitly assumes that perception of audiovisual phenomena can be described unproblematically by semiotic models built on linguistic communication. It follows that the audiovisual sequences are dealt with as 'texts', 'discourses', and so on. Language is thus the primary mental model for the processing of visual and acoustic information. This does not mean that the model is not modified when dealing with visual information; a distinction between the iconic-analogue sign, the indexical-synechdocic sign and the arbitrary-symbolic sign is introduced, following Peirce *et al.*

There are, however, some problems connected with the consideration of audiovisual communication exclusively in terms of 'signs' understood in analogy with linguistic signs, because much of the communication is based on representations of phenomena existing without a socially produced communicative intent. Linguistic signifiers are made by man and with a communicative purpose; furthermore, they are arbitrary, and are phenomenologically understood as signifying 'something else'.[3] I am able to experience the 'arbi-

---

[3] Cf. Todorov's cautious definition of a sign in Ducrot and Todorov (1979). He emphasizes the social aspect of the sign and, with good reason, refuses to call 'smoke' an indexical sign of fire except if made one by a community of users.

trariness' of dog, *chien*, *càne* or *Hund* as signifiers of a four-legged domestic
animal of which I can produce analogue images or a set of propositions determining the dog. When I see a dog in real life, however, I do not primarily see
the dog as a signifier of something else: the dog simply is. When we make a
film showing a dog we make two things: a 'mechanical', analogue representation of the dog on the film, and a 'communicative act', by which the dog is
represented in a special way, linked to a specific context and possibly provided with special meanings. In the photographic image, the analogue representation is normally not 'reduced' to a purely distinctive level ruled by the
communicative intent in the same way as linguistic communication is. Many
arguments about iconic representations draw on examples such as road-signs,
and drawings, representations which might be produced by a technique based
on the communicative function. But vision and photographic representations
not only communicate 'distinctive features': even minimalist representations
like cartoon dogs often provide more visual information than is necessary for
a simple communicative 'recognition', and most representations provide a
quantity of visual information not necessary for identification alone.

The claim that language should be the privileged model for understanding
communication is often linked to a claim for culturalism: the way in which
we perceive the world is culturally 'coded'. Whorf's descriptions of the means
by which language influences the way we understand the world gave credibility to the idea that the main features of the brain were culturally coded. An
even stronger argument for culturalism was put forward by Eco (1989),[4] in
which he criticizes concepts of 'iconism' and 'analogism'. His point is that we
learn visual similarity in the same coded way that we learn language. As an
argument against the naturalness of visual perception, Eco attacks what he
calls six 'naïve notions' concerning iconism (191 ff.). One of Eco's examples
of naïve iconism is that the iconic sign has the same properties as its object.
As an example he discusses the question of contour: if we draw a horse by
making a black line of the outline of the horse we represent it by a property
which it does not have (it is a mass, not an outline). Therefore the line is a
graphic convention 'which allows one to transform, on paper, the elements of
a *schematic conceptual or perceptual convention* which has motivated the
sign' (p. 194). But Marr (1982) has pointed to the perceptual processes such
as zero-crossings, and primal sketch which make the outline of the horse
'belong' to the horse by innate perceptual processes, by ecological conventions, in the same way as the property 'brown' belongs to it. Eco further criticizes the 'naïve notion' that the iconic sign resembles its object despite a
difference in scale (for instance an image of pyramid in relation to a real, big
pyramid). Within limits, rescaling is, however, also an innate process. Eco's
arguments presuppose a very primitive notion of perceptual-cognitive

---

[4] The chapters on visual communication were published in French in *Communications*, 15 (Eco
1970) and preceded by Metz's more cautious foreword to that number.

processing, because he demands 'identity' between image and 'real thing', instead of presupposing an ability to make the 'best available match to existing templates stored in memory'.

Some of the basic skills needed to understand film and television are identical with those necessary for natural visual perception (Greenfield 1984; Messaris 1994). A face or a tree is immediately recognizable by means of innate perceptual mechanisms plus fundamental human experience, even for people without any previous experience of film or television. Furthermore, except for some problems with stereopsis, the retinal impact of the film image can be indistinguishable from the retinal impact of 'real-world images'. Fundamental aspects of the seen, such as space, object, motion, and colour, exist in such a form that to say that they are 'analogue' *signs* of space, object, motion, and colour located in a signified elsewhere violates the 'naturalness' and 'innateness' by which they are perceived.

Although the phenomena 'making meanings' in consciousness are 'calculations', or 'information processes', and as such can be simulated in computers, they possess at the same time qualities (that is, they possess meaning as a felt phenomenon, the perceptual *qualia*, the emotions) which are linked to the phenomenon 'consciousness' which cannot be separated from the realization of the calculations in a 'specific type of computer' of flesh and blood. As pointed out by Searle (1984), the specific biological realization of the calculations in man's embodied brain is an important aspect of consciousness. Vision, hearing, touch, and taste have innate specifications, so that, although all the perceptual modalities rely on the same type of neuronal firings, the brain architecture and its relation to the world specifies semanticized types of functions. The use of the double articulation in language and the division of signifiers and signifieds has been detrimental to an understanding of meanings and semantics (although for the opposite reason to that which underlies the 'poststructuralist' position), namely that the model has prevented serious theoretical and analytical work being undertaken into the way in which these phenomena are fused in many types of perception and cognition.

Constructivism in perception works within a framework that is built in by a process of evolution, and it is therefore important to distinguish between an 'arbitrariness' built in by evolution ('if we had senses like bats, we would see the world differently'), and an 'arbitrariness' constructed by social means. The social constructedness of the world represents certain features and structurations of the seen, interwoven with non-cultural aspects (space, object, light, colour, shape, and motion as built-in *'Anschauungsformen'*, as stated by Kant). To take a constructivist position does not mean that we disregard some aspects of vision taking place by bottom-up procedures. In ordinary picture-viewing situations we will have, as Panofsky among others has pointed out (1955: 40), what he calls a pre-iconographical level of perception. On this level, the elements can have structural and textural elements which are *iden-*

tical with the elements that would have resulted from seeing in real life. The greenness of the colour green in the image, the triangularity of some shapes, the spatial orientations, and so forth are not signifiers of green or signifiers of triangularity, and in that sense they are not just 'analogue' but *identical* elements, triggering the same neuronal firing patterns as when we see these phenomena in a non-image world. An analogue representation contains some identical elements (for example, angle) and some non-identical elements (like scale, aspects of texture, etc.). In film, some aspects of the perception of the relative motion of a figure in relation to a ground are identical with real-life perceptions: we need no procedures of transformation. Therefore, important aspects of perception of visual phenomena are *not* dependent on cultural codes. However, the 'natural' aspects of perception and cognition do not dictate any normative aesthetic.

The 'natural level' in (audio)visual communication is integrated into many different systems of representation, cinematic modes of representation (such as narrative schemata, and enunciation), cultural systems creating macrostructures in audiovisual sequences, and so on. We can raise problems of representation. What reality-status do these perceptual phenomena have: that of a picture? a photograph? a real life experience? We can also raise illocutionary questions: what are the intentions behind the (re)presentation in this film or this picture? In relation to these questions the picture elements will become 'signs', pointing to an 'elsewhere', an activation of schemata which make up the basis of our evaluation, for example of resemblance, or those providing the basis of evaluations of iconological or iconographical meanings. However, this does not make the identical or quasi-identical features into signifiers at their own local level, although they will also participate as elements in the level on which questions of reference and resemblance are raised by our interpretational acts. Questions of 'resemblance', for example, do not cancel out phenomena of identity. A triangle in a picture is not a picture of a triangle, it is a triangle; the geometrical configurations of two eyes and a mouth in a picture are not only a representation of forms, circles, ovals, and relative position as they would be if facial features were indicated by non-analogue means; but some of the structural features of a face exist in the picture.

Part II

Narratives as Basic
Mental Models

4

Cognitive Identification and Empathy

In this chapter I shall demonstrate that emotional empathy and cognitive identification play a crucial role in the reception of visual fiction, and also that cognition and emotion are two different aspects of one information system. An example from *Psycho* will illustrate the means by which cognitive identification causes empathy, because cognition is intimately linked to motivation. I shall analyse the intersubjective status of emotions and describe the cognitive labelling of emotions as a narrative strategy. I shall also discuss the way in which narrative processes can be described as homeostatic systems, that is, as an alternative to the psychoanalytic description of narration as driven by 'narrative desire', and I shall examine the applicability of two concepts of homeostasis, *telic* and *paratelic* motivation, as tools for describing visual fiction and entertainment.

CHARACTER IDENTIFICATION IN FILM THEORY

The earliest views of identification in film theory seem also to be the most up-to-date. In 1916 Hugo Münsterberg described the ways in which spectators become emotionally involved in film:

On the one side we have those emotions in which the feelings of the persons in the play are transmitted to our own soul. On the other side, we find those feelings which may be entirely different, perhaps exactly opposite to those which the figures in the play express. (1970: 53)

The spectator 'shares' the emotions of many of the persons on the screen and simulates these so that 'all the resulting sensations from muscles, joints, tendons, from skin and viscera, from blood circulation and breathing, give the colour of living experience to the emotional reflection in our mind' (ibid.). But to other fictional characters our emotional reactions will be different types of distancing or rejection. Other classical film-theorists express similar points of view. Thus Balázs:

In the cinema the camera carries the spectator into the film picture itself. We are seeing everything from the inside as it were and are surrounded by the characters of the film. They need not tell us what they feel, for we see what they see and see it as they see it . . . our eyes are in the camera and become identical with the gaze of the characters. They see with our eyes. Herein lies the psychological act of 'identification'. (1970: 48)

Münsterberg and Balázs saw identification as positive; other theoreticians point to character identification but see it as problematic, either as connected with illusion and dream, or as part of a state similar to hypnosis. Bazin (1967: 98 f.) describes character-identification in film by a comparison to theatre: 'A member of a film audience tends to identify himself with the film's hero by a psychological process, the result of which is to turn the audience into a "mass" and to render emotion uniform.'[1] Bazin thinks that in the theatre the spectator relates directly to the different actors, whereas in film the viewer's relation to the world represented is mediated through protagonist-identification. Kracauer quotes with acceptance various critics who describe the way in which the film-goer has less conscious control than the theatre-goer, for example (1961: 159 *passim*), and although he does not specifically deal with character identification, it could be inferred that identification is an aspect of film which lowers the spectator's conscious control. Mitry is more positive: he describes the way in which the viewer, by participation and identification, simulates the different characters through 'associative projection' (1990: 126 f.). We do not assimilate the character, but provide him with our intentionality, motor reactions, emotions, and so on, so that we can live out our non-realized potential: he is our double. As such, the experience may have elements of catharsis. But the compensation is unreal: the hero *assume ce moi que je n'ai pas su être*, which sounds like an existentialist rephrasing of a Freudian concept of 'daydream'.

In the 1960s and early 1970s, the modernist, 'materialist', and psychoanalytic schools within film theory were even more sceptical of character-identification and its alleged ideological or illusionistic nature. The viewer's cued mental reconstruction of fictional spaces, acts, thoughts, motivations, and other elements was thought to be a way in which the viewer was lured into ideological forms of representation. Film-makers and critics ought to 'lay bare' the narrative devices and thus transgress the ideological representations. The influence of Lacanian psychoanalysis on film studies strengthened scepticism *vis-à-vis* fictional structures. For Lacan, only the first rudimentary perceptions (including basic proprioceptions) are 'real'; the more sophisticated mental models created during socialization are increasingly 'unreal', the 'imaginary' order is founded on 'misrecognition', and the 'symbolic' order on repression. Somehow Lacan presupposes that the basic level of perception-

---

[1] In a curious way Bazin's conception of theatre is quite contrary to Brecht's. Bazin illustrates his description of theatrical identification with an example: in the theatre the chorus-line girls excite the spectator in the same way that the girls would do in ordinary life, whereas in the cinema the spectator is calmed by identification with the hero. For Brecht a break of 'illusion' would create distancing, whereas for Bazin this would create real-life relations not necessarily characterized by *verfremdung*.

consciousness is beyond systems of representation and has a transcendental truth, which creates a foil for describing the alienations of higher mental life. Metz (1982) followed a Lacanian approach and was mainly interested in identification with the film image as such; he did not deal with character-identification, which he called a 'secondary identification' (1982: 96).

A particularly negative relation to character-identification was implied in the so-called 'suture' theory as put forward by Oudart and Dayan (Dayan 1976). According to this modernist approach, the framedness and centredness of the image (painted, photographed, or filmed) is an ideological construct, the view of 'the absent one'. The viewer might become suspicious of this foreign control by noticing the framedness of the image and be conscious of 'the absent one', but classical cinema hides the clues, providing a reverse shot which psychologically motivates the image and the frame by pointing to a person looking at the phenomena in the first shot. The first shot is therefore made retroactively into 'just' the field of vision of a given character of fiction, so that this 'fake' motivation veils the absent one. Thus to tell a story about persons, motives, perceptions, or other such elements, could be seen as merely a huge cover-up operation, so that the viewer fails to notice that the picture was made by somebody else, and is prevented from having the freedom just to look at images.

Branigan represents another type of rejection of 'identification'. For him, as for structuralists like Barthes, identification relates to an anthropomorph level, whereas he prefers to describe a kind of Chomskyan set of rules which generate our understanding of many films; the viewer has, by extensive viewing, extracted a small set of rules which make up the elements in a 'Logic of Reading' (1984: 16 ff.). At the same time he rejects rather different theories of identification (Aristotelian, Brechtian, or Lacanian) by stating that an approach based on 'identification is too broad. Identification often neglects textual features or simply dissolves them in a search for psychical mechanisms' (p. 17). The objection assumes that descriptions of identification will lead to 'reductionism', based on the problematic assumption that attention to identification necessarily competes with attention to textual features. Bordwell's (1986) critique of identification is 'by silence': his description of narration omits most story phenomena. His cognitive-constructivist theory is written as an alternative to mimetic theories of narration. These are focused on the story, and not on the way it is told or the means by which reception plays a role, and common-sense conceptions restrict themselves to anthropomorphic categories of understanding: narration consists of tales about humans or living creatures, and their wishes, acts, and so on. Bordwell's viewer is an entity totally separated from the hypothetical world of fiction, performing activities like 'guessing', 'hypothesis-making', and 'construction'. In Bordwell (1989b), however, personification (of characters in fiction, of addresser, and of viewer) plays an important role as a schema for constructing meaning in films, albeit not in viewers but in critics, just as Bordwell and Thompson (1990) make use of the concept of identification.

I would like to deal more extensively with the interesting critique of character-identification put forward in Carroll (1990: 88–96). Carroll argues against the idea that the viewer wholly or partially duplicates the protagonist's mental and emotional states. His main counter-argument centres on the observation that the viewer's state of mind is often quite different from that of the protagonist. According to the examples given by Carroll, there are two main reasons for this. First, the viewer's level of information is often different from (mostly higher than) that of the protagonist. Secondly, the emotional response of viewer and protagonist will be different because of their different positions. An example of a situation with a difference between protagonist-information and viewer-information is the first shark-scene in Spielberg's *Jaws*. At one point in the scene a young girl is enjoying a swim, whereas we know that a monster shark is lurking nearby and are therefore frightened. So, according to Carroll, there can be no identification, because our emotional state differs from that of the protagonist.

The question of character-identification is, however, not an either/or one. The canonical way of telling stories is to follow a protagonist; discrepancies of information between viewer and protagonist are therefore the deviation, not the norm. Even when, as in the situation in *Jaws,* we possess more information than the girl, we feel fear in simulation of how we think we would feel if we were in the girl's position and knew about the threat. If we took the shark's point of view we would be delighted at the prospect of food; if we were sadists, we would look forward to enjoying the girl's agony. The types of activities we would look forward to would differ yet again if, instead of taking the girl's point of view and thinking of ways of escaping, we thought of ways of catching her (like the butterfly- and girl-catcher in Wyler's *The Collector*). And if we thought that girls were masochists, we might be quite delighted at the prospect of a scene of ultimate abandonment to the other. Our understanding of a scene depends on the types of emotions and the type of motivation evoked, and the types of emotions evoked depend in turn on our understanding[2] (for a description of identification as activation, see also Plantinga 1994).

[2] S. Heath (1985) interprets this scene ambiguously. On the one hand he sees a parallel between the boy chasing the girl and the shark doing likewise (male sexuality as sadism, female sexuality as masochism); on the other, the devouring of the girl is linked to dismemberment (meaning that the shark represents a kind of *vagina dentata* and the girl represents the boy's penis). This interpretation implies a shift of identification. The first part of the scene has an identification with shark-boy as dynamic subject, attracted by and 'devouring' an object; the second part has an identification with boy/girl as possible object. It implies the mapping of a mental model: sexual intercourse is comparable to eating. Both identifications imply arousal, but with the two different labels of telic desire and saturated fear-pain. If we do not choose identification, the scene would be complex-saturated. The possibilities of complex identifications with film events would not

This does not mean that discrepancies between protagonist-information and viewer information are unimportant; on the contrary, they can be important tools for creating, destroying, or relocating identification. In *Jaws*, the discrepancy of information is created in order to increase the emotional response, for example by evoking a terrifying helplessness *vis-à-vis* the invisible dangers of the world, and the information gap is only temporary: the girl will be confronted by the shark. Other discrepancies of information can be constructed in order to diminish identification by presenting points of view other than the protagonist's. But, correspondingly, in 'real life', people do not always have complete empathy with themselves; we can take an Olympian view of our own real-life problems, be absent-minded, hate ourselves and/or identify with the points of views of others, or be ashamed of ourselves. For excellent reasons, the model of oneself must be very much simpler than the mental totality of which it is a subset (Johnson-Laird 1988: 360 ff.) and, in order to control the model, we need cognitive and emotional points outside the model-self.

Carroll proposes the word 'assimilation'[3] instead of identification, meaning that a character's understanding and evaluation of the situation can be perceived 'without becoming, so to speak, possessed by him'. The phrasing understates the intensity with which people often feel love, jealousy, hate, or fear by identifying with symbolic representations, but most people would understand the same thing by identification that Carroll understands by assimilation. Identification does not exclude a certain distance, just as we do not fully 'identify with ourselves': normally we are not totally obsessed by ourselves, but are able to look at our own emotions with varying degrees of distance. The model-self is created as a discrete subset of the total set of phenomena concerning the self, and has strong social and imitative elements.

Carroll further argues that the position of the viewer is different from that of the protagonist. According to Carroll, if a protagonist is threatened by a monster, the feeling of fear is an egoistic one, whereas the audience-emotions are altruistic, feelings for other people. But to use altruism in such a situation is beside the point, because it would imply that the spectator disregards his own interest in order to feel sympathy with the protagonist, whereas the two interests are, in fact, quite compatible. The viewer can see the problems of the protagonist as symbolic representations of his own 'egotistic' interests; he is not competing with the protagonist for sympathy or attention. Normally, therefore, producing altruism in fiction requires a symbolic representation of the conflict. In films like *Cyrano de Bergerac* or *Roxanne* there is a real conflict between experiencing an egotistic jealousy toward the silly fool who

---

differ from the possibilities of complex identifications in 'real life'. The point in this connection is that cognitive, motivational, and emotional dimensions are linked; if Heath chooses deviant identifications it changes his understanding and emotional response.

[3] Carroll (1984) uses 'allegiance' as an alternative to 'identification'.

cashes in on the noble work of long-nosed Cyrano, and an identification with Cyrano's altruistic sacrifice of his own interests on behalf of others. Here the viewer's 'interests' are represented by the same symbolic situation, and therefore these different interests compete: symbolically it is impossible to get the girl and be altruistic at the same time.

EMPATHY, UNDERSTANDING OF OTHERS, AND CANONICAL NARRATIVES

As mentioned above, many film critics have described identification as an aspect of ideological representation. In an evolutionary perspective, however, our ability to empathize with, identify with, and cognitively simulate the situation of other members of our species is linked to the evident survival-value of these prosocial activities. Higher animals and humans try to understand and simulate the feelings, motives, and cognitive focus of other members of their species. Studies of monkeys indicate that perception of other living beings is a special mental function. Perret, Harries, Mistlin, and Chitty (1990) analyzed monkey reactions to different types of body movements by direct insertions of electrodes in neurons in the temporal lobe. They wanted to investigate the response in monkeys to seeing humans move in different ways. One experiment analyzed the effect on monkeys of seeing a person walking either backwards or forwards, and it showed that some special neurons fired much more strongly when the human walked forward than backwards: that is, the hardwired response was also an 'interpretation of significance', because a forward movement is ordinarily more significant than a backward movement. The experiment found that the monkeys had special neurons sensitive to an object-centred description of moving persons. Object-centred means that the direction of movements is understood not in relation to the viewer, but to the orientation of the person; a movement of the arms away from the body of the observed person gave greater response than one towards the body, even if this meant that a movement towards the body also meant a movement toward the observing monkey. And, further, the research team found special neurons sensitive to goals of action. Monkeys observed a person walking in different directions around a room. Special neurons fired much more strongly when the person moved toward a door leading out of the laboratory than when he or she did so in any other direction.

This is indirectly a comment on views like those of Metz, for example, that there is a primary identification with the cinematic image 'as such' which expresses the viewer's pre-Oedipal identification with his own omnipotent act of perception and a secondary identification with characters. The secondary identification is described by de Lauretis (1984) and Doane (1987) as 'Oedipal', as is the Propp-Greimas narrative. But the findings seem to indicate that, for example, the ability to process movements of persons according to basic models, such as an object-centred and goal-oriented 'comprehension' of the movements of a person, is relatively automatic and fundamental and based on innate circuits, and is not a result of a cultural process.

When the monkeys react strongly in connection with a cognitive evaluation of the purposive, goal-oriented movement toward the door, it is not specified whether the reaction is just a reaction to 'a possible major event' or linked to some monkey interests. But the main point is that a viewer's cognitive analysis of at least basic movements and goals, including object-centred analysis, is a relatively automatic process and the strong neuronal activity is probably 'felt'. The experiments of Malmo and others might indicate that the processing of goals and acts would activate motor-control systems, and the processing would then be 'felt' as 'tensity'. When people are 'fascinated' by films, this may be an effect of the number of movements and purposive acts represented in them.

In the canonical narrative like the folk-tale, we have a prototype of the way in which anthropomorph beings symbolize and control the connections between their acts, emotions, cognitions, and goals in a hypothetical world. A key to understanding the viewer's reconstruction of a narrative is the procedure by which he cognitively 'identifies' himself with the agents of fiction, using mental models and schemata from everyday psychology. Part of the motivation for the reconstruction is provided by empathy, that is, the viewer's cued simulation of emotions in identification with an agent of fiction. Cognition is intimately linked to emotions. Our cognitive abilities are not disinterested: on the contrary, our cognitive software is developed through evolution as a tool for implementing the preferences of a given biological entity. The superior connection between cognition and emotion is that of *motivation*, as exemplified by the narrative film in which the cognitive activities are motivated by basic human preferences including: food, security, erotic gratification, and social acceptance, and by the emotions and affects which are linked to these preferences.

The cognitive activities first serve to produce emotions and affects because the relation between the preferences and a given situation demands cognitive analysis. A given situation can only be evaluated as 'dangerous', for example, by cognitive analysis. The cognitive activities then produce mental models for reducing the affects and emotions. Therefore, a story-oriented (or fabula-oriented) basic model of the viewer's construction of the narrative sequences (covering the Step 3 and Step 4 procedures in Chapter 2) can be described as follows:

Cognitive analysis of a given narrative situation → evaluation of the situation in relation to the preferences of a fictive being, the result of this evaluation being mentally and often 'physically' represented by the viewer as 'affect', 'emotion' (in empathic identification with the being) → the viewer's mental simulation of and anticipation of plans for carrying out cognitive, communicative, and motor schemata in the fiction, aiming at reducing negative and increasing positive emotions and affects for the fictive beings → cognitive analysis of and affective representation of the actual fictive development and its consequences for the fictive being (such as joy, relief, disappointment, and frustration).

Interacting with the phenomena described in this basic model are other phenomena connected with the viewer's reconstruction of the enunciatory aspects of the visual sequence of fiction, like discrepancies between the point of view of the viewer and that of the fictional agents; changes in the structuration of time and space, that only exist as discourse-structures for the viewer, are stylistic features that cannot be described within the framework of the world of fiction (see Chapter 9). But it is very probable that a story that has linear and progressive time and is centred on the experience of a single being is a mental base-model, as shown by research into canonical story-schemata (Mandler 1984). Narrative and enunciatory sophistication can rearrange material in terms of its temporal appearance and its structures of identification, for example, and this has been the focus of attention in classical theory of narration;[4] but these sophistications acquire their special meanings as deviations from the canonical story-format.

COGNITIVE IDENTIFICATION WITH SUBJECT-ACTANTS

The comprehension of narrative schemata presupposes that of its acting and conscious beings, its 'actants', to borrow and customize the terminology of Greimas (1983).[5] The comprehension of actants has a cognitive as well as an affective aspect, corresponding to two types of mental operations performed by the viewer, *cognitive identification* and *empathy*. I shall first describe the way in which these operations function in connection with simple narrative sequences, and then discuss whether such narrative sequences are tokens of basic mental models.

   Acting—and usually also conscious—beings, or actants, are the core of simple narrative sequences. Usually such sequences adopt the point of view of one single actant, called main character, hero, heroine, or protagonist. This actant may be an abstract construction, a personification of several people or, creatures of abstract principles like Humanity, the American people, and Evil. I shall call the 'centring being' the *subject-actant*.

---

   [4] From Henry James and Lubbock via, for example, Booth (1965), Stanzel (1955), Lämmert (1965), and Genette (1980), to Bordwell (1986) and Branigan (1992).
   [5] Greimas distinguishes between actant and acteur (and 'role'), the actant carrying anthropomorph functions, whereas the acteur is an entity of manifestation which can have several actantial functions (cf. also 1970; 255 f.). I use 'actant' as a term describing a mental model of a concrete or abstract anthropomorph or zoomorph agent or patient in fiction, as constructed by the viewer, not as a semantic entity.

The sheer presence of a living being at the beginning of a visual or verbal narrative will normally be sufficient to centre the story around this being. Our 'attention is caught' by the actant: the universe represented is conceived as a kind of figure-ground. Obviously, our attention may also be caught by various *objects,* but this kind of attention can only be maintained over an extended period of time if the object has consequences for a living being (or for an anthropomorphic entity, a robot, for instance), to which consciousness, motives, and acts are ascribed. When watching a visual representation of phenomena without any centring anthropomorphic actants, we often 'lose interest' owing to lack of emotional motivation for the cognitive analysis of the perceived, a fact which many makers of experimental films have discovered when presenting their films to a mass audience.

When the viewer's attention has been caught, the application of a set of cognitive procedures follows. These will be labelled *cognitive identification:* the viewer will try to simulate the subject-actant by constructing the subject-actant's perceptions. He will try, for example, to construct the field of vision of the actant by generalizing his/her own perceptual experiences into an objective and transformational model: what would I have seen if I had been in the same place as the actant? This activity presupposes the construction of abstract models of the world.[6] The viewer will further construct the actant's body-surface sensations in so far as these are indicated by the context (for instance, if the actant is being hit or, tickled).

Finally, the viewer will try to construct the subject actant's emotions, affects, and proprioceptive sensations, based on context (a man close to a tiger = fear; a man caressed = pleasure), or of acts (a person hitting another person = anger). The so-called Kuleshov effect, created by juxtaposing the same close-up of a face with different object-shots, has often been interpreted as a means to manipulate by montage. However, what the experiment 'says' is that a fine-grained assessment of a given state of mind relies on interpretation of context. Whether a face expresses pleasure by the prospect of freedom or by the prospect of soup cannot be learned by facial expressions alone,[7] and we will also understand the finer nuances of our emotions by their object and context. However, the partly innate vocal sounds for signalling emotions (see, for example, Sundberg 1982), the likewise partly innate 'body posture' and 'body language', and, most of all, the facial expressions[8] provide powerful

---

[6] This probably relies on innate wetware circuits in the posterior parietal area of cortex; cf. e.g. Kolb and Whishaw (1990: 418 ff.).

[7] Cf. Kuleshov (1974: 192 f.). Pudovkin (1970 edn.: 168) gave a somewhat different description of an experiment supposed to have been performed with Kuleshov (the same 'neutral' face contextualized with 'plate of soup', 'coffin with dead woman', and 'girl playing with teddy bear' was remembered by the audience as expressing three quite different emotions). Whether Pudovkin's version is a confabulation or not is hard to say; but the point, that evaluations and memories may be influenced by context, is indisputable: e.g. Motley (1993).

[8] For an overview of research into the interpretation of body language and facial expression cf. Burgoon, Buller, and Woodall (1989). Since Darwin's classic study *The Expression of the*

means for cueing basic emotions. The centres for the regulation of facial expressions are placed with other evolutionarily late features in the anterior part of the cortex, and it is generally believed that facial expressions for basic emotions such as happiness, sadness, anger, surprise, fear, and disgust are innate and therefore transcultural (see Ekman and Friesen 1975). The facial expressions of fear, sadness, joy, or other emotions often directly evoke the displayed emotions in the beholder. In visual narration, close-ups of persons that either indicate their emotions or their perceptions (and thus the possible emotional impact of the objects of their perceptions) play a very prominent role (see Carroll 1993). Classical film-theory laid great emphasis on the role of close-ups of facial expressions as a central means of cinema and its communication of emotions (for example, Balázs 1970: ch. 8), possibly in combination with close-ups of body reactions (such as those of the hands). In genres like television melodrama, such emotion-expressing close-ups are one of the cornerstones of the narration; in genres like musicals, reaction shots play a very prominent role. Considering the enormous role of facial expressions as communicative cues of and inducers of emotions in interpersonal relations, the Lacanian reduction of the 'facial problem' to mirror-stage phenomena (and to 'desire of the other') seems to have a limited explanatory value.

The viewer, furthermore, tries to construct the preferences, plans, and goals of the subject-actant and to assess the means and possibilities of implementing these plans and goals. The narrative world is then structured from the point of view of these preferences and goals.

Narrative theory often uses the concept 'focalization' to describe the focus of attention of a given representation (Genette 1980: 198 ff., Branigan 1992: 100 ff.). Centring by identification is, however, not quite congruent with focalization, which is often used to describe the type of access we have to a given sequence: are we inside the mind? do we look through the eyes of or do we just have an exterior view of a person (sometimes linked to distinction between degrees of 'subjectivity' in representation)? Centring by identification implies that the viewer activates anthropomorph schemata-orienting emotions or, goals. This may be done by different types of focalization, for instance by following the deeds of an actant, by using his perceptions (for example, looking 'through his eyes'), or by sharing 'his' thoughts; and this will make a difference to the location of the focus of attention (exterior world–interior world, distal activation–proximal activation: see Chapter 6). But the difference may not be one in degree of 'objectivity': to follow one person and his interests for ninety minutes creates a 'subjective' point of view. The centring

Emotions in Man and Animals (1872), there has been a quantity of literature about emotions and facial expressions as a means of communicating emotions. Cf. Izard (1991: 33 ff. and *passim*) for descriptions of the communicative function, Ekman (1973), and Ekman and Friesen (1975). Cf. also the many descriptions of facial expressions of emotions in Izard (1991).

may exist even when the subject-actant is absent: if we witness villains plotting against an absent hero, we feel fear, for instance, because we 'identify with', focus our attention on, the interests of the hero.

Focalization in a traditional sense is often an important guideline for cognitive evaluations of ranges of information when this information cannot be accessed by a given person because of his point of view. It may *not* provide information of the type of identification activated (see Browne 1982: 1–16), and it may not provide a clue as to the degree of subjectivity (understood, for example, as emotionality in a given situation) which can be evoked by many different means.[9] We can compare two 'subjective' situations: the blow on the head in *Murder, My Sweet* and the backtracking in *Gone With the Wind*, showing Scarlett O'Hara on a hilltop in the sunset (analyzed in Chapter 11). The first situation has an internal focalization (showing the working of the protagonist's perceptual system), the second an external optical focalization; but both aim to provide the subjective experience of a protagonist. Furthermore, it is not possible by enunciatory means alone to discover whether a given situation provides an objective, impartial representation or not. In most fictions it is the holistic, anthropomorph schemata which create the superior framework for our understanding, fusing, for example, extradiegetic mood-evoking music, acts, goals, special angles, and colour. In order to understand the effects of different narrative stategies we need to understand the means by which the canonical models of anthropomorph-identification work.

It is important to emphasize that cognitive identification (and empathy) are normally established at a very general level. In films about animals or in animated cartoons we can identify with animals; that is, we reconstruct their wishes, plans, and needs; but we do not mentally construct special 'quadruped', 'winged', 'finned', or 'beaked' mental models except in very special situations where the context demands the rudiments of such models in order to make a situation comprehensible. It is easy to make such identifications with beings very different from ourselves, because the specific motor realization of mental models normally takes place at a non-conscious level of the brain. If we wish to walk, we are normally only conscious of phenomena

---

[9] Branigan states that 'a narrator offers statements *about,* an actor/agent acts *on* or is acted upon; and a focalizer has an experience *of.* More precisely, narration, action, and focalization are three alternative modes of describing how knowledge may be stated, or obtained' (1992: 105), and these are useful distinctions if emphasis is put on the means by which viewers obtain knowledge. The problems surface when a focus on perceptual processes, for example, is made into a privileged way of gaining access to experience. The distinction between actor and focalizer is reflected in the distinction made on p. 101: 'Focalization (reflection) involves a character neither speaking (narrating, reporting, communicating) nor acting (focusing, focused by), but rather actually *experiencing* something through seeing or hearing it,' and experience is in a problematic way contrasted to 'awareness'. We may, however, gain access to experience based on inferences from acts, not just from 'awareness'.

such as speed and the general trajectory which the walk-movement has to follow, and of a general action-tension. But we are not conscious of the individual muscle-innervations, or of the way that we first move one leg and then
the other. Likewise, we only have a very general awareness of our body. We
do not have constant mental representations of our toes, ears, breast(s), or
other specific body parts: they only attract attention on special occasions.

Correspondingly, the cognitive identification with other human beings will
typically take place at a relatively abstract level. It is the focusing or centring
of the presentation which rules our type of identification: normally everyday
events as well as narrative representations will be moulded at a very general
level, at which the differences between men and women, children and adults,
or different races does not prevent the centring of the presentation from ensur-
ing a common ground for cognitive identification and empathy for many
viewers. Seeing a film about Gandhi, I, as a European, can easily make a cognitive identification with him, because I follow his perceptions, thoughts,
communications, and acts, and these are understandable according to general
patterns, such as that of the opposition between social humiliation and social
acceptance. In reading Jane Austen's novel *Pride and Prejudice,* men can easily follow the main lines of reasoning, acts, and motivations, although the central character is a woman. Certain situations may demand more specific
cognitive models of identification, when, for instance, class-culture or gender-
specific mental models are a precondition for identification. But these models
are specifications of more general models, and do not, as might appear from
certain aspects of the current culture-race-and-gender debate, constitute
totally discrete identities. Human beings are not totally identical, they are
moulded by concrete experiences; but neither are they millions of islands of
total otherness and specificity. A reason for emphasizing 'otherness' is often
a wish to explain suppression, discrimination, and exploitation as a lack of
understanding, as if the reason for these phenomena were mainly cognitive in
isolation from emotions, and not a difference in interests understood as a
fusion of cognitive and motivational factors.

Cognitive identification is thus carried out on the basis of mental models of
living beings, and there exist, therefore, several levels of specification of cognitive identification. The most basic levels are the most general. They only
presuppose abilities such as the ability to perceive remote objects, to experience tactile and interoceptive sensation, to feel simple motives, affects, and
emotions, and to understand uncomplicated plans, goals, and acts. Fiction and
plays serve as learning-processes for these mental models (Winnicott 1961),
and narrative patterns serve as the main 'objective', intersubjective models of
human behaviour.

The salience and activation-power of fictions may be enhanced if the 'texture' of protagonists has a close match to that of the particular viewer.
Children are specially activated by films showing other children; people from

Taiwan experience extra pleasure in watching Taiwanese films; people familiar with John Wayne will be more activated than people unfamiliar with him.
Thus the universality of superior narrative-mental models does not exclude
activation by thematic and 'textural' preferences. Some narratives or parts of
narratives can further presuppose much more complex and specified 'subject'
models in the viewer as preconditions for full cognitive identification, in the
same way that our knowledge of ourselves or others may be rudimentary or
complex.

COGNITIVE IDENTIFICATION, EMPATHY, AND MOTIVATION

What is meant by empathy is a viewer-activation of affects and emotions in
identification with the interests of a fictive being.[10] Although cognitive identification need not necessarily imply empathy (that is, implying that the viewer
simulates the actual or possible emotional states of the protagonist resulting
from his cognitive analysis of a given situation), empathy will very often be
the consequence of a prolonged cognitive identification. The reason for this
is simple. The mental apparatus is primarily developed as a tool for implementing the preferences of the subject. The senses safeguard us against dangers and register possible objectives, such as food or mating, which are then
transformed into plans and goals and carried out by the motor system. There
will therefore be a very strong relationship between motivation and cognitive
activities. If a given preference finds its way into the consciousness, the consciousness will immediately begin to seek scripts[11] for implementing that preference. Conversely, cognitive scripts will activate the corresponding emotions
and preferences if these are previously known by the subject. The cognitive
system is cause-seeking: when it perceives certain behaviour this will trigger
the search for causes of that behaviour, its 'motives'; and, if empathy is established, these will be represented by their emotional tone.

Affects and emotions play a crucial role in long-term memory, probably
because the consciousness does not work according to 'abstract' and disinterested mechanisms: perceptions and cognitive sequences are stored in order to
be used to support the future implementation of the living being's preferences,
and this support has both cognitive and motivational dimensions. 'Tiger' is
not only stored in memory as 'yellow creature with black stripes' but also
with affective values which will support adequate acts (for instance, fight or
flight) when a tiger is seen. The affective values therefore, are crucial for the
encoding and affective marking of the perceptual elements of memory.
Psychologists like Hamilton have argued (1988) that cognition, motivation,
and affect are three aspects of one information-processing system, in which

---

[10] For an overview of empathy research from Adam Smith onwards, see Zillmann (1991).
[11] My use of the word 'script' is borrowed from Schank and Abelson (1977).

the three aspects are only separated from each other by the ways in which they appear in consciousness. As I have noted previously, all cognitive sequences have an affective-motivational 'tone', which can vary in strength and structure (such as the intensities, tensities, saturations, and 'emotivities' described in Chapter 2), and quality (love, hate, sorrow, and so on). During fiction viewing the viewer performs hypothetical 'as if' simulations of situations; and the empathic tears shed during melodrama-viewing are real. If we were not able to respond to fictional hypotheses by emotional activation we would probably not be able to respond emotionally to hypothesized, imagined, but possible real-life events in the future, nor use the imagined as motivation for present acts.

Besides the cognitive reason for empathy, which is the integration of cognition in a holistic system of representation and motivation, empathy also has evolutionary roots in the social structure of humans. It is the opinion of many researchers into the evolution of emotions that empathy has a genetic basis caused by the clear survival-value of social bonding resulting from emotional ties (Izard 1991: 395 ff.). Social co-operation, simple types of division of 'labour' (whether hunting or child-rearing), learning processes by imitation, and social communication based on an understanding of the motives of others presuppose empathy.[12] A description of the processes of identification as based on 'narrative desire' does not explain the many types of fiction film which, for their emotional effect, rely on human bonding by empathy.

In order to see the way in which cognitive identification, empathic identification, and motivation interrelate, I shall analyze a short sequence from Hitchcock's film *Psycho*. At one point in the film a young woman is killed. At the time of the killing, the identity of the murderer cannot be established with certainty, although the primary suspicion of the viewer is directed toward the mother of a perhaps rather mentally disturbed and voyeuristic young man, Norman Bates, played by Anthony Perkins. Later the viewer witnesses the young man removing the body from the motel-room where the murder has been committed, and trying to destroy all evidence of the crime. He drives the dead woman's car, which contains her body, to a swamp, and pushes the car out into the swamp. The car slowly sinks, but when it is halfway down into the mud, the sinking stops momentarily, after which it starts again until the car has totally disappeared. We might imagine that the normal viewer's empathy and moral sense would make him hope that the endeavour of the young man will fail, so that the circumstances of the murder can be cleared up and the guilty punished. We would, for instance, expect

---

[12] To describe evolution as 'the survival of the fittest in the struggle of life' is in some respects a misrepresentation, as selection takes place at the level of the species, not the individual. The Freudian description of evolution takes its point of departure in power struggle and has the mother–child relation as the main 'prosocial' emotional relation.

the viewer to be pleased during those moments when the sinking comes temporarily to a halt, and to be sorry when the car sinks again shortly afterwards and disappears into the swamp. But the typical reaction of the viewer is different. The viewer worries during the short halt in the sinking and experiences a feeling of relief when the car starts to sink again. The viewer has cognitively identified himself with the young man over a longer period of time, and has, during this period, been 'forced' to 'actualize' the emotions which are presupposed in order to give coherence and meaning to his acts ('I must wash off the smear of blood', 'I must dispose of the body and the car', and so forth). This type of identification and motivation is built in by Hitchcock (see Truffaut 1984: 269–72). If the viewer had other points of identification, for instance a sympathetic detective or a concerned friend or relative, that character could anchor the empathy of the viewer and thereby reduce the empathic elements in the cognitive identification with the young man. But the first part of the film has only provided Norman Bates and the young woman as points of identification and empathy. When she dies, a vacuum is created which the young man partially fills; and when the film later presents new points of identification, the sister and the lover of the murdered woman, this 'unnatural sympathy' with the young man fades away.

Many films, such as gangster films, show corresponding developments in which cognitive identification evokes and actualizes sympathies which conflict with the viewer's normal feelings. When Dix Handley in Huston's *The Asphalt Jungle* is confronted with a witness whom he threatens by using non-verbal language, we emotionally identify with Handley's threats, because we have been cued into cognitively identifying with his point of view, although our better 'I' might object to the behaviour. The precondition for cognitive identification leading to empathic identification in opposition to normal values is, of course, that no other clear points of identification are articulated. The sceptical might object that the reason for identifying with such persons as criminals in visual narratives is that they appeal to suppressed wishes; and in some cases this might be true. But it is not valid as a general explanation: we identify with Norman or Dix because the films have cued us skilfully into reconstructing a situation in which the rational act is to avoid negative consequences. It is not subconscious and irrational drives which are set free, but, on the contrary, an individual rationality which is 'set free' from the rationality of social, supra-individual norms.

Even under normal conditions there will be a certain degree of cognitive identification with villains and opponents. We will try to guess at and to emulate the motives and plans of a villain; for instance, 'the villain is probably preparing an ambush' or 'the wolves are probably hungry and will soon try to eat the hero'. This capacity for understanding opponents is clearly necessary in order to orient oneself in the world, and it does not imply empathy because of the short and fragmentary nature of the procedure of cognitive identification. The understanding of the opponent's 'point of view' will normally only be as elaborate as is needed for coping with the given situation. The attack by wolves on a person is not primarily perceived as 'hunger' but as 'aggression', a term which fully exemplifies the way in which the cognitive, motivational, and affective dimensions are interwoven. If a film were made 'from the point of view of the wolves' in which man represented merely 'food', there would be a strong change in the emotional, cognitive, and motivational structure of viewer-reception (possibly resulting in cognitive and emotional dissociation: see Chapter 10).

OBJECTIVITY OF EMOTIONS AND COGNITIVE LABELLING OF AROUSAL

In the following, I shall discuss the degree of intersubjectivity in emotions and affects, and their relation to cognitive evaluation, and then expand my discussion of the cognitive labelling theory. Emotions and affects are often described as quite subjective and personal, and therefore beyond precise analysis. If subjective means merely 'something which characterizes neural states', this is obviously true: stones do not have emotions. But if subjective means 'something which eludes objective and intersubjective analysis', it is a problematic description. The conception of a scientific analysis of meanings and aesthetic phenomena has its roots in the analysis of the visible and audible world, probably because this exterior world, and the senses representing it, have been thought objective and intersubjective. If we look in a textbook on semantics for descriptions of what meaning is, it will typically offer examples of referential meaning by suggesting signifiers of objects such as 'tree' or 'cow', which are available for intersubjective visual inspection.

Any sense-experience will have two poles: its external (or internal) cause, and the perceptual apparatus perceiving the phenomenon. A perception of a red cow will be caused by an object reflecting certain light-waves, which in the perceptual apparatus will be represented as 'redness' and which will be constructed with a certain outline. If no perceptual apparatus is available there will be no representation of the cow; and, in another perceptual system, say a colour-blind one or one unable to construct outlines, the representations will be different. In that respect, all representations and phenomena of consciousness depend on the 'subject' and its system of perception. But the perception of colour is not 'subjective' in the sense that, given similar perceptual systems, it is not intersubjective. It has been argued convincingly by Dennett (1990), for example, that the concept of some mental *qualia*, subjective qualities in one's experience which give non-objective information, is meaningless. It does not make sense to divide the information into two parts, one objective (emitting light-waves of a certain length) and one subjective (the 'redness' of red). The 'redness' of red does not give any information except that it is a special way of representing certain perceptions, certain inputs. The way in which the contour of a cow is represented in the consciousness is dependent on the perceptual system; but, at the same time, it is an objective representation of the cow. The representation of the external world is thus not simply an analogical representation of the exterior world: forms of representations like colour and contour are special, human ways of 'objectively' representing the world.

In the same way, emotions and affects are caused by interaction with the physical and human environment. Very often we can objectively and inter-subjectively perceive causes, and, given a knowledge of the standard system of perception and evaluation, can infer their emotional impact. If we see a person being threatened with an axe, we can infer his fear in the same way as we can infer his seeing 'green' and 'wheelbarrow' when exposed to the sight of a green wheelbarrow. I have no stronger guarantee that other people mentally experience 'green wheelbarrow' in the same way that I do than that they experience fear in the same way as I do. The intersubjectivity of the mental representations is in both cases based partly on the assumption that everybody has the same system of perception and the same mental equipment, partly on the fact that it is possible to communicate with others about these phenomena without serious difficulty. There are persons who, because of colour-blindness or a special affective structure, experience given inputs differently, but this will probably reveal itself in the course of communication. Emotions and perceptions are developed through experience, and any statement concerning human perception, meaning, and experience should, in principle, specify what type of observer socialization or programming is presupposed in the description. But for practical reasons we often have to imply standard assumptions about the film-viewer, for example, for which a given statement is valid (and choose not to have long lists of assumptions, from the viewer not being colour-blind to the viewer not being a psychopath or an infant).

Affects and emotions are represented in a person by psychosomatic intensities or, levels of arousal. Furthermore, these intensities or levels of arousal are experienced with their hedonic value (pleasant–unpleasant) by means of a cognitive evaluation and labelling of the level of arousal. The physiological basis for emotions and affects is relatively unspecific, and acquires its specifications by means of cognitive analysis of the context of the arousal. I would like to expand my presentation of the cognitive-labelling theory given in Chapter 2. The theory was first suggested by the psychologist Stanley Schachter, and a brief outline of the theory is as follows (see also Schachter 1971; Gross 1987: 433 ff.; and Izard 1991: 35 ff.): some given perceptions cause physiological changes which generate a consciousness of physiological 'arousal'; but the precise interpretation and the consequential labelling of the arousal is a cognitive process based on an interpretation of the given situation. The 'same' physiological arousal and excitement can thus have different 'labels' in different contexts. Schachter carried out experiments with people who had been injected with adrenalin: some were placed in contexts that made them 'label' their arousal as anger; others in contexts that made them 'label' their arousal as euphoria. Dutton and Aron conducted an experiment in which the experimental subjects, young men, were placed on bridges over a river while they were interviewed by a pretty young woman who presented them with an ambiguous picture of another woman and asked them to invent a story inspired by the picture. One group was placed on an extremely unstable suspension bridge 230 feet above a canyon, while another was placed on a solid wooden bridge upstream. The stories from the group on the unstable bridge, young men who were supposedly aroused by the dangerous circumstances, contained far more sexual imagery than the stories from the people on the wooden bridge. An arousal, which to some extent was caused by fear, was reinterpreted and consciously or non-consciously relabelled as sexual, based on the other clues in the context of the picture and the interviewer.

Unlike a psychoanalytical description, the cognitive-labelling theory does not presuppose a strongly content-specified drive or libido which is then reinterpreted or veiled. A larger set of emotions and affects makes up an arsenal of 'mental models' that can specify a smaller set of psycho-physiological states of arousal. In many action and suspense films, arousal is evoked and then relabelled. This is the case in many Spielberg and Lucas films, in which arousal is produced by dangerous situations (for example, in several Indiana Jones films in which characters stand on decrepit and unstable suspension bridges) and then later relabelled as erotic arousal or as tenderness.[13] In many Westerns, arousal is created by a sexual situation and then relabelled as aggression in a subsequent fight-scene. A psychoanalytical explanation would recognize manifestations of sexuality that then express themselves directly or are sublimated into, or frustrated by, all these arousal situations.

Cognitive analysis and labelling are to a large extent based on input from the intersubjective world, and therefore the trained and informed observer has an opportunity to predict which labelling a person will perform in a given situation, equal to that of the person directly involved in the situation. P. M. Churchland (1988: 76 ff.) has argued convincingly against the view that people possess a privileged knowledge of themselves as a result of introspection, and he cites the psychologists Nisbett and Wilson in support of the view that much of what passes for an introspective report is really the expression of one's spontaneous theorizing about one's reasons, motives, and perceptions, when the hypotheses produced are based on the same external evidence available to the public at large.

Applied to film and media research, this means that there is no difference in principle between deciding what emotions a given film scene will evoke in

---

[13] The relabelling is correlated with functional changes: fear and erotic desire are antagonistic.

the agents and/or in the spectator, and deciding other strategies of perception and cognition in the film: all these inferences of viewer-impact are equally certain or uncertain. When, for instance, we watch a film showing a feudal war, in which arousal, caused by the danger of body mutilation and death, is not labelled as 'fear' but as 'heroic euphoria' by the feudal values expressed (perhaps supported by the general motor-activity-generated euphoria simulated by the viewer), or if we watch a film about Christian martyrs which labels a pain-induced arousal as euphoric beatification, or if we watch a film that takes place today and describes the experiences of a masochist, we can partly reconstruct the mental models and the cognitive-labelling processes of the film, and thereby experience the emotions of the protagonists by empathic identification. The 'unusually' labelled emotions will perhaps not have the same vividness and 'salience' as they supposedly would have had for a hypothetical knight in the Middle Ages or a Christian martyr, for whom the film would activate many emotionally charged memories; but many perceptual and cognitive activities likewise demand special abilities in order to be fully and intensively conscious. The cognitive labelling of arousal is therefore an objective and intersubjective mental process. Some film themes and some film plots will be 'uninteresting' or 'repellent' to certain viewers, and the lack of emotional appeal will cause an absence of motivation for cognitive identification, just as a lack of cognitive appeal will cause an absence of empathic representation; cognitive and affective processes presuppose each other, and variations in the viewer's cognitive preferences are linked to those in the viewer's emotional preferences.

As we have seen, there is no reason to presume that, in principle, the mental representation of the colour 'green' or the outline of a cow is more objective than the psychosomatic representation of 'arousal' and its different emotional 'labels'. The cognitive labelling of this arousal is to a large extent determined by the context, and, to interpret this, we use schemata in which the cognitive aspects are fused with the affective. Therefore, when a viewer tries to understand a given film, the empathic 'simulation', the psychosomatic representation of affects and emotions, participates on the same level as other mental reconstructions of, for example, a perceptual nature. The intensity and the nature of this empathic simulation are to a large degree dependent on the focus of the representation. If we mainly or exclusively follow the experience of one being the empathic intensity will be great; whereas if we follow the experiences of many different beings the intensity of our empathic identification with each of the beings will, of course, be less, just as a small green spot of colour in a large picture will lack the intensity of a large area of green.

Analogous to the perception of three-dimensional figures, but in contrast to the perception of colour, empathy as a rule presupposes a dominant 'hypothesis', a subject that anchors the identification. Gestalt psychologists often use ambiguous pictures in which, for instance, a given picture may be perceived as an old hag or as a young girl, or another given picture either as a staircase seen from below or from above, but never as both at the same time. These pictures illustrate the top-down aspects of perception. In the same way, a given narrative can yield one type of cognitive and emotional experience if we identify with one actant, and another if we identify with another actant (as when children sometimes read a fairy tale 'from the point of view of the monster'). But we cannot at a given moment view a narrative from the point of view of two antagonist actants while experiencing the same intensity of identification with both actants simultaneously, although we can shift identification. After having seen the ambiguous stairs 'from above' and 'from below' a couple of times, we 'know' that they can be seen in two ways; but this metaknowledge lacks perceptual 'salience', just as the metaknowledge that we can experience the Dracula story from the point of view of Jonathan Harker or from the point of view of Dracula lacks the emotional intensity which characterizes the singular identification. A major reorientation of the emotional identifications in a story is normally only possible by changing the cognitive structures, like the narrative changes (the identification with Dracula) in Dragoti's *Love at First Bite*, which transform the Dracula narrative into a romance. Ambiguous identifications lead to nonlinear, non-narrative, associative-saturated forms of experience which surface, for example, in Murnau's *Nosferatu* and Herzog's *Nosferatu the Vampire*.

EMOTIONS, AFFECTS, AND MODELS OF NARRATIVE HOMEOSTASIS

Narrative sequences are by definition process-oriented. In order to create a process, the beginning of a narrative must describe or bring about a disequilibrium. The starting-point for a narrative sequence is what Propp (1968) and Greimas (1983) call the (initial) lack, and what one could also call the first actual or potential narrative disequilibrium. According to Greimas this lack is often a lack of knowledge, power, or goods; Carroll (1988)[14] has emphasized lack of knowledge (question–answer) as a fundamental narrative structure. Whereas Greimas sees the disequilibrium as caused by the subject-actant having some preferences which are not satisfied for the time being, Carroll emphasizes the lack of knowledge in the viewer. Greimas' model does not consider discourse structures, whereas Carroll's question–answer structure does not consider the fabula structures. In a psychoanalytical framework the lack or the disequilibrium has been interpreted as 'castration', just as all the forces and motivations which drive the narration toward equilibrium have been interpreted as 'desire'. Such a framework of interpretation creates a

---

[14] Carroll's term for the question–answer structure is 'erotetic', and functions rather like Barthes' *'hermeneutic code'* (1972b) and 'function' (1977b: 92), whereas it is less general than Greimas' narrative model.

number of problems for the understanding of many narrative phenomena. Preferences for avoiding danger, for removing an opponent, for social recognition, for sexual gratification, for food, shelter, and other requirements are different and equally possible motivational forces of narrative transformations, but they are rooted in different socio-biological needs, and cannot be subsumed under general labels like 'desire'.

The psychological-motivational description of the narrative sequences as movements from disequilibrium to equilibrium is a theory of homeostasis. The word was first used in this sense in 1932 by Walter Cannon in order to describe the physiological mechanisms of regulation which manage to keep some variables fluctuating about a certain level, for example the regulation of the body temperature around 37° C. But this line of thought was known earlier, for instance among German physiologists like Wundt, who inspired Freud in his early ideas concerning drive, *Trieb*. Transferred to narrative sequences, homeostasis implies that the viewers, in empathy with the preferences of the subject-actants, will try to maintain a base level of 'tension', so that 'lacks' will be registered as increased levels of excitation, hedonically experienced as un-pleasure. This high level of excitation will trigger expectations of symbolic narrative mechanisms of reduction of excitation. Both as a psychological theory and as a tool to explain narrative sequences, a simple theory of homeostasis suffers from certain flaws. That narrative tension and excitation should always be hedonically evaluated as un-pleasure, and that only the final denouement and tension-reduction should be evaluated as pleasurable, does not fit the intuitive experience of the hedonic tone of, for example, many suspense narratives.

In his book *The Experience of Motivation: The Theory of Psychological Reversals* (1982; see also Evans 1989), Apter has put forward a theory that tries to solve some of the problems arising from the psychological theories of homeostasis. His main point is to suggest the existence of not one but two motivational systems. One, which Apter calls the 'telic' system (that is, goal- or telos-seeking), system corresponds very well to the tension-reducing system as described above. In this system, high arousal is evaluated as unpleasant, low arousal as pleasant. But to this Apter adds another motivational system, which he calls 'paratelic' (which could be described as 'means-oriented'), in which low arousal is evaluated as unpleasant, high arousal as pleasant. The paratelic motivation is process-oriented, as, for instance, in the positive arousal some people experience from motor activity for its own sake (for instance, in jogging and other types of sports). The control of the application of the two systems is a cognitive labelling procedure. An arousal caused by 'danger', for instance, will be controlled on one side by a telic cognitive system, which aims at reducing danger and, in that way, arousal, and on the other side by a paratelic cognitive system, which aims at an increase of arousal (because within certain limits, arousal serves as a support for the necessary motor activity). At the same time the systems are functionally cooperative and antagonistic. Low arousal will be labelled telically as relaxation or pleasure, but paratelically as boredom or displeasure. High arousal will be labelled paratelically as excitement or pleasure, whereas telically it will be labelled as fear. When Apter calls his theory one of 'reversals' it is because it implies rela-belling. The labelling of low arousal as relaxation can reverse into a rela-belling as boredom, just as the labelling of high arousal as pleasurable excitement can reverse into a relabelling as fear. Apter sees these reversals as means of keeping the level of motivation within certain upper and lower limits. By under-stimulation the relaxation reverses into boredom, by over-stimulation the excitement reverses into fear.

The concepts of telic and paratelic motivation and cognitive labelling have an explanatory value for visual fiction and entertainment. Many fiction and entertainment elements—for instance, many forms of humour and comedy—have a non-narrative, non-teleological character, and their effect is typically to produce an increase of arousal rather than of relaxation, for example when viewers become more and more excited during a preposterous comedy. The reception of these forms of fiction and entertainment is therefore not easily explained by a simple tension-reduction model; the viewer is exposed to both arousal-creating and arousal-reducing elements, and their labelling of the arousal as unpleasure constantly reverses into pleasure and vice versa. The embarrassment created by a sequence of awkward situations is constantly transformed into laughter, and this laughter not only reduces the sympathetic, telic arousal, but also produces an increased level of parasympathetic arousal, as expressed in terms like 'to die of laughter'. We want still more embarrass-ing, funny episodes; and, although the viewing creates relaxation in a telic, motor-based sense, we become increasingly aroused.

Narrative fiction also relies on paratelic arousal. Although the overall effect of suspense fiction is to create relaxation, and although our expectations are telically geared toward a tension-reducing denouement, over long stretches of time the narrative sequence paratelically increases suspense and arousal. This semi-suspension of telic demands on arousal-reduction is partly made possible by the fictional framing of the experience: because we know that the horror story is made for pleasurable consumption and is not a live report from the real world, we consume it by identifying with and simulating the story as true, but, at the same time, we relabel part of the arousal as paratelic-pleasurable by framing the story as fiction, as hypothesis, as a game from which we can bale out. But many people actually experience a stimulus from extremely dangerous pastimes like mountaineering, so the hypothetical aspect of fiction-consumption is not a necessity for a pleasurable experience of dan-ger: it can rely on the paratelic mechanisms. One might, too, note the increase in the use of the disgusting in splatter films and music videos as examples of cognitive-hedonic relabelling of arousal.

So far, I have mainly dealt with the story—the fabula—and with viewer identification with subject-actants, as the basis for my description of empathy phenomena. In many ways, the *syuzhet* empathy is brought about in analogy with this 'canonical' identification and empathy. When we agree to watch visual fiction, we accept a set of rules of experience and establish a viewer-persona, a mental model of the viewer as spectator of fiction, and this viewer-model, this persona, feels suspense, happiness, fear, and sadness as if witnessing similar phenomena in the non-fictive world. In simple narrative forms, the subject-actant and the viewer-persona are merged, whereas more complicated narrative forms have every possible variety of distance between viewer-persona and actants. All fictional forms of identification and empathy are hypothetical simulations of non-fictional types of experience.

A CRITICAL DIGRESSION ON THE USE OF 'VOYEURISM' IN FILM STUDIES

One of the central theories in film and television studies has been a Freud- and Lacan-based theory of voyeurism and fetishism arising from the Freudian concept of castration. This theory has been the basis from which viewer identification and emotional response have been described. Metz's article 'Disavowal, Fetishism' (included in Metz 1982), Mulvey (1989), Silverman (1983), and Krutnik (1991) are examples of this theory. The theory goes something like this: seeing a naked woman, the little boy thinks that she has been castrated, and this makes him anxious, especially because he thinks that his father could do the same to him. He can try to look again and again in the hope that he was wrong and that women do have penises. But he can also try to suppress what he has seen, and make a 'positive' representation of woman by fetishism, for example, by a metonymic representation of the female sex (such as worshipping garters, and shoes) or by turning the whole woman into a fetish. For both sexes an acceptance of the fact of castration will mean the acceptance of the paternal power to castrate and thereby an acceptance of the 'reality principle'. The theory can be historicized, castration then becoming a phenomenon within the 'patriarchal ideology'. Patriarchal ideology is, among other things, characterized by phallic, rational unity, and can be undermined by heterogeneity. A psychoanalytical description of sexuality is primarily a hermeneutic description of the thoughts which people may have when they perceive anatomical differences between the sexes, and also a description of possible steps in their development which describe these thoughts, seen from the point of view of an individual. Sexuality described neither as patterned schemata of social interaction, nor as psychosomatic patterns which mould behaviour.

That some people at certain times in the past, and in the present, have believed that women are 'castrated' men is probably very true; but as an overall description of beliefs held in 'patriarchal societies', for example, the psychological theories of castration are quite incredible. Except for the last two centuries, most children have grown up under conditions in which they have witnessed copulation among animals (and often human copulation) from their earliest infancy. Most 'patriarchal' societies have few restrictions relating to verbal descriptions of the facts of life. In feudal Europe, for example, children could see pictures of copulation even in churches. For these children, the anatomical differences between men and women, and between male and female animals, would be understood in act-terms and functional terms: anatomical differences which had their *raison d'être* in copulation and procreation. A Freudian-style speculation would have no meaning for these children, because how can copulation and procreation be possible if the two sexes are not provided with two complementary organs?

Sex-related behaviour is a biosocial system which can be described at a social macro-level, not just at the nuclear-family micro-level. Sexuality characterizes a large number of the world's species; it is an innate system, the evolutionary basis for which is defined at the level of the species (mixing gene codes), not at the level of the individual. For many higher species sexuality is furthermore integrated with offspring-rearing, and, for some strongly social species, like humans, it is integrated within a broader framework of social systems of species and group interaction.

Copulation is behaviour which a given individual can perform with individuals of the opposite sex in competition with individuals of the same sex and using various types of 'negotiations' (from consent to violence) with the potential partners. As a social system, sexuality relies heavily on visual, acoustic, olfactory, and tactile communication: the individual has to send and receive 'messages' of attractiveness, and has to interpret 'messages' of consent or rejection. Furthermore, s/he has to send and receive 'messages' to and from individuals of the same sex regarding 'possessive restrictions' on possible configurations of sexual relations. The actual intercourse only takes up a fraction of the time used in communicating and negotiating mating wishes, mating intentions, and mating rights, by humans and many other species. Human 'voyeurism' and 'exhibitionism' do not need special explanations, like fear of castration, but are functional elements in the gathering of information about and communication of sex-related, sex-triggering aspects of anatomy. Furthermore, visual access to the naked body forms part of the social systems for negotiating right to and/or consent to 'sexual behaviour'. The given norms for a neutral degree of nudity will determine the part of the body which articulates a voyeuristic or exhibitionistic behaviour; a beach environment will have norms for the degree of nudity which signals a 'consent' quite unlike the norms of the workplace. The 'battlefield of consent' has been different in the past: in the nineteenth century, showing an ankle might be interpreted as a signal of 'consent'.

Many films appeal to voyeurism in the trivial sense that the viewers are allowed visual inspections of other people in circumstances of 'symbolic consent' which they would not have in everyday life. An important element in pornographic films is the communication of signs of pleasurable consent, by sounds and body-language, to sexual approaches. In detective films intellectual curiosity is often directed towards observing and scrutinizing sex-related phenomena, and these films (as in Hitchcock's *Rear Window*) are concerned with the mental simulation of emotionally highly charged phenomena related to body existence, such as death. The combination of two phenomena like sex and death, both of which in isolation are infused with strong emotions, will often increase the emotional charge. However, this does not make death identical to castration.

But films do not normally appeal to voyeurism or exhibitionism in the special sense of whether the viewer is interested in whether Faye Dunaway has a penis after all, or whether Marlon Brando has been castrated. The essence of striptease in films is not an uncertainty as to what will be revealed, but a game with symbolic consent. The emission of signals of consent is also to some degree a 'real consent', because accepting a role which involves a certain degree of nudity and/or expression of sexual content is also a 'real-life event' involving the actors' real-life 'morality' or their star image; for example, the way in which Julie Andrews' 'Victorian' star image is used when she strips in the Blake Edwards film *S.O.B.* Different communication institutions (film, television, video, and stage) and different audiences have different moral norms, and emission of sexual signals is part of a series of complicated social negotiations. Exhibitionism on film often relies heavily on reaction-shots in order to cue the 'proper' emotional response. In Verhoeven's *Basic Instinct* a glimpse of female pubic hair is cued as exciting and as emitted from a position of power, in which visual consent is opposed to physical consent, by a series of reaction-shots. Pleasure by a relabelled arousal originating in exhibitionist shame (cued by reaction-shots of middle-aged or elderly people) is an element of *9½ Weeks* and its clones. The emission of sexual signals is a symbolic or hypothetical act and therefore not equivalent to actual consent. Individuals can emit sexual signals to a large group of people or to the general public without any intention of performing physical sex acts with all or any of the spectators, as is indicated in the ambivalence of the sexual meaning of 'tease'. To emit sexual signals is an act aiming to influence the addressee, and whether it will be interpreted as a sign of consent or of sexual power will depend on the addressee's interpretation of the context.[15]

[15] For a critique of Mulvey's use of the terms 'active-looking-masculine' and 'passive-looked-at-feminine', and her use of Freud, cf. Keane (1986).

5

Intentions, Will, Goal, Consciousness, and Humanness

This chapter first describes the way in which some phenomena, such as flexibility, intentionality, free will, and empathy, play an important role in the understanding of what humanness is, and also shows the way in which humanness is often described negatively, as something lacking, in non-human figures of fiction such as robots and monsters. The chapter then describes some essential features in the cognitive constitution of man's mental model of himself and this model's importance for understanding the structure of the canonical narrative. The description is compared to psychoanalytical models such as the 'mirror stage'. The chapter goes on to analyze the way in which models of non-humanness in many film genres are used not only for representing negatively evaluated phenomena, but also to represent social and superhuman phenomena. It concludes with an analysis of the role of repetition in narration.

HUMANS, ROBOTS, MONSTERS, PSYCHOPATHS, AND CLOWNS

A recurrent theme in B-films as well as ambitious films is a deeply philosophical one: how to determine the essence of humanness. But whereas the ambitious films often, although not exclusively, try to define humanness by verbal means, action-and-suspense films, comedies, and farce often deal with the subject by illustrating it through character and plot. This determination can arise from contrasts and differences to other living beings, as when humanness is determined by delimiting it in relation to a beastly otherness that has its own *raison d'être*, but the determination is often subtractive: the essential human features are implied by describing certain human-like but 'non-human' actants, who retain some features comparable to those of humans but who still lack some 'essential' human features. Traditional 'non-human' figures of subtractive contrast are the clown and the monster; but, during the last two centuries, robots and psychopaths have increasingly complemented these figures as modern versions of monsters.

Massive viewer-interest indicates that the phenomenon of 'humanness' has very strong cognitive and affective appeal. It is fair to assume that the viewer in his everyday life also undertakes a continuous interpretation, categorization, and mental construction of the world and himself based on some essential criteria of humanness, and that these interpretations play a very important role in his affective experiences and affective motivations for actions. It is, of course, of vital interest for humans to know whether they are confronted with an obsessive psychopath, an instinct-ruled animal, or with an individual who is able to understand, that is, to make a full model of his environment. Countless numbers of horror films describe the affective result of possession, in which a family member, relative, or friend suddenly becomes an 'alien', such as a monster or a robot. A main theme in visual fiction is, further, the articulation of 'human bonding', contrasting the bonding, by caring and relating, with the psychopathic lack of affective bonds.[1] The representations of humanness also contain strong normative elements. In *Modern Times,* Chaplin shows us the way in which work on the assembly line is an inhuman, robot-like existence, and the representation expresses some normative views of what humanness is.

The subtractive–contrastive determination of humanness has many aspects, but themes like consciousness, empathy, emotions, memory, ethics, intentionality, flexibility, and free will are central. In a given film all these themes or their subsets may be present, and may be more or less correlated. The delimitation from 'non-humans' is not necessarily sharp, just as the delimitation from higher animals is fluid. A further complication is that 'non-humanness' often comes in two variants: the negative variant, in which it is connected with the subhuman, and that in which the non-human features are connected with the superhuman, whether evaluated as positive, negative, or complex. For example, a stereotypical tone of voice or 'empty, staring' eyes may be signs of animal-like automatism, but may also be signs of a ritualistic, 'superhuman' behaviour recognized by us from religious and political behaviour or from certain types of news, or the signs may express a positively evaluated contact with 'deep layers of the psyche', as in orgiastic emotional states or those of trance.

As the viewer, like the person in everyday life, does not have direct access to the mental life of other beings, the ascription 'degree of humanness' must take the form of interpretive hypotheses based on the expressive signs that these beings emit and on an interpretation of their behaviour. Expressive signs and behaviour have to fit into certain mental models for humanness. In what follows I shall present an outline of some typical examples.

---

[1] In genres as different as war films, science-fiction films, and melodrama, problems of 'bonding' have a greater explanatory value than those relating to 'desire'. Many love stories deal more with bonding than with 'sex' in a narrow sense. Although we might say that the term 'bonding' is 'loose', covering most pro-social phenomena, it nevertheless provides an alternative framework to 'desire' for understanding the impact of visual fiction.

1. Automatism and schematism versus flexibility

Normally, schematic behaviour and schematic communication are sure signs of non-humanness: clowns walk with rigid steps and speak in a ritualized manner. Non-human cognitive schematism deviates from human flexibility either by lack of feedback in response to new information (as we find in Don Quixote's fight with windmills) or by excessive feedback, as when all new impulses cause a reflex-like change of behaviour or line of thought (see, for example, the policeman in *Bringing up Baby,* whose lines of thought and associations are manipulated by 'Katherine Hepburn' to such an extent that they become a 'reflex' of whatever she mentions). The gaze of the non-human being is staring and inflexible, as if the 'monster' were incapable of feedback or of making a conscious mental representation of the seen (see, for instance, Steve Martin in *The Man With Two Brains*).

The robot is controlled by simple models of behaviour and speaks with a toneless, non-modulated, and stereotypical voice. The psychopath is controlled by very few mental schemata comprising obsessional thoughts which often lead to ritualized behaviour, as shown in the super-cliché of American films about sex crimes in which the offender is ruled by a simple 'pattern of behaviour'. Humanness is, then, by implicit inference, characterized by the flexibility that is a prominent feature of the powerful human bio-computer. But the registration of this computer-power is not only a cognitive phenomenon: the registration of non-human 'one-track minds' impels a strong emotional impact, with reactions varying from fear and disgust to amusement (or, in relation to children and certain animals, a reaction of 'tenderness').

2. Teleological, intentional, and voluntary behaviour versus causal behaviour

By teleological and intentional behaviour, we understand a form of behaviour that is not controlled by simple stimulus–response schemata but by more complex mental models, in which goals, plans, and objects are imagined and present in the consciousness, in contrast to nonconscious, causal behaviour. Complexity in behaviour and communication is often taken as a sign of voluntary control. Whereas flexibility is visible, intentionality is a model of interpretation, which is often the mental equivalent of flexible behaviour. If we see a human being or an animal watching an object closely we ascribe consciousness, a conscious, mental representation of the object, to the being. Part of the horror in the film *Psycho* is caused by Norman Bates' eyes, which are contextualized by the bird theme; their inflexible stare makes us wonder whether his eyes serve as instruments for a conscious mental representation. Wide-open eyes in dead persons, or persons in coma or trance, can produce the horrible experience of a gaze without intention or representation. Because of their importance for social communication, strong emotions are connected with the kinds of behaviour that express teleology, intention, will, and conscious representation.

If an animal or human being inflexibly pursues an object, we ascribe a lower degree of consciousness to the being than if it undertakes complex manipulations of objects. Causally ruled behaviour is interpreted as based on simple, hardwired, and therefore non-human schemata. Films about vampires or possession and enchantment typically describe the transition from a teleological-intentional to a causal form of behaviour, in which the fellow-being is no longer represented in a conscious way, that is, with normal complexity, but only as a stimulus; for instance, as the 'trigger' 'blood', which causes schematic behaviour.

3. Emotivity and empathy versus non-emotivity

Even if there exist relatively universal signs of emotional states, like crying, laughter, and anger (Ekman 1973), these are also partly mental models that the viewer uses to understand the inner life of persons in the exterior world. In contrast to intentionality, 'true emotions' must be spontaneous manifestations of emotional schemata, not 'false emotions' displayed by an actant who calculates his emission of emotional signs according to certain intentions. There is thus a certain demand for a 'reflex-like', 'causal' pattern of reaction. However, if the emotions repeat simple schemata to an excessive degree, they are perceived as non-human and non-spontaneous in the commonsense psychology of films: for example, when Norman Bates' emotional life is ruled by one fixed emotional pattern, or when clowns begin to cry or laugh by reflex. In films like Ridley Scott's *Blade Runner* it is crucial to ascertain whether the emotions are programmed as simple stimulus–response schemata or whether they emerge as consequences of complex, non-programmed experiences.

In contrast to emotions, empathy demands a cognitive element: in order to understand a form of behaviour or an emotional expression like compassion, it is usual for the situation of the fellow-being to be represented mentally in a conscious way. Loss of intentional, cognitive representation leads to a loss of empathy; but intentional, cognitive representation does not necessarily imply that a non-human also possesses the characteristic 'empathy'. The plot in Siegel's *The Invasion of the Body Snatchers* builds on the assertion of a break in the link between cognitive, intentional representation and empathic compassion in the robot-like copies of humans who illustrate non-humanness in the film, although the film tends to suggest a certain loss of intentional representation in the people whose minds have been replaced, which is shown by a certain degree of mechanical behaviour and inflexibly staring eyes. In Kubrick's *2001: A Space Odyssey,* the computer-monster HAL 9000 possesses, besides rudimentary emotions, a cognitive, intentional representation of human beings, but without any empathic identification: when confronted by HAL's emotionless, video-camera stare directed toward human beings, the viewer feels fear at the 'mechanical sight'.

Common elements in mental models of humanness, as described above, are flexible behaviour based on mental representation of the object world, and empathic relations to fellow creatures. It is a commonplace pointed out long ago by Aristotle that man is a *zoon politikon,* a social animal. Social co-operation has had a positive survival value for humans, and many of their higher skills depend on this cooperation and on communication. Social inter-action demands advanced capabilities for cognitive and empathic identifica-tion: there are strong (and probably rather hardwired) emotions linked to deviations from prototypical humanness. Deviations indicate potentially threatening non-communication.

Furthermore, it is characteristic of the models of humanness that human-ness is depicted as a 'felt totality'. The individual human being is made up of innumerable cells, many organs, and a large number of mental schemata. The component parts have a relatively non-human autonomy, as in the functions of stomach, heart, or secretion of saliva. Similarly, the individual mental schema is a 'mechanical program'. The cognitive recognition of and affective relation to humanness and life are linked to a certain level of holism based on complexity and variety. Therefore, if we isolate the component parts and functions from the totality, the components are very often felt to have a non-human quality which is normally connected with lower life-forms, things, and mechanical devices. It follows that if we isolate pupil contractions and expan-sions from the human totality by means of an ultra close-up, if we isolate and amplify heartbeats, or allow a 'robot' to walk in such a mechanical way that it exposes the lever-mechanisms in the movements, the viewer will register the non-human features as a felt strangeness. An aspect of the felt totality is neg-atively described by discrepancies between the conscious and the non-conscious parts of the brain; and an important element of body-based comic situations consists of showing a mismatch between intentions and body real-ization, as when a clown trips over unintentionally or drops things, implying that the body and mind are experienced as severed.

Representations that focus on the relative autonomy of interior parts of the body are often experienced as particularly non-human. The inner body is nor-mally inaccessible to direct surveillance and manipulation, and is controlled by autonomic processes. In many relatively recent films, like Cronenberg's *Shivers* and Scott's *Alien,* strange organisms make a forced entry into the body interior, vampirize from within, and in this way bypass the outward-directed senses and the apparatus of motor acts of the host subject. Films like *The Exorcist* further demonstrate the way in which autonomization (and, by that, fragmentation) of bodily functions is linked to the autonomization of mental functions. Vomiting, cramps, and other autonomic reactions are paralleled by a mental fragmentation. The religious metaphors of 'obsession' in this film, and in other films and stories, demonstrate the way in which bodily and mental dysfunctions and the lack of central control are at the root of ideas concerning diabolical causation. In horror films particularly, bodily and mental malfunctions, from cramps to obsessional thoughts, are explained by the construction of diabolical agents. Lack of central control is felt; that is, it is mentally constructed, as if the processes were under the influence of an alien and non-human agent.

Using the concept of *le corps morcelé*, the psychoanalyst Lacan (1977: 4) has tried to describe aspects of the experience of bodily fragmentation. His main explanation is to see it in the framework of a typology of development, in which the experience of the fragmented body is a transitional stage between that with an undifferentiated experience of the relation between subject and world, and that in which the mirror-image provides the subject with a holistic model of itself. Seen from a cognitive point of view, the experiences of fragmentation and autonomy are a permanent possibility. The numerous bodily and neural modules have many sources of dysfunction, on the module level, and in the top-down integration of the bodily, neural, and mental models, and the different perceptual modalities, into a totality. Genres like horror and comedy use malfunctions of integration in order to create arousal.

WILL, GOAL, AND SELF-CONSCIOUSNESS

In the previous passage I have dealt with the human 'model of totality' by describing the effects of deviations. In the following I shall describe some major features in the construction of the human being's 'holistic' mental models of himself. The Lacanian description of the 'mirror stage' is a rudimentary description of aspects of such a model. At a certain point in the development process the mirror-image or the sight of other people causes the individual to recognize that these images, which enter from the exterior world, are those of himself. He creates what Lacan calls a *gestalt*, that is, a mental model, which helps him to orient himself in the world and to coordinate his motor activities, and which forms a link between the interior and the exterior world. Lacan believes that this mental model has several negative effects. It creates a fictive, false unity, and it alienates the individual by placing the model in another mirror-image or mirror-person (1977: 2–7). The problem about Lacan's description is especially linked to his use of words like 'imaginary' and 'imago' (1977: 2). He misuses the two different meanings of the word 'imaginary', that of something having a 'visual form', an image, and that of something 'made up', an image as something more 'unreal' than the reality that it depicts. The mental model of the 'I' of the interior world (*l'organisme, l'Innenwelt*) is, according to Lacan, an image of the body as an object in space (*realité*, *l'Umwelt*), seen from 'within' as something exterior, and, as it is a model, an 'imago' (in the first sense), it is 'false', invented, fictitious (in the second sense). It seems that Lacan implies that a model constructed from within (for example, from sense-data coming from touch, or from the body interior) would be less false. But internal sense-data are just as much 'fictitious' or 'imaginary' as are external sense-data, or just as 'real'. Pain from a wound or pleasure from a part of the body are just as much mental constructions as are 'visual body images'. Although Lacan begins by pointing to the function of 'body image' (a model aiding motor control), he 'forgets' this functional role because he then goes on to describe the means by which visual capabilities develop more quickly than motor control, so that the visual anticipations create all kinds of 'imaginary' 'fantasms'.

We might, then, think that a third stage in the development of the child is the point at which he gains full motor control and then, by the feedback of experience, develops a more precise idea of the relations between body–mind and world. But Lacan's treatment of this phase concentrates on describing a relation to the father-image and fear of castration. Lacan's theory of the three stages or layers, the 'real', the 'imaginary', and the 'symbolic', is therefore bizarre. The term 'real' covers the primitive way in which small children perceive the world (probably with tactile information playing an important role); the more sophisticated mental models connected with vision in the next stage are less 'real', more 'imaginary'; and the last stage, the 'symbolic', connected to language and acoustic information (the name of the father) is determined by arbitrary signification and an even more 'alienated' and unreal state, as the symbols refer to something absent and lacking. Nevertheless, the symbolic stage appears to work, albeit based on a fundamental alienation. The mental 'models' end up with no direct function as to the way the subject orients himself in the world, only an indirect function as creating repression and as the foundation of representation in the system of unconscious 'signifiers'.

However, one of the reasons for the widespread acceptance of Lacan's mirror-stage description within film studies is that it highlights a set of very real problems and a set of central themes in films: how are the different perceptual modalities, such as proprioception, and sight, and the models of the subject in a (social) time-space, 'fused' into a holistic experience? Why do 'mirror' problems have a prominent role in an experience of 'dissociation', for instance in situations involving motivational conflicts and strong reorientations such as sudden loss or emergence of possible emotional relations to objects, identity-forming behaviour, social recognition, and so forth? Why is a dissociation often felt as a defamiliarization in relation to 'images of the self'?

A starting-point for the understanding of this form of holism is the evolutionary appearance of an objective (i.e. object-centred) representation of the physical world, connected with new ways of controlling behaviour in higher animals and especially in human beings. In simple stimulus–response creatures there is no objective representation of the world. Marr (1982: 32 f.) refers to descriptions made by German scientists of the system of vision in the common housefly, in which there is absolutely no representation of the world, but only a few built-in stimulus–response patterns. Such systems make possible 'ego-centric' movements (that is, movements that take the body of the subject as the point of orientation, as when we turn to the right or to the left), and also stimulus movements, which are triggered by a given stimulus from the envir-onment. In contrast to this, human vision continuously creates a mental map of its surroundings, an objective representation of space as existing indepen-dently of the viewer. It not only represents phenomena which eventually lead to acts, such as 'poisonous snake' or 'apple', but also represents clouds, water, moss, or trees, that is, a superfluous amount of information from which we can select data for further processing. Furthermore, the map of the space and the representations of the objects tend to be non-egocentric and objective; that is, the maps and models represent space and objects in a way that is indepen-dent of a specific egocentric point of view, so that objects can be recognized from new angles and space and positions calculated from hypothetical and/or future points of view. Movement can now be aimed even at invisible, calcu-lated sections of space. The movement is not controlled by stimulus–response schemata, but by schemata formulated in the same 'language' as the objective representation of space. Models of movements, of acts, are planned; that is, they are simulated in the mental representations of space. However, this pre-supposes that one's own body is represented in the objective, cognitive map.

Johnson-Laird (1988: 356) discusses several features which are characteris-tic of the human consciousness. One is that it functions as a superior opera-tional system. The concrete and detailed control and implementation of muscle innervations, for example, take place on a non-conscious level. We have no consciousness of the numerous muscle innervations which enable us to skate. But we have a 'conscious' high-level operational control of our behaviour via a much more general program. This program could, for exam-ple, look like a script in the sense in which the term is described in Schank and Abelson (1977), that is, a 'narrative' or a summary of a sequence of acts. Important aspects of 'storytelling' could be seen as developing out of the pro-cedures we use when planning.

According to Johnson-Laird, another essential feature of human conscious-ness is the ability of the embodied brain to make a model of itself. Because this model has to be contained in the human brain itself, it follows that it must necessarily be much simpler than the brain. Johnson-Laird sees the func-tion of this model as linked to its ability to improve the quality of the acts of which humans are capable, whether these be physical, such as steering the body around in space, or mental, such as solving a problem.

The mental models of the consciousness are primarily 'phenomenological', representing exterior space, with the inclusion of agents and objects in this space. The raw material for these mental models consists of perceptions. If, for instance, we watch people skating, we invent a skating script, possibly worked out as an interior 'film' with very low resolution, which can function as a master program. The program can be used for the understanding or the recollection of the behaviour 'to skate', and also as an operational schema if we ourselves want to skate. To let the behaviour be ruled by conscious, voluntary, 'film-like' programs is very different from involuntary behaviour, in which perceptual input or act-generating impulses (for example, in migration) are directly transformed into behaviour.

To control behaviour via conscious and objective mental models based on perceptual input has obvious advantages. First, the transmission of the specific behaviour is cut loose from a transmission via gene codes. I can imitate skating without waiting for a change in the genetic code to build skating into my repertoire of possible behaviours. Culture-transmitted programs can be modified and supplied in a short period of time. Secondly, the objective, analogue models of the world are probably much simpler to use for more complex problems than endless masses of specific stimulus–response schemata.

If we compare Lacan's theory of the mirror-stage with theories of mental models there are similarities. Lacan hints at the advantages for motor coordination of making a gestalt, a mental model. But humans in Lacan's concept somehow do not belong 'out there' in the *Umwelt*, and he is not interested in mundane matters, such as how and why they act 'out there'. The feelings and emotions are not connected to elements in models of persons acting and relating in space, but to the way in which some hermeneutic inner self relates with misrecognition to the world. Contrary to that, mental models describe the way in which we act in the world by importing features of it, using aspects of it as tools. Models for Johnson-Laird and metaphors for Mark Johnson are not just representations, they are 'tools', concepts that owe a great deal to the computer revolution that has diminished the clear-cut opposition between mind and matter.

An essential aspect of the mental models is the construction of the above-mentioned model of the person himself. The model acquires its elements partly from the exterior world, partly from the inner world. The conception of the person as an 'acting figure' in space is acquired from the exterior world by imitation: the person uses his visual perceptions of other persons as model schemata. The conception of abilities to perceive, to feel pleasure and pain, and to think, to intend, and to will are acquired from the interior world. But the content of the thought processes is mainly represented in forms from exterior space. If, for instance, we imagine that we are taking a specific walk, we imagine ourselves in the third person as objective figures moving through space. Similarly the imagination used in more abstract thinking will employ model images of phenomena in and acts performed in an exterior, objective space, which is marked linguistically by the use of figurative language. We 'look at problems with new eyes'; we 'find new ways' (Johnson 1987; Lakoff 1987; Lakoff and Johnson 1980). The figurative and metaphorical aspects of language make it reasonable to assume that, from an evolutionary point of view, 'abstract' thinking has developed on the basis of the concrete scripts of acts and scenes which have gone through a process of extraction of 'essential' features that could be used as models for other mental processes. The scripts have had their field of application expanded by retaining some features and abandoning others. When Kosslyn (1980) describes the way in which a person is able to imagine that he is 'rotating' or 'scanning' a given complex of mental images, this implies that the mental processing of images takes place as a simulation of perceptual processes with external objects. Besides scripts of actions, we thus also have 'scripts of perceptions', which enable us to carry out acts of hypothetical perception, that is, imagination.

That normal self-awareness is based on an objective model of the self sheds some light on a notorious flop in film history, Montgomery's movie *Lady in the Lake*. The whole film, except the narrator sequences, is shot using 'subjective camera'; the effect, however, is not an intense 'subjective' identification with the protagonist but, on the contrary, a feeling of alienation, because there is no objective model, a body, on whom to anchor feelings of identification (and there are not—as in real life—any body-sensations to anchor the objective model of the self). The 'subjective' camera view cannot therefore be experienced with complete cognitive and empathic identification by the viewer: it is experienced as the view of an alien. In order to make the vision of the protagonist 'realistic', the camera moves rapidly around as if it were reconstructing rapid eye-scanning. But the brain does not normally experience saccadic movements or abrupt turns of the head: the brain 'normalizes' and creates continuity out of the discontinuous input (contrary to the view put forward by many critics of the 'Classical Hollywood Style'). As I shall describe in more detail in Chapter 6, 'subjective experiences' are often characterized by being intense and saturated, but unfamiliar and strange compared with normal self-awareness.

Lacan-inspired film theoreticians like Metz and Baudry have seen the reception of the narrative film as related to dream mechanisms and as relying on the viewer's narcissistic fascination with his or her imaginary mirror-image. But from a cognitive perspective there are fairly good reasons to assume that the narrative film in particular is related to the higher mental models which regulate thinking and action, and which model the 'subject' in an objective space. The visual model of the self, which Lacan connected with mirror-fascination and tried to explain within a sexual frame of reference, must primarily be understood as having developed as a precondition of a neural system for controlling the motor system by non-egocentric, objective models and coordinates of space, which demand a projection of the self into these cognitive maps.[2] However, for motivational reasons such a control is intimately linked with emotional structures. As noted in Chapter 2, the neurologist Damasio (1994) has described as a hypothesis the way in which the brain in the right somasensory area constructs an image of the present state of the body. This affective body-image is linked to pre-frontal regions, which will normally cognitively and affectively assess present or hypothetical situations involving the person. This seems to be just the function needed to explain the neurological basis for the cognitive-affective model of the self.

The visual model of the self as an object in space is equipped with a set of schemata of dynamic functions used for the mental simulations of motor acts and the mental simulation of acts of perception: as described above, the simulations can either be used for planning concrete, physical acts or used figuratively as tools for 'abstract thought'. The dynamic functions of the self are introspectively perceived as voluntary acts, contrary to low-level autonomic 'acts', like cramps and twitches, described in the first part of this chapter. But what is implied by the concept 'voluntary'?

One essential precondition for calling an act 'voluntary' is that it is one of several possible acts, or is *felt as being* one of several possible acts. If stimulus A automatically causes response B, we describe the behaviour as involuntary: for example as instinctive or autonomic, like the regulation of heartbeats. Only if stimulus A can cause a set of alternative acts B_1 to B_n would we speak of voluntary acts. Another essential feature of the concept 'voluntary' is that the alternative acts and their mental 'scripts' are present in outline in the consciousness, or are felt to exist as an option. That is, a given stimulus causes the mental computer to run alternative act-scripts with more or less conscious intensity before it selects the optimal act based on the preferences and resources of the given embodied brain. From this point of view, voluntary acts presuppose a mental 'loop' inserted between stimulus and response, which makes it possible for the mind to compare and choose between different alternative responses. The 'winning script' will then play the role of the operational system as a mental model for the behaviour. In our identification with agents of fiction it is, however, sufficient that we *feel* that a given situation and a given behaviour have alternative options in order to activate voluntary-telic mechanisms and to be experienced as voluntary.

When no conscious loop in the processing of alternative acts is present in the mind, we characterize the behaviour as 'mechanical', 'somnambulistic',

---

[2] If we find a 'sexual source' for the affects connected with the model self-image, it may be because the mental models and necessary cultural schemata for human behaviour are primarily learned by imitation of the behaviour of the other members of the species. It is therefore very likely that *Homo sapiens* and other higher animals have a powerful innate need to model themselves on the image of the other members of the species. The many hours that people spend in front of film and television screens are specific manifestations of this need for perception of and mental imitation and simulation of the rest of the species.

'instinctive', 'intuitive', or 'absent-minded'. Behaviours that are evaluated introspectively as, for example, intuitive or instinctive can be the result of non-conscious simulations of alternatives. The difference between voluntary and involuntary acts may be one of processing strength. In routine acts we lose 'concentration' and 'consciousness' (especially of alternatives): see, for instance, the examination of automated behaviour in Eysenck and Keane (1990: 118–31). From this perspective, 'consciousness' might be characterized as a strength in the perception and in the simulation of programs of acts, which explicitly or implicitly make alternative acts possible. This strength is characteristic of the mental processes which hypothetically or actually aim to carry out voluntary acts.

Another way of looking at voluntary acts is by emphasizing that the end attains a relative autonomy *vis-à-vis* the means; that the goal, the telos, can be mentally represented and fixed as a mental constant, causing the means-loop to come up with some possible scripts for implementing the goal. Although eventually even a teleological system of operation is reduced to a 'causal system', for example by the processes setting the goals, the very complexity of the voluntary, teleological operational system causes it to be felt as a *humanness-defining* feature which, as discussed at the beginning of this chapter, is charged with strong emotions.[3] Aspects of the problem of 'will' are connected to the problems described by intentionality within phenomenology.

The voluntary, teleological models of the subject are fundamental to narrative schemata, because narrative schemata are based on the mental models of everyday life. Narrative schemata can be described in two different, but connected, ways. The first way is to describe acts by 'push' models, in which attention, will, or muscular tension are seen as forward-directed vectors 'pushing' the processes ahead toward an open, undecided future. Claude Bremond's narrative model (1966; see also Culler 1975: 205–12 and Rimmon-Kenan 1987: 22 ff.) is a push-choice model: a given point in time in a narrative sequence opens a set of possible acts and possible outcomes. A situation in which the hero is confronted by a monster makes possible either fight or flight. If fight is chosen, the outcome can either be victory or defeat. Bremond mostly describes binary choices, but (as in many computer narratives and real-life-simulating films) we may, of course, have a multiple choice at each point in the narrative, just as we may have many possible choices in the 'mental loop'. This way of looking at the narrative process emphasizes the paratelic aspects of the process, although Bremond is imprecise about this because his description is not constructed as a model of the reader's reception of the processes, but as a system of immanent textual structures. The viewer basis of the narrative text's 'openness' is described in Bordwell's (1986) cognitive theory of viewer reception of narrative films. His models are also 'push'

[3] For a discussion of teleological and intentional systems cf. Lycan (1990) and Dretske (1988).

models, in which the attention and expectations of the viewer are searching forward into an unknown narrative future. Iser's Husserl-based description of the 'reader-*protensions*' into the narrative future uses a similar model (1980: 108 ff.).

The openness–undecidedness described above is different from Eco's (1984: 47–66) and Barthes' (1972*b*) concepts of openness and *lisibilté,* 'readerliness'. First, it is a model of the way in which viewers perform an ongoing (re)construction of the virtual undecidedness in narrative events, which is not necessarily in conflict with a strong 'textual' control in the cueing of the ongoing reconstructions of uncertainties: a cliffhanger is a temporarily open situation which will be resolved later. Secondly, there is no normative aspect in words like 'open', 'undecided', and 'closed'; narrative openness and closure are aspects of fundamental mental models of acts, and although people may have individual preferences as to whether they like narratives in which, for example, the protagonists wander around without finding the Holy Grail, and with many uncertainties as to motives, time, place, and so forth, or whether they like texts in which the Grail is finally found, both structures are equally determined by the audiovisual input and thus cued by the addresser. Openness in a modernist sense cues processes of reception that are just as controlled and determined as closedness.

The second way of describing the activities of the subject and the narrative process is by means of 'pull' models, models of goals and motivations conceptualized as exterior-future-preferred states. Here the telos is a constant and the means are variables. Greimas' (1966) narrative model describes the narrative process by means of final, teleological causation. The final scenarios of plenitude, of possession of knowledge, money, sexual gratification, security, and so on are the narrative constants that determine the selection of means, the processes of transformation, by which the different types of lack are liquidated. Greimas described this process in an objectivist manner as semantic logics ruling the narrative processes; but the final, teleological causation can also be explained as a textualization of the psychological processes of teleological motivation, in which mental representations of goals replace stimulus-type causation. This way of looking at the narrative process emphasizes the telic aspects of the process.

Figure 5.1 shows the interrelatedness of the forward-directed processes of narrative expectations, hypothesis-making, motivation, and goal-setting, and the 'backward-directed' influence of goals which, when set, are felt as causal determinants of the narrative and the narrative actants.

In narratives, as in real life, the goal-structure does not consist of one but of several goals that can be independent of or dependent on each other, or mutually conflicting. A given end-goal can presuppose a larger or smaller number of sub-goals (see Ortony *et al.* 1988: 35 ff.). The cognitive loops in narratives can therefore be complicated by increasing the number of goals and

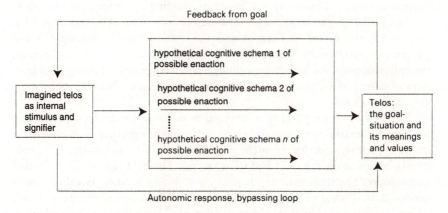

Fig. 5.1 Loop of choice, imagination, and guesswork. The model illustrates the way in which an imagined goal is a cause, an internal stimulus, but is perceived as a goal ahead in time–space, and also illustrates the way in which the subject tries out hypothetical schemata and mental models for achieving the goal, the telos. In some cases the relation between start and goal is automatic and involuntary.

the number of possible schemata linking each situation to a goal. In *Raiders of the Lost Ark* Indiana Jones has the possession of the ark as the superior goal, but has to formulate a series of sub-goals (going to Nepal and Egypt, for example). These sub-goals demand series of sub-sub-goals, like the act of going into an aircraft, and at the bottom of the goal-directed hierarchy we find the singular muscular series, like moving the hands towards an object. We need the tense knowledge of the superior levels of goals in order to understand the individual telic acts.

The narrative can emphasize different aspects of the push–pull process with different results. A narrative can excel in focusing on processes of choice, as in certain action-adventure stories, or on an endless hypothesis-formation, as in crime and other types of fiction that rely heavily on what Barthes would call the 'hermeneutic code' (1972b). Signifiers and evidence can be underdetermined, so that no single result, no single signified, can be determined, which means that the hypothesis-loop can continue forever. This will relocate the viewer's attention from constructing a telic fictional fabula to a paratelic preoccupation with the process of construction. Films with many interpretational problems, like Orson Welles' *The Trial* or Roeg's *Don't Look Now*, possess a paratelic, mental intensity and are felt as lacking 'reality'. The effect is, in some respects, the mental equivalent of jogging, because the subjective charge is caused by the 'freedom' of the process-orientation by the fading of the exterior telos. The hypothesis-loops can be totally short-circuited by using ambiguities or by contradictory input, often with the result that the narrative goal-oriented and process-oriented aspects disappear and the reception process is switched into a lyrical mode of building up perceptual intensities and networks of similarities and saturated associations. The cognitive-loop process can also be totally rejected as in the comic answer to ambiguities and paradoxes: rejection by laughter. But emphasis can also be put on the goal, the pull-processes, so that the hypothesis loop, the paratelic experience of freedom of choice and chance, is undercut by determinism. This is especially the case in melodrama.

The hypothesis loop can be minimized or removed by strong deterministic narrative schemata or by narrating the conclusion of the story first, as is often the case in *film noir,* for example in Wilder's *Double Indemnity.* This *noir* drama begins as the fabula is almost at an end. The hero is mortally wounded and recounts the story into a dictaphone just before he dies. His dictation is used as a voice-over to images in the narrative. The main narrative is shown as a canonical one, but it is told at a point of time in the narrative which is embedded between its near-end and its end (near end → canonical narrative → end). This means that the arousal caused by the love–crime plot cannot achieve a full voluntary–telic outlet. We know the tragic ending throughout our viewing of the story. Furthermore, if we try to forget, and try to construct the love story in a telic, voluntary, and open way, the voice-over reminds us constantly of the fact that this is a 'causal', 'dead' repetition of a past chain of events. The arousal can therefore only attain an autonomic outlet by feelings of melancholia, possibly also perceived in a Step 2 process of lyrical associations. The images and events gain in saturation, but lose in tensity and suspense by the blocking of a telic-voluntary outlet.

The voluntary, intentional, and teleological processes are the main models and procedures for linking the acting, intending, and thinking subject to an object-world. These processes and models constitute the objectivity of the world, its existence as a goal for cognitive or physical manipulation, as when we pinch ourselves to ascertain whether we are dreaming or awake. In films, therefore, the feeling of reality will be correlated to the representation or simulation of voluntary, intentional, and teleological processes. Procedures which undercut the representation and simulation of these processes will therefore lead to a feeling that the experienced exists in a more 'unreal' mental reality.

I have argued above in favour of the hypothesis that 'the model of the self' as an object in space has been an evolutionary necessity in order to construct an operational system ruled by objective time-space coordinates. The feeling of consciousness and the 'conscious identity' are linked by empathy to the model and its characteristic functions, like voluntary acts and voluntary thinking. This also applies to our identification with subject-actants. If their capacity for voluntary acts and thinking is blocked, this leads to a feeling of alienation, strangeness, and unreality in the viewer, as experienced in watching horror films and science fiction, for example, when a person with whom we have a sympathetic relation suddenly becomes possessed by alien forces and behaves according to a 'fixed pattern'.

Our simulation or construction of a given situation as characterized by freedom of choice and hypothesis-formation is represented in the visual appearance of the actants as a 'feeling of life and familiarity'. The breakdown of this construction can be observed in the feeling of alienation and 'death' which we feel, for instance, when we look at old news taped on our private video recorders. It is not only the signifier, the audiovisual input, which has changed (although there is a reduction in quality in the VHS image), and even 'live news' may be partly or totally taped (if we do not know that what is supposed to be live is actually produced by old tapes, we cannot take this into consideration and cannot represent its pastness by means of feelings).

When we look at live news we mentally construct an open world in which the future, from the next word of the anchor to the outcome of the events spoken of, can be simulated by real hypothesis-making and as real-life acts. But, when we know that we are confronted with AV tapes, because we can manipulate them by pressing buttons for pause or still, fast forward, and other operations, we change our hypothesis concerning the mental construction of the event, registered as a more melodramatic feeling of pastness, decidedness, causality, and unfamiliarity. We can no longer mobilize a simulation of voluntary possibilities of interference, change, and undecidedness. Action adventure films often cue us to construct their worlds as voluntary and undecided, whereas a *film noir* like *Double Indemnity* provides the same saturated, fatalistic feeling that we experience when we look at old news or at home-made videos of our private lives, which we know cannot be constructed as openundecided. The feeling of 'strangeness' *vis-à-vis* the moving pictures can be emphasized in many ways, by a black-and-white image or by voice-over, as in *Double Indemnity*, where the blocking of the reconstruction of free will and undecidedness caused by revealing the conclusion first is underlined by the linguistic marks of pastness in the voice-over of the subject-actant.

The 'free will' provides a means to certain ends; but, as discussed in the section on filmic representations of clowns and robots, the experience of free will as such is also an end in itself and provides paratelic pleasure: for example, the pleasure we take in participating in sheer narrative undecidedness and under-determinedness. But the opposite, the 'robotic' giving up of free will, can also be evaluated positively, especially in connection with representations of social integration. Musicals and 'dance films' are very often based on the integration of the individual 'will' into larger, ritualized social schemata (see Altman 1987), which are represented on many levels, from motor behaviour ruled by musical schemata (such as the chorus line) to stereotype 'archetypal' patterns of sexual union in comedies of love. Phenomena like parades are mental models that integrate the 'free will' of the individual into models of social subjects. Many war films, or those showing life in the barracks, are mainly focused on representing relations between the free will of the individual and that of larger social institutions. The military farce has a comic distance to the robotification of the individual, whereas the heroic military melodrama often worships heteronomy and telic integration. Representations of religious and political ceremonial events often use schemata indicating 'robotism', because they try to construct a mental model of 'higher forces' using political or religious humans as mouthpieces. Science-fiction film is a genre in which such representations of non-voluntary subjectivities can take place. Following the abuses of, for example, a Nazi or a Stalinist *mise-en-scène* of social integration there has been a tendency to reject all representations of social integration and 'submission' as fascist. A more cautious approach would be to observe that representations of individuation, as well as of social integration, and emphasis on common denominators, have their fascination that can be used or abused.

TERMINATOR II, EMOTIONS, AND FREE WILL

To exemplify the problems of free will versus autonomic reactions, let us take a closer look at the semi-melodrama *Terminator II*. The film begins with a typical Step 3 scene. A terrible nuclear war destroys Los Angeles, and also most of the globe, in the year 1997. We witness in particular the way in which a number of children in a playground are burned to death by the thermonuclear heatwave. We further witness the way in which the few survivors of the globe are hunted by terrible robots. The viewer is put into a state of high arousal, labelled fear and grief. But voluntary reactions seem to be totally blocked, because we are told that this is a precise recording of a future event in the history of mankind. We spectators in the 1990s do not have an undecided future ahead of us. Logically there can be no teleological and voluntary acts, no guesses of outcomes. Everything is preprogrammed and causal. We can only shiver, cry, or react with various types of involuntary reactions of the autonomic nervous system.

But then the *Terminator II* narrative hints at a miraculous return to a canonical telic voluntary narrative. Forces from the future try to interfere with their past, which, at the same time, is the approximate present of the viewer and the protagonists in the main part of the *Terminator II* narrative. An angel-robot, who looks not unlike Frankenstein's monster, arrives in present-day California to protect a future Messiah, young John Connor, who may be able save mankind from the robots; so acts and thoughts again make a difference. Nevertheless, the spectator is provided with two mental or narrative models: one melodramatic and causal, the other telic-voluntary. The uncertainty as to which model is the true one (after all, to change the past is bizarre, and contrary to common sense) provides an optional model of autonomic response. Throughout the entire film the possibility hovers that free will is impossible.

This uncertainty is strengthened by the presence of a devil from the future, who is apparently not ruled by normal causal laws: he can change shape at will. Teleology and calculation presuppose some rules by which one can calculate and interfere with the world, but the 'Devil' seems to be beyond human rules by being beyond physical and biological laws. In horror stories like Dracula the breakdown of one set of rules leads to the establishment of another: Dracula can be controlled by garlic, wolfbane, a cross, silver bullets, daylight, and stakes driven into his heart while he is sleeping in a coffin. As a result of these new 'laws' the canonical narrative can be restored by allowing intentions, calculations, and acts. The same situation takes place in *Terminator II*. Nevertheless, the uncertainty as to causal rules creates arousal and terror in the protagonists and in the viewer of the film. No matter what actions the 'good guy' performs to destroy the 'evil guy', they seem to have no effect. For this reason, the viewer is back to square one and can only react by autonomic responses, like tears.

Perhaps that is not a bad reaction after all. *Terminator II*, like many recent science-fiction films, speculates as to what constitutes humanness and subjectivity and indicates two criteria. The first criterion implies flexible and voluntary acts and thoughts, and these are almost learned by the robot Schwarzenegger: his permutations and generation of new sentences seem flexible. But the second criterion is the possession of emotions, of the ability to cry, and this is still a human privilege, as the film states over and over again.

NARRATION AS REPETITION AND AS ACTIVE CONSTRUCTION

Whether fictions are experienced as telic, paratelic, or autonomic is not only related to the anthropomorph narrative level but also to the experience of the audiovisual sequence as such. There are two ways of describing a given mental realization of an audiovisual sequence or a text: it can be described and experienced as a subjective telic construction taking place in a present which points to the future, or as an 'objective' mental effect of the input of a fixed program of meaning constructed in and concerning the past. Viewing points to the future as well as the past, and this dual function is connected to a similar duality in all narrative phenomena (see Richoeur 1981 and Brooks 1984). To establish the 'narrative track' in a story, film, or piece of music is at the same time to establish a narrative future and a repetition. To say, 'Once upon a time,' or to play a couple of bars of music, or to show a sequence of moving pictures is to produce active expectations about a time to come in the future, to establish a sequence of signifiers pointing to the signified. At the same time, the 'reader' is passively carried along by the external system of physical signifiers produced in the past. Even the face-to-face storytelling depends on the reproduction of narrative schemata and linguistic structures. Thus narration and music possess a duality of repetition and enactive freedom in the subjective (re)actualization of the narrative track;[4] an activation of the repetitive aspect in the addressee will activate paratelic or autonomic experiences, whereas an activation of enactive freedom will activate telic experiences.

A live storyteller's main function is to act as a medium for the story in its two aspects: as a fabula, a telic sequence of states and acts, and as a prefabricated set of schemata and signifiers. The author or storyteller is not the prime addresser of the story: the marks of enunciation are, phenomenologically speaking, 'inserted' into the story (see Hamburger 1973: 136). Furthermore, the reader is not marked as addressee in the same way as in ordinary conversation, but s/he reconstructs the narrative, fictional hypothesis. Benveniste-inspired descriptions of audiovisual fiction are used by many critics,[5] but these anthropomorph descriptions of the communication process are not even primary in literary narration from the point of view of the reception process. A narrative sequence comes from without, through the senses, but the reader will reconstruct and personalize the 'impersonal' input by making emotionally charged mental models, and only under special circumstances will the narrative otherness acquire focal attention as an exterior voice-over to the reconstruction. Many people experience a strong feeling of alienation when they hear their own voice on a tape-recorder: the voice has become dead and strange, a third person's voice, disconnected from interior, subjective connections (for instance, from the enactive qualities of speaking normally experienced in holistic fusion with acoustic patterns), and the loss of (motor) modality makes the voice more 'unreal'; in the same way there are means by which the narrative 'track' can be brought to focal attention.

When someone sings a song, the 'track' is more obvious than when, for instance, he is speaking; even if the song says 'I', this 'I' is said from another position, it is a persona speaking; the 'I' is inserted into the 'track', 'fused with a subjective current', indicating that the 'I' performs a *transitory role*.

---

[4] When Benjamin (1977) describes the way in which the technical reproduction in film leads to a loss of aura compared to previous periods and types of art, he forgets that most temporal art is based on repetitions of schemata. Although one might argue that the actor in a play compared to one in a film has an 'auratic' presence, both film and theatre are based on script repetitions, which may either be felt as repetitions or as having a unique presentic quality.

[5] For example, Casetti (1990, 1995), when he uses 'I', 'you', 'it', as a framework for understanding addresser, addressee, and that which is represented in films. Structuralists anchored their distinction between story and discourse in Benveniste; cf. Todorov (1966: 126), in which story evokes a reality and some events, whereas discourse points to a narrator telling the story to somebody; Todorov claims that his concept of discourse follows Benveniste. For Benveniste, however, an important aspect of the concept of discourse is to see language as a 'speech act' (although he does not use the term; cf. 1971: 258–66), analyzing discourse and 'subjectivity', not from the point of view of 'subjective colouring' of story, but as aspects pointing to the role of language as an agent, similar to the concepts of Austin and Searle dealing with language as acts.

Contrary to a 'narrative' 'he' or 'I', which is an enactive figure telically reconstructed on an objective 'ground', the paratelic, 'lyrical' 'I' will be fused with the 'ground', and the empirical 'I' fuses with the lyrical 'I', so that the 'medium'-persona surfaces. The song will therefore be perceived as more 'enunciated' than the narrative, but not addressed by a real-life colloquial 'I'-addresser; and, furthermore, the lyrical 'I' is not object-directed.[6]

Branigan (1984) and Bordwell (1986: 21 ff.), among others, have indicated the problems involved in describing the film as enunciated; the existence of an addresser, a personal dispatcher of the message, is not central to film-reception. Burgoyne has put forward a theory of impersonal and personal narration as representing two options (Stam *et al.* 1992: 117), whereas Metz advocates an impersonal enunciation,[7] an impersonality on top of which possibly several forms of more personal enunciation take place. One might say that the film is constructed 'out there', as a physically manifested sequence of light and sound (often a result of teamwork, in which many people cooperate to make a film), and constructed according to schematic conventions. 'Personal points of view' and specific themes or stylistic features can be inserted into the broader social and physical phenomenon of 'track of percepts', and thus convey the message of a 'personal addresser'.

These points of view discuss the problems of narration by showing that there is no overall personalized addresser. But the above-mentioned problem of the viewer's relation to the ' inhuman track of signifiers, of clues' remains, a problem that concerns the viewer's 'enunciation', his active construction of the film. This problem is even more pressing in the media that have a 'mechanical' reproduction than it is in literature, in which the reader himself sets the pace. An audiovisual track, a text, or a piece of music is, in a sense, not only told from a position *par derrière,* after the fact, and reconstructed, experienced as telic and open by the addressee; it is also experienced as something already filed in a dead track of signifiers. The problem is quite clear in past-tense voice-over narration, especially when this narration, as in many *noir* films, is performed by a subject-actant. If the text of the voice-over had been read as literature or heard as live storytelling, the reader-listener would have performed an active-telic reconstruction despite the markers of pastness. But the voice-over in film makes it possible to fix the experience of the time of enunciation as different from the time presented in the visual narrative. The voice indicates and fixes a feeling of temporal distance to the images. By this activation of an experience of pastness the visual narration loses some of its telic qualities, and the images become more 'dead' and saturated.

---

[6] Cf. Hamburger (1973: 278), which states that the lyrical 'I' is not directed at the object except the object as experience (*Erlebnis*).

[7] Metz (1991). This book discusses Branigan's and Bordwell's position extensively, and the position stated in ch. 1 (the film coming from a place of origin, the 'foyer') is deliberately modified in the final chapter.

From a point of view of socialization, the voice and its production of a sequence of signifiers are always the reproduction of the voice and the track of other people. When a child learns how to speak and express itself it is trying to make a subjective-enactive copy of what it has passively heard from other people and from the physical environment. The voice of the 'I' becomes an acting-out of the voices of the others, an insertion of the enactive 'I' into the social track, thereby providing a cognitive and affective identification with, and personalization of, the track.

As discussed earlier in this chapter, to plan and to carry out movements is to imitate the objective models of acts that can be learned by looking at other people. Film is therefore comparable to language in being 'active mimesis', a reconstruction of visual or verbal sequences and episodes. By a partial cognitive and affective identification with the film we feel that we reconstruct both a role and the language of other people, in the same way as when we have recently established a new type of behaviour and still 'feel' that we are only 'acting' as, for example, a vice-president, performing in accordance with objective 'vice-president' schemata just as we would if we re-enacted Hamlet schemata or sheriff schemata. But, by a full cognitive and affective identification, the feelings of schemata-exteriority and schemata-repetition disappear, and the reproduction is experienced as voluntary, telic, and taking place in progressive time, a 'now' going towards the future. Parodies allow the schemata to surface again.

The ability to synthesize the different aspects and modalities of experience may disappear. Jackendoff (1987: 301) has described the way in which a dissolution of the unity of experience takes place, causing feelings of estrangement and objectification. He quotes a case study in which the patient is unable to synthesize the visual perception of a person speaking with the acoustic perception of what the person is saying: 'I noticed that the mouth moving did not belong to what I heard any more than a—than if one of the old talkie pictures would make sense if the voice tape had been the wrong tape for the conversation.' Because of the patient's lack of ability to synthesize the different modalities of consciousness, *in casu* image and sound, these appear as 'physical tracks', indicated by the film metaphor used in a 'live' situation, in which the patient's everyday perceptions have become a sound-track and a visual track, felt as having no inner connection. Coppola's *The Conversation* and de Palma's *Blow Out* highlight the problems of modality synthesis and the feeling of estrangement caused by these problems; sound and image are not 'naturally' fused for the 'detective' sound-technicians of the films, and the technical problems of linking sound to image is at the same time felt as a problematic, mental 'modality synthesis' creating defamiliarization. Vision is more closely connected to exterior space than sound, and, in general, the use of sound is therefore important for providing the images with telic or paratelic qualities. Although identification with acts is the main procedure by which the 'track' is made 'live', the film relies heavily on dialogue and music in order to construct a 'live' experience.[8]

As a consequence of the above, there are three main ways in which the viewer can receive the audiovisual track:

1. The audiovisual track is perceived as a 'strange' sequence of repetition and pastness, with which the viewer has no telic, voluntary, or empathic identification

The effect can be caused by simple means: for example, the film-stock can be mutilated in such a way that the viewer experiences the film as a 'dead' collection of items, and thereby feels the 'tapes', the 'canned' repetitive aspect of the representation, as a 'pastness quality'. Many modernist film-makers have inserted phenomena connected to the material existence of the film, or, like Bergman in *Persona,* have allowed the film to get stuck and burn in the film projector. Black-and-white sequences are now often used in order to evoke a 'canned', repetitive experience. But the feeling of repetition and pastness can also be caused by a cognitive or affective inability in the viewer to make an active telic-voluntary reconstruction. The subject matter may be strange *vis-à-vis* the viewer's qualifications and tastes (possibly as a calculated effect by the addresser in order to evoke feelings of 'estrangement' in the viewer, as in Lynch's *Eraserhead*). The viewer may have seen the film so many times that he finds it impossible to make a 'live' reconstruction because of a total lack of felt uncertainty of what is going to happen, being quite certain of events even down to minute details (parallel to those occasions on which people have heard a piece of music on a record too many times to be able to make a 'live' reconstruction of the music, which is 'felt' as a past and mechanical experience).

2. The audiovisual track is reproduced by a dynamic–paratelic and autonomic 'now', comparable to singing a song and identifying with a rhythm of dynamic repetition

We do not identify with a fully active–voluntary position in the construction: we identify with anonymous agents and symbiotically repeat patterns (as in the discussion in Chapter 2 about people who are able to sing but unable to speak, a phenomenon which seems to indicate that song relies on a brain mechanism different from that controlling normal telic speech). We copy the audiovisual track without simulating the future situations of the track. Musicals rely on these kinds of experience, especially in chorus-like scenes. In Chapter 6, I shall discuss phenomena of repetition, like oscillation.

[8] Cf. the critique of a pure visual definition of film in Altman (1985) and Kozloff (1988: 8 ff.).

3. *The audiovisual track is reconstructed by voluntary, telic, cognitive, and affective strategies*

This is done as in the normal way of reproducing the track, as if it were not a repetition but a sequence of open-undecided situations.

These three ways of experiencing the audiovisual track will often be mixed. In order to make a minimally qualified guess as to the outcome of a narrative, and thus to keep his cognitive loops running and maintain the telic qualities of the story, the viewer must possess a set of schemata suitable for guessing the outcome. The 'feeling of freedom' in the guessing of the outcome is, in a sense, the choice between several possible repetitions, several possible schemata. The viewer will sometimes have an interest in 'reactivating' the patterned-unfree aspect of the fictional experience, for example as a means of defence against too much excitement, by saying, for instance, 'this is just a story', or 'I know that a story of this type will end happily'. Young children like the minute repetitions of narrative schemata: they have not yet fully learned the schemata, and therefore cannot have the full pleasure of schema choice and the hypothetical construction of a narrative future by means of 'past' schemata. They therefore need the concrete memory of the concrete story-line as a future-producing device, whereas adults can construct a future of goals and mediating acts by a more or less non-conscious narrative competence.

Films and verbal fictions based on 'lyrical'–'associational' principles of construction are often more suited to repeated consumption than fictions based on strongly narrative construction principles. Patterns of narrative structures of expectations–realizations are often fully grasped at the first viewing, whereas possible configurations of associational meanings in, for example, lyrical films cannot be grasped in one viewing, so that the basic 'repetitive' aspects of the lyrical mode are further strengthened by the potentially endless new ways of structuring the associations. This is similar to the consumption of music (and music videos), in which repetitive consumption of a given product is the norm, whereas in narrative films it is the exception.

6

Subjectivity, Causality, and Time

In this chapter I shall first examine the way in which subjectivity in film is often produced by causality and restrictions that refocus attention to proximal sites of experience. I shall then characterize the way in which temporal experiences are subjective, but cued by a set of cognitive and affective parameters in the diegetic world, and shall demonstrate the means by which temporal experiences provide modal tones to visual fiction.

SUBJECTIVITY IN VISUAL FICTION

A stumbling-block for the understanding of subjectivity in film has been what I call *the paradoxical 'rule of thumb': in visual fiction the use of subjective and anthropomorph narrative schemata, like intention and will, provides an experience of 'objectivity', whereas the use of 'causal-objective' schemata provides an experience of 'subjectivity' linked to the activation of intense or saturated networks of associations.* The reason that subjectivity may be experienced as paradoxical is that, according to prevailing romantic anthropology, the 'subjective' and 'human' are defined as the opposite of the restricted, rational, and causal world. If, however, we look at the means by which we produce 'subjectivity' in film, we soon find that subjectivity is often linked to 'restrictions and delimitations'. Subjective camera means that there are strong constraints as to where the camera can be placed (it has to simulate origination in the eyes of the protagonist); subjective representations put constraints on our ability to see, as when a scene is overlit or very dark, and thus reduce the amount of visible detail, or show the object from a sub-optimal (that is, uncharacteristic) angle, thus making it difficult to perceive its identity. The constraints may trigger an emotional build-up that provides the subjective feeling.

In 'objective' narratives, the senses are transparent and function as tools for carrying out the mind's preference and for perceiving the distal object world, whereas subjective and possibly dreamlike narrative sequences are ruled by 'causality', autonomic processes beyond human control. The senses are ruled by external causalities or by a causally induced malfunction, like the subjective vision of a drunk in *North by Northwest,* vision being affected by a blow on the head as in *Murder, My Sweet* (see Branigan 1984: 80), or representations of persons suffering from mental illness or personality disorder; and all this activates a proximal, subjective experience. Visual 'distanciation' by means of long shots is often felt to be subjective, because it shows protagonists or objects as elements of passive, causal scenarios. 'Subjective' visual distortions show the way in which the actants or viewers are ruled by external or internal causality, but the experience becomes proximal.

The constraints put on vision by a low-definition, 'romantic' image (for instance, a foggy or hazy space) might, of course, be interpreted as 'freedom' (making unlimited top-down hypotheses possible), not as a constraint; and this option of interpretational 'freedom' is one reason for links between *de facto* visual constraints and experiences of 'subjective freedom', another being activation of proximal (subjective), intense and saturated experiences caused by the difficulties of making a smooth projection onto a distal image-world.

AFFECTIVE TRANSACTIONS BY CUEING OF DISTAL OR PROXIMAL ATTENTION LOCATION

As mentioned in my discussion of reality-status in Chapter 1, the evaluation of whether a given phenomenon by the viewer is experienced as located in exterior space, on the corporeal rim, or in the body–mind interior is an important aspect of its experienced qualities. All phenomena of consciousness exist in the embodied brain, whether they are the perceptions of a tree or a memory, so that the location of an experience as 'exterior' or 'interior' is dependent on a cognitive evaluation by the brain that experiences the result as a focus of attention ('this exists in the world' or 'this exists in my mind') and as a felt quality. The narrative schemata can influence the evaluation, and in that way influence the location of attention and the felt tonality of an experienced phenomenon, as illustrated by slow motion, in which temporal slow-down relocates the experience of the 'same' images from an exterior to an interior 'space', and changes the emotional tone. I shall call a process by which a phenomenon is relocated from being experienced as an aspect of a body–mind to being experienced as an aspect of the exterior world a *projection,* the reverse process being an *introjection*. An example of a projection is a situation in which we see something that we first believe to be a dream or a hallucination, but that we then discover to really exist. An example of an introjection would be seeing a *film noir* and feeling that the wet streets are not 'real', but represent mental states. My use of the terms 'introjection' and 'projection' is therefore different from the use made of these terms in psychoanalysis: they relate to two modes by which we map reality.

The affective sources of an experience are the perceptual system, the central nervous system, and the chemical substances of the human body, but the affects can be relocated by projection and introjection (for example, pleasure can be seen either as an aspect of the sensuous system of the subject or of the

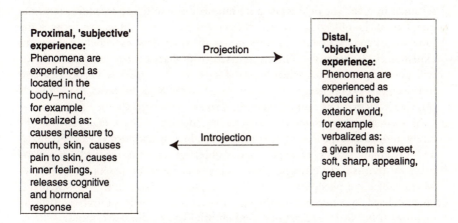

Fig. 6.1 Projective and introjective transactions. In connection with perceptions and acts, qualities will often be experienced as belonging to the object, whereas blocks of acts or passive 'object-roles' will introject the experience so that qualities will be experienced as activated in the subject.

object). The technical term for a stimulus as a transmission from objects in the exterior world is *distal stimulus,* as opposed to the term *proximal stimulus,* which describes it as a process in the perceptual system. Audiovisual media have to represent all types of sense stimulation in audiovisual form. The remote senses are developed as tools for orientation and for making hypotheses about the environment and possible future acts in relation to one's preferences. Possible consequences for senses of contact and body senses are represented 'in the visual image' as a distal stimulus, not as a possible proximal stimulus. If we look at an apple, we may say 'it looks sweet', meaning that if we ate the apple, our gustatory senses would send a 'sweet' signal along. But the future effect on the non-remote senses is mentally represented, projected, onto the visual representation: even when eating we would mentally model part of the experience as belonging to the object—'it tastes good'—and not comment on its effect on our gustatory receptors. Projection is therefore linked to the way in which different perceptual modalities are integrated in representation.

Only under special circumstances will the subject's attention highlight the subjective side of a given phenomenon. What projects the representations to the object-representations, and especially to the visual images, is the possibility of hypothetical or actual mediating acts. But by the blocking, or absence, of mediating acts, the subject's attention will shift to subjective representations. In 'I feel hungry' we have a mere absence of mediating acts, unlike the refocused description: I want to go to the kitchen for some food. In the paratelic 'I feel so much in love', the process is more important than telic procedures (and the qualities of the object). However, the typical cause of a subjective focus is the blocking of enactive mediations, as in passive situations, especially if these are experienced as negative. The experience of a sharp, threatening instrument will generally put phenomenological focus on the subjective processes and introject the experience of the anticipated body pain, whereas the subject's positive anticipations will be mentally projected toward the object.

By switching between active and passive modes of representation the different modes and genres of fiction can produce transactions between distal and proximal modes of experience. Subjective experiences and sensations may, by the use of active narrative schemata, be projected onto the object world; objective phenomena may, by the use of passive narrative schemata, be refocused, introjected into being experienced in their subjective form as qualities (intensities, saturations, and emotivities) of the body–mind.

A special variation of these transactions is connected with the reality-status of the objects (and subjects). An image of an object in visual fiction can be labelled as a real or possible object existing simultaneously with the subject-actant, and it can then actualize enactive relations. But the image can also be labelled as a memory, dream, or picture of a dead person, and will then actualize passive-perceptual relations. This distinction is connected to the difficulty of being aware of the proximal visual stimulus. The processing of the visual input in the eye–brain is totally non-conscious: we cannot experience our retina activity or the stages of constructing an image, and only indirectly—for example, by special input like some types of abstract painting—can we have an 'upstream' experience of seeing the stimulus in a less elaborated form (see Chapter 2). In *Wild Strawberries* Bergman makes extensive use of the effects caused by short-circuiting the separation of different levels of reality. The protagonist, Borg, interacts with his own memories and (day)dreams, and the ambiguous cues of the reality-status in these sequences provide cognitive dissonance and affect.

The way in which the images originating in the interior are cognitively represented as different from images of real objects is by another system of representation: by 'labels', made of feelings of reality or unreality, attached to a given image (Jackendoff 1987). By employing words like 'dream' and 'memory' ('I experienced the situation *as if* it were a dream'), we try to make an intersubjective representation of the cognitive feature 'feeling of unreality' which indicates the proximal-neural existence of a given experience without an immediate distal cause and thus without an immediate object of action. The subjective experience only possesses intense and saturated feelings, but no tense ones. Thus a local sound-off in films is often used as a cue for an evaluation of unreality: objects can be seen but not heard, and this triggers the evaluation that objects which can be seen but not heard, under circumstances when they normally possess both modal qualities, are 'subjective', and therefore do not possess an optional tactile quality or the corresponding motor quality. This is represented in abbreviated form in the brain as a *feeling* (of a special reality-status). Fictions play with reality-status to evoke such feelings. Procedures like *mise en abyme,* which short-circuit evaluations of reality-status, are used to evoke feelings, although they pretend to say something about representations and epistemology in general.

DREAM AND SUBJECTIVITY

Dream has become paradigm or metaphor for all strong subjective states of consciousness. Dream processes are, however, mostly different from processes of the waking state due to quantitative factors. Relatively controlled associations are called fantasy: uncontrolled associations are called dreamlike, and if they are strongly charged with positive or negative affect, they are called a wish-fulfilment dream or nightmare. If a film depicts a given situation with a moderate degree of modification of the normal, prototypical visual categorization and depiction, the representation is called subjective, but if the distortion is very powerful—as, for example, in some German expressionist films, like Wiene's *The Cabinet of Caligari* or Leni's *Waxworks*—the distortion is called dreamlike (Eisner 1973; see also Petric 1981: 1–50 for an overview of dream effects in film).

Hobson has (1988 and in Petric 1981: 75–96) put forward a theory concerning dreams. According to this, an essential function of dreaming is to activate even those parts of the brain that are rarely used by a *random* activation of the brain (triggered by the firing of special cells and linked to the rapid eye-movements). The dream processes try to make sense of these random elements, and may create untraditional associations. Activations of many different memories of perceptions often produce a heterogeneous, 'bizarre', and emotionally charged material, from which dream processing tries to create associative connections and meanings, although many dreams are simple and easily comprehensible. In contrast to Freud, Hobson does not believe in an original, first level of clear and coherent dream sense, which is then 'scrambled' by the secondary elaboration to avoid censorship. The bizarre features indicate an incomplete mental synthesis of the heterogeneous material. Hobson understands the synthesis as a narrative activity, perhaps by applying standard narrative schemata.

The association processing of the dream state distinguishes itself from that of the waking state by a degree of subtraction of control. By this lack of control during dream-processing, the subjective aspects of the mental processing become visible. Normally consciousness appears as distal, as object-related. A given phenomenon will acquire its meaning, for example, by associations to many non-conscious, memorized perceptions of related phenomena, but the associations to the previous perceptions are absorbed in the present perception or present memory. In the dream processes, associations will often be made from quite heterogeneous material and may result in an incomplete synthesis. Although association is a phenomenon that only exists in the data-processing of intelligent systems, the associations will normally be consciously experienced as phenomenally tied to the object-world. Only under special conditions, as in the waking perception of heterogeneous dream associations or art representations, will they be experienced as subjective features, or aspects of mental data processing.

As noted above, subjectivity in visual fiction may be caused by perceptual distortions, or by distortion of the narrative sequence, or by a combination of both. Given an appropriate context, deviations from the 'objective' representation of space and objects will be perceived as an expression of a subjective factor.

Deviating lighting, like over-exposure or under-exposure, special colours, or fluctuating light will often form part of the representation of subjectivity (because of an underlying viewer-assumption of a normal, unmediated, and objective access to the object-world). The same is the case with deviating camera-focusing, deviation from normal structure of space, or deviating camera movements and deviating cutting and masking, which prevent the construction of whole objects and spaces, and, which furthermore underline the conditions of perception and point of view.

These deviations can typically be understood as deviations from a normal perception of the exterior world: the ability to construct stable objects and spaces and to construct unambiguous and realistic points of view is diminished, and the general body–mind state interferes with perception. The deviations can be motivated: the fluctuation of light is caused by clouds, moving leaves, reflections in water, a flashing neon sign. The director can diminish the subjective effect by emphasizing a motivation (including a psychological motivation related to state of mind, or character deviations like 'psychopath') or can, as in impressionist and expressionist films, enhance the subjective effect by lack of explicit motivation, which may be implicitly evaluated as a special subjective *vision du monde* by the viewer.

Several deviations may be interpreted as simulations of deviating central mental data-processing: deviating scaling, size, and isolation of a detail from a complex-composite totality. Considerable deviations from normal size can be part of a representation of subjectivity, as in Hitchcock's Dali-inspired dream sequence in *Spellbound*, which features gigantic playing cards. Scale deformations are often combined with isolation of a detail from its links with a complex whole, as in the strong subjective effect produced by extreme close-ups of lips or eyes, for example. Considerable deviations of scale can partly be caused by extreme positions of perception, as in high-angle or low-angle shots, double exposure, multiple-exposure, dissolve, and montage. If a single picture is constructed by mixing two or several pictures from different points in time or space there is normally no possible external source for the frames, and they will therefore be interpreted as expressions of a mental association. Correspondingly, fast sequences of different shots or stills will be interpreted as mental associations. The exterior reality will ordinarily consist of heterogeneous and complex objects. The eyes exist in an immediate context of perhaps nose, eyebrow, or forehead. A door exists in an environment of wall, floor, ceiling, and so on. If, as in the dream sequence in *Spellbound,* we see a curtain of eyes, the eye-curtain 'mimics' the association files of consciousness: one might compare Jakobson's (1960) dictum about the poetic function as projecting the axis of equivalence onto the axis of combination. In a subjective, 'dreamlike' film like Hitchcock's *Vertigo,* a whole network of metaphorical associations is established, as discussed in Chapter 11. Many music videos create a subjective, dreamlike effect by using a network of associations produced by visual similarities and a lack of stable narrative structures. Repetitions can have the same function as metaphorical similarities by producing associations that are cut loose from a directed, progressive time–space, and therefore can only realistically exist in the mind.

Deformation of canonical narratives may often lead to 'felt subjectivity'. Felt objectivity and 'distality' in visual fiction depend on the viewer's ability to produce mental models of the seen in relation to unambiguous, coherent, and teleological person–act–time–space schemata, as in a canonical narrative. These schemata possess inner 'logical' relations: we cannot make mental models of acts if the space and its objects possess incalculable properties, or if the time-structure is fragmentary, or if motives and goals are unclear. The existence of schemata of acts plays a key role in felt objectivity; if they are missing, feelings of subjectivity and dreaminess will be created. This is easy to understand in nightmares and horror situations, when perceptions are disconnected from schemata of acts and gradual build-up of affect. The subjectifying blocking of enaction by the modification of normal causal relations takes place, for example, in ghost stories, in which we isolate visual from tactile qualities by creating ghosts with visibility but without tangibility or vulnerability. However, positive experiences can also provide a 'dreamy' experience. This can be the case, for example, in certain episodes in musicals, when there is a disproportion between effort and reward, or a sudden reversal from misfortune to fortune. The intense positive experience of sudden glory, sudden bliss, or sudden pride creates an emotional 'flooding', which is felt as a 'daydream'. Standard narrative schemata of hypothetical and implemented acts consume part of the motivating affective charge by projection into distal hypothetical acts, and, when the mediating schemata are missing due to sudden reversals, the situations become highly charged and are labelled 'dreamy'. Canonical narratives typically evoke distal experiences; the absence of a teleological quality is an indicator of unreality, as in slow-motion, when the decrease of directedness evokes feelings of unreality and of subjective or dreamlike states.

The urge to find meaning in phenomena according to certain mental schemata like purpose, telos, or causality is, I suppose, a built-in feature of the functioning of the brain. By curbing or blocking the viewer's construction of a link between the input and the narrative schemata, a double subjective saturation is created. First, there is the saturation created by the associational network, and the felt meaning-intensity caused by this (described by Pribram: see also Chapter 2), and, secondly, there is the saturation caused by the curbed or blocked narrative schemata, which evoke a 'paratelic', subjective feeling of meaningfulness, of meaning as a process, rather than as a finished, established result. Paradoxically, the feeling of meaningfulness can be in a reverse relation to the amount of actual meaning, of constructed schemata and references. The feeling of meaningfulness is a motivational force that can often be mistaken for meaning, as in the dream situation, in which the brain desperately tries to find meaning in bizarre associations and is driven by this very feeling of meaningfulness.

The paratelic, process-oriented aspect of the meaning-construction in dreams and subjective states is perhaps also a result of the disappearance of what the neuropsychologist Shallice (1988) calls the 'higher-level control' of will, attention, intention, and so on. The meaning construction is therefore made by lower and more automated schemata. The persons in film-dreams are often experienced as robot-like, controlled more by causal than by teleological mechanisms, because their movements and acts do not seem to be integrated by clear goal concepts and goal-images. Nightmares are often characterized by a dissociation of perception or lack of voluntary motor control, or by disparate, diffuse, or ambiguously labelled schemata of possible acts or goals.

Some films try to use the Freudian model of dreamwork as a concept for making dream-like film sequences, by providing an unambiguous meaning with a 'scrambled', enigmatic surface; the films then provide 'keys' by which the viewer can unscramble the surface and discover the meaning of the dream. But such dream sequences (for example, the 'Freudian dream' in *Spellbound*) are often not felt to be entirely convincing and successful as dream simulations. They lack the affect intensity and the association intensity of films which have a cobweb of associations and similarities and in which no clear, unique, and unambiguous meaning can be established. Many films produce 'subjectivity' and 'dreaminess' by totally dissolving the objective time-structure; but the very moment we find a key to reconstruct a fabula, an objective time sequence, the feeling of subjectivity and dreaminess disappears.

THE FIRST DREAM SEQUENCE IN *WILD STRAWBERRIES*

I shall illustrate the creation of subjectivity in film with a dream sequence from the beginning of Ingmar Bergman's film *Wild Strawberries* (1958). We see the selectively lit head of an old man asleep, and on the sound track a voice-over of an old man tells us that he had a strange dream about being in an unknown part of town. Then the old man walks around in a non-goal-directed way in an empty, over-lit street marked by strong shadows. He looks at a large clock with no hands, then looks at his own watch, which has no hands either. His facial expressions suggest that he finds this puzzling. Later, the old man sees another man from behind, and, when the man turns, he has a peculiarly 'astringent' face with closed eyes. The stranger falls to the ground like an object, his head disappears and blood pours out in a nonhuman and excessive way, as if a bucket of blood has been spilt. A hearse without a driver is then shown from different points of view, and the viewer has difficulty in orienting himself and mapping the street-location, in deciding which shots are seen from the old man's point of view and what the exact time structure is.

The hearse hits a lamp-post, and hammers repeatedly, almost catatonically, at it, whereupon it falls to pieces; the hammering wheel disintegrates and rolls away. A coffin falls out and the lid falls off, and an apparently stiff hand appears; it moves and grasps the hand of the old man. Soon the face of the dead person is seen: it is the face of the old man himself, but the two faces are seen with different lighting and from different angles. The film cross-cuts between the two affect-charged faces, which are increasingly seen in ultra-close up, so that their eyes and mouths are enlarged and isolated from a larger context. The sequence is closed by cutting back to the old man, who is asleep but wakes up shortly afterwards.

During the dream sequence there are relatively few sounds. Amplified heart-beats, the footsteps of the old man, church bells, sounds of hooves, for example, gain salience as a result of the 'ground' of silence. The sounds are used as affect-evokers for the visual representation by the isolation of the singular sound-schema from a 'ground' and from a full, realistic fusion with the visual representation. The separation of sound and image is already established by the voice-over, which separates the 'internal subjectivity' of the voice from its invisible, objective source (an image of the narrator); the voice is only visually represented by the images of the old man in another time and other spaces (physical space as sleeping, mental space as dream-walker). The amplified heartbeats must come from within, but belong to another time than that of the voice-over, and they cannot fuse with the external, distanced I-images of the sleep-walker. The fragmentation of the sound structure, and the isolation of sound from image, create affect.

An important source of the unreality of the dream-space is the lighting. Over-exposure makes objects poor in resolution, and the lack of detailed texture renders them 'abstract', for example by the marked contrast between the white surfaces of the walls and the darkness of the gates. The shadows from visible and invisible objects look like objects themselves because of the lack of grading of intensity, and make it difficult to distinguish between objects and lighting. The space is therefore perceived as a mental image, as a memory image with few details or from the intermediate, uncompleted processing of a percept (Marr 1982) before final, objective analysis has been completed.

The objects in the space have several strange details, from the watches without hands and the strange man, made up of a combination of human features and object features, to the hearse without a driver. Time is also strange: its linearity is broken, for instance by the fact that the dream-I, living in one time, can meet himself as dead, that is, existing at a later point in the time sequence. The dream-I is relatively paralyzed, whereas the corpse-I is active, although without clear intentions. The other acts of the sequence have involuntary, repetitive, and non-telic qualities: the stranger falling and the carriage without a driver, combined with the cutting, increase the involuntary impression of the acts by shifts between points of view and format without clear anchoring of the shots in a subject and without logical enunciation procedures. Ultra close-ups isolate central features of the face, eye, nose, and mouth, and their expressions of affect, from the body totality.

The dream sequence has a network of associations centred in the phenomena of decay and death. The stranger 'spills' blood on the street, the handless watches are 'defective', the lamp-post and the wheel are fragmented, a horse falls, a coffin falls, the stiff dead hand is a body fragment, the close-ups are body fragments, and the bell ringing is an isolated sound fragment without any visible source. The dream-like qualities of the network of association are linked to the isolation procedure: the visual and acoustic perceptions acquire affective salience by isolation from realistic contexts and, at the same time, are linked by mental categories, such as decay and death, caused by involuntary mechanisms. The network of associations is simultaneously the raw material for producing the allegorical meaning of the dream sequence; *memento mori*, but this allegorical meaning is the least dream-like aspect of the dream sequence, because its unambiguous simplicity threatens to order and motivate the dream and in that way discharges the representation by making schemata for the heterogeneous material. (This accords with Freud's concepts of the relation between consciousness and the unconscious: the affects are linked to images and episodes, but the intensity of the affects can be reduced by integrating images and episodes in higher, conscious patterns.)

The saturated, subjective aspects of the sequence are based on distortions of perception, time, space, objects, and acts. The meaning of the dream is obvious: it deals with old age and the fear of 'castration' and death. The art of Bergman consists in giving perceptual salience and affective intensity to these prototypical human experiences. Through the process of socialization, the affects are tied to many experiences stored as images and episodes in the long-term memory, and Bergman's achievement is that he activates the charged network of images by combining common-denominator affect-charged images in a new and surprising or stimulating way.

SUBJECTIVE AND OBJECTIVE TIME

The purpose of the following paragraphs is to examine some of the temporal schemata by which the emotional affects of visual fiction are created. I shall discuss the reasons for which classical narrative descriptions of temporal duration, those of Genette (1980)[1] and Bordwell (1986), must be modified in order to characterize experienced time. I shall also delineate the way in which the experience of time is derived from different types of mental processes and their relation to the modal qualities and 'experienced tones' of time. Temporal experiences come in a limited number of prototypical configurations; representations of these may be called 'psychomimetic' in order to underline the point that such representations are not just 'style'. The temporal forms are often, for instance in the melodrama, an integrated part of the emotional experience, and the perceptual flow in film may give experiences that parallel 'tempo' in music and that provide 'kinetic' experiences.

Classical narrative theory presupposes that time is a single phenomenon: that of clock time. The prevailing opinion of laymen, poets, film-makers, and experimental psychologists is, however, that time is not just one but several related phenomena, of which one phenomenon is clock time, whereas the different types of experience of time constitute other phenomena (see Aumont *et al.* 1992). When we say, for example, that we 'feel' time to be short or long, we are not just using a metaphor but also a concrete description of an aspect of the way in which we construct and evaluate perceptual phenomena.

The aesthetic experience of time in visual fiction is not directly linked to the clock-time speed of projection, but to *time as constructed during perception and cognition*. I would like to summarize some experimental results concerning time perception as presented by Dember and Warm (1979: 306 ff.), for example, beginning with the filled-duration illusion: if we compare an evaluation of the length of two time-sequences, one consisting of a continuous signal (light or sound), the other of two short bounding signals surrounding an 'unfilled' interval, the filled intervals are perceived to be longer. Judgements of absolute duration are directly related to the signal's intensity, but have no

[1] Cf. also Lämmert (1965) and Chatman (1978).

effect on relative evaluations. Monotonous tasks are experienced as longer than interesting tasks. Perceived duration varies inversely with the muscular effort expended in a task, and expands when elements of danger or painful stimulation are introduced into the situation. It has further been argued that perception of time requires processing or attentional capacity, and that distraction from attending to time (by the need to process a task) decreases the experience of duration. Ornstein has further put forward the theory (1972: ch. 4) that the experience of length relates positively to the amount of information linked to a given time period.

Friedman (1990: ch. 6, *passim*) has discussed the way in which the construction of temporal schemata is often a bottom-up process: when necessary we construct more global temporal schemata based on fewer global experiences (in analogy to the way in which we construct the fabula out of *syuzhet*[2] clues). We do not have an objective temporal model of, say, the story of our life; we have to construct it based on remembered landmark[3] episodes, important episodes such as before or after graduating, before or after going to China, and so on. Genette cannot presuppose a 'background' of objective temporal duration as a backdrop in relation to which we feel the speed of the discourse: this will only be activated when cued, and the means by which a given type of construction takes place, and under what circumstances, will now be analyzed.

The construction of the concept of a single, universal category of time took place over a span of many centuries, and the period from the Renaissance to the end of the nineteenth century was especially important for constructing time as a single phenomenon. Some reasons were practical, linked to the co-ordination of many different, interacting social activities. Kern (1983: 12 ff.) has shown[4] the way in which railways created a need for national, continental, and global timetables, and therefore a need for global time. Global television news and global division of labour have augmented the need for representations of global synchronous time.

In fictional sequences, with many lines of action presented by such devices as alternation, and crosscutting, temporal relations like synchronicity or flashback are not automatically defined or salient for the viewer, because a global time-schema need not be defined. The viewer will only try to map the temporal relations between the different story-lines if these are important for understanding the interaction between them. Macro-temporal structures are, as a rule, constructed by a bottom-up process inferred by cues in the individual scene.

The experimental results (besides being informative for the following discussion of temporal experience in visual fiction) are presented in order to

---

[2] Cf. Bordwell (1986).

[3] For a description of the image-schema 'landmark' cf. Lakoff (1987: index entry, 609).

[4] For a description of the history of concepts of time cf. also Wendorff (1980).

emphasize that what we colloquially refer to as 'subjective phenomena', such as perception and the mental processing of phenomena, are objective in the sense that many of them vary systematically and according to input for all humans. If, for example, people are exposed to painful or dangerous experiences they all experience the time of the exposure as longer than clock time, and the experience is thus an objective consequence of the way in which mental evaluation of time takes place.

TEMPORAL SCHEMATA AND MODALITIES

Experienced time is not an independent parameter among the other cognitive and affective processes during viewing: on the contrary, it is derived from and felt as an aspect of other mental activities. The viewer's cognitive and emotional reconstruction of time in the fiction film consists of several activities, and the following outline indicates some of the activities in the viewing of fiction to which the experience is linked. First, experience of time is linked to cognitive processes evaluating causal chains in the (diegetic) world, based on schemata of 'objective time structure' and linked to the construction of the fabula. Experience of time is linked to the perception and schematization of events taking place in a scene, in order to evaluate the 'speed' of acts and processes; and to valenced[5] expectations of the outcome of 'events' in the diegetic world. Fourthly, it is linked to the felt salience of the perceptual-cognitive processes of the perceptual input. It is linked to the form of the narrative processes—for example, sequential (telic, paratelic, or autonomic-rhythmic) as against associative form—to their frequency, and to the subjective location of the experience (whether interior or exterior). These dimensions articulate the modal aspects of time. And finally, experience of time is linked to the activated type of reality-status. These different time 'experiences' interact, but in a complex way.

Experience of time is linked to cognitive processes evaluating causal chains in the (diegetic) world, based on schemata of 'objective time structure' and linked to the construction of the fabula

To understand the causal links in acts and processes in the diegetic world, the viewer has to formulate a more or less sketchy chronology, based on a large set of logical and heuristic inferences which are themselves based on 'knowledge of the world', from causal chains and temporal cues (like sunrise, or the age of protagonist) to a general knowledge of history or geography. These temporal schemata are cognitive constructs and do not as such possess strong

---

[5] For a description of the term 'valenced' cf. Ortony, Clore, and Collins (1988: 18 ff.).

'experienced salience' as to felt duration: the four-million-year ellipsis in Kubrick's movie *2001—A Space Odyssey*[6] is not necessarily experienced as more elliptic than one lasting forty years. Months may be skipped without the viewer feeling the ellipsis, unless something important for the understanding of the present situation is missing. In two versions of a story of reasonable length, in which the first has scene–ellipsis–scene, whereas the second has scene–episodic sequence–scene, the second will be felt as more 'elliptic' than the first, although the opposite is the case. The temporal 'stretch' will be felt in the second case, because the passing of time possesses perceptual salience. This 'stretch' might—using the terminology of Sternberg and of Bordwell, as presented in Bordwell (1986: 82)—be described as a 'diffuse' and 'flaunted' ellipsis; but that would be rather misleading, because it is not, strictly speaking, information necessary for the construction of the fabula that is left out. The 'episodic' ellipsis mainly withholds 'perceptual information' which would be necessary for constructing a perceptual experience of continuity. It is the elliptical activation of schemata of perceptual continuity that leads to a feeling of the passing of time in the episodic sequence.

Thus it is only under special circumstances that the relations between the objective chronology of the fabula and the discursive stretch are essential for generating temporal experiences similar to tempo in music. The reason for this is that the construction of the fabula chronology is a 'logical' one, from smaller and perceptually concrete components (such as scenes, or elements of knowledge) to global, 'abstract' schemata. When we reconstruct the chronology of the fabula we do not necessarily visualize the chronological story as if it had the same degree of perceptual concreteness as the scenes by which the chronology is made. A logical activation of a temporal ellipsis (such as, 'What did the alleged murderer do in the temporal ellipsis?') does not necessarily activate an 'experience of time'.

Experience of time is linked to the perception and schematization of events taking place in a scene, in order to evaluate the 'speed' of acts and processes

In scenes closer to the speed of an 'uncut', 'pro-filmic' event, several dimensions are directly linked to perceptual time–space–process schemata. We have schemata which time-map the standard speed of some acts and processes, like a man or an animal running, waves rolling, or objects falling. Even minor deviations from standard expectations are immediately felt as 'slow-motion' or 'fast-motion'. Motion schemata are linked to an objective time sequencing:

---

[6] If the cut makes a strong impression, it is not only because of the temporal ellipsis, but because the gap is 'flaunted' by the paradoxical graphic match of the metamorphosis from bone to spaceship, counterpointed by the earth/heaven, small mass/large mass contrasts, and a dynamic upward motion in contrast to a weightless floating.

a man running, shown with a 20 per cent slowdown, is still moving much more rapidly than a walking man; and yet this is felt immediately as 'slow' motion. The motion in a poetic scene in Widerberg's film *Elvira Madigan*, showing the lovers running in a meadow, is only slowed down very slightly, and yet the difference can be felt. The specific schemata of the way in which limbs move relative to one another at different natural speeds evoke specific objective time-expectations (see Humphreys and Bruce 1989: 103 f.).

This is quite different from cutting in a scene. Excluding the use of jump cuts, we may compress an act by showing samples of the act-schema or the situation-schema. There is no precise time-schema for the 'normal length' of entering a room, reaching a chair, sitting down, discussing problems, or leaving; the temporal expectations that could measure reduction or expansion are not well-defined. The role of act-schemata is even more obvious in a one-person act-sequence. A person is not ordinarily seen walking up all the steps of a staircase: we are shown a sample, or we are just shown the start and finish, for example; the awareness of compression is diffuse (see Burch 1981: 6 f.). These diffuse standards for 'speed of scene' will provide a backdrop for pace. However, the standards might be dependent not only on experienced real-life length but also on narrative competence, because viewers can 'chunk' elements of act-schemata by experience, contrary to the absolute standards for perceptual processes.

We might think that speeding up an act, either by cutting or by extreme fast-motion (or dissolves), would be equally 'artificial', but it is not experienced in this way. Climbing up the stairs has two aspects: there is a 'goal-schema', coming from the ground to a certain goal at the top, and there is a perceptual sequence, 'local' connections between act-schemata and perceptual schemata, perceptions of the process of ascension. To compress by cutting in the act-schema is felt to be more 'natural' than to compress the perceptual sequence. In other words, *a sequence of acts and a scene can be represented mentally in a temporal-'logical' schema, a mental model of time as one-dimensional space; but a sequence of acts can also be mentally linked to changes in a two- or two-and-a-half-dimensional space, measured by interior timing devices. The one-dimensional model is a second-order construct, using space as a model for acts and processes, and has a relative scale; compressions or dilations provide a more or less diffuse experience of speed as with: 'fast-paced' or 'slow-paced'.* A given fiction can generate its own temporal scale for act-schemata: a science-fiction film may have a scale geared to millennia, whereas a thriller may be scaled to minutes. But *the two- or two-and-a-half-dimensional models work directly on time–space-perception; compression or dilation is felt as a tampering with time–space.*

Slow-motion, fast-motion, dissolves, and jump cuts are felt as modifications of perceptual time–space. Because most people regard the perceptual time–space as an objective phenomenon, the viewer is led to formulate an expressive hypothesis: modifications of objective perceptual time–space express subjective and felt aspects of the experience. Or, put another way, the stretch or compression of perceptual time–space will be felt as intense or saturated.

A special borderline phenomenon between the two ways of representation, perception of time–space and construction of episode–act–goal schemata, is visible in phenomena related to flicker, stroboscopic effects, and flicker fusion. Wertheimer conducted an experiment in which two vertical lines divided by a short distance were presented sequentially (Nichols 1981: 297 f.). The lines were perceived as existing simultaneously if the temporal intervals were very short, while different types of apparent motion appeared at medium intervals; if the intervals became longer the two lines appeared as successive, that is, they were perceived as two discrete 'episodes' or spatio-temporal samples.

The temporal duration at 'scene level' therefore possesses two dimensions, one correlated to act–situation schemata and the other correlated to perceptual time–space schemata. The first dimension will be experienced (to a certain extent) as tempo, whereas the second dimension has additional 'modal' qualities (probably the felt dimension of the short-circuits in integration of the object, the location, and the motion-perception systems).

If we turn to Bordwell's summation of duration (1986: 83 f.) we find that the problems in his presentation derive from the fact that *syuzhet* time is often a diffuse phenomenon: as an experienced phenomenon it often has a non-perceptual goal-schema form. To establish continuity–discontinuity, and to establish whether something is left out or not, is impossible in precise temporal terms. This becomes obvious in his description of temporal compression. As an example of compression, Bordwell uses Tati's *Playtime*:

A night-to-dawn carouse in the prematurely opened Royal Garden is rendered in forty-five minutes of screen time. But there is no point at which we can isolate moments, let alone hours, as having been ellided by the syuzhet. . . . Thus the sequence presents at least six hours of fabula and syuzhet time without, strictly speaking, omitting a second! We can only say that the sequence has concentrated, or compressed those hours into about forty-five minutes of screen time. (1986: 82)

This analysis presupposes that there is a 'real' *syuzhet*-time lasting six hours, although we only see acts lasting forty-five minutes. To make such a 'real' *syuzhet*-time is apparently to fuse *syuzhet* and fabula, because what is compressed? No acts, no perceptual sequences, only pure clock-time has been omitted; the eventual feeling of acceleration which might take place for the viewer when the main character leaves the restaurant and shortly afterwards the viewer witnesses the daybreak, does not imply that the viewer retroactively experiences the night as more fast-paced and compressed, but instead provides an experience similar to our own when we have been intensely occupied with a piece of work and suddenly discover that hours have passed, and thus have to synchronize two different time-sequences (experienced time and clock-time). It makes little sense to say that *syuzhet*-time is compressed in *Playtime* in the same way that we experience a 'perceptual compression' (as when several days of a plant's growth are compressed into minutes).

The problems do not decrease when several act-schemata, manifested by cross-cutting, are tied together by a common situation and interlocking goals. Bordwell (1986: 84) describes an episode in Griffith's *The Birth of a Nation*:

The little band in the cabin is only moments from annihilation, and the Klan must ride several miles to rescue them. Cutting to the galloping rescuers prolongs the cabin siege (expansion by insertion), while cutting back to the cabin motivates the omission of very long stretches of the Klan's ride (ellipsis). This example, not at all extraordinary, shows the way in which the tension of crosscutting proceeds partly from the fact that syuzhet and style have given each line of action a different durational span.

In what sense is the cabin siege 'expanded by insertion' (in the form 'fabula time' < *syuzhet*-time = screen duration)? Is the *syuzhet* siege supposed to continue progressing in time, although we do not see the situation, whereas the Klan's ride as a *syuzhet* phenomenon stops (the ellipsis for this being: fabula > *syuzhet* = screen-time) as soon as we cut back and lose visual contact? The problems are derived from the fact that the correct description of the first cut is that it is a flashback to another act-series but is experienced as synchronous, because it 'expresses' the tense expectations of the besieged and of the empathic viewers. Such a description may, however, blur the distinction between *syuzhet* and style, because a new category would arise: emotion-expressing insertion (fabula = syuzhet < screen duration/style), and suddenly we would, from Bordwell's point of view, be 'back' in something which looked like an impersonal enunciation theory, exactly what his constructivism intended to replace.

However, it seems inevitable that *in order to describe the 'expressive' and felt qualities of duration, we need to make a distinction between perceptual time and act–situation time, and the way in which they relate to each other.* The ambiguity of *The Birth of a Nation* cross-cutting is that the perceptual qualities of the Klan's ride-insert is experienced by the viewer to expand the act-time of the besieged, although there is no increase in clock-time, and the insert therefore has certain psychomimetic features ('Where can they be? When will they arrive?'). In the same way, it is reasonable to assume that the use of slow and fast motion is not only a 'stylistic' feature but also has certain psychomimetic qualities. It would be an unnecessary objectivist prejudice to make a categorical distinction between representations of a (normal) exterior reality, *syuzhet*, implicitly provided with mimetic qualities, and representations of typical 'mental' dimensions of experiences, called 'style'. The same kind of objectivist distinctions are found in enunciation theories, in which all representations of 'subjective' experiences are regarded as 'enunciatory' phenomena, implicitly contrasted by, say, a standard mimesis of exterior acts. However, simply allowing the camera to follow a protagonist could be regarded from a super-objectivist point of view as a 'subjectivist' bias, as opposed to merely letting the camera represent without indicating any 'human' preferences at all.

This leads to our next parameter: time and expectations.

Experience of time is linked to valenced expectations of the outcome of 'events' in the diegetic world

When we have positive or negative expectations connected to an event or an outcome, we feel the tensity of the expectations to be partly 'temporal'. The time feels 'long', it 'drags on' when we wait for the final shootout, but 'rushes along' during a happy climax. As anecdotal evidence, I can record my own surprise at seeing the unpleasant snake-pit scene in Spielberg's movie *Raiders of the Lost Ark* for the second time and discovering that it was much shorter than remembered; my memory of the scene represented the 'felt duration', not screen duration. Arousal felt as tense will stretch time. The experience of speed will therefore be strongly influenced by level of arousal and by whether this arousal is felt as tense or saturated.

Arousal experienced as tense will expand experienced time. The experience of tempo and pace will therefore be strongly influenced by the level of arousal which a given sequence evokes in the viewer and whether it is experienced as tense or saturated.

The problems created by working with clock-time alone can be exemplified by Bordwell's analysis of the famous plate-smashing scene in *The Battleship Potemkin* (1986: 85 ff.). He points out that, although most viewers and critics take it for 'an extensive expansion', this is not clear upon closer analysis: either it is an ellipsis in which the event is cut by one or two seconds, or an ambiguous expanded mix of two different gestures. But, given the pressure of time and the context of other joltingly overlapping shots, 'the viewer comes to expect a nervous, vibrating treatment of fabula time as the film's internal norm, so that perplexing shots involving movement tend to be slotted into the most probable category'(1986: 88). The problem arising from this explanation is that when people are asked, or ask themselves, the question of how long the actual screen-time of the shot was, they will consult the 'memory of their impression', which was filed not to answer the question but as a cued response to the scene, as 'long' compared with the prototype of 'length of an act of plate-smashing'. 'Nervous', 'vibrating', and 'long' are aspects of the salience and modal qualities of the 'experience of time', and this is the basis on which the viewer can make inferences as to the length of screen-time: they have no written notes stating the exact clock-time. The content of the scene, the affects which it arouses in the viewer, will influence temporal evaluation; they are not just cognitively confused by the other montage sequences in the film, although this aspect also matters.[7] The filing in memory of the affective importance of a scene by 'temporal length' is a normal and built-in mechanism.

The experience of speed and 'rhythm' in a film will be influenced by fluctuations in the emotional charge of the sequences, so that if a film alternates between scenes of equal screen-time but widely different emotional impact, it nevertheless creates experienced shifts of tempo.

Experience of time is linked to the felt salience of the perceptual-cognitive processes of the perceptual input

The salience is composed of many different factors, and nothing very general can be said. The same *syuzhet* can be given the same clock-time length by a complex montage of shots from different angles, as in the telephone-booth scene in Hitchcock's *The Birds*, or by just one shot; and the experienced time will often be 'stretched' by a complex representation,[8] although if it becomes too complex there may not be any attention-capacity left for attending to the length of time. Evidently if the same image is seen for minutes it will ordinarily be experienced as 'long' during viewing (if evaluated as painfully dull) but will eventually be remembered as shorter because of the lack of features to recall (as in the above experimental indications of the difference in remembered length between a 'filled' and an 'unfilled' interval). But some of the features creating salience presuppose special viewer-skills and special motivation. Resnais' film *L'Année dernière à Marienbad* may be experienced by some viewers as long and dull, the voice-over narrator as monotonous. But others would enjoy finding clues to a reconstruction of fabula and to the mysteries of the visuals, and these people would experience the voice-over narrator as an 'irruption of discursive magma' in the way that Genette felt about Proust. A standard Hollywood film may be experienced as salient for some viewers, whereas the scenes would be quickly 'chunked' and filed by other viewers, experienced as trivial variations of well-known patterns and therefore filed in memory without any perceptual salience.

---

[7] Cf. also Eisenstein's description of the problem of the emotional qualities of time experience (1968: 25 ff.).

[8] Cf. Burch (1981: 52): 'the viewer's estimate of the duration of a shot is conditioned by its *legibility*. . . . an uncomplicated two-second close-up will appear to be longer than a long shot of exactly the same duration that is swarming with people, a white or black screen will appear to be longer still'.

Experience of time is linked to the form of the narrative processes—for example, sequential (telic, paratelic, or autonomic-rhythmic) as against associative form—, to their frequency, and to the subjective location of the experience (whether interior or exterior). These dimensions articulate the modal aspects of time

As discussed in previous chapters, the canonical narrative has a forward-directed, telic experience of time, linked to the tense expectations of outcome. But if the narrative process in salient episodes loses the telic aspect, we would describe the temporal form as paratelic. In these circumstances, the grand final chase in *The Disorderly Orderly* becomes paratelic; it loses its voluntary aspects and becomes a gratifying flow of experiences in which the capacity for structuring a future, a goal, shrinks, and time becomes a dynamic 'now'. The expressive song interludes ('I love you, I love you') in musicals are paratelic if they are felt as being strongly salient 'in themselves', and are not merely a retardation. This dynamic presence is mostly linked to undecided phenomena. The passive paratelic experience is created if the outcome is known (as, for example, in *Double Indemnity*). In this case the *syuzhet* is mentally constructed as a passive repetition, and the temporal experience tends to lose its linear-tense form and become saturated.

In the lyrical mode the linear aspect of time may be lost, and we may have 'timeless' experiences. Certain types of stream-of-consciousness in lyrical films or in music videos (Larsen 1990) have an associative and 'perceptual', 'achronic', many-dimensional time-experience. As mentioned above, Ornstein explains this by saying that many items are activated, and that both short- and long-term memory are activated. Earlier segments of the film are not thrown away as merely input to fabula construction: the memories are kept active by association. The present is experienced as a 'now' and at the same time as an 'echo' and 'mirror-image' of the past via metaphoric or metonymic associations. Resnais' *Hiroshima, mon amour* and *L'Année dernière à Marienbad* activate different temporal sequences simultaneously by association, and this phenomenon, of course, is only possible 'in memory'. The associative 'long-term-memory'-activated experience of time is often described as 'oceanic'; in psychoanalysis it is described as a regression to an early stage of development, before the split between subject- and object-world takes place. An additional explanation is, however, that association and memory are basic structural aspects of the way in which we experience reality, as in Jakobson's (1960: 251) famous dictum that 'the poetic function projects the principle of equivalence from the axis of selection into the axis of combination'; furthermore, to experience time in a modality connected to achronic associations rather than to a one-dimensional, telic time is sufficiently explained by the mechanisms of memory. A Bergson-inspired description of time-experience in film has been put forward by Deleuze (1991: ch. 4 and *passim*); he connects time *per se* with achronic associations, temporal crystals from which all linearity has disappeared. This theory makes time an essence and not a derived experience, and deprives the achronic modal experience of its definition by contrast to other, for example linear, experiences of time.

A special type of association is frequency (as described by Genette 1980), by which the association is established between identical, repeated elements; frequency also influences the form of temporal experience. Repetitions change the form of time-experience from linear-tense to 'spatial-associative' saturated form, unless the repetitions are perceived as 'rhythm', as temporal-cyclical repetitions of the 'same act'. As pointed out by Mitry (1990: 171 f.), visual phenomena as such are, by their close connection to spatial representation, not especially rhythmic. Rhythmic phenomena in film are often created or strongly supported by music, speech, and rhythmically represented or rhythmically enacted motion.[9] Rhythmic phenomena have traditionally been perceived as closely connected to the autonomic processes of the body (such as heartbeat, breathing, and basic motor schemata in which there are symbiotic fusions of subject-agents and objects).[10] In action, rhythm often emphasizes whole-body movements and coordinated limb movements more than independent limb movements.[11] This would explain the role of rhythm as the most important form of representing a 'non-telic', 'non-object-directed' activity. Rhythm points to the internal sequencing and 'clocking' of the body–mind, not to an external object. Although rhythm is directed, 'creating future time', it does not create a 'space ahead'; rhythm is anchored in a 'body in time' and, in a sense, is pure signification, highlighting the process of subjective expression. The 'meaning' is totally bound up with the subjective embodied consciousness. The embodied consciousness expresses itself by repeating 'the same' in time, thus expanding in time without any exterior goal. For this reason, rhythm manifests pure causality in the paratelic expansion of the subject in the world, instead of a 'teleological' striving of the subject toward the world.

[9] The experiments with abstract visual rhythms in, for example, the works of Eggeling, Ruttmann, Fischinger, and Richter around 1920, are felt as most rhythmic when an anthropomorph- or zoomorph-motion rhythm is 'felt' as an aspect of the abstract visual rhythm.

[10] A critical résumé of the research and hypotheses concerning the connection between rhythm and the involuntary motor system is made in Mitry (1963), especially in the third part, 'Le Rythme et le montage' (287 ff.). Cf. also Mitry (1987). For a cognitively oriented description of rhythm see Jackendoff (1987: 253 f.). He rejects a simple relation between metre and biological rhythms, but, on the other hand, emphasizes the close connection between music and the motor system (236 f.).

[11] The whole-body and coordinated limb movements partly rely on older, subcortical structures, whereas independent limb movements (and, even more, finger movements) rely on neocortex, cf. Kolb and Whishaw (1990: 257 f.). Part of the modal tone of the experience of different types of movements may somehow be linked to the difference in the mentally activated type of movement.

The way in which repetition destroys the telic qualities of movement is exemplified in a sequence from *L'Année dernière à Marienbad,* in which the female protagonist lies down on her bed. The act is repeated four times, first from the right-hand side of the bed (seen from the viewer's point of view), then from the left-hand side, then from the right-hand side, and finally from the left-hand side again. The first time, in which the act is still unique, continues to have telic qualities, but the repetitions and symmetrical reversals are experienced as passive, non-telic acts, so that in the last 'repetition' she is experienced as if she were somehow 'falling': by this point she is not really making a telic act any more. Rhythmic and repetitive phenomena are often experienced as 'expressive', characterizing the source of the activity rather than the goal. An example of this is found in Wenders's film *Paris, Texas,* in which there are several sequences of a man walking, and, as the viewer is unable to guess the purpose of his walking, these movements are experienced as 'repetitions' and expressive characterizations of the man. Dance sequences are experienced as more 'expressive' than people chasing each other. The non-telic aspects provide a more atemporal quality to rhythmic and repetitive phenomena.

As previously mentioned, frequency may be manifested in a special form as 'durative', which implies that acts and processes are mentally represented by atemporal concepts. The basic form of duration is the perception of space. A space in which no changes take place will be experienced as 'timeless', just as time–space is transformed into a purely timeless space when moving pictures are frozen into a still. The atemporality indicates that the experience has lost its unambiguous localization in the exterior space, or its distal qualities, and is now experienced as 'interior' as well, that is, as a mental image. In principle, motion and change need not be a precondition for localizing the experience in exterior space, as many spaces 'in reality' would be totally unchanged for extended periods of time. However, in 'real life', changes of focus of attention will mostly be a subjective compensation for the changeless object-world, whereas this possibility is more limited during film viewing. The change and permanence rate is often directly linked to the chosen format: a sudden bird's-eye view of the burning gas station at Bodega Bay in Hitchcock's *The Birds* functions as a timeless abstraction, because the dynamic elements shrink and the static ones expand. Besides the effect linked to 'prototypical format' of human identification, the long shot will also tend to turn process into state if the unchanging 'ground' gains in relative weight.

The still is the extreme durative, but often a certain dynamic element is retained in the durative representation, in which case the experience of duration becomes an autonomic, passive flow. A typical way of producing a dynamic durative is by using an episodic montage-sequence, possibly constructed by using dissolves (which transform a space of perception into one of association). Situations and processes lose their connection with an exterior space, and the viewer is passively moved. Metz (1972) has pointed out the durative use of episodic sequences. In classic American films durative montage sequences were, for example, used to illustrate the concert tours in *Citizen Kane* and *The Band Wagon*. The temporal progression of time is cut loose from its links to concrete places and concrete participants, and has become a 'pure process' of success or failure, experienced as a partly mental process. Some episodic montage-sequences and dissolves destroy the viewer's ability to anchor the motion in an exterior, objective space and, by that, induce an interior achronic 'flow'.

Experience of time is linked to the activated type of reality-status

Some types of representation activate forms of experience which indicate a certain 'reality hypothesis': this chain of events can be experienced as taking place in a possible existing, physical world (this is frequently the case in the telic, canonical narrative). Other types of representation, such as paratelic and autonomic narrative schemata, may cue a reception in which the events and phenomena of the exterior world are experienced as symbolic representations of mental events. In the previous section I dealt with the problem of iterative and durative phenomena from the point of view of 'abstraction', but these phenomena can also be described from the point of view of 'reality-status and its temporality'. The experience of 'exterior reality' is mostly connected to an experience of perceptions and acts as being unique time–space configurations. If the singular act is experienced as an exemplification of a general, supra-individual schema, the temporal experience tends to be an activation of the temporal dimensions of the domain to which the schema is applied. If a singular act is an exemplification of 'the conditions of human life', the temporal experience will be linked to scales of 'human life', not to the scale of the illustrative act.

The effect of change of reality-status can be exemplified by Laughton's *The Night of the Hunter*. A central sequence in the film is a journey made down a river by two children in a boat. The journey attains 'mythic' dimensions: the diurnal cycle is strongly marked by emphasis on night, daybreak, and dawn. There is a strong and explicit use of 'framing', 'silhouetting', and contrast-strong, texture-poor images, not fully motivated by the light-source (moonshine, and dawn), cueing an experience of abstraction, just as the description of man–woman oppositions emphasizes the prototypical. The compositions made by deep-focus photography (whether of animal life or human life) are experienced as symbolic. The diegetic world and its acts are experienced as an exemplification of supra-individual schemata, and the temporal dimension is scaled by the extension of concepts of 'human life'. There is an emphasis on autonomic motion (a boat drifting, or moved toward the rush of the bank), and a 'self-conscious' use of extradiegetic, emotion-evoking song, activating paratelic or autonomic modality qualities.

The iterative-durative phenomena in montage-sequences like the ones in *Citizen Kane* and *The Band Wagon* are made by synthesizing phenomena on the level of the individual temporal experience, whereas *The Night of the Hunter* extrapolates, from the singular sequence of events, a supra-individual level of prototypical repetition: the viewed is experienced as one of many tokens of the mythic prototype; a given act 'repeats' the prototypical schema. On the immediate fabula- and *syuzhet*-level there are no spectacular expansions or compressions. Only by an analysis of the structure of the perceptions and associations of the narrative will it become obvious that these structural elements activate temporal schemata of 'human life' leading to an experience of temporal expansion. Similarly, an analysis of reality-status and its scale is presupposed in the conventional use of a freeze-frame as a means of making 'narrative closure' at the end of a film. The freeze-frame represents a slight pause from a clock-time point of view, with 'style-time' still running for some seconds while fabula- and *syuzhet*-time have stopped (although it could be argued that style-time divided by zero-fabula-time would converge toward infinity). However, the way that closure by freeze-frame is often used and experienced is as a shift in reality-status, in which the frozen situation activates a durative mode of experience.

A special role in evaluation of reality-status and thus of temporal status is connected to the opposition between light as a property of 'solid' objects and as a phenomenon drawing attention to itself; or, to put it another way, objects as possessing such qualities as colours, and luminosity as 'immanent' properties as against objects as only light-reflecting surfaces. Several clichés in *film noir* are produced by partly dissolving a space made up of solid objects with identities of their own by making their appearance depend on illumination in a spectacular way. Using venetian blinds, we may create linear patterns on the surfaces of space, so that the appearance indicates the source of light and the trajectory of light through space before reaching the surfaces, whereas the objects play a minor role in moulding the experience. By oscillating neon signs we may create a similar situation, in which the reflected light points to its source, not to the reflecting objects. We may visually quote a 'natural' oscillation by showing reflections on water surfaces or by filtering the light through moving leaves, or a cultural oscillation by showing a dance-hall with stroboscopic lights. All these effects dissolve the 'reality' of the space, making the experience more achronic. In the Episode 24 of *Twin Peaks* David Lynch uses oscillating, flashing white light to dissolve time and space. We expect the effect of such oscillating light to be 'episodic' in analogy to a montage series (whether of stills or of moving images), with at least a partial anchoring of the series in space; but the effect is a 'ghostly' perception of two-dimensional images, experienced as mental and not linked by temporal schemata 'out there'. Two face-illuminations viewed in succession are not experienced as a face moved from point A to point B in the intermediate period, but as achronous exemplars existing in or projected into the viewer's mind.

Another way of expressing the redefinition of reality-status of space, from consisting of light-emanating objects to being the effect of light, is that space has become a source of perceptions, not a space of possible acts, whereby its lyrical or passive–melodramatic aspects become evident.

All these different types of temporal schemata and temporal modalities interact and create temporal experiences that are often compared to those of music. There is a certain explanatory value in the comparison, although it is important to emphasize that this is on the level of 'experience' rather than on that of technique, because the temporal experience in visual fiction is derived from anthropomorph mental schemata, not from 'pure', desemanticized, perceptual qualities.

Part III

A Typology of
Genres and
Emotions

7

A Typology of Genres of Fiction

This chapter will describe a model representing genres of fiction, based on viewer identification with active and passive positions in narratives and on different types of cognitive and affective identification with the narrative actants. I shall then outline a typology of genres with their different proto-typical emotional effects.

THE DIMENSIONS OF FICTION-RECEPTION

There seem to be three main dimensions of fiction-reception that mould the affective states of the viewer.

1. The 'real-life' contextualization of fiction consumption

The first dimension concerns the viewer's relation to the 'real-world' context of reception. Whether the consumption of fiction takes place in a cinema or in a private home (alone or with other television or video viewers), the viewer can alternate between identification with the real-world context and the fic-tive context, although not in a simple either/or manner. The restraints which are put on the interaction between the viewers in a theatre context tend, of course, to produce a greater emotional involvement in the fictive event com-pared to, for instance, a home-viewing situation in which the viewers are free to eat, talk, and do the housework (see for example, Morley and Silverstone 1991). But different genres of fiction also presuppose and generate different viewer-relations to the fictive event and the real-life context. This is most evi-dent in comedy, during which the spectator will experience the feeling of being part of a community, that of the audience, by sharing laughter in the theatre at what is taking place in the fiction. Musicals frequently simulate 'live performance' in order to activate 'real-life' viewer-participation. A real-life contextualization is also noticeable in the types of 'modernist' fiction that try to enhance, destroy, embed, or frame the fictional experience by indicating the circumstances of the consumption or production of fiction: Brecht, for exam-ple, tries to produce *Verfremdung*, distance to the fictive events. In his fiction introductions on television, Hitchcock speaks to the viewer about the contrast between the viewer's easy-chair and the dreadful fiction events themselves.

The viewer experience of fiction is thus influenced by contextualizations of it; some of the problems associated with this are often described as 'positioning of the spectator'.

2. *The articulation of the viewer's modes of perception and modes of cognitive and empathic identification with fictive agents*

Important for the mode of perception is an evaluation of whether the seen or heard has its source in, or represents, an exterior hypothetical or real world or an interior mental world (or belongs to intermediary positions), or whether the source is ambiguous. If the perceived is constructed as belonging to an exterior world it cues the mental simulation of an enactive world; whereas, if the perceived is constructed as belonging to a mental world, it cues a purely perceptual–cognitive, proximal experience. Equally important is the relation to agents of fiction. The viewer may perceive the agents with the same emotional distance that typifies his relation to inanimate objects, but he may also make a cognitive and empathic identification with them. If the agent with whom the viewer identifies is in active-telic situations, this will 'reduce the distance' to the viewer, by bringing the viewer's focus of attention 'out' into the hypothetical world and creating modes of perception which are focused on distal modes of representation.

If the viewer identifies with an agent in passive situations, characterized by perception and/or paratelic or autonomic acts and processes, this will focus attention on proximal and interior modes of representation. However, whether this will lead to a 'reduction of distance' depends on certain empathic and hedonic factors. A positive evaluation of the situation will normally evoke fusion of perceptual and emotional representation: the viewer is emotionally carried away, and can diminish the distance between the passive agent and himself in a symbiotic experience. If, on the other hand, the situation is negatively evaluated, the identification with the agent often becomes 'purely perceptual'; the agent is the preferred focus of attention, but perceived to be 'unfamiliar' and 'distant', and the saturated feelings evoked by the situations are also felt to be 'unfamiliar'. The purpose of this is clearly defensive: the mind dissociates perceptions and emotions in strongly negatively charged situations, as when people involved in catastrophes experience them as happening to somebody else.

A good example of dissociation of perception and emotion is Carl Dreyer's *Vampyr;* the dissociation is linked to a lack of enaction and 'strange' subjective images. The main character does not usually act, but listens and observes, even seeing himself as a body in a coffin. The phenomena in the film are represented with incomplete modality-definition, as shadows or silhouettes, or even as mirrored shadows, reversed and upside-down; object-identity is dissolved by the existence of several copies of the same person in one frame, and the fictional universe is ruled by supernatural causality. The sinister plot ensures that the many subjective images are felt in a perceptual distance as unfamiliar, and that they cause viewer-experiences saturated with *Angst*. As I shall demonstrate in more detail in the following chapters, subjective, saturated images are most often felt to be 'strange' and 'unfamiliar': familiar images are located in the exterior, objective world.

3. The narrative structure of the world of fiction

The third dimension concerns the narrative structures within the fictive world, and the relations between fictive subjects and fictive objects. This has been the object of classical narrative theory.

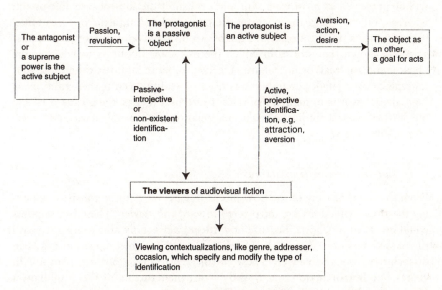

Fig. 7.1 Model of dimensions of importance for genre constitution: the upper-left-hand corner shows the passive narratives, in which viewers identify with protagonists as objects; the upper-right-hand corner shows the active narratives, in which viewers identify with active protagonists. The intermediate arrows show projective and introjective transactions, linked to type of identification.

These three dimensions interact and make up the framework of the emotional transactions between viewer and the fictive world. The transactions can be divided into the following two main types.

i. Enactive-projective transactions

Affects and empathy are projected from the viewer toward simulations of an exterior, fictive world of objective models of living beings. The emotive sources of affects in the central nervous system and body of the viewer are projected towards phenomena represented as belonging to exterior worlds. These projective transactions are manifest in action-adventure fiction, with its quest for enticing objects and the destruction of aversive opponents. The aesthetic effect of these transactions is the creation of tension, desire, aversion, and significant and meaningful depth. The effect of enactive projection is the creation of a certain symbolic realism and objectivity, because these are closely related to the ability of anthropomorph subjects to deal with perceptual phenomena by means of enactive manipulations of objects. The difference between a world of physical objects and an interior world of dreams, thoughts, and memories, is that the first world can be modified by physical action. For this reason a fairy-tale, which in some senses is quite 'unrealistic', will be perceived as possessing symbolic realism if the subjects are able to act; whereas, other quite realistic stories are perceived as 'fantastic' or 'dreamlike' if the 'subjects' of the stories are unable to do so. Todorov (1975: 37 f. *passim*) has shown that stories in which there is some doubt as to whether the phenomena are 'real' or unreal are perceived as more fantastic than those that take place on a single, unambiguous level of reality, even if this reality is as 'unrealistic' as it is in many fairy-tales. I interpret this as being caused by the blocking of mental models of enactional relations by a problematic and uncertain reality-status.

ii. Passive-introjective transactions

From the point of view of the flow model in Chapter 2, these consist in blocking the flow. Affections are introjected toward the viewer. These transactions could be called psychotic, because now the viewer is only able to identify with the passive position, that of the object, whereas the subject-position has been dissociated from the viewer. These introjective transactions are manifest in genres like horror fiction and tragedy, with their threats of the annihilation of exterior objects of identification. The aesthetic effect of these transactions is that they create emotivities and affective saturation. Furthermore, the effect of passive-introjective transactions is to produce a certain irreality and mentalism, because they position the viewer in a passive-perceptual relation to perceptual phenomena (experienced, for example, as dreams, memories, and hallucinations).

Whether phenomena are perceived as located in a (symbolic) real space or a psychological one, and whether the affective charge of a perception is located in the object or in the perceiving subject, are matters that are regulated by narrative transactions; these transactions demonstrate the connections between subject- and object-relations, and the relations between perceptual and affective quantity. The dimensions of fiction can be illustrated as in Figure 7.2.

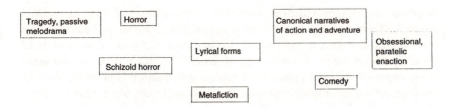

Fig. 7.2 The main genre-types in a spatial distribution, in which left means passive, right means active, down means distanced, and up means identification. Lyrical forms are in the centre.

These dimensions point to some characteristic narrative types: narratives, that emphasize the dimension of action, as opposed to those that emphasize the axis of passivity and passion (like the classical tragedy, or a modern melo-drama of the passive kind). There are two mediating forms: (paranoid) hor-ror, in which the position as object is not accepted, contrary to a real tragedy or melodrama, and obsessional enaction, in which the canonical relation between subject and object loses a number of its voluntary aspects. There are, further, several types of fiction that have their structural centres in modifica-tions of the identification between viewer and protagonists. Comedy tem-porarily suspends identification; schizoid fiction dissolves the holistic frame for relating remote perceptions and body-perceptions; metafiction establishes filters between viewer and fiction. Finally, lyrical 'fictions' result when a film has no anthropomorph narrative schemata.

GENRE THEORY, GENRE TYPOLOGY, AND GENRE MOODS

We may now consider a more detailed analysis of the affective impact of dif-ferent types of visual fiction. As objects I shall use a selection of genres and genre moods, because it seems that genres like canonical narratives, horror, comedy, and visual lyrics/music videos have strong and characteristic emo-tional effects. My hypothesis is that the main genre-formulas and moods of fictive entertainment are often constructed to produce certain emotions, by allowing the viewer to simulate one from a set of fundamental emotions linked to basic human situations. Mass fiction, in particular, is produced, con-sumed, and distributed in certain categories, and it seems intuitively evident that one of the pertinent features distinguishing these categories is a set of affect-producing narrative patterns (such as horror, romance, and comedy), especially if film-genres are seen in the historical perspective of 'popular gen-res of fiction since around 1780'. The reason for this is not that there exist some essentialist, innate genres. The lyrical mode and the canonical narrative are as close as we get to innate, 'hardwired' genre-like mental models. The emotions and certain structural aspects of the way in which they are evoked are probably innate; but to use emotion-producing features as a guideline for constructing fiction is a 'pragmatic' decision, like using the western part of the USA as a setting for a certain type of fiction. The practical reason for making emotion-evocation a principle of generic construction is probably that, to produce fiction for a global market, the producers very often need to create clear-cut and relatively universal narrative motivations. It is easier to communicate expectations of 'romantic love', 'pleasurable horror', or 'good laughs' to a mass audience than it is to communicate an 'interesting narrative about conflicts between Greek Orthodox priests and ecologists in Lithuania', although an iconology or certain themes, like the Western, can also have a relatively widespread appeal.

Before establishing a typology of genres, I shall briefly discuss the different ways in which the phenomenon of genre functions and the different ways in which generic analysis has been made.[1] The word 'genre' generally just means a category or a set of categories used to describe some general features in works of fiction. Works of fiction are complex phenomena, that can be analyzed, and therefore categorized, in many different ways.

First, genre can *exist* in different ways. The producer of a given work of fiction may have some notions of general schemata serving as models for producing a given work; the distributor may market products according to certain genre-labels; the critic may use certain categories in his guidance to consumers; viewers may use certain genre schemata to structure their total consumption or as schemata to be used during viewing; and the researcher may use historical or systematic genre-categories to organize a vast quantity of material. These different modes of existence interact. The way that the viewer experiences the film is not independent of the way that it is marketed or produced, but viewer schemata change in the course of time; while marketing tries to predict which categories are correlated with which preferences and for which segment of the viewing public, and tries to obtain feedback, for instance from the box office.

Secondly, genre-categories can be *constituted* in many different ways: they can be based on time ('historical films'); time and place (Westerns); types of action and themes (detective fiction, war films, love-stories); addresser-intention (avant-garde films, art films); and they can be constructed with a large time-horizon (claiming to map all films or all types of fiction), or a small one ('screwball' comedy).[2]

Each set of criteria has its own particular usefulness. The usefulness of a genre typology based on emotional reaction is that it increases an under-

---

[1] For a discussion of different points of view regarding generic film analysis, see Grant (1986), Neale (1980), Altman (1987: 1–16), Bordwell (1989*b*: 146–51), and Neale (1990).

[2] Cawelti (1976) and Schatz (1981), for example, have advanced historical genre descriptions. Cf. also Frye (1957).

standing of the way in which the cueing of emotions takes place as a choice within a set of structural options that mutually define each other. Although a given genre has a basis in mental and bodily mechanisms, it is not an essence, but acquires its specific effect in contrast to the other generic options. A typology based on emotional reaction also corresponds to an important aspect of the basis on which viewers in a given situation choose a type of fiction (I want to see something funny, or something passionate, or something that terrifies me). The generic expectations of dominant emotional impact further play an important role in the viewers' reconstruction of a given film. When de Palma's *Blow Out* suddenly changes from canonical narrative to melodrama almost at the end, it creates an emotional disorientation in the viewer.

The focus of the present typology centres on a description of cognitive-emotional schemata and functions, existing in viewers and producers and playing an important role in combination with other genre-categories defined, for example, in terms of time and place. The typology is made up of prototypes (in the sense of the word used by Lakoff 1987 and Johnson 1987):[3] some films are more central to a given prototype than others. The types can further be combined in many different ways (mixing of genres is not a 'postmodern' invention).

One aspect of emotional response which is outside the scope of the present typology is 'familiarity'. As mentioned earlier in my analysis of perceptual input, feelings of familiarity–unfamiliarity play an important role. A given set of elements of fiction will therefore have an affective value for the viewer connected with the number of times the viewer has been exposed to a set of features (in fiction or in ordinary life). People who have seen many Westerns have a positive feeling of familiarity connected with western iconology (certain landscapes like Monument Valley, certain objects like horses, guns, and wagons) and with the narrative formulas of the Western. People who have seen many films featuring Ernest Borgnine have a feeling of familiarity connected with him. People living in France have feelings of familiarity connected with certain types of faces, houses, or language types. People who have seen many avant-garde films have a positive feeling of familiarity with certain types of heterogeneity. Familiarity as a 'reception-psychological' phenomenon can be treated in general terms, but its genre-constituting features can only be studied by concrete historical analysis, because they are constituted by the specific experiences of specific groups of people.

Genre, according to this typology, is merely a set of dominant features of a given fiction, which shapes the overall viewer-expectations and the correlated emotional reaction. Although a canonical narrative like an action-adventure

---

[3] The term 'prototype' is developed from Wittgenstein's concept of 'family resemblance', a group of phenomena like a family, who resemble one another in various ways although there need be no single collection of properties shared by everyone in the family.

film is mostly concerned with tense acts, the hero is often put in a situation which instead resembles that of a horror narrative or a melodrama, and similarly canonical narrative may have lyrical sequences. As genre is often determined by a global or dominant narrative pattern and correlated emotional tone, we need a term to describe the local, situation- and sequence-bound narrative pattern and its correlated emotional tone; I shall use the word *mood* to describe the local pattern and its affective tone (despite the passive associations of the word):

Genre: *dominant pattern of emotions/expectations/narrative functions*

$\longrightarrow$

mood 1→ mood 2→ mood 3→ $\longrightarrow$ *mood n*

The dominant pattern of expectations activates the emotional response and focuses levels of attention: even when the hero in a canonical-action feature is trapped in a snake pit, we do not wholly despair, but continue our active attitude. Had the genre expectations been melodramatic, we would have started to cry; had they been comic, we would have started to laugh; had they been horror, we would have shivered. Shifts of mood allow the creation of complex emotional configurations (for instance, traditional complex configurations like tragi-comical), and the creation of emotional contrast. *The effect of shifts of mood is related in some way to what M. C. Beardsley has described as the kinetic pattern of music.*[4] Furthermore, some genres rely on devices and moods from other genres in order to be able to make their affective transactions; comic fictions, for example, often rely on canonical narratives for the creation of empathy and tensity which is then comically negated.

ASSOCIATIVE LYRICISM

The 'zero'-point of fiction is the symbiotic fusion between viewer and the viewed, perceived as a saturated-metaphorical lack of or minimal articulation of difference between viewer and 'fiction', subject and object, body and mind. To create a lyrical sequence we have to reduce or totally block the possibilities of constructing a stable hypothetical time-space with well-defined agents and objects.

One parameter of this is the presence or absence of a subject-actant. By totally removing the presence of an agent as a focus of attention, or by reducing a given agent's ability to act, and emphasizing the agent's perceptions and

---

[4] Cf. Beardsley (1958: 184): 'I propose to say that a musical composition has . . . *kinetic pattern:* it is the pattern of variation in its propulsion, or intensity of movement . . . music, as a process in time, has varying regional qualities that can be described, metaphorically, by terms borrowed from physical motions: the music is rushing, hesitating, pausing, picking up speed, becoming calm, driving ahead, overcoming resistance, building up inertia'.

expressions of emotions, we reduce the possibilities of making an objective time-space. If there is no agent to whom a given shot can be anchored, this could be interpreted in an objectivist sense as a pure 'analytical' or 'descriptive' activity, but could equally (for example, when depicting 'natural beauty') be interpreted in an aesthetic and subjectivist sense as an expression of a Kantian purposiveness without purpose, by which the space loses its qualities of 'space of acts' and becomes 'space of purposeless subjective perception'.

A second parameter is the presence or absence of the possibility of constructing stable object-identities. Normally, objects are perceived at a certain level of attention, at which the objects are constructed as a specific concrete–heterogeneous set of features, perceived as types or individualized tokens. But the concrete identity of an object can be diminished by activating associative connections, especially if this takes place at a lower or a higher level than the typical level of focus of attention. If we juxtapose images of 'eyes', 'flowers', and 'sun', we will create metaphoric associations between the objects by means of a 'lower' level than the typical focus of attention. One feature, 'roundness', is the basis of the association, and this 'breaks up' the perception of the discreteness of the singular, composite object; the object is experienced as a set of features associated with similar features in other objects. This activates 'lyrical' associative networks in consciousness, in which the objects are linked at feature level (say, roundness). The juxtapositions can also be made according to 'emotional' common denominators, ranging from a series of traditional emblems of love, like roses and moonlight, or emblems of horror, to more specific emotional series, or those anchored by emotional reaction shots or music. Associative connections can further be established at a higher level, by 'grouping', abstraction, and symbolism, often as a 'poetic level' in a narrative film.[5] In *Citizen Kane* the 'rosebud' symbolism subsumes many different concrete-composite acts and situations. The category of 'nature', as opposed to 'culture', both groups and abstracts the concrete-composite situations in the films of Jacques Tati, so that the viewer has to activate some 'higher', abstract (non-perceptual) categories in order to make sense of the films. 'Gold' and 'quest' abstract the concrete narrative level in *The Treasures of the Sierra Madre*. All narrative films consist of a combination of a thematic-achronic and a narrative-diachronic level, but in some films the thematic-achronic level abstracts and subsumes the concrete-composite narrative and creates feelings of atemporal, allegorical meanings and truths that are lyrical-saturated rather than narrative-tense. In musicals we often see lyrical-paratelic sequences based on 'abstraction': the concrete love-narrative is interrupted in order to abstract it into 'love' in general.

A third parameter is the mode in which we gain visual access to the object. The normal processing of visual input often filters aspects that belong to light

---

[5] Cf. Greimas' seme-lexeme analysis (1983); also in Grodal and Madsen (1974).

as a medium and to the proximal and central processing of the input. Light and shade are only interesting as cues to the spatial dimensions and the identity of an object, and are 'thrown away' during processing. Local variations in light intensity are also 'normalized'. The objects are understood as 'light-emanating essences', not as 'surfaces on which light is reflected'. If the fact that we only see objects through the medium of light is brought to focal attention, it will break down the normalization and evoke a 'subjective impression' (as in impressionism, expressionism, or *film noir*: see Chapter 6). If the processing *per se* of the perceptual input is brought to focal attention, it will also create a 'subjective impression' (see Chapter 6) by making the 'spatial' source of the perceived ambiguous, as in soft-focus or out-of-focus photography, in which the source is both 'out there' and 'in here'; this will break down object-identity because the phenomena are not unambiguously placed in objective space. Consequently, this type of perception may activate subjective associations because it appears to exist and to acquire its identity in the mind.

Whether the 'lyrical' networks of associations will be felt as 'intense' or 'saturated' depends on the degree to which the topics have generally known emotional values or are provided with emotional 'relays' (for example, music) in the film. In *Film Art* (1990) Bordwell and Thompson distinguish between abstract formal systems and associational formal systems, but both rely on a paradigmatic/associational system, the main difference being whether or not saturated feelings are activated.[6]

Because of its lack of enactive agents and distinct objects, lyricism is, of course, non-narrative, and its main 'dynamic' means are visual rhythm and oscillation, supplemented by motion from the represented world (especially the 'romantic' world produced by the motion of wind and waves). In popular culture, the lyrical mode always exists in symbiosis with the enactive-paratelic tensity of music or prosody which provides 'kinetic dynamism' to the network of associations. Written poetry has never attracted many readers, in contrast to an immense interest in (popular) songs; visual 'poetry', except when provided with a musical background or a motivating narrative, attracts even fewer viewers. Pictures without sound are often experienced as 'distant' and 'unemotional'. The later silent film relied on live music in the cinema to compensate for this distance, and to 'anchor' the emotional interpretation of the seen.[7] Visual 'poetry' has existed since the beginning of cinema, with early major works like *Ballet mécanique* (1923–4) and *Un Chien andalou* (1928); but visual poetry only became a popular genre in the 1980s, when it was fused with popular music in the music video. In visual fiction, the lyrical form is therefore mostly used as a device embedded as a mood in narrative fiction,

---

[6] Cf. also Bordwell (1980).

[7] Cf. Altman (1992) and Gorbman's discussion (1987: 39 f.) of Adorno/Eisler's hypothesis of the shadowiness and ghostliness of images without sound.

and nearly always motivated, for example as 'hallucinations' (*Altered States*), dreams *(Vertigo)*, or 'visions' *(2001—A Space Odyssey)*.

A borderline type of lyrical and narrative mode is what might be called 'synechdochic lyricism', centred on the process of identifying with images of humans. The perception of the viewed is still one of saturation, but the problem of the perception of identity is moved 'out there', to the image of the 'I' as other, as body and especially as face, as opposed to the 'I' as 'interior' perception. The viewer tries, by means of acts of perception and cognition, to solve the riddle of self-as-other. In a voyeurist-fetishist film like *The Rocky Horror Picture Show,* the show itself emphasizes the arbitrary nature of the signs of sexual difference: they are empty, physical, and interchangeable signifiers for the affections of the spectator. Sexuality is a mental model which provides certain schemata of cognition and action and certain schemata of empathic identification; and, if empathic identification is absent, the signifiers will be felt as 'meaningless'. Drag films like *Tootsie* exploit this phenomenon by showing that what is normally projected as an essence quality is a mental hypothesis for social behaviour enabling certain biological processes. Now, *Tootsie* has sufficient narrative structure to enable full identification with the two narrative roles, so that the viewer can separate the 'real' male role from the fictive-hypothetical drag role. However, in many music videos the shift of gender identity (or, say, identity of race or age) is so swift and so ambiguous that a narrative and empathic identification becomes impossible, so that the mental-subjective and perceptual aspects of the roles become the dominant mode of existence in the viewer, whereas they lack tense telic meaningfulness.

CANONICAL NARRATIVES OF ACTION

This genre is by far the dominant genre of visual fiction, and has been the paradigm for the classic narrative models of Propp, Greimas, *et al.* The typical time-structure is one of simple chronological progression, and the dominant enactions are voluntary and telic. The basic or canonical narrative genre is brought about by an enactive cognitive and empathic identification with a fictive subject and its hypothetical or actual relations to fictive objects and phenomena. The viewed is no longer saturated: the affective and emotional experience of subjective qualities is projected metonymically onto the object and onto the fictive 'space' separating an enactive fictive subject from an object. Under optimal conditions, the viewer loses self-awareness: he is fully absorbed and projected into the narrative world. Instead of saturation, the fiction becomes soaked with tense enactive desires and aversions. Through his identification with the subject-actant, the viewer's relation to the fictional world develops two main forms that can be combined: either as a positive desire aimed at positively evaluated objects and qualifications such as knowledge, power, respect, and money or as a negative desire aimed at controlling or destroying objects and agents. The canonical narrative often has a closed structure, with a beginning (subject lacks object), middle (action), and end (object repossessed), frequently emphasized visually by a fading-out in symbiotic fusion by means of slow-motion and still pictures. The schemata can also be combined in narrative hierarchies, as in the different types of serials in which the single episode has a relative closure but the episode is also part of a larger narrative or thematic framework without closure (this, of course, is more dominant in television fiction than it is in the cinema).

Canonical enactive fiction is the narrative schema used in fiction types like fairy-tales, erotic comedy, and standard action, adventure, and romance narratives, as well as in many 'realistic' types of narrative. Canonical narratives can be subdivided into several types. One subdivision can be made according to whether the narrative emphasizes physical or 'cognitive' enaction. Straightforward crime fiction with a progressive time structure is very similar to action fiction, except that physical acts alternate with or are replaced by cognitive acts and 'cognitive tensity' (in contrast to psychothrillers, for example, which have a dominant progressive–regressive time-structure and more saturated sequences). Another subdivision distinguishes between the narrative as fully telic or as having major paratelic sequences. Musicals are often straightforward telic narratives, interrupted by paratelic sequences of singing and dancing.

OBSESSIONAL FICTIONS OF PARATELIC COGNITION AND ENACTION

There are some types of crime fiction and 'thrillers' in which the viewer becomes increasingly alienated from an identification with the fictive enaction and with the fictive protagonist. The acts lose their voluntary aspects and become obsessional, as when, for example, a chase after an object seems to be driven by involuntary and non-conscious mechanisms. Consequently the paratelic activity does not appear to be motivated by the qualities of the objects. *The Maltese Falcon* begins as a classic detective quest for a murderer, combined with the hunt by a group of criminals for some valuable objects, symbolized by the Maltese falcon as the supreme good. But the chase for the valued object ends by being a quest without any real object, and without any real possibility of a 'closure' by 'possession'. In David Lynch's *Blue Velvet* the young 'detective' is obsessed with clues and with thinking about clues, but they have no meaning 'in themselves', only as signifiers; their meanings, the 'objects' and acts they refer to, are opaque. The signified, the objects and meanings, seem to be deferred into infinity, so that any connection between signifier and signified becomes difficult to establish. The paratelic, process-oriented aspect dominates the telic. An important device for creating paratelic effects is 'abstraction' produced by repetition: the individual acts and objects are represented as mere exemplifications of more abstract schemata. The transformation of a narrative sequence from a telic to a paratelic form by representations of repetitive acts is linked to the 'obsessional' aspects of the acts, but also to a change of reality-definition in the object of the quest. Examples are *The Maltese Falcon* and *The Treasure of the Sierra Madre,* in which the diegetic world is undercut by a redefinition of the reality-status of gold from being a physical object to being a mental phenomenon. The redefinition of telic to paratelic acts by a redefinition of the reality-status of the object transforms the narratives into proto-lyrical, symbolic and allegorical patterns.

Signifiers, like the clues in ordinary crime fiction, attract attention by being indexed and bracketed by the visual narration, like the famous key in Hitchcock's *Notorious.* In this way they lose their standard affective charge and the meaning normally produced by their connectedness to the immediate context. Instead they become tense, with indexical directedness toward 'the meaning', which is quickly grasped by the ordinary film-goer. The clues in classic crime fiction, whether of cigarette ends, hair, or fingerprints, are trivial and meaningless in themselves; but they acquire a deep and tense meaning by their metonymic relations to absent objects and meanings.

However, in obsessional, paratelic crime fiction the clues are like pointing fingers, understood as a process of signification, not as a result of it. The 'obsessive' and paratelic use of clues 'short-circuits' the process by blocking the relations between means and ends. The clues and acts lose their telic, tense qualities, and become more lyrical, intense, and/or saturated by the toning-down of any possibility of conceptualizing telic images and situations. The voluntary aspect disappears: if there is no possible telos, there is no guideline for voluntary decision, and the narrative evokes feelings of involuntary models for identification with the subject-actants. The most famous example of the transformation of a clue into a saturated 'symbol' is, of course, 'rosebud' in Welles' *Citizen Kane,* which starts as a signifier of hidden meanings and, because of the impossibility of fixing definite meanings to the word, ends as a saturated symbol, condensing meanings by the cobweb of associations built up during the film.

Obsessional fiction can be seen as transitional, falling somewhere between the enactive genres and the passive and passionate genres as a result of ambiguous oscillations between seemingly goal-directed, telic subject-actants and paratelic subject-actants. This transitional status is also marked in the temporal structure. There is a conflict between the forward-directedness of the acts of detection and the backward-directedness of the criminal past unravelled by the detection. The temporal order is often blurred to such a degree that it is difficult to know what is present and what is past. In a psycho-thriller like Hitchcock's *Marnie* there is a straight progressive–regressive structure, a progressive narrative in which we learn, step by step, about

Marnie's past, until the past has been reconstructed and the progressive action can be brought to a halt. The regressive past, as in *Marnie*, is often a retrogression into mental structures, memories, traumas, and dreams. However, in intellectual 'detective stories', like Resnais' *L'Année dernière à Marienbad,* it is difficult to ascertain whether the narrative goes forward or backwards in time and whether the past or the present are subjective constructions; crime fictions like von Trier's *The Element of Crime* make it equally difficult to construct a chronology, and therefore also to construct models of reality and schemata of acts.

At a certain point in the substitution of voluntary enaction with obsessional enaction, projection toward a distal world stops, leading to 'psychotic' forms of fiction. The fiction regains 'saturated' aspects, and instead of experiencing tension linked to the experience of a suppressed action tendency by means of voluntary motor outlet, the viewer may respond to the threatening passive position by involuntary motor-outlet.

MELODRAMAS OF THE PASSIVE POSITION

The genres and moods of fiction discussed above presuppose that the reader identifies himself with the protagonist of enaction. But in fiction of the melodramatic type, for example, the actant of identification is predominantly a passive one, an object-actant. The identification is therefore predominantly perceptual and empathic. The passive melodramatic actant of identification is controlled by alien agents, and the alien signifiers of enaction are partly or totally incongruous with a 'human model' and with ordinary voluntarism, as, for instance, in many romances and melodramas in which grandiose superhuman or subhuman agents control the events in the narrative.

The grandiose agents could be phenomena of nature such as sea or wind, or of a superhuman culture, with superhuman agents like complicated machines or social institutions in science fiction and in other fictions of the sublime, or phenomena representing metaphysical agents, like Destiny or God. In this way the viewer will be moved, touched, and so on: metaphors that express a passive perception located by the viewer on the corporeal rim or in the autonomic body-interior. Phenomenologically the direction of signification moves from a remote point of enactive signification, via a fictive object of identification, toward the viewer, in whom the emotions trigger autonomic responses. The fictive identification-'object' loses its corporeal delimitation. This loss may take place directly, if the passive protagonist is overwhelmed by a grandiose principle of enaction (destiny, whether destiny is positive as when lovers are united by the fortune-machinations of plot, or negative as when social or natural catastrophes negate an active position); or indirectly, when this principle engulfs an object of desire for a fictive person (such as the death of a baby, or a lover), and thereby annihilates its position as enac-tive subject defined by an object.

The second possibility may lead to static melancholia, as described below in 'Schizoid Fiction, Moods of Grief, and Static Melancholia'. To become a melodrama of the passive position, the identification-object must possess a certain degree of passive acceptance of the narrative fate. If the 'patient', the object, passively confronts the evil actions of the alien agents, as in paranoid horror-fiction, the emotional tone of the film changes. Active resistance to 'fate' creates a genre emotion. The 'catastrophe films' of the mid-1970s were often a mixture of melodramatic-passive emotion caused by a dramatic red alert combined with active-constructive tenseness.

The temporal aspect of passive melodrama is often one of pastness or atem-poral repetition, or 'iterative-durative'. A paradigm of this romantic melan-cholia is *Gone With the Wind*, in which grandiose subjects like History, Passion, and Nature (the 'wind' blowing the human leaves) move the objecti-fied human beings (for a more extensive analysis of the film, see Chapter 11). Both Daphne du Maurier's romantic melodrama *Rebecca* and Hitchcock's film version of the book are intent on creating the passive position from the very beginning, by emphasizing that the story is told *par derrière*, in a mood of loss, dream, and repetition. Loss and melancholia are also important func-tions in 'soap operas' and prime-time melodrama, as a means of introjecting emotions normally projected onto luxurious and beautiful settings. A viewer emptied by active projections of affect toward the object-world may need to reject an active relation to the world in order to be 'filled up again', even if this means giving up real-world possession for a mental possession of the objects as 'lost' in the world of action but stored in the long-term memory. Such use of a melancholic passive position has even pervaded a police drama like *Miami Vice* (see Grodal 1990).

Many 'naturalist' fictions are examples of a melodramatic passive position. Social institutions such as high-rise buildings (Guillermin's *The Towering Inferno*), mines and railway networks (Renoir's *La Bête Humaine*), 'degener-ation' and alcohol (Sirk's *Written on the Wind*), mental obsession (von Stroheim's *Greed*), or the body as an alien drive, are grandiose enactive prin-ciples,[8] and the objectified human beings are moved along and empathically 'move' the viewer. The rhythms of pulse and breathing are metaphors for enactive principles placing an objectified consciousness in a passive position (and, for example, body-rhythms can be mapped onto machine-rhythms, or vice versa). Frequently, body-rhythms and music-rhythms are connected. It is not without reason that melodrama means drama with music; but whether the rhythm of music represents enaction in an active or a passive position is deter-mined by contextualization.

---

[8] Cf. also Kracauer's description of the 'instinct theme' (1971: 96 ff.) *passim*.

FICTIONS OF HORROR

Fictions of horror are narratives in which the viewer identifies with a relatively 'passive' fictive object, who nevertheless has a relation of aversion or
ambivalence to the alien enactive forces of the narrative. The viewer models
the reactions of fear and possible defence. Prototypical narratives of horror
are versions of the Dracula legend or a film like Siodmak's *The Spiral
Staircase*. In the latter, the viewer identifies with a mute girl threatened by a
murderer, and, although all the hypothesis-machinery of possible defensive
acts is activated, lack of information and lack of 'offensive capabilities' make
the feelings of fear dominate the active strategies.

In the paranoid film, the viewer identifies with a perceptual 'object' which
has an ambivalent synecdochic-antithetic relation of paranoia and horror to
the 'subject', the villainous antagonist. Voluntary motor-reactions are often
negated by paralysis in the 'victim', and motor-subjectivity is only perceived
as an aspect of the exterior antagonist, 'the Other', whereas the viewer is overwhelmed by involuntary motor-reactions because of the lack of processing of
the input into active schemata. The viewer shivers, trembles, makes vasomotor contractions, breaks out in goose-pimples, and has other autonomic
reactions. This is a compromise between an active and a passive position, and
represents a 'negative' way of activating the viewer's awareness of his body.
In a sense, it is a perfect fictional structure for the creation of strong psychosomatic reactions, because it generates active as well as passive reactions. But,
to be pleasant, the high level of arousal in the horror fiction has to be hedonically re-evaluated, temporarily 'reversed' into a positive evaluation.

The inability of the 'agent' to act may be motivated in different ways. It
may be by purely physical means, as in Poe's tale *The Pit and the Pendulum*,
in which the hero is locked up and threatened without having any direct contact with the antagonists, and similarly in claustrophobic stories about being
buried alive. Or it can be motivated psychologically, as when the victim is
spellbound, or by the antagonist's being 'hypernatural' or 'supernatural'.
Hypernatural antagonists are typical of science-fiction horror, in which the
antagonist, as in *Them!* or *Alien*, works in a sophisticated way, supposedly
within the framework of the laws of nature. The supernatural antagonists,
however, work outside the laws of nature and are often characterized by specific modality-definitions: for example, they are visible but not tangible, or
they can be heard but not seen or touched. Horror is therefore caused by the
combination of the aversive nature of the antagonists and the breakdown of
systems of causality enabling acts to have effects on them. In supernatural
horror-fiction (for example, Gothic fiction, like the Dracula formula), the
ambivalent passive position is often transformed in the end into enaction by
use of symbolic-ritualistic causation, by rituals of metonymic chains of signi-

fiers (spells and prayers) or the rituals of Cross, garlic, and mutilations of the body of the Other.

The mechanisms of a 'paranoid' passive position can be illustrated by the phenomenon of fear of the dark. When the visual projection of emotions into a (deep-tense) space disappears, it produces for many people an increased awareness of the other more intimate senses of the body (touch, proprioception, hearing) because of the disappearance of enactive projection. When a person is afraid of the dark, this body-perception is heightened by production of imaginary enactive principles: weird subjectivities are 'out there' in the dark, trying to touch the terrified individual. The simulation of this experience in fiction can be explained as an effort at trauma containment by repetition in a controlled and distanced position.[9] But this is not the whole truth: real pleasures are released by a paratelic euphoric relabelling of the high level of arousal and the high level of autonomic body response. The use of the ambivalence of fear and pleasure associated with the passive position is well-known in amusement parks, with their instruments for breaking down enactive subjectivity, the roller-coaster being a prime example. The enactive control and projection are overruled and destroyed by the big Other of the roller-coaster.

Horror-fiction narratives have enjoyed widespread popularity, especially since the period known as pre-Romanticism, when the genre of Gothic fiction was created (see Punter 1980); these works were often written by women like Ann Radcliffe, author of *The Mysteries of Udolpho* (1794) and *The Italian* (1797), as articulations of conflicts between the active and the passive position. In 1897 Bram Stoker renovated the genre by enhancing the contrasts in his novel *Dracula*. Here the intellectual enaction and corporeal delimitation of modern London and modern England are strongly contrasted with pre-modern and infantile experiences of passivity symbolically emerging from feudal Transylvania and connected also with a brutal Renaissance aggression and unrestrained personal acting-out of impulses. The passive protagonists are threatened by the possibility of being eaten and touched; they are unable to fuse perceptual phenomena (such as ghosts) in over-determined wholes that can then be objects of enaction. In cinematic form, horror fiction caters for an audience of young people, and this accords very closely with the basis of the horror formula, which resides in an ambivalence between the active and the passive position and the problems of corporeal delimitation *vis-à-vis* the Other (that is, the other sex) in puberty.[10] For adults the genre is more likely to be viewed as a pleasurable antidote to 'neurotic' hyper-enaction, or as a thriller element in crime fiction.

---

[9] Grixti (1989: ch. 6) describes the relation between fear and cognitive control.

[10] Cf. Twitchell (1985: 87 f.) in which Van Gennep's theory of *rites de passage* is used in order to explain the link between horror fiction and puberty. A comprehensive registration of sexuality in horror fiction is made by Hogan (1986).

Horror fiction is also used as an affective antidote to hyper-projection and a 'reified charge' of desired but unattainable objects. The reified affections projected into the home and its beloved objects are 'liquidated': made liquid for introjection by destruction. Monsters or criminals destroy the hyper-charged belongings and, by the destruction of signifiers, the emotional charge is activated. Spielberg, in particular, has specialized in the destruction of transitional objects such as toys, and dolls as a tool for activating and 'recycling' the emotional charge of the objects of childhood and/or everyday life.

SCHIZOID FICTIONS, MOODS OF GRIEF, AND STATIC MELANCHOLIA

In melodrama of the passive position the viewer is moved and touched by grandiose enactive principles and abandons himself fatalistically. Although he has given up an active constructive attitude, he maintains an empathic identification with the object and its fortunes or misfortunes. But in schizoid horror-fiction the viewer 'evacuates' his empathic identification with the object of horrible misfortunes, although his attention is still 'focused' on the 'object' by a limited cognitive identification. This creates a schizoid viewer-situation, in which the viewer's relation is 'voyeuristic', that is, perceptual without empathic or fully cognitive identification. Several scenes in Lynch's *Blue Velvet* are schizoid horror: the viewer is supposed to look at scenes of violence in a perceptual-saturated state and without empathic identification.

The 'schizoid' withdrawal of empathy can be seen as one of several defence reactions (laughter being another) which function as an antidote to empathy (if we invariably felt total empathy for all five billion people on the planet, and maybe also empathy for animals or plants, we would suffer and would be unable to articulate our own interests). In 'good old films', genre expectations might well ensure that if a subject-actant is a 'nice guy' who evokes empathy all will turn out well for him, unless melodramatic markers indicate a passive, but motivated, tragic ending. But in modern schizoid fiction there is no such guarantee: several people dying in *Alien,* for example, are 'goodies'; the transformation of 'goodies' into zombies in *Dawn of the Dead* is not wholly justified by 'old standards' of poetic justice. If we do not wish to be hurt as viewers, we would do well to withhold our empathy. To do this, however, we may need some genre markers preventing us from making empathic identifications, thus transforming our construction of the film into perceptual-saturated patterns, because when the evil forces are let loose in psychotic fiction no protagonist is safe. There are, of course, also sadistic components in the consumption of schizoid fiction. To watch films like Cunningham's *Friday the 13th* presupposes that the viewer partly enjoys the destruction of the summer-camp inhabitants, and enjoys the negation of the pro-social Scout ethics; the protagonist aggression in action films is mostly 'motivated', and viewer-pleasure by the antagonist's suffering justified, whereas we are implicated in abnormal points of views in, for instance, splatter films.

In some respects schizoid fiction resembles synechdochic lyricism in its dominance of saturated perceptions, especially of the human face and body. The difference is that, whereas the synecdochic fusion with a perception of a human model 'out there' is constituted from an active position by the viewer, who is trying to put the pieces of the identity puzzle together to form a complete model of an empathically charged person in objective space, the schizoid position is a passive one, in which strong, invisible enactive forces mutilate and destroy everything in the fictive world.

The classic schizoid narrative is the split-personality story, like Stevenson's *Dr Jekyll and Mr Hyde*. The reader identifies by voyeurist distance with the hollow shell, Dr Jekyll, whereas the active subjectivity belongs to the repressed enactive principle, Mr Hyde. Similarly, the relation between Sherlock Holmes and Moriarty/Moran develops into schizoid horror, especially in 'The Adventure of the Empty House', which contains a scene in which a wax bust of Holmes is mutilated. Schizoid fiction is more affectively saturated than paranoid fiction, with its ambivalent evaluations of negative body experiences, because the relentless mutilation of objects of identification demands a withdrawal of identification and affective charge of all signifiers on the screen, to leave only 'empty shells' of what could optionally have been affectively-charged figures of identification. The process is easy to observe in Hamsun's novel *Hunger* and in Carlsen's film version, in which the point of identification has been withdrawn from the body-image of the protagonist and transformed into an identity mostly built up around the remote sense of vision. Visual perception of the protagonist's body and its sensual aspect of touch, taste, and interoception are not connected in such a way that they form part of a 'holistic' experience.

Schizoid fiction is especially widespread in modernist literature and in the schizoid visual-horror fiction of the last twenty years, a period in which there has been a trend away from paranoid toward schizoid horror-fiction in mass as well as in avant-garde films. Modernist literature in particular uses such fiction for the depiction of alienation and objectification, and Robin Wood has argued that even horror films like *The Texas Chainsaw Massacre* (mainly viewed by a lowbrow audience) are descriptions of patriarchy and capitalism.[11] I believe that their primary effect is to block empathy and to evoke saturated emotions. This can be done in order for the viewer to experience something about the non-fictive world, and also in order for him to experience the schizoid emotions (and the reason for this may be more or less ethical). For obvious social reasons, the schizoid genre is not appropriate for prime-time television or for family films, for example, unless 'framed', for

[11] Wood (1986: 87–94).

instance as 'human-interest documentary' or 'psychological realism'. However, elements of the genre are very often integrated into music videos and thrillers.

The tragic 'object' destruction in schizoid fiction is often strongly sequential: the evil thing or the social killer performs an endless sequence of murders and mutilations. But if a sequence of losses is slowed, so that a kind of empathy can be established before destruction, the film can create experiences of melancholia: states in which beloved objects are lost, but remembered in a passive way. This activates saturated feelings of grief by means of 'images' to which we can only have a 'perceptual' and 'empathic' but not an enactive relation, as explored in my analysis of *Miami Vice* (1990). The difference between moods of melancholia and tragic melodrama is that melancholia evokes saturations, whereas melodrama may equally evoke a dynamic autonomic reaction like tears. Static melancholia is a lyrical effect, and is often used in music videos.

COMIC FICTIONS

In some respects the comic modes and genres of fiction resemble its other 'psychotic' genres, but their effects are totally different. The comic effects are based on a rejection of empathic identification with subject-actants or rejection of cognitive schemata. Comic rejection is combined with strong autonomic outlet; there ensues laughter, even tears, and the vasomotors dilate to allow circulation of the blood. In this way the body creates a corporeal autonomy: it can experience satisfaction without an object. The comic is, in certain respects, a parasitic genre *vis-à-vis* the other genres. It releases affective charge projected by other means. Classic comedy has an intrigue and actions which are in some respects very similar to canonical narratives: subjects in tense quests for objects. But, in comic fiction, the tense charge is not released by letting the protagonists achieve their goal, but by a viewer-reaction: viewers laugh at protagonist failures, thus rejecting empathic identification with the protagonists and their acts and motives.

The rejection of diegetic identification is often compensated for by integration into a new real-audience identity by means of shared laughter. This is brought about automatically in a theatre, and is simulated in television shows by recorded laughter. Establishing real-world identification is important for triggering comic rejection, because, if identification with the fictive objects of disasters (persons rendered objects by body-mutilations or loss of a beloved thing or person) is established, the situation may become tragic-melancholic or schizoid. (It is well-known that paranoid and schizoid horror can be viewed either in a comic or tragic-psychotic mode, depending on viewer contextualization, as in the cliché 'I don't know whether to laugh or cry'.) Intake of alcohol by the viewers will often transform other genres into comic fictions. It is equally important to reject identification with an 'alien' mechanical enactive subjectivity and the lack of motor control that characterizes comic figures.

One of the means by which comic rejection is produced is by 'mirror' incongruence. Clowns have enormous red mouths and boots, underlining their status as physical objects beyond a human scale. In this respect the comic film resembles pornography, which blows up the physical dimensions of sexual parts of the body, thereby producing a maximum distance between viewer and body-object.

METAFICTION: DISTANCIATION, REAL-WORLD EMBEDDING, AND FRAMES

Except for comic rejection, the above-mentioned emotive structurations of fiction have been based on the responses of a viewer plunged into the world of fiction. There are, however, several modes of distancing based on a contextualization, a 'positioning' of the viewer in different 'extradiegetic' and more or less real-world contexts. The simplest mode is the 'exhibitionist' break of a representation-hypothesis, allowing protagonists on the screen or stage to address the viewer, and, by that, turn him into a real-world addressee. The address may be either explicit or implicit, as in entertainment shows, in which actors suppress mutual interaction in order to direct their eyes and words toward the viewers. Romantic fiction has in many ways heightened emotional projection into worlds of fiction, and romanticists have used the antidote of romantic irony, the breaking of 'illusion'.[12] This creates a real-world relation of interlocution, with all its forms of emotional charge, instead of creating emotions articulated within a hypothetical framework. The focus of attention is partly shifted to the viewer, and activates a 'proximal' self-awareness similar to the shift of attention we feel when suddenly spoken to in 'real life'. 'Live programmes' or simulations of 'live events' in fiction try to activate a participative, proximal, addressee self-awareness.

Mentally, the viewer needs to have two or more frames of meaning active at the same time: a proximal 'self-awareness' connected to subjective or objective associations and mental operations, and a 'distal' mental simulation of the hypothetical world. Activating the fiction and also the viewer 'self-awareness' may create an overall increase of activation, but will distract some attention from both frames.

Many authors, playwrights, and directors have attempted radical ways of breaking the spell of fiction and its salience in order to create what they conceive as realism. Brecht was one of the most outspoken (modernist) critics

---

[12] Cf. Wellek (1955: 309).

of the fiction of direct emotional involvement. The theatre should be didactic, he believed; and, in order to be so, distance and estrangement, *Verfremdung,* should be produced in the relation between spectator and fiction. A distance to the fictive world on the screen or stage can be produced by contextual 'frames' and embeddings that force the spectator to double his position of reception by creating an awareness of the reception-situation. Fellini's *8½* uses a wide variety of frames, embeddings, and other means of distancing, symbolically indicated at the beginning of the film by scenes of a traffic jam, with sound off and people caught incommunicado, creating an 'aquarium-like' effect. This blocking of enaction and empathic identification may have been part of a schizoid fiction, but the film then proceeds to show the making of a film, the film that becomes *8½.* It tries to create distance by showing that this is a film, a representation, not real life. The emotional effect of this distancing is to block enactive tensity and create saturation.

The embeddings of distancing can, for example, be contextual 'frames', like art, genre, reality, or markers of real-world author-director intention. The viewer of framed 'metafiction' has to look at the fiction via a 'persona' image of himself implied in the markers of reception context, for example by identifying himself with a viewer of art film or a scientifically detached observer of the sordidness of human nature. The attention and affective charge focused on special frames and on the viewer-as-observer persona will absorb part of the disposable attention and function as an emotional buffer or filter.[13]

Despite the strong critical interest in so-called 'transgressive values' in 'self-conscious' forms of fiction, metafunctions have been important devices in fiction for centuries (see, for example, Sterne's *Tristram Shandy*). The affective impact of the self-conscious distancing is often more important than the cognitive effect of the frequently rather uncomplicated devices producing the distancing.

The buffer zone created by the framing is sometimes a necessary defence mechanism to protect the reader or viewer.[14] The disruption of the affective bonds between reader and the read, viewer and the viewed is a 'modern', objectivist separation of subject and object. Realists and naturalists have often seen themselves as doctors making a 'clinical' analysis of their fellow-men and society, and this can be viewed as the production of a distancing reading position to counterbalance the affective impact of the new realism in fiction. To learn to appreciate certain types of fiction is not only to learn to 'understand' them but also to produce the necessary affective structures of reception. Lynch's *Blue Velvet* or Roeg's *Bad Timing* motivate their representation of sadism and near-necrophilism as descriptions of voyeurism, and therefore create a 'persona' for the viewer who is 'not just looking', for example, but

---

[13] Goffman describes the function of 'documentary' as an emotional buffer frame (1986: 70 ff.).

[14] As, for example, in the naturalism of Zola seen from a historical point of view.

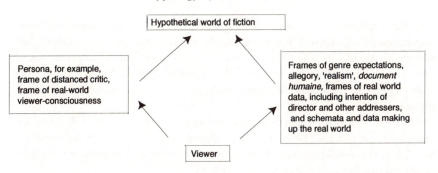

Fig 7.3 Metafictional filter frames inserted between viewer and the diegetic world. The filters may be special viewer-positions and/or special labels put on the visual product.

is acquiring 'knowledge about the nature of voyeurism' (*Bad Timing* lays bare this motivation yet further). There is no sharp line between distance created by visual, verbal, or acoustic marks in a film pointing to its reality-status as a representation (for example, by revealing camera or frame, or letting the film address the viewer) and distance created by marks of genre motivation.

Resnais' *Mon Oncle d'Amèrique* is in some respects an example of a self-conscious remake of the naturalist mode of representation, and illustrates the way in which naturalism may serve as an emotion-filtering meta-frame. The film provides 'samples' of different aspects of social life in France: country–city, upstairs–downstairs, new social types, old social types. We follow the lives of three people, but through frames creating emotional distance and cognitive analysis. One prominent frame is the real-life French scientist Henri Laborit, who, in inserted documentary sequences, tells us about animal behaviour, and the conditioning of rats, and their relevance for understanding human behaviour. An important part of our attention and emotional involvement is filtered by this 'frame', so that episodes and life-stories are shown as exemplifications of basic behaviour-schemata. We reduce our emotional involvement with the people who are conditioned by their biological structure, upbringing, class, and so forth because we see them through the emotional filters created by Laborit's and Resnais' 'cognitive insight'. Parallels between human and animal life (which in other contexts may function as a 'symbolic-metaphorical' extension of the diegetic life-world, providing it with mythical depth by rich associations) indicate the frame of knowledge. The bio-psychological angle is supported by self-consciousness in representation: the film points directly to the pre-existence of its scenes at the beginning of the film, as a moving 'iris' reveals many stills, thus existing achronically at the beginning (and the film ends pointillistically by showing the importance of distance in our perception of the seen). The film also shows samples of 'typical objects', such as a sewing-machine and a bicycle; this procedure further supports an 'anti-realist' experience of the film as being a collection of 'samples' selected by analytical and didactic procedures. Inserted film-sequences of old French films (especially those featuring Jean Gabin) are shown as models for the protagonists' behaviour and world-interpretation, and as sociologically and ideologically 'typical' mental forms. Films and stills have no 'facticity' of their own, but express socio-psychological processes.

Thus the emotions evoked by the narrative do not acquire full tense or autonomic forms; the 'filter' frame produces intense and saturated associations, and the distal fictional phenomena are experienced as proximal aspects of the viewer-persona activity.

'Affective realism' is based on a particular prototypical 'human scale of representation' which presupposes a certain amount of empathy and enaction. Creation of distance, in order to represent 'objectivity', will therefore often backfire. If, for instance, the hostile forces are grandiose, the representation will perhaps be experienced as similar to a 'dreamlike' state, complete with motor block, and will possibly be perceived as melodrama, static melancholia, or schizoid horror. I shall return to this problem in Chapter 11, in connection with elements of distancing in melodrama.

Schema 7.1 Genres and Moods in Schematic Form

lyricism	Perceptual, nonlinear time, networks of associations, fusion of world and mind, intensities or saturations by proximal focus of attention, no telic enaction, possibly paratelic or autonomic 'motion'
canonical narrative	Telic voluntary enaction, linear time, construction of objective world, cognitive and empathic identification with 'subject', tensity, distal focus of attention
obsessional narratives	Paratelic/involuntary enaction, often progressive–regressive or non-linear time, some saturations and proximal focus of attention
melodramas of passion	Perceptual, causal enaction, autonomic reaction, construction of subjective world, cognitive and empathic identification with 'object', fatalistic fusion of 'subject' and 'object', often 'retrospective' or non-linear time, saturations and autonomic response combined with proximal focus of attention
horror	Causal enaction, autonomic reaction, construction of subjective world, cognitive and empathic identification with object, aversion between subject and object, mostly linear time: tensities, saturations, or autonomic response, proximal focus of attention

schizoid	Causal enaction, construction of subjective world, cognitive identification with object, often non-linear time, fragmented space, intensities and saturations, proximal as well as distal focus of attention
comic	Causal and autonomic action, rejection of empathic identification with object, rejection of objective world, autonomic response
metafiction	Mediated identification with subjects and objects via cognitive and empathic 'frames' (personae, all types of schemata), several focuses of attention

Part IV

Laughter, Distance,
Horror, and Tears

8

Comic Fictions

This chapter argues that comic fictions and slapstick rely on cued viewer-reactions. It also argues against the different theories which attempt to find immanent, formal features distinguishing comic from other fictions. Viewer-reactions depend on a strong emotional arousal and on the performance of a reality-evaluation which is, as a rule, connected with an autonomic response: laughter.

A group of different fictional forms is normally given the common genre-label of comedy. Although comedy in principle is perceived as a narrative structure, by no means does it have a well-defined delimitation from other genre forms, such as action-adventure or romance (Neale and Krutnik 1990). The application of the genre-term 'comedy' is used to characterize some types of fiction that are produced for the purpose of evoking a comic effect for the viewer, rather than to describe clear, common, structural features. Mast's typology of comedy plots (1979) shows the structural diffuseness of the term 'comedy', and the difficulties of delimiting it from minor forms like slapstick. I have therefore chosen to use the term 'comic fiction' instead of the term 'comedy' in order to underline the reception process and its effect on the viewer.

'Comic fiction' is, in some respects, a diffuse joker term, like 'comedy', because comic reactions are elicited by a large and heterogeneous group of fictions. But the term 'comic fiction' highlights the dipolar aspect of the phenomenon: one pole represents the comic and humour as types of reaction correlated with pleasure, while the other represents the structural phenomena which often elicit laughter. The same phenomenon can be experienced as frightening or funny, depending on the contextual markers and the viewer's specific disposition of reception. An analysis of the comic will therefore be double-sided, comprising a description of the psychological mechanisms which are characteristic of the comic and connected with certain types of pragmatic behaviour, together with a description of the typical phenomena which elicit a humorous response.

LAUGHTER AS A HYPOTHESIS OF REALITY-STATUS AND AS AUTONOMIC
RESPONSE

Just as the characteristic feature of horror fiction is that it evokes fear in the
addressee of the visual and/or verbal message, the characteristic feature of
comic fiction is that it evokes a certain reaction in the addressee. The reaction can be weak, expressed by a smile, or strong, expressed by a roar of
laughter. One way to try to determine what constitutes a comic reaction is
therefore to describe the psycho-physiological reactions of smile and laughter
and, at the same time, the characteristic phenomena which evoke the psycho-
physiological reaction. As man is the only animal capable of laughing, it is
possible that laughter and humour are connected with the higher cognitive
faculties which distinguish us from other species.

The body-parts primarily involved in the smile and laughter functions, that
is, the face and the respiratory passages, are also involved (via facial expressions and language) in higher social communication, which has reached per-
fection in humans. Smile and laughter also have communicative functions, as
well as functions connected with voluntary cognition. Newborn babies have
smile reflexes, whereas their capacity to laugh is developed later. To smile
consists of the contraction of certain facial muscles, and this leads to a greater
or lesser laying-bare of the teeth and mouth. According to van Hoof and
others, the smile has developed from the prosimian and monkey grin which
functioned as an expression of fear, into the grin of the apes for whom it
assumes the functions of submission, appeasement, and affection (see
Chevalier-Skolnikoff 1973). Laughter consists of rhythmic contractions of the
diaphragm and the respiratory passages with corresponding utterance of
sounds, and the ape 'root' of this is the 'play face'. In man, smile and laughter have become a continuum, whereas 'grin' and 'play face' have distinct
functions in apes. As discussed in Chapter 1, 'play' and 'hypothesis' are members of a family of specifications of reality status, just as showing appeasement and affections by simulating a fear reaction is a 'communicative
hypothesis'; the common denominator of 'grin', 'play face', and the human
smile–laughter continuum seems to be the redefinition of reality-status, often
with the purpose of expressing and communicating non-threat and non-
aversion.

Searle (1969) has described language from the point of view of speech-acts.
Searle describes illocutionary speech-acts like promises and naming, in which
language has not only a representative function, but also functions as an act,
whereas perlocutionary speech-acts describe language from the point of view
of its impact on the addressee. We could describe the psychological aspect of
the comic as the way smile and laughter function as special, illocutionary
speech/mental acts performed by the viewer, and by which a phenomenon is

evaluated as 'not fully real'. The textual pole of the comic is represented by the perlocutionary strategies used to elicit the illocutionary viewer-act. The advantage of speaking of laughter as an illocutionary act is that by so doing we separate the reaction from its cause. One person laughs at an event that makes another person cry; the reactions are different, the cause is the same, but the laughing person has redefined the reality-status of the cause.

The main function of smile and laughter as messages consists in signalling such messages as non-aversion, and sympathy; but, paradoxically, the two reactions can also convey the opposite message, such as laughing scornfully or making somebody looking ridiculous. The philosopher Hobbes even considered a feeling of superiority, a 'sudden glory', to be the central aspect of laughter. Why does the same reaction signal two seemingly opposite messages? A preliminary answer is that the positive-conjunctive as well as the negative-aversive use of smile and laughter signal an unthreatening relationship between subject and object, either because the subject feels some sympathy for the object, or because the subject experiences, or signals the experience, that the object is 'without any importance' and therefore not worthy of genuinely aversive reactions. A common denominator for the 'positive' and the 'negative' use of smile and laughter could be 'relaxation', pleasure by a reduction of a tense object-world-directed or self-directed attitude.

Smiles, and especially laughter, are normally understood as relatively involuntary reactions; we can if we wish produce a fake smile or laugh (a sham smile, a forced laugh), in order to try, for communicative reasons, to simulate bodily reactions. But, unlike infectious laughter, which suggests that genuine laughter can be triggered in a passive addressee by his hearing the laughter of another person, the willed and intended emission of smile and laughter is evaluated as not genuine; smile and laughter ought to be connected with involuntarily controlled, affective processes. There are good reasons for this: the genuine smile uses muscles controlled by the autonomic nervous system, and the voluntary smile has to use different facial muscles (see Damasio 1994: 139–43). The emphasis on autonomic reaction in laughter and smile differs from the common evaluation of the emission of signs of, for example, hate and other types of aversion; for those, the communicative emission of signs of hate can be based on anything from a spontaneous to a calculated reaction, but the degree of spontaneity does not play a major role in the evaluation of the reaction.

Reactions of laughter therefore seem to demand a certain switching-off of conscious and voluntary forms of reaction. This is evident from the fact that laughter demands social circumstances and a certain passivity in the laughing person; Freud (1960) drew attention to the fact that, to evoke laughter by jokes and funny stories, the person who is supposed to laugh should be a listener, a person other than the teller of tales and jokes. The conscious and goal-directed effort and control required in telling a story seem to be incompatible with the passive and non-conscious, trigger-mechanisms of laughter. From this fact we cannot, however, infer that the comic depends on irrational and non-cognitive processes; most cognitive, rational processes are non-conscious.

In Chapter 5, I analyzed the way in which voluntary reactions presuppose objective mental models in which a model subject produces teleological cognitive relations and motor relations directed to models of goal-scenarios and target objects. Involuntary reactions do not presuppose objective models and do not require imagined or perceived external objects. As a preliminary hypothesis I suggest, therefore, that the mechanism of laughter has been developed in connection with problems in the functioning of the mental architecture using objective, teleological, and voluntary mental models. The bale-out markers in the playful mode of a hypothetical status of behaviours have been generalized, so that all mental phenomena can be marked as 'hypothetical = non-real', and so that laughter, among other functions, serves as an 'escape-button' in relation to the voluntary system of consciousness, including empathic identification.

I thus assume that laughter, like other types of autonomic response, is a reaction to overload, an 'escape-button alternative' to voluntary reactions. The basis of the overload is, as for other autonomic responses, a general psychosomatic agitation: arousal. I further assume that the reaction of laughter is an illocutionary act, which says that: *the cause of the arousal is for the time being hypothetical, it is 'not real' ('not real', meaning 'not for the time being a cause of voluntary acts with full intent')*.

The advantage of these hypotheses compared with other explanations of the comic is that they clearly separate three matters: the cause of the arousal/overload; the arousal; and the reactions to the arousal.

Two basic comic situations are shock by surprise and reaction to extremely painful or embarrassing situations. In slapstick comedies the viewers are surprised and 'shocked' when the 'bad guy' suddenly turns up at an unexpected moment or from an unexpected direction. We are surprised by the punchline of a joke. We make mock-frightening sounds to children. We laugh when a clown hits himself with a hammer or falls off a chair. These different situations all cause strong arousal, but they do not necessarily cause laughter. On the contrary, small children may feel frightened and start to cry as a result of surprise or painful situations. The same cause and the same situations often lead to different reactions. Furthermore, the many different causes of laughter have only one element in common: they create a degree of arousal. It is therefore important to distinguish between causes and reactions.

Compared with Freud's theory concerning the joke, my hypothesis of the comic as a redefinition of reality-status has the advantage of being more general. It does not presuppose that arousal is connected with suppressed drives or with super-ego functions. Arousal can be connected with a broad spectrum of phenomena, from perceptual shock and cognitive overload to empathy, fear, and sex.

The temporal redefinition of reality-status by laughter may serve many different purposes, not just aggression. Freud claimed that an essential aspect of humour is aggression, and this position has been reasserted by Neale and Krutnik (1990, for example: 75 ff.). The comic-aggression position is linked to a claim that, when somebody laughs, narcissism triumphs and denies reality itself, for instance by repressing castration and death. The problem about this attitude is that it links a temporary redefinition of reality-status to a denial of reality itself (and fails to recognize the role of smile and laughter when positive interpersonal relations are established).

In order to examine difficulties inherent in the Freudian approach to understanding reality, I would like to return to the phenomena of playing, planning, and hypothesis-making discussed in Chapter 1. When playing, animals and humans try out various behaviour patterns, such as 'hunting', 'playing mothers and fathers', and so on. When 'planning', humans try out different possible acts. Playing, hypothesis-making, and planning are not fully 'real' acts and they can be fun; but, at the same time, the hypothetical acts are part of a cognitive mastery of reality, not a repression of it.

The special types of hypothetical situations, stories, and acts that we call comic all evoke arousal, and sometimes the cause of arousal is sadism, lack of empathy with the sufferings of the clown. But, at other times, it is the acting-out of desires or tender feelings, and the reactions may possess tones of desire or tenderness. On yet other occasions it is the playing with words or the result of the advent of surprising new events that is central to the comic situation. Nothing in general can be said about the relation between the comic and aggression, or whether the comic serves as an insight into, or the suppression of, reality. Freud's, Neale's, and Krutnik's problematic assertions derive from the misleading romantic dualism of pleasure versus reality, which haunts many theories relating to media products. Pleasure and unpleasure, or pain, are positions in an innate motivation-system supporting survival. Pain, death, or 'castration' are neither more nor less 'real' than pleasure.

Many descriptions of comedies assert that the comic reaction is connected to a basic narrative feature, for instance the existence of a sudden change or reversal (often called 'peripeteia'), as in the punchline. The triggering of the involuntary reaction often seems to presuppose a surprise or shock, an overload of the voluntary system. We know the ludic use of surprise and shock in its simplest form in the above-mentioned games, which involve surprising, mock-frightening acts that result in pleasure. A sudden and unexpected stimulus cannot immediately be subject to a full cognitive analysis, and the surprise thus creates a strong arousal. But the surprising event is very quickly provided with a label and a corresponding autonomic response: either the stimulus and the arousal are labelled danger-fear, or the opposite, resulting in laughter. One of the most basic forms of comic surprise in visual fiction is the appearance of a person or an object at an unexpected time or from an unexpected direction, as used in action comedy and silent film. More complicated types of shock are produced when a given line of thought or a given interpretation of a situation is suddenly and radically changed in the course of the narrative progression, so that what has led up to the point of surprise looks rather like misdirection. This creates arousal; first, because the tensity of the telos-directedness of the first line of thought has been 'set free' by the sudden discrediting loss of its target image; secondly, by the arousal resulting from the cognitive overload caused by having to regroup the representations. This also takes place on the narrative macrolevel: at the conclusion of *The Treasure of the Sierra Madre,* the gold dust, for which three men have worked and suffered for many months, is blown away, and this sudden disappearance of a tense goal elicits laughter, as the men are left to regroup their representations of past, present, and future events and goals.

The overload can have strong affective dimensions, as when the authoritarian general suddenly loses his trousers and appears as an ordinary human being. It can often be produced by short-circuiting cognitive processes, as when a word with several meanings first seems to possess one meaning and then suddenly another. The overload can be intensified if one of the meanings of the ambiguous words or representations 'in itself' is heavily charged with affect, as in the case of sexual ambiguities. The bad narrator and the bad director allow the addressee time to guess the outcome and to establish possible mental representations, so that the shock-effect and the laughter-effect disappear. An overload-relabelling theory of laughter has the advantage *vis-à-vis* a psychoanalytical theory (which regards the effect as caused by unconscious, repressed material): it can explain why many events and phenomena evoke laughter, although they do not contain any repressed material.[1]

A turning-point of shock will often be a precondition for the build-up of arousal resulting in a powerful reaction of laughter, but many arousals resulting in reactions of laughter are caused by more continuous phenomena, typically situations in which the viewer possesses information that the protagonists do not have, and can therefore, over an extended period of time, witness the foolish consequences of wrong hypotheses. This is the case in a scene from *The 39 Steps* in which an innkeeper interprets the closeness caused by handcuffs as a sign of love, whereas the viewer knows the truth (see Carroll

---

[1] Actually such a theory is closer to one line of Freud's own ideas developed in the conclusion of 1960, in which he broadens the perspective to the comic and humorous, which he explains as savings in energy of representation and empathy. These ideas are more general than his main approach.

1991). The numerous comic fictions based on mistaken identity over a prolonged period of time do not generally have marked turning-points. It is the high level of arousal in combination with the comic label and the autonomic response that is the distinctive feature of the comic, and shock is one means of producing arousal; however, the opposite of shock, namely expectations of comic events, can have the same effect. Many comic sequences are marked from the beginning as 'passive, comic hypotheses', for example by exaggerated gestures and movements and/or by lack of goal-directed elements. These markers reduce the cognitive and affective identification, and the viewer does not need special points of distancing. In *The Man With Two Brains*, Steve Martin carries out two brain operations at the same time, using exaggerated and jerky movements; we do not consider the scene to be a fully goal-directed act, but rather a series of expressive, paratelic acts characterizing the person; and we can therefore laugh during his activities, without first mentally identifying with the person and project and then being jolted by shock into a comic mood. When we watch a comic chase like the one at the end of Tashlin's *The Disorderly Orderly,* in which those involved very quickly lose all control over the outcome, we soon give up our voluntary reactions and our teleological modelling of the events and laugh at them, and in this way bale out of the impossible job of making full, realistic sense of the sequence. We could say that the whole film is made up of peripeteias, but then peripeteia becomes just another word for a new event which produces arousal. It is therefore not a necessary element in the comic, and can be substituted by other events producing arousal.

THE COMIC AND LAUGHTER AS ESCAPE-BUTTONS FOR MENTAL OVERLOAD

Many researchers, such as Kant, Schopenhauer, Freud, and Koestler (see Horton 1991: 5 f.), have pointed to a relation between the comic and paradoxes and incongruences. Freud (1960) sums up some of the typical theories, such as 'playful judgement', 'contrast of representations', and 'sense in non-sense'. More recently, Greimas has described humour in jokes as caused by a break of semantic isotopy, that is, the coexistence of two incompatible systems of meaning within the same section of the text (1966: 70 f.), and I have described elsewhere the way in which the break of isotopy could be described as a double isotopy, a dominant and a dominated, the latter being brought to our attention by the joke (Grodal and Madsen 1974). Greimas' joke-example deals with the signifier 'toilettes', in French having two signifieds, 'fashionable ladies' wear' and 'water closet', which yield two widely different interpretations of a given utterance. One person states his admiration for a stylish party and its beautiful 'toilettes', the other interrupts with the remark that he

has not been there yet. Whereas the misunderstanding and the correct understanding in *The 39 Steps* is obvious to the viewers right from the beginning,
the two interpretations of the clothes–toilet ambiguity each have a kind of
probability, and the last statement might be interpreted as having a polemical
edge. Koestler and Palmer have argued that the comic is very often based on
'false syllogisms', two statements that at one level are contradictory but at
another level compatible, because the reasoning seems to have a touch of
probability.

   If the brain is confronted with a problem which has two or more equally
probable but different solutions, or two heterogeneous representations, it
could, in principle, proceed to endless calculations. This is sometimes the case
in certain reactions to ambiguous signifiers in horror films and thrillers, in
which we have more unknowns than equations, so that some viewers either
react by endless speculations or by the invention of 'superstitious' hypotheses.
Laughter may function as an escape-button in relation to paradoxes, ambiguities, equally probable alternatives, and so on by cutting the Gordian knot,
that is, by rejecting the mental calculation, just as we sometimes have to turn
off the computer if it is running wild and producing endless calculations. The
story about Buridan's donkey, which died of hunger because it was unable to
decide which of two equally attractive heaps of hay it should eat, shows the
possibly paralyzing effect of choice and cognitive loops.

   That a given comic situation has contrasts, sense in nonsense, paradoxes,
and so forth does not mean that it represents 'irrational' or 'paradoxical'
problems in an absolute sense. A widespread but erroneous conception of
'rationality' understands it as an essence, a fixed standard, that we can use
independently of the actual situation and the time that is at our disposal for
rationalization. But John R. Anderson (1990b) has pointed out that rationality has a 'price' in the given situation, consisting of the amount of information to be gathered and the calculation-time we will spend on a given problem.
As we are always placed in a situation of limited resources, we must ask ourselves how much calculation-time, calculation-capacity, and information-
gathering we are willing to spend on a given problem in order to acquire the
optimal basis for a decision. Often it will be necessary to make a quick
decision. Seen against this background, many comic grotesques are not
expressions of mysterious and irrational phenomena, but expressions of the
pleasure of accepting the shock-like 'incomplete rationality', and rejecting a
serious calculation of the problems involved. Incomplete rationality is produced continuously, because rationality takes time and the amount of information often surpasses the actual processing-time available. For good reasons,
the consciousness must make fast decisions in the period of transition; new
turns, new interpretations, which, given a longer period of decision, would be
totally rejected or rationalized into a holistic framework of interpretation,
could for a short time assume abnormally high probability or appear to be

paradoxical, because lower cognitive functions do the processing. The comic bale-out mechanism is an efficient way of making mental priorities, and can also be used with a ludic purpose.

Pleasure is often connected with invalidating oppositions and alternatives. Thinking demands energy, tenseness, and concentration, for instance by the energy used in rejecting non-pertinent connections and associations; any goal-directed, sequential line of thought needs a constant rejection and blocking of all alternative trajectories. The invalidation of choices and rejection of alternatives will therefore be experienced as relaxation, and may be labelled positively (although it is important to bear in mind that tensity can also be labelled in this way).

Some researchers, such as Palmer (1987: ch. 2), have claimed that the basic structure of all humour is the paradox. To Palmer, the absurd core of humour rests on a pair of syllogisms, of which one is true or probable, whereas the other is false or improbable but has a certain surface-probability. This description is problematic for two reasons. First, humour and the comic are primarily mental reactions, not formal structures, and, as we have seen, phenomena like the paradox can cause widely different reactions. Paradox is therefore one among several factors that elicit laughter, given that textual clues and/or viewer disposition favours a comic reaction. Secondly, many phenomena that often provoke laughter, for example a surprising appearance from an unexpected direction or clownish deviations from prototypical appearances (long noses, big lips, big feet, clumsy acts, and flatulations) do not fit particularly well into the syllogistic form. These phenomena could perhaps be described by means of syllogisms, but are more simply described as different types of deviation that for various reasons evoke arousal, whereas the way in which the arousal is labelled is similar.

That the labelling of the overload is central to the comic, whether it is caused by affective, cognitive, or perceptual means, is even more obvious when the comic is seen in connection with other members of the entertainment family. Many market-place fun activities produce overload by surprise and strong perceptual stimulation. The continuous change of direction on a roller-coaster ride creates continuous changes of orientation that break down a teleological intentionality, so that we can only abandon ourselves passively to the changes, with pleasure or unpleasure. Halls of mirrors and surprising, mock-frightening phenomena have the same effect of creating overload. In normal, intentional states of consciousness there is a tense directedness toward an object of perception or cognition. It takes time to shift program, and a sudden surprising new input causes a strong increase in arousal, which only after a while can be processed cognitively.

THE COMIC AND LAUGHTER AS ELEMENTS IN REACTIONS OF PLEASURE

A characteristic feature of smile-and-laughter processes is that they are the primary concomitant phenomena of pleasure situations. Laughter is also characterized by an autonomic reaction: vasomotor dilation, which brings blood to the surface of the skin and produces the well-known flushing associated with joy and laughter. Smile and laughter thus belong to those parasympathetic reactions which accompany incorporation, corporeal restoration, and from relaxation, and which arise, for example, from motor activity, and from the parasympathetic, integrative aspect of erotic processes.

I shall make a digression here to deal with pleasure and unpleasure in general, thus expanding my analysis in Chapter 2, because of the importance of hedonic features in the understanding of the comic. The almost hegemonous conceptualization of pleasure in the humanities has for decades been a variation of the early concepts put forward by Freud (before he made his hypothesis of the death instinct). From this Freudian point of view, unpleasure has its cause in repression, in the interference of social forces and natural conditions alien to the embodied psyche, whereas pleasure is the basic condition of the non-repressed individual. Freud's descriptions take their point of departure in the development of the individual, so that although interference with the individual's wish to achieve pleasure might in principle be described in functional terms, the concrete descriptions have a dual structure of pleasure-principle versus reality-principle understood as a social and cultural interference. The dominant neuropsychological conceptualization of pleasure and unpleasure is quite different. Pleasure and unpleasure mechanisms are regarded as built-in, oppositely directed, stop-go mechanisms that serve to maintain the psychosomatic homeostasis. Important centres for the regulation of sex, temperature, thirst, and hunger, as well as the basic aversive reactions, are located in the brain-structure hypothalamus (Vincent 1990: 150 ff.). The 'needs', as expressed in these centres, are specific, but, at the same time, these central states seem to be part of the dipolar system of assimilation–approach–attraction as opposed to 'dissimilation'—avoidance–attack–exhaustion, states that are manifested peripherally as well. It is therefore untenable to motivate all types of inhibitions with mental categories of social origin; although the specific inhibition may be socially conditioned, the mechanisms of inhibition are innate and have no special links to sexuality.

The body and the consciousness have some aversive functions, which can be subdivided into passive and active aversions. Passive-aversive functions prevent unwanted substances and objects from entering or penetrating the subject. The aversive function can be the immune defence system; it can be 'disgust', or vomiting of unwanted, perhaps, poisonous, substances; regulation of appetite, so that excessive weight is avoided; pain, to avoid body mutilation; and aversive reactions supporting the avoidance of unwanted sexual penetration—invagination—or of unwanted information. The higher forms of passive, aversive arousal are typically hedonically labelled unpleasure; they activate the sympathetic nervous system and support the voluntarily controlled, striated muscles, but will also often find an autonomic outlet, as in fear.

'Aversion' may also have an active form in all the activities that imply telic (or paratelic) schemata and active-voluntary use of striated muscles or sequential-telic cognitive procedures, from thinking about chess problems to playing ball-games, from pursuit of mating partners to killing and destroying. These activities also activate the sympathetic nervous system. The typical hedonic labelling is context-dependent: if the activity is 'felt as' voluntary, the experience of the aversive activity is predominantly labelled pleasure; but if it is 'felt as' a quasi-passive, forced activity, the experience is predominantly labelled unpleasure, although, as we have seen in melodrama, for example, re-evaluations take place.

Body and mind also have some conjunctive and incorporative functions that ensure that necessary substances, objects, and information are internalized in the psychosomatic system. The functions of incorporation are, as stated above, supported by the parasympathetic nervous system and lead to a relaxation of the voluntary, striated muscles, and they are hedonically labelled as pleasure, although pleasure may also have points of satiety that lead to a relabelling of relaxation as unpleasure.

The active-aversive and the incorporative reactions are meanwhile functionally linked: tense food gathering or hunting is linked to eating, and the tense erotic directedness toward a sexual object in 'outer space' is linked to parasympathetic erotic reactions that destroy tense-aversive reactions. Although the link seems to be a means-end link, the old questions of whether we live to eat or eat to live, or which came first, the chicken or the egg, point to the fact that 'tension' and 'relaxation' are states within an ongoing fluctuation; and although 'incorporation' and 'relaxation', for instance in smile and laughter, are often conceived as more genuine pleasure than tense coping, this hedonic evaluation depends on the 'fluctuating' context, as in the unpleasant eating-vomiting scene in Monty Python's *The Meaning of Life*. Switching from tense activities to 'relaxed' activities or the reverse is therefore primarily a switch of program, whereas the hedonic tone will be provided contextually. The 'relaxation' caused by the disappearance of the goal of the gold in *The Treasure of the Sierra Madre* could have been contextualized with a negative hedonic tone, so that the program-switching laughter would be tragihysterical, instead of being given a more positive hedonic tone as opening up 'paratelic living' in a Mexican paradise.

Laughter, the comic-playful cognitive re-evaluation of the reality-status of phenomena, is one of the main program-switches by which a given mental representation can be evaluated as 'non-dangerous', 'not cause for acts', and 'non-real' in the sense that it does not trigger voluntary acts. Because most of these switches are evaluated as pleasant, laughter is mostly a pleasant experience; but hysterical laughter clearly functions as a safety-valve for unpleasant events by judging them unreal, and hysterical laughter is probably no more pleasant than crying.

Most parasympathetic reactions of incorporation are closely connected with the contact senses of touch, taste, and smell, and the problems of how to activate parasympathetic reactions in audiovisual fiction are therefore greater than those of how to activate sympathetic reactions of aversion that are more closely connected with the exterior world and the remote senses of hearing and seeing. Most pornographic films are unable to trigger full parasympathetic reactions, because the activities take place 'out there' (and, in these films, attempts are often made to circumvent the problem by staging masochistic, passive situations in order to tone down voluntary reactions). Although food has become a major topic in many recent films, such as several directed by Greenaway, and is perhaps the main subject of commercials, viewer reactions are probably not parasympathetic. The comic is the main type of parasympathetic simulation of pleasure suited to fictional representation because of its 'switch function', and because it relates to exterior or voluntary cognitive phenomena, but by a process of negation.

Many different functional fields (such as food, sex, and body integrity) share the fundamental mental models of incorporation versus dissociation. For this reason, aspects of one field of behaviour can be a model for another field of behaviour. These models have various names: taxonomies (Greimas), paradigms, and mythical structures (Lévi-Strauss 1967), or mental categories (Lakoff). Appetite for food can be a cognitive and an affective model for sexual desire and vice versa (Grodal and Madsen 1974: 182 *passim*); a wish for motor exercise can be interpreted sexually. The given context determines which category/taxonomy will be the basis for the dominant field of attention and which category will serve as an illustrative metaphoric mental model for the dominant field.

Laughter can exercise its function as program-switcher by negating one program to open another. In *Bringing Up Baby*, Cary Grant is a scientist working on the restoration of a dinosaur. The work as such has many gratifying elements: Grant is genuinely excited when he finds out that a missing bone in the construction of the dinosaur has been found, so this telic activity is not painful on the whole. Nevertheless it has some unfree aspects, linked to his rigid fiancée and her ambitions. The scenes of laughter and ridiculousness open the way for a new project: sexual union with Katherine Hepburn. In the final scene their happy confessions of mutual love lead to the destruction of the dinosaur. The cause of arousal by this destruction of many months of tense work is that the object is denied 'reality' by comic illocution; the arousal is fused with eroticism and arousal caused by fear of falling (by the rhythmic rocking of a ladder). But that does not mean that the pleasures of recreating dinosaurs were only anal, super-ego unpleasures, or that the fear of falling from the ladder was only sexual inhibition. The plot makes the comic mood serve as a switch from a program of work to one of love, but, had the plot been constructed in another way, the comic could have been used as a switch from being lovesick to being involved in gratifying work.

THE COMIC AND LAUGHTER AS REGULATORS OF EMPATHIC IDENTIFICATION

The mental states and processes connected with smile and laughter play an important role in the regulation of empathic identification. When, as discussed in Chapter 4, we relate non-interactively to a fellow being, we try to produce an emotional simulation, which may vary from total 'compassion' to total rejection. When a clown is put into painful situations, small children and some adults will react with total compassion and cry out of sympathy with the clown and his pain. Given the right markers, however, the typical audience will reject an empathic identification by laughing at the clown. This rejection is rather brutal, but the laughing mechanism of rejection-empathy is probably a necessary defence developed as a stop-mechanism, parallel to the development of the sophisticated human faculty of self-consciousness and empathy. An all-embracing empathy with the sufferings of fellow human and animal beings would probably lead to dysphoria and permanent depression. Total compassion would also block the ability to recognize that man is not only a consciousness, but also an object among other objects in space. When clowns beat each other over the head, or when cartoon figures are transformed, smashed, or moulded into the most improbable shapes, it is not fair to evaluate these activities as merely sadistic. The empathy-break of comic situations enables a cognitive exploration of the materiality and object-status of man.

Although the basic mechanisms of empathy are probably innate, the specific regulation of empathy is certainly social. We do not have the same lack of inhibition about laughing at the deformed or disabled as people in previous centuries did. Lynch's film *The Elephant Man* illustrates two different norms of relating to deformed people: the historical early rejection of empathy, as expressed by the audience at the fair, and the empathic attitude, expressed by the educated and upper classes. Because of the social character of the regulation of empathy, comic fictions and comic situations are especially dependent on a social contextualization of reception. Whereas the effect of horror films might even be strengthened by a solitary situation of reception, the effect of the comic is enforced by a social negotiation of the rules and limits of empathy, for instance by shared laughter in the cinema. As I have pointed out elsewhere, most television producers prefer to add recorded laughter to the sound-track of situation comedies, in order to control the optimal situation of reception, whereas a track labelled 'fear' is never added to horror films; music and special sound-effects serve as expressive means of evoking the right emotional response, but these means are not anchored by staging a hypothetical situation of reception.

Palmer (1987) has argued against an element of emotional insulation in humour and jokes. He considers humour as functioning by a logical discrepancy between two opposed 'syllogisms', each of which has a certain degree of probability. Palmer calls this effect 'the logic of the absurd'. He argues, for instance (p. 17), that the laughter-evoking features of a story (about a woman at the zoo who falls over in front of an orang-utan which threatens to have intercourse with her, whereupon her husband advises her to tell the animal that she has a headache) only consist in the logical-absurd, not in emotional features. Many women, according to Palmer, find the story funny, and Palmer does too; and it is important for him to assert that we do not necessarily have to be sexist in order to laugh at the story. His main argument is that it is impossible to believe the story: no husband would behave in this manner, and therefore the situation is absurd. Later, he argues that absurdism serves as 'insulation' to avoid empathic phenomena being taken seriously, and in this way we can laugh at the unreal. Palmer's point of departure resembles a modernist reversal of Freud's position: Freud's point is that the joke-work 'insulates' the discharge of tendentious pleasure from the sanctions of the social, super-ego structures of inhibition. Palmer's reversal consists in saying that the formal elaboration in the joke and in humour insulates us from a serious interpretation of funny stories, because the joke-'work' (the formal elaboration) with its absurd blend of probability and improbability, insulates us from interpreting the content (for example, possible strong elements of aggression, pain, and obscenity) as real.

The hypothesis of the absurd insulation does not seem to be convincing. By such a concept of reality all the meanings in figurative and allegorical forms of representation would be 'unreal', because they differ from everyday realism. The funny story has two opposed descriptions of sexual behaviour: a 'natural' behaviour, in which women voluntarily or involuntarily take a position of lordosis while being mounted by strong males, and a cultural behaviour, in which sexual intercourse is blocked by the combination of female aversion and male resignation. The story first evokes sexually charged pictures, but then admits that private reality is very different. In the punch-line of the story, the fictive narrator further admits that he does not resort to rape, but accepts a female rejection. The content is far less absurd than many other figurative and allegorical tales and legends which could evoke a religious mood (Jesus is God, Jesus is human, Jesus is dead, Jesus is alive).[2] Despite Palmer's criticism, Freud's empathic and moral point about jokes is still the best hypothesis: the jokes, the elaborations in the funny texts, may, under certain circumstances, provide social acceptability for thoughts and imaginings that would be rejected under others.

The hypothesis of comic insulation presupposes that absurdity and irreality are of the meanings of the narrative, not properties of the mechanisms of reception. Laughter and humour are, however, 'performatives', acts by which the laughing person rejects implications of the reality of and the responsibility for the stated meanings, a kind of bracketing procedure or a frame which provides social acceptability, for example with respect to a temporary withdrawal of empathic identification. If a clown hits his finger with a hammer, the clumsiness and pain as 'meaning' are not absurd; they are real, but the situation allows us to avoid taking them 'for real'.

The bracketing procedure of laughter allows the phenomena to exist in consciousness as special mental models that, for instance, give social sanction to a temporary withdrawal of empathic identification. The conditions of the brackets allow the models of behaviour to be used for autonomic pleasure, but they are not to be applied in a way that hypothetically or actually simulates voluntary motor behaviour. Many cartoons comprise representations of hate, aggression, violence, and lack of empathy, and the 'comic' markings indicate that the behaviour is not supposed to be applied in real life, although the use of violence and lack of empathy are not themselves especially uncommon or unreal aspects of behaviour.

The comic transformation implied in the empathic side of comic performatives therefore implies a mental simulation of the sequence:

Subjective goals of action → motor response → object

transformed into a mental simulation of the bracketed sequence:

(Subjective goals of action → motor response → object) → autonomic response by laughter.

The mental evaluation of the status of reality of a given experience is thus not necessarily a function of its actual reality,[3] but of its consequences for mental and physical acts: I could experience many descriptions of the construction of cosmic space as unreal, because they have no consequences for my physical actions or for my ordinary cognitive processes. But, for an astronomer, a given model of space might create order in many instrument-readings and in many observations recorded in professional contexts, and therefore the model would be experienced as real for him, especially if it also implied hints as to the potential for new practical activities.

---

[2] Cf. Olson's criticism of founding the comic only on the concept of paradox (1968: 9 ff.).

[3] Cf. also the effect on reality-evaluation made by various drugs or alcohol, which are often concomitant with laughter and seem to point to 'reality-evaluation' as a specific mental function.

Laughter is a built-in, innate faculty; but the signals, formats, themes, and so on which allow the reaction of laughter depend on social negotiation on many levels. Laughter can also be a phase of transition to a cognitive and empathic reorientation, as when laughter is transformed into ridicule, which is then transformed into real, strongly aversive acts, such as the demonstration in the novel and film *Lord of the Flies* of the way in which ridicule functions as a transitory stage between civilized behaviour and primitive sadism. 'Comic brackets' can be placed or removed, in accordance with contextualizations and the dispositions of the addressee.

Both cognitive and empathic identification are involved in the comic relation to human models, to representations of the human body, and especially to representations of the human face. Any culture has prototypical concepts of the visual image of humans, and deviations from this will typically cause fearful aversive aggression or comic rejection. The gallery of deformed persons in horror fiction and comic fiction contains an endless number of monsters. Comic figures like the clown with big lips and big feet, Cyrano de Bergerac with his long nose, and the Elephant Man with his deformities, differ more from the monsters of horror fiction by the contextual cues like genre-marks or reaction-shots prescribing the empathic reactions of the viewer than by anything essential in the representation of the monstrous.

The affective mechanisms are closely linked to cognitive mechanisms in the way in which we perceive (and model and mould) the relation between individualizing and typifying/prototyping facial features. Facial features normally serve as the basis for identifying a given, specific individual, and there is probably a special innate brain module for this activity that often demands very difficult distinctions and categorizations in order to distinguish small differences (see, for example, Ellis and Young 1988: 87–111 for a description of face-recognition processing). The cognitive process of identification is therefore in itself activating and stimulating,[4] and feelings of familiarity and unfamiliarity are a prominent aspect of the process. The facial features will meanwhile also be identified as specific realizations of the prototypical features of the species *Homo sapiens*. Pascal noted that seeing two similar faces makes us laugh, and Bergson (1911) tried to explain this by saying that we laugh at the 'repetition' because life does not repeat itself. This is not quite true: our individual features are variations of common features. Stereotyping and repetitions may evoke quite different reactions. Make-up, coiffure, and

---

[4] Neale and Krutnik (1990: 77 f.) have used a Lacanian theory of alienation connected with the 'mirror image' as an explanation for comic interest in the human face and body. As I have noted in Chapter 5, Johnson-Laird has, however, explained the role of an objective model of the self which does not imply an obligatory alienation. The self-evident social role of a strong interest in the face and body of other members of the species is characteristic of most higher animals, and the role of the face as a prime communicator of emotions is a better framework for understanding the phenomenon than is 'alienation'.

clothes are often the result of a minute balancing-act between individualizing and prototyping. Clown masks and erotic make-up are often based upon stereotyping, but with very different purposes. We laugh at the clown because we reject stereotyping, the robotizing of human beings, and affirm individualism and voluntarism; whereas erotic make-up, besides providing salience for the individual user, is often used for triggering responses connected with a model of man as a member of a species, performing stereotype, non-voluntary, sexual acts. In films, identical twins are frequently used to create an effect by contrasting individualization and stereotyping. They can be used for very different purposes; in the psycho-thriller or science-fiction film identical 'twins' are mostly used for creating fear in the viewer, resulting from their loss of individuality, for example linked to 'robotization' or to a disconnection of appearance and mental equipment (as, say, when a bad twin performs acts ascribed to a good twin) which renders stable representations impossible. The uncertainty of identity creates cognitive and empathic problems for the viewer. In comedies and musicals, 'twins' are often used to create pleasure by the dismantling of individualism, for instance in the 'funny episodes' in which they even speak in an identical way.

I have presupposed above that laughter serves as an instrument for the rejection of empathic identification of, for example, the grotesque deviations of the clown from prototypical humanness. This in turn presupposes that the grotesque acts and failures of performance have been the responsibility of the clown. However, if the clown is an impersonator parodying other human beings his purpose is not to reject empathic identification with himself, but with whatever is the object of the parody. Scholars like Bakhtin (1968) have described a 'popular' culture of laughter from a point of view that emphasizes an identification with the grotesque transgression of normal standards of humanness, because these standards are regarded as restrictions on free behaviour. The essence of the Bakhtinian grotesque, which he describes as typical of folk culture, is the pleasurable identification with the body *vis-à-vis* the rigidity of consciousness (or rigidity of the upper classes), and the conceptualization of the way in which the body is a component of huge cycles of time, nature, and biology.

We could reject this conception by pointing out that, without a central nervous system, the body is a rather rigid and dead thing. The concept of 'body' in Bakhtin and others is crude, and considers the body as something existing without sophisticated mental control, in some respects synonymous with autonomic responses and paratelic behaviour and the opposite of voluntary telic processes which are regarded as more 'unbodily'. A 'Bakhtinian' body-act would be, for example, a person farting in front of 'rigid' upper-class people, a violation of social taboos that may be said to emphasize 'body culture' and a suspension of control; but all slapstick responses, like those of clumsy people falling, are just as much fun, only directed at people lacking control. Comedy, the comic, and the grotesque very often represent reality from a point of view of a *juste milieu* to which most viewers and listeners belong (see the genre theory of Frye 1967), and reject phenomena which they regard as 'below' themselves (for example, intellectually or socially) and, equally, phenomena above themselves; the comic attitude often denies 'deviators' the 'right' to belong to the human community. There is no reason to believe that laughter and humour are especially conservative or radical phenomena; they are fundamental mechanisms that can be used for many different purposes.

In parodic grotesque, the grotesque elements fulfil a different role from the one they play in 'plain' grotesque. Parodic grotesque underlines the patterned and thereby the mechanical elements of the features they exaggerate and deform, for instance by upscaling certain features or by simplifying certain schemata of thoughts and actions. The impersonator shows his human flexibility by his ability to represent grotesquely, and, in many modernist films, Fellini's for instance, the clowns are artists dressed up like 'the people'. The free and human performance of the imitator is actually a cognitive and intellectual performance, and does not represent body against mind, because the parodies are calculated representations of other people.

THE COMIC, LAUGHTER, EMPATHY, AND VOLUNTARY ACTS

I have dealt above with the laughter-triggering factors that have their main source in static phenomena, such as appearance. In the following, I shall analyze the elements in the cognitive *processes* that cause a reaction of laughter. Many of these processes are defective functions in relation to the optimal or prototypical cognitive-processing procedure. If the optimal voluntary cognitive processes are characterized by a flexible choice between several possible scripts and schemata, there are two quite different possibilities of malfunction: on the one hand, the suspension of flexible choices in favour of a schematic rigidity; on the other, a suspension of schemata and higher control in favour of totally random mental processes.

One source of fun is the incongruity between conscious, voluntary intention and the possibilities of a motor implementation. A basic element in 'slipping-on-a-banana-skin' funniness is that the people concerned do not have full motor control of their bodies. Whereas body (that is, non-conscious parts of the nervous system) and consciousness in the perfect act seem to be fused and are sometimes experienced as immaterial, for example in a perfect ballet, the mechanical and the object-like appear as a clumsy disproportion between intention and implementation. As the problem of integration of intention and motor implementation is often most intense in childhood, this source of laughter is frequently evaluated as childish. Bergson (1911) stated that laughter is triggered by involuntary and mechanical rigidity in behaviour and thoughts; man is treated as a thing, the equivalent to a domination of body over mind.

Another source of fun and laughter is the suspension of free will and of flexible and plastic behaviour, which is replaced by a deterministic, causal mental activity. This may happen in two quite different ways, either as schematic, obsessional mental activity, or as totally unpredictable and unsystematic mental activity. One of the basic forms of schematic behaviour is represented by obsessional patterns of movement, as in John Cleese's *Silly Walks* in the Monty Python Show, which represent a medley of the endless variations of significant, obsessional walks in silent-film comedy, with Chaplin's characteristic walk as the prototype. Dance is also mainly a motor activity, in which it is easy to register that the body-movements are an implementation of a relatively fixed program. But, whereas dance is mentally evaluated as the expression of a free choice in following fixed social schemata, comic movement is interpreted as if lower motor programs controlled the behaviour in a reflex-like manner. In parodies of various genres of fiction there are often several general exhibitions of the formulaic generic determinism. The world of a certain genre of fiction, which is ordinarily interpreted as and simulated as a platform for free and spontaneous behaviour, is represented by mechanical patterns and fixed conventions in the parodic versions.

Another basic type of mental schematism is represented by obsessional thoughts, sequences of thought which must be manifested, irrespective of the circumstances. In *Dr Strangelove,* General Ripper interprets all phenomena in the light of his obsession about the Communist pollution of 'bodily fluids' by the addition of flour to the drinking water. Don Quixote possesses a set of heroic schemata which he uses to interpret reality irrespective of the input. A variation of obsessional thought is the false hypothesis of explanation which reveals the mechanical in 'top-down' procedures of comprehension, and which often leads to non-communication. Carroll (1991) has pointed out the comic effects between the clash of two different interpretations of the same phenomenon, as in the scene in Hitchcock's *The 39 Steps* in which the main characters arrive at an inn handcuffed to each other, and the people at the inn misinterpret their close body contact as an expression of love because they do not know the true circumstances. The understanding of reality which is normally experienced as coming into existence by means of a flexible, but unambiguous, 'data-driven' bottom-up procedure, now falls apart. The world is seen as consisting of ambiguous phenomena, which only assume unique meanings by rigid top-down procedures. The misunderstandings reveal the mental mechanisms.

A modified variation of obsessional thought consists in construing the viewer's vantage-point so that the viewer has far more information than the comic protagonists in the film. The subject-actant walks along, occupied with his own thoughts and activities, and does not see an uncovered manhole which the viewer sees. From our knowledge of the conventions of comic fiction we know that, if there is a manhole, somebody must necessarily fall into it. The discrepancy between our knowledge (creating a position of possible voluntary acts to be avoided) and that of the protagonists makes their behaviour more deterministic; 'accidents' are transformed into law-abiding fate.

Another word for schematism is pattern *repetition*. The repetition of acts, words, or pictures is a characteristic feature of many comic fictions and slapstick productions. Repetition may occur synchronously, in space, as when several people move in the same significant way, or as when the cars in Tati's *Mon Oncle* drive in parallel and make synchronous turns, either identical or strictly symmetrical. These spatial patterns, however, typically appear in visual sequences that are marked as lyrical, melodramatic, or horrifying (and Tati often balances humour and the lyrical). More often the comic repetition is manifested in time. An example among thousands is an episode from the film *The Return of the Pink Panther*. Inspector Clouseau freewheels backwards and ends up in a swimming-pool. When his new car later starts freewheeling backwards, we know with near-certainty that it will end up in the same pool: and it does. The schematism of repetition is an expectation of genre, and creates a double structure of expectations and hypotheses in the viewers: on the one hand, the viewer expects that acts and utterances will be repeated with a rigorous schematism; on the other, the viewer knows that such a repetition is quite improbable in real life. That Clouseau would end up a second time in exactly the same pool has, in real life, a probability factor of zero. The repetition is therefore a 'logical short-circuit', which we as viewers laughingly reject because otherwise we would experience a change to superstitious beliefs and thus a change of genre (to horror, or religious melodrama).

Obsessional pattern-repetition annuls voluntary, teleological behaviour and thinking, and replaces it with causal stimulus–response behaviour and thinking. Repetition and automatism can evoke other subjective effects besides laughter: they can lead to a lyrical-melodramatic abandonment to automatism, reactions of horror, or superstitious adherence to certain non-voluntary rituals.

Whereas the humour of schematism rejects total linearity and causality, the humour of 'random behaviour', as manifested, for example, in much zany humour, is an expression of the reverse principles of organization. Here total unpredictability is combined with uncontrolled associations and metaphors. The associations may be mental but they can also be factual, as when a subject-actant continually changes his line of thought and his concepts under the impression of new events, and new input. From the point of view of higher mental control, the humour of randomness is also a humour of causality, because the persons are powerless victims of the impact of causalities in the external world or in their own mental files. In Hawks's *Bringing up Baby* we witness the ridiculous change of thought patterns in a police officer who is victimized by being unable to resist following all the false leads given to him by other people. In order to enjoy ludicrous and 'wild' associations, the viewer is dependent on contextual clues for labelling these associations as ludicrous and therefore made for a ludic use, because real madness would demand quite different types of reactions.

The structure of mental-association humour is closely related to the principles of poetic genres. The associations follow not linear, directed trajectories, but all types of similarities, visual or linguistic paradigms, from grotesque nonsense rhymes to visual associations, such as an attempt to cook shoelaces as if they were spaghetti: see Arnheim's (1971: 144 ff.) and Carroll's (1991) analysis of the use of visual metaphor in silent film comedy. Often only special marks offer a clue as to whether a given sequence should be construed as lyrical abandonment or comic rejection. This can lead to confusion in the reception, as in the evaluation of certain Chaplin films as 'sentimental' because of the lack of separation in signals of either a lyrical or a comic reception.

The construction of sequential meaning implies a reduction of associations. We need to curb the full range of possible associations and material features of A in order to produce the specific *quid pro quo* reference of A to B: such a procedure creates tensity. The curbing of the perceptual and associative aspects of signifiers is easiest to register in arbitrary language, but iconic and pictorial language also has its schemata of reference, for example references to functional relations that downgrade the perceptual qualities of a given figure. This is negatively illustrated in the visual metaphor, which allows visual similarities of form to dominate functional relations and non-visual qualities (such as smell and taste) which establish the meaning. The lyrical use of associations accepts saturated associative meanings, whereas the comic use is a ludic recess of hypothetical acceptance combined with comic rejection by making the associations 'unreal'.

THE COMIC, LAUGHTER, AND NARRATIVE SEQUENCES

The basic structure in the construction of a narrative sequence consists in goal-directed acts, the purpose of which is to create a telic reduction of arousal and tension. Consequently, the comic and laughter have no direct means of contributing to the construction of narrative structures: on the contrary, laughter often replaces narrative actions, contrary to aversive feelings such as fear and hate, for example, which directly motivate acts. Typical comic situations are created by non-comic narrative sequences, as when Stan and Oliver try to push a piano uphill, a non-comic teleological project, and the comedy only starts when they lose control of the piano, which runs downhill again. Of course, we could say that failure is an act, too; but the comic is not the failure, it is not a goal within the narrative, but a cued reaction in the viewer as applied to the narrative. Inspector Clouseau's endeavours as a police detective follow the rules and patterns that are in principle characteristic of the detective genre, whereas the comic is only engendered by his impossible and clumsy attempts at detection, and only as an extradiegetic viewer-reaction. The comic effect only comes into existence if we curb or deny our cognitive or empathic identification with the subject-actants, and temporarily reduce our evaluation of the desirability of their goals.

A distance to the active goals of the agents is especially important in 'black comedies'. In a black comedy, like Kramer's *It's a Mad, Mad, Mad, Mad World,* the agents are driven by their lust for money, and the grand finale tries by many different means to provide the viewer with a distance to this goal. Far more striking is the comic-ironic distance to means and ends in *Dr Strangelove*. An especially refined dissolution of pleasure in the goal is found in *The Man With Two Brains,* in which a brain surgeon falls in love with a female brain in a jar, and, when he finally succeeds in transplanting the brain into the body of his beautiful, but evil wife, it turns out that the 'brain' is an obsessive eater, which, within a few weeks, has eaten so much food that the beautiful body has swollen to large and not-so-beautiful proportions.

The exception, which modifies the rule that the comic and laughter do not functionally create narrative drive because they destroy the motivation of acting and reject the goal, is the representation of the conflict between autonomy and heteronomy, between aversion and attraction, in the 'falling-in-love' situation; feeling erotic pleasure also implies giving up freedom and personal integrity. The classic pattern of comedy is modelled on a sequence of events from the moment when two young people fall in love, via the obstacles to their union, and culminating in their marriage. In this sequence of actions there are two motivating aspects, desire and pleasure, connected to the remote-sense aspect and the contact-sense aspect of sexuality. Desire is linked to sexuality as a motivating element in object-directed acts, as we find to be the case in action adventure and romance genres. These acts are seen from the perspective of one person: the hero or the heroine performs a sequence of acts with the purpose of gaining the possession of the desired object, and the acts are, in a sense, aversive, because they emphasize the motor control of the subject over the object. Genre constructions of desire, seen from the point of view of the object, may be aspects of horror and melodrama, in which the object of identification voluntarily or involuntarily gives in to the 'foreign agent'.

Aspects of pleasure are linked with cognitive and affective problems that are, in turn, connected with the 'shift of program': the transition from aversion to incorporation, from voluntary to involuntary reaction. The prototypical design of this 'shift-of-program' problem is the eternal theme of comedy, 'lover's quarrels', which we find from New Attic Comedy via

Shakespeare's comedies to modern film comedy. A and B are in love, but at the same time they will not give up their (other) voluntary, goal-directed pleasures. In *Bringing up Baby* Cary Grant is attracted to Katherine Hepburn, but he is simultaneously tied to a set of positive voluntary acts connected with his work. In *Double Wedding* Myrna Loy is attracted to William Powell, but also experiences gratification connected with her work as a businesswoman. Even though some realizations of the 'lovers'-quarrel' type of conflict may seem to indicate that the conflict is a Freudian one between duty and desire, super-ego and id, this is not the main dimension of the conflict. A simple reason for this is that, as argued elsewhere, not all activities with a positive hedonic value are erotic; Grant's pleasure in his work in *Bringing up Baby,* for instance his joy in finding the missing bone of a dinosaur, cannot be described as merely sublimated sexuality, but as an activity with some gratifications of its own, which competes with erotic attraction for his attention. The other activities (seemingly) put him in control of voluntary cognitive and real acts, whereas love seems to threaten his autonomy, as it threatens that of Myrna Loy. The aspects of autonomy are probably supported by the desire-curbing built-in mechanisms of aversion which I have described above; they constitute one pole in a dual-polar control system.

For this reason, the two seemingly opposed functions of the 'lovers' quarrel' comedy, the (biologically based) attraction to the love-object, and the series of degradations of it, pull in the same direction, although it might appear that the degradations are demotivating. But laughter, caused by frequently continuous mutual degradation, serves to make the other unthreatening, and therefore has a conjunctive narrative function. *Double Wedding* clearly illustrates these mechanisms, because the film contrasts romantic, act-oriented models with the comic-cognitive-oriented aspects of the *mise-en-scène* of love and desire. One couple is characterized by weak wills and interests, so has to be provided with romantic mental models, here the 'Valentino-Sheik' model of male conquest, and female surrender. The other couple suffers from an excess of will autonomy, and the development of their relations shows continuous degradation and ridicule, culminating in a Bakhtinian mass orgy of ridiculousness, in which Myrna Loy and William Powell look increasingly foolish. The climax consists, among other things, of their being knocked out, she felled accidentally by one of the wedding guests, he hit by a pan, so that—unconscious—they drop down beside each other on the bed. Laughter and degradation are the mechanisms which destroy the deadlock of attraction and aversion by making the other unthreatening, and they destroy the voluntary, telic mechanisms in such a way that a parasympathetic incorporation can take place. In the same way, *Bringing up Baby* is one long series of ridiculous scenes aimed at paralyzing the telic mechanisms and creating situations of paratelic, non-aversive leisure.

As discussed earlier, smile and laughter are not only subjective reactions,

9

Metaframes as Emotion-Filters and Brackets

For many years, high-culture texts have been occupied with the moulding of relations between fiction and addressee (reader, viewer, or spectator) and with highlighting fiction as an encoded system of meaning different from real-life systems. 'Avant-garde' fiction has often been 'metafiction', fiction that lays bare its devices and makes the relation between addressee and fiction visible in a critique of clichés of representation. In this chapter I shall make a short analysis of Godard's *Pierrot le Fou*, in order to show that changing the modal quality of the emotions is an important aspect of a metafictional laying-bare of devices. In recent decades, popular fiction has also used metafictional devices to an increasing degree, and special formulas, for example certain cartoons, have used metafiction for an even longer period. I shall illustrate the way in which metafiction is used in popular fiction by making a short analysis at the end of this chapter of an episode, *The Dream Sequence Always Rings Twice*, from the television series *Moonlighting*, and shall then discuss the emotional function of 'cliché'. First, however, I shall expand my earlier descriptions of the means by which a metaframe, an awareness of 'extra-diegetic' and 'metafictional' phenomena, influences the viewer's cognitive and emotional relation to the narrative.

'Frame' is a word with many meanings and functions. The basic meaning is the image schema: boundedness of a two-dimensional space, as in 'film frame', the name of the individual photographic image in a film. Immediately however, this schema leaves us two opposed meanings: first, of frame as a container (see Lakoff 1987: 272), supporting internal relations in the contained; and, second, something cutting off relations to whatever is beyond the frame. The cutting-off can further be understood as negative (something left out or masked-off) or as positive, frames as brackets leaving unwanted elements outside the frames. Whether 'frame' is interpreted as establishing internal relations or excluding something may be cued by a given representation, but is also related to 'viewer attitude'. A 'suspicious' or 'hostile' viewer will focus on the exclusion, whereas the accepting viewer will focus on the framed. The critical viewer wants to have cognitive and voluntary control, whereas the accepting viewer prefers to abandon himself while watching a film.

Focus of attention as a 'protected area' in which special hypothesis-systems are isolated, for the time being, from general norms, behaviours, beliefs, and associations. The viewer-reaction to the isolation can be positive or negative	Focus of attention as a masked off fragment of a totality, a synechdoche, activating the absent, masked elements (off-space, missing, or hidden parts of objects). The viewer-reaction will often be an activation of saturated associations of lack or 'invisible', diffuse plenitude, the associational equivalent of tense enactional goal-schemata

Fig. 9.1 Focus of attention either as a bracketed area or as an area defined by a masking of surrounding space.

Frame has further become a model for attention described by means of the attended: it is thus (as described in Chapter 3) an image-model for focus of attention and/or the determining framework of the attention. To some extent, the framework as focus of attention will equate to a hypothesis system of categorizing and grouping. As focus of attention it may further be understood within a three-dimensional 'figure-ground' model: the frame(work) is a ground that establishes a distance to the figures of attention. By this means it functions as an activator of 'broader areas of attention', and as a cognitive or emotional filter: the given figure, the given phenomenon, is understood by means of a special frame that highlights some phenomena and leaves out others. Some of the main structures in 'frame' are then:

1. As picture-frame establishing an autonomous whole, a container supporting internal relations, possibly functioning as bracket, a container protecting the contained against something by this isolation;

2. as window, which either positively makes the vision of an elsewhere possible or negatively masks some aspects of an elsewhere. The masking may point to its source, the 'camera', and activate the masked-off space;

3. as spatio-temporal 'focus of attention', an index, a pointer-mechanism;

4. as hypothesis system or frame-work and as a hierarchically superior 'embedder of embedded material'; and

5. as 'cognitive' or emotional filter.

Central to the different uses of frame are: frame as inclusion or a container, versus frame as exclusion as a mask, with filter as a special mask; and frame as a system that produces a dual focus of attention, possibly with one of the focuses of attention controlling the other, as in Figure 9.2.

REALITY, FRAMING, ATTENTIONAL SALIENCE, FREE WILL,
AND COUNTER-CINEMA

Film and television screens can be described as focuses of visual attention emitting cues for constructing a hypothetical or actual time-space. The cues

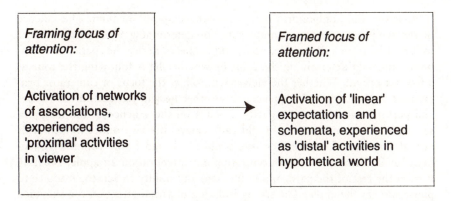

Fig. 9.2 Dual focus of attention provides an overall activation. It diminishes activation of tense emotions as a consequence of the redefinition of reality-status of the framed focus from being a real-life hypothesis to being a schema hypothesis.

in the focus are produced by the addresser; the viewer cannot actively control the signals from the screen, only decide whether he wants to provide attention and to reconstruct the emitted. In real-life situations, the direction of visual attention is a 'free act', often linked to other functions like the actual or virtual possibility of interaction with the object world. The real-life situations are furthermore located in an open and non-directed world (see Kazanskij 1981: 107). If we see an apple on a tree, we can consider picking and eating it, or can allow our eyes to move metonymically from apple to branch or leaves, or to another person. Our experience of whether a film is bounded or not depends on whether our expectations follow the temporal, forward-directed flow, so that the capacity limitations on attention will let us follow the centre of the audiovisual time–space flow, or whether our attention will focus on the frame of representation. The central problem is not that of spatial boundedness, but of control of direction (see Perkins 1974: 71) and thus the control of the spatio-temporal sequence in respect to possible fields of vision and possible enactive relations. The problem is therefore whether the control of direction is felt as determined by the viewer's preferences or as a limitation imposed by the addresser, and whether the control is carried out positively, by the salience of the spatio-temporal sequence, or negatively, by activating the viewer's experience of the frame as masking possible desirable vistas. The film may even try to cue attention to the spatial boundedness. In Greenaway's *The Draughtsman's Contract*, the main character is a painter using a 'drawing machine', a frame without canvas but with wires dividing the frame itself into subframes. The fragmentation of the field of vision into small bounded rectangles draws attention to the frames of representation in a metacommentary.

However, film, unlike drawing, is a spatio-temporal medium. The salience of the temporal sequence is important for determining whether the viewer feels that he is on a dull guided tour, and begins to notice the spatial and temporal schemata determining the tour, or whether he is following the tour as a free act of will. Whether the viewer will follow the focus of camera or protagonist in the temporal sequence, or whether he will refocus on the frames and perform meta-activities, partly depends on the salience of the *temporal* sequence. A person in a real world can achieve affective outlet by actual or virtual actions and perceptions. We could block and frame voluntary openness, for instance, by fully concentrating our attention on an apple, isolating it from the rest of the garden, and blocking our ability to act, for instance to pluck and eat the apple. The strong isolation of visual attention for extended periods of time, which in real-life situations is relatively rare, is an important element in visual representations. Film may represent objects cut off from immediate metonymic relations to a broader, open life-world. This procedure of framing and isolation enhances the perception of the intense and saturated network of associations, but reduces the application of tense sequential schemata; it enhances the perception of space, but weakens the perception of telic or paratelic time. In *The Draughtsman's Contract* the film moves toward becoming a series of stills, a series of 'tableaux'.

One dimension of salience and attention in visual fiction is linked to the salience *of the world as such,* irrespective of whether what is viewed is part of a hypothetical world or not. When people watch an interesting documentary or other non-hypothetical material, they invest a degree of attention which depends on the felt salience of the seen. Another dimension of attention and salience is linked to *the hypothetical system and the framework*[1] *of attention as such.* Central to the salience of such systems are their possible relevance for a living being, that is, that the framework activates *the application of anthropomorph schemata* by presenting living agents who feel, memorize, wish, or act as a central part of the hypothetical world. A wish to break the spell of the narrative cinema is often related to the hypothesis systems involving anthropomorph beings, and the affective activation caused by this.

Objections to fiction, possibly linked to preferences for metafiction, take different forms, according to whether the objections are directed at the use of anthropomorph schemata, at hypothetical systems, or at the salience of the audiovisual sequence *per se.* Some of the most radical viewpoints in the 1960s recognized the problem of salience as such; even if anthropomorph schemata and hypothetical systems were abandoned, art would still cast a spell on the addressee, and those who held such viewpoints consequently worked toward abolishing art to make room for 'life'. In connection with Godard's *oeuvre,* Peter Wollen (1986) has characterized 'counter-cinema' according to seven

---

[1] Framework is here used in the sense of 'a set of assumptions supporting understanding', as used by Goffman (1986) and Minsky (1988: ch. 25 *passim*).

dichotomies: narrative transitivity or intransitivity (logical coherence/incoherence); identification or estrangement; transparency or foregrounding; single or multiple diegesis; closure or aperture; pleasure or un-pleasure; and fiction or reality. One of the reasons given for the use of counter-cinema is the Brechtian one, that is, that it enhances the viewer's cognitive abilities by blocking the emotional appeal. Wollen considers that, by disrupting the emotional 'spell' of the narrative flow and thus refocusing the viewer's attention, the attention might be totally lost, and further suggests that there might be an element of suspicion towards art as such in the Brecht-Artaud tradition. He indicates indirectly the issue that was a major topic in Chapter 2 of the present book: a strong motivational link between cognition and emotion. Nevertheless, for Wollen this point is an aside; he mainly takes a modernist stand (shared by many postmodernists) not only in finding emotional involvement in anthropomorph schemata or hypothetical frameworks problematic, but also in questioning the salience of (film) art *per se*. The verbal intricacies necessary to argue against making visual sequences too fascinating and gratifying become apparent when Wollen argues for *un-pleasure* as a strategy for counter-cinema, although as a transitory stage.

It could be posited that a central element in counter-cinema was motivated by preferences for certain emotional modalities just as much as by cognitive goals. The first aspect of this is the question of voluntary control. Certain types of salience and cues are felt by some viewers to represent an unpleasant 'alien' control (expressed in words like spell and illusion), something (for example a standard narrative schema) that forces itself into the viewer's attention. Dealing with complicated intertextual references, complex narrative patterns, and narrative lacunae and incoherence is felt to be an active, voluntary activity. The emotional 'tone' of this type of cognition is preferred to one having a greater element of involuntary abandonment. The complex web of associations possibly evokes passive experiences of being 'overwhelmed' by saturated networks, but this overwhelming richness is positively experienced as a response to one's *own* associations, albeit cued by the film. One way of understanding a 'readerly' text in a Barthesian sense is that it sophisticates the control of the addresser by letting the text be experienced as the addressee's own work.

DEFAMILIARIZATION AND DISTANCIATION

To isolate and fragment has been an important device in modern art, sometimes in order to show that it is the 'frame' or the ' art institution' itself which creates a work of art. Framing and isolation make the work of art an object of concentrated attention, thus increasing the affective charge by removing metonymic relations. Arnheim (1957: 25) states that 'isolation makes for weight'. The erotic effect of dressing is often produced by framing and isolating certain parts of the body from the body totality. Music videos are frequently made by isolating many phenomena and then combining them in a sequence. The combined sequence consists of isolated objects without metonymic real-life relations, and therefore possesses a high degree of affective charge. To isolate in order to increase the aesthetic effect of a given object is part of what was called de-automation and defamiliarization, *ostranenie*, by the Russian formalists. De-automation was a procedure for breaking down the 'automated' reception of artworks, in order to reactivate attention and create new salience.

Sklovskij (1965) points out that the purpose of art is to create perceptual salience. Ordinary life often creates non-consciousness: a person may forget, when dusting a room, whether he has already dusted the sofa, because the process has become automated. Another example is the way in which rhythm in a song heard during work makes the job easier by automating it. Sklovskij uses the latter example to illustrate that rhythm functions as a device for co-ordinating motor activity and saving energy, but he also uses the example to link muscular rhythm with prose, whereas the function of rhythm in poetry is different. In art, the perceptual process is a purpose in itself, and art prolongs the perception of an object and makes the process difficult in order to trigger attention. Art is the liberation of perception from automatism by which the object is not perceived as a part of space, but acquires a maximum of intensity and duration. Sklovskij emphasizes that narrative structure functions by blocking and retarding. He wishes to liberate perception from space and provide it with an intense, temporal existence, but in some respects the procedure of defamiliarization achieves the opposite: the perceived is not part of a temporal sequence, but acquires 'duration', which is a 'spatial' way of understanding time as extension, not as a sequential process of change. The intensity is created by blocking the telic aspects of objects as part of processes; rhythm becomes a percept, not a paratelic or telic process; the description of narrative structure highlights retardation, not the functions and schemata of directedness which make the retardation of the directedness possible.

Sklovskij attempts to show the way in which artists may create perceptual salience by *ostranenie*, whereas self-conscious artists like Greenaway also point to the process of reception by trying to highlight devices in the art itself; both 'metapositions', however, lead to 'perceptual-spatial' understanding of art as isolation cut off from temporal-telic schemata. Although the dominant explicit motivation for defamiliarization and self-consciousness in art film is often perceptual and cognitive, a preference for intense and saturated lyrical emotions might be just as important for the viewers. In Chapters 10 and 11, I shall examine ways in which defamiliarization can be used as a cue for emotional responses of a 'non-lyrical-perceptual' kind, and shall link these with an analysis of melodrama and horror. It is the concrete uses of 'defamiliarization' that specify the type of effect to be achieved. This is obvious if we look at the way that Eisenstein, for example, uses defamiliarization to create a higher emotional charge in the representation and expressive, melodramatic, and opera-like qualities of film (see Wollen 1972). Montage, unfamiliar camera angles and framings, or close-ups of facial expressions could, from one point of view, be interpreted as defamiliarization of standard perceptions and systems of representation. The salience is, however, contextualized in such a way that it supports emotional expressions, not cognitions about reality-status or the 'role of representation'.

Defamiliarization is a tool for drawing attention to a given representation. The effect therefore tends to be perceptual or lyrical, by cueing the viewer into a perceptual fusion with objects cut off from their normal contexts and 'higher-order' systems of meaning. Eisenstein used similar effects, contextualized to evoke emotions. Brecht, however, redefined defamiliarization in a way that became clearly directed against *'Einfühlung'*, empathic identification, and (a certain kind of) emotion. He had a term for 'defamiliarization' in a formalist sense as a means of evoking a new salience in the artwork (see Steinweg 1972: 159 f.), but it was his concept of *Verfremdung*, in which defamiliarization had strong components of distanciation, that became one of the most influential normative aesthetic concepts of the twentieth century. Its purpose was to emphasize the cognitive and didactic aspects of art and play down their emotional impact by reducing spectator identification. According to Brecht, traditional 'dramatic' theatre (Aristotelian, romantic, or naturalistic) aims at mimesis and direct emotional involvement by spectator identification with the drama, whereas the epic theatre provides insight and blocks spectator identification. Consequently, he attacks Aristotle's notion of catharsis. Although Brecht denies that his concept is a rejection of emotions, it nevertheless implies a certain puritanical rejection of theatre as entertainment (see Esslin 1961: 123 ff.).

One aspect of *Verfremdung* is a normative emphasis on non-fictional didactic communication. Another aspect concerns 'self-consciousness' and *Verfremdung* as means of creating emotional tones and modal qualities. Brechtian distanciation activates intense and saturated experiences in clusters of associations felt in a more 'proximal' mode by the viewer than canonical narratives would be. An example of this is 'break of illusion', that is, a diegetic character speaking directly to the audience. This could be called 'distanciation', but, at the same time, it is an activation of the viewer's self-awareness, like that of a person who, having followed a lecture or a conversation, is suddenly spoken to and has to perform a 'switch of program', activating self-centred knowledge structures, affective-motivational structures, and a general 'proximal tone' within the experience, instead of distal, object-oriented structures of experience. During Godard's *Pierrot le Fou* Ferdinand turns around and addresses the viewer during a car drive, and the change brings about a short-lived activation of the viewer's self-awareness, creating a polar system combining a diegetic focus of attention with a self-awareness focus that is more emotional than cognitive, as it provides a 'feeling' in the viewer, rather than any new information.

GODARD AND THE LYRICAL EFFECT OF 'SELF-CONSCIOUSNESS'

Godard's *Pierrot le Fou* is a good example of a self-conscious metatext working with a Brechtian *Verfremdung*. By means of inserts like 'cinema' written all over the screen, and by addressing the viewer and laying bare the devices, the film advises the viewer not to accept it as reality: probably no viewer would do so. But calling attention to the constructedness might influence the way in which the viewer invests emotions in the narrative. These warnings to the viewers can be seen as 'emotional' rather than cognitive: the emotions are staged and therefore false. Interwoven with the emotional/narrative theme are several more general themes of cultural and political criticism to which I shall return shortly.

The narrative is in most respects a straightforward and 'banal', double-triangle love story: a poet (male) loves a woman and leaves wife and bourgeois lifestyle behind; the lovers wander around until the woman finally leaves the poet for another and is subsequently shot. Like Goethe's Werther, the young 'poet' chooses to take his own life, although in a more spectacular way: by blowing himself to pieces with dynamite. The film thus has a basic canonical and anthropomorph narrative schema into which the viewer can let his emotions be moulded. Usually there are unambiguous emotional structures providing explanations for the acts and emotional states of the actants (love, jealousy, fear, hate, boredom, despair, and bitterness). Although acts motivated by the emotions are sometimes slightly unorthodox, the majority follow orthodox act-schemata and goal-schemata (fighting, caressing, transportation by car, by foot, by boat, and so forth, in order to reach, say, goals of avoidance or possession). Sometimes the sequencing of the schemata becomes scrambled at the scene level, as in the 'murder' scene in Marianne's flat early in the film (see Bordwell 1986: 318 ff.). Very often the acts become paratelic-playful for a short period of time, but mostly this is psychologically motivated: young lovers playing in woods, with cars, with, for young people, typical exploratory and playful relations to new or possible schemata of behaviour. The overall narrative structure could, however, be termed canonical. Consequently, this should stabilize the cueing of emotions made at the microlevel (by readings of facial expressions and 'Kuleshov' contexts). The narrative would then be a romance, in which an active position (alternating with lyrical-paratelic or lyrical-autonomic inserts) is transformed into a romance of passive positions, quite traditionally prophesied by thematic inserts even in the 'active' sequences (for example, Ferdinand glancing in his car mirror and saying that he looks like someone who is about to drive over a precipice). The thematic, emotion-supporting use of Duhamel's extra-diegetic music underlines the romance aspects, and the inserts of *chansons* allow the telic plot (as in opera and musical) to be interrupted by paratelic songs. The visual descriptions of nature are characterized by traditional 'romantic' components: moon, running water, fire, and blue sky.

At the same time, the film contains a number of elements stating that any behaviour and any description is 'merely' a manifestation of cultural schemata. The prime 'proof' of this point is made by explicit mappings between sets of literary schemata and the diegetic world of the film. The film is sometimes segmented into 'chapters' provided with a thematic résumé of represented emotions (hope, despair, bitterness, or a season in hell). Scenes are provided with literary parallels, for instance by indicating that the scene which follows echoes Stevenson, Faulkner, Hemingway, or Verne, or by inserting a medieval romance told in 'brackets'. The words and the writings of the 'poet-philosopher-writer' Pierrot-Ferdinand comment on, index, and bracket the diegetic world and its emotions. 'The words' control 'the things', the schemata control the experienced: Ferdinand prefers reading and writing to feeling and experiencing, a preference expressed in the lovers' quarrel that breaks up the romance. A second field of foregrounded schemata comes from mass culture and advertising: the persons do not, in a romantic sense, express their inner selves: their emotions are 'spoken' by cultural codes (Godard 'illus-trates' Barthes 1957, who analyzes the schematic 'ideological' aspects of mass culture). The emotions and sentiments in this film are moulded by popular genres, such as crime fiction, the romantic *chanson*, slapstick, and *film noir*. A third field of foregrounded schemata is cinematic convention, for example unambiguous space, voice-over (by using dialogical voice-over), or rescue deadline schemata (when Pierre has to rescue Marianne from the 'bad guys' and seemingly runs in the opposite direction of the location of his beloved, an action emphasized by a pan leaving the running hero and finding Marianne). The film comments on the effect of the standard genre film by showing an interview with the B-action film director Samuel Fuller, who says that the film is a battleground for love, hate, action, and violence, death: in a word, for emotions.

A strong version of the underlying argument in the film could be that as our cognitions and emotions are moulded by social schemata and coded sig-nifiers—cinema, literature, popular culture, and art—we live an unauthentic life compared with a possible Rousseauist world with its potentially unmedi-ated way of experiencing and communicating. A weaker version of the under-lying argument might be that these specifically bourgeois representations should be supplanted by better ones.

The sheer presence of humans in basic situations (such as love, loss of beloved, jealousy, and fear of opponent) activates basic affective reactions in the viewer. The emotional function of the dual focus of attention on acts and emotional moods, as well as on schemata of representation, is not a 'deconstruction' of the emotions, but has its primary effect in their modalization. It produces paratelic or autonomic effects by modifying the telic goal schemata, and in that way transforms part of the tensity into intensity, saturation, and autonomic response. In many respects, therefore, the 'self-conscious' effects support the lyrical and the passive romantic effects, rather than destroying them. Few, if any, spectators believe that an aria in an opera or the dance patterns in a ballet are a direct mimesis of everyday life. The aria 'expresses' an emotional attitude, makes it salient and vivid for the spectator, and the spectator measures its 'expressive mimesis' by evaluating whether it evokes appropriate emotions (passion instead of embarrassment); its expressiveness is partly linked to its explicit indication of schematic behaviour. For this reason, when Marianne starts singing in a schematic fashion on a number of occasions, the viewer quickly realizes that a motivation of 'direct mimesis of everyday life' has to be abandoned. At the same time the song is psychologically motivated, and the viewer abandons a more specific hypothesis, that this is a representation of an episode in Marianne's life, for the more general hypothesis, that it is about a young woman's expression of feelings. In one episode the lovers burn their car under tableau-like conditions, with dead people lying at or sitting by wrecked cars but attracting no attention from the protagonists. As the dead people are not procured with any diegetic motivation, the viewer has by association to motivate their presence on a more general level (something about death, modern life, and so on) and to connect this to the emotions evoked by the lover's journey; the dead people may therefore be a cue for making a more abstract-complex network of associations.

The activation of associative networks is a common procedure in the film. The viewer has his cultural fields of association activated by continuous reference to Velasquez, Picasso, Hemingway, Faulkner, Fuller, and television documentaries about the Vietnam war. The associations have no common denominators at low levels of abstraction, only at high levels like 'art', 'feelings', 'war', and this further strengthens the lyrical tone of the film. The *Verfremdung* and intertextuality serve to activate extra networks of association and therefore evoke intense and saturated modalities of experience. As these are constructed by the addresser and reconstructed in the viewer, the focus of the experience will, despite the romantic break of illusion and the activation of real-life contexts by *Verfremdung*, be more 'subjective', as the associations and evoked emotions exist in 'consciousness' and not in the diegetic world. At the same time the representational *ostranenie* will bring vividness to the perceptions. The emotions will eventually be experienced within a viewer-frame, a persona, like 'viewer of avant-garde film', which would also make the experience more 'subjective', centred in the viewer, not in the viewed.

Now, if *Verfremdung* in the film had been closely linked to a specific political goal-structure, for example, the evoked emotions might have activated 'real-life strategies'. This would be a consequence not of an undermining of diegetic 'illusion' and the critique of representation, but of specific rhetorical strategies linking the experience to political goals, just as a documentary can activate either general enlightenment or social intervention. A possible political effect of *Pierrot le Fou,* as experienced in 1965, could be linked to overt political statements (for example, the symbolic sketch showing Marianne as a Vietnamese object of American aggression) rather than to 'distanciation' as such.

The film further raises the question of the way in which it is possible to mentally 'break the illusory spells of representation and semblance of reality'. In a crude sense, all the frames projected onto the screen have the same 'real-life' reality status, whether they provide the message 'Cinema' in big letters or tell a love story. Nobody is fooled into believing that the screen is a window into a real, physical world. The only way of really 'breaking the illusion' is by dullness. From a certain point of view, many strategies of 'reflexivity' can be said to achieve the opposite: to strengthen the 'illusion' by trying to break down the 'ground' on which fictions can be experienced as hypotheses with a special reality-status. This is done by denying the 'naturalness' of non-fictional experiences: life is a dream in a dream in a dream, the world is a text, a set of representations, a film, a or story, and there are no valid hypothetical representations of 'reality'. The implication of this is that the world is not primarily represented as a source of perceptions and a goal for acts, but as 'a state of consciousness', and should therefore be approached in a lyrical-associative way. It further activates the viewer's proximal or proprioceptive 'feeling of himself' during viewing.

The problem of creating distanciation to 'film as such' is connected with the way in which we establish reality-status. The audiovisual perceptual sequence possesses a 'givenness' and a perceptual coherence in relation to which we cognitively and affectively specify reality-status. Even if we know that something has been put together by montage and special effects, the knowledge and feeling become specifications for the perceptual holistic given. The antagonism between metadistances and a holistic fusion of the level of perception is exemplified by Reiner's *Dead Men Don't Wear Plaid* from 1982, and Stone's *JFK.* The first film is a very 'self-conscious' modern *film noir,* shot in black and white, in which clips from old films (*Notorious, The Big Sleep, Double Indemnity, The Killers,* and many others) are spliced with new footage in such a way that Steve Martin interacts with Ingrid Bergman, Bogart, Grant, and others. Of course we notice the trick, and our processing of this (with questions like what film? what scene?) uses part of our attentional capacity and diminishes the tensity of the narrative. But, nevertheless, the many shots with their numerous specifications 'fuse' into a holistic experience of a film. In the same way, in *JFK*—a docudrama about the Kennedy assassination— several shots in the film have been taken from documentary material and exist as such in the film, and we notice the special reality-status of these shots. The documentary material activates special mental procedures and associations, but nevertheless the film fuses into a holistic experience.

When a film is being viewed, the audiovisual sequence has an experiential reality and a perceptual 'presence' which is specified in relation to such attributes as reality-status by continuous cognitive-affective evaluations in many dimensions, such as: 'this is a dream' experienced by one of the protagonists'; 'this is an expressive dance'; 'this is documentary footage'; 'this is a montage of shots from *Notorious* and shots made by Carl Reiner'. However, when the film is being viewed, the perceptual sequence, 'the film', is the basic framework of the activation of the experience of 'reality as such', as a result of its presentic perceptual qualities. A total distanciation from 'the film as such' as an illusion would therefore be experienced as a temporary distanciation from 'reality as such' as an 'illusion'.

FRAMING AND FILTERING OF EMOTIONS BY EXTRADIEGETIC AND DIEGETIC MOTIVATION

Motivation is a central way of cueing the focus of attention. If, for example, we look at an 'unmotivated' scene of torture, isolated from a possible motivational context, we may experience the scene with strong, unstructured, and saturated associations. We may also look for an extradiegetic motivation: this scene is made by a sado-masochist in order to evoke sado-masochistic feelings. If, however, the scene of torture has a narrative motivation, this shifts the focus of attention and of expectation. When Stallone is tortured by Communists in *Rambo,* the scene is experienced through the motivating frame. One part of our attention is directed at understanding and emotionally rejecting the motives of evil Communists, another at hopes and ideas of escape, while a third empathically perceives the painful scene. The motivation and the narrative context, with their virtual options of a possible change of situation, have directed our focus of attention, and some saturated associations have been transformed into tense schemata based on enactive identification. Sexual scenes may be presented as isolated, cueing undirected saturated associations, but may also be provided with a diegetic motivation that directs the attention toward the characters performing the acts and the goals of the acts.

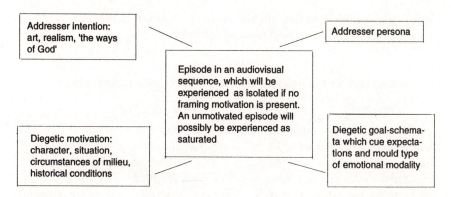

Fig. 9.3 Motivational frames, like addresser intention, diegetic motivation, addresser persona, or diegetic goal-schemata, are filters, while isolation effects and saturated associations are possibly activated by lack of motivational frames.

The attention may be further redirected by introducing extradiegetic motivations like addresser motivation. During the pornography trials in the 1960s, several producers of erotic fictions claimed that erotic scenes should not be seen as literal descriptions of carnal activities, and therefore cannot be said to entice diegetic identification, but should instead be seen as expressions of a special artistic vision, so that the literal meaning of the texts is only a clue to the deeper system of signifiers in the mind of the artist. The erotic film *Deep Throat* (1972) provides montage sequences that signal a 'higher', 'artistic' motivation for the film. Strong 'naturalistic', 'realistic' descriptions of pain, poverty, or mutilation are often framed by extradiegetic motivation in order to diminish addressee-identification with the fictive protagonists and their suffering. This is either achieved by means of an addresser intention, for example that the director intends to make a 'human document' (he wants, say, to show the suffering of people in the Third World), or by producing an equivalent addressee persona, that this is to be received, for example, by a 'modern', 'scientific', and emotionally detached viewer. Historical narratives can motivate strong descriptions of sex and violence, and the motivation allows the viewer an increased identification with the viewed by isolating the narrative from standard norms.

Motivation as frame can thus serve as an emotional filter, in order to diminish empathic identification (by activating extradiegetic associations and creating a dual focus) or in order to perform modal transformations. Framing by motivation is not a procedure for 'hiding something', similar to the psychoanalytical concept of 'secondary elaboration'. The basic way in which phenomena exist in fictions is as part of a motivating context. An isolated existence as cause for undirected and saturated associations is (excluding lyrical films) the exception, not the norm. Motivation is therefore a choice between options of frame and focus of attention.

NATURALIST DETERMINISM, REALISM, AND OTHER GENRE PATTERNS

Generic schemata may increase the level of affective charge by making the world of fiction less open than the standard conception of the real world. Barthes has described what he calls narrative functions, phenomena that are functionally linked to later phenomena, as when the purchase of a revolver is correlated to the moment when it will be used. He further describes 'indices', phenomena indicating character traits, 'atmosphere', and other elements (Barthes 1977b; see Tomachevski 1965). A conventional use of 'functions' and 'indices' raises the addressee expectations and experience of 'meaning' supported by the bounded-guided attention cued by the audiovisual sequence. Barthes' functions and indices would be described within the terminology of the present book as narrative schemata, associative schemata, and categorizations.

The viewer's relations to the schemata raise an intricate cluster of problems that can be divided into those related to temporal expectations and achronic categorization as such, and those related to degree of viewer knowledge of, and 'consciousness about', schemata and formulaic categorization. To create temporal expectations presupposes at least a minimal schematic structure in the fiction and in the viewer. If a given situation in fiction were totally open and undirected, the reader/viewer would not be able to make any guesses as to its links with an ensuing situation. The viewer's expectations could lead him in many directions, but could also supplant temporal expectations with achronic associations. To increase temporal expectation therefore presupposes a number of schemata, each with some probability. The more we strengthen the schematic relations between a given situation and possible future situations, and the more we limit the options, the more we increase the activation of tense or saturated experiences—up to a point. Expressed 'negatively', this means that the schemata 'isolate' the situation from total openness. A small set of possible outcomes will be the target of the concentrated expectations, and will, given proper motivation, activate strong 'obsessive' emotions.

Genre schemata and also stereotype schemata from everyday life provide such activation of a limited set of expectations (given that the outcome of these expectations has some salience). In highly patterned narrative formulas like those of *film noir,* the general outline of the narrative will be quite predictable. A considerable number of its elements would be 'functions' in Barthes' sense. The determinedness and temporal directedness of the audiovisual sequence caused by the media have thus been further raised by the content. Nearly all phenomena have a clear, patterned, sequential 'function'.

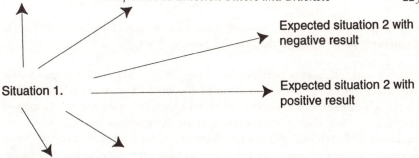

Expected situation 2 with negative result

Expected situation 2 with positive result

Situation 1.

Fig. 9.4 Vectors of possible outcomes. Schemata may make some results more probable and thus evoke tense or saturated expectations controlled by these situations, here situations 1 and 2; whereas outcomes for which the viewer and the film do not have ready-made schemata, here the unmarked arrows, do not contain tense or saturated expectations.

Likewise the visual phenomena would be indices, pointing to formulaic categorization (night = horror, passion; white horse = hero).

The smooth operation of the activation of expectations by formulaic schemata is undermined from two sides. The activation of expectations and affective charge can be decreased by total *automation,* so that the viewer performs the mental processes without much conscious attention and emotional activation. However, the schemata as such may also become so obvious that they attract the biggest share of the attention. The experience would stop being a simulation of 'life'; attention to meta-activities (like registering what device is used and when) might create an affective distance to the viewed and filter empathic identification.

Realists of the nineteenth and twentieth centuries have tried to tone down narrative patterns and simulate an open and undirected world by increasing the level of description, especially of objects, in order to make the reader or viewer feel that he is located in a world of unbounded and undirected metonymy. The single object or feature in a realist text does not possess the high level of symbolic directedness and affective charge of, for example, romantic literature. An object is connected to other objects and features by a web of metonymic relations. The selection of elements in realist fiction seems to be motivated extra-textually: a given element just happened to be there when the camera passed by, metonymically connected to all the other phenomena, and will not appear later. The singular percept is not categorized.

Kracauer believed that films

tend to capture physical existence in its endlessness. Accordingly, one may also say that they have an affinity, evidently denied to photography, with the continuum of life or the 'flow of life', which of course is identical with open-ended life. The concept 'flow of life', then, covers the stream of material situations and happenings with all that they intimate in terms of emotions, values, thoughts. The implication is that the flow of life is predominantly a material rather than a mental continuum, even though, by definition, it extends into the mental dimension. (1961: 71)

Consequently, Kracauer prefers 'the found story' (1961: 245 ff.); his models are 'street life' or the patterns created by the wind on a surface of water, stories in which nature or a kind of social nature is the subject-agent. As long as the 'details' have only a static-photographic existence as facticity he has no problems with 'realism' (contrary to Barthes, as we shall see); it is only when narrative systems of motivation for the motion arise that he has to opt for supra-individual agents moving the seen. His conception of 'realism' therefore leads towards the passive lyrical-associative melodrama. In a paradoxical way, his 'realist' approach accords with a formalist approach in shunning representations with strong anthropomorph elements and structured by individual intentions.

Whereas some realists depict 'real life' as open, others, the 'naturalists', describe a highly 'deterministic' world (in which causes lead to effects) or supra-individual telic processes. This means applying sequential schemata. The objective of describing the phenomena as 'just existing' and real is in conflict with the objective of describing the phenomena as elements in chains of causes and effects or chains of global acts and goals, because the description of deterministic or telic processes will have consequences for the emotional evaluation. As we saw in Chapter 7, a 'naturalist' film like Resnais' *Mon Oncle d'Amèrique* tends to become metafiction in the sense that the diegetic world lacks 'realist facticity', and empathic-enactive identification is filtered by the frame. The diegetic world consists of exemplifications of a super-schema, and this is often emphasized by the voice-over commentary of the 'real' scientist, Laboris. Kubrick's *2001—A Space Odyssey* has a similar socio-psychological frame, of man's expansion by aggression, and a similar distance to the diegetic world.

The paradox of 'realistic existence' versus objective causality and determinism in fiction is a concrete paradox in naturalism, because the efforts to describe a scientific and determined world are often emotionally experienced as melodrama of the passive position. The individual will is supplanted by supra-individual schemata experienced in analogy to romantic fate. Zola's naturalist novels describe a world of strict determinism on the social and psycho-biological level, and the role of 'scientific laws' has a narrative function similar to 'fate'. In Renoir's *La Bête Humaine,* based on a novel by Zola, the railway system and sexuality are two 'forces' which acquire the same function as 'fate' in a romantic melodrama. Another example of the way in which a naturalist 'flow of life' is experienced as a melodrama is John Ford's *The Grapes of Wrath.* In order to show that the Joad family forms part of two great historical processes, one a deterministic process of exploitation, one a telic process of creating a just society, the film uses romantic, socialist, and biblical schemata. This transforms the phenomena from existence as emblems of extratextual reality into elements in dynamic mental models of 'social existence'. The closing long shots of Tom Joad walking along a ridge, and of migrant workers driving along a road, use a mental model of telic-paratelic 'motion along a trajectory without a specified goal'. The model is symbolic in the sense that the perception of the motion is linked to a more global understanding of the acts as representative of greater forces, not as random samples of items that just happened to be there, and the use of the model in these shots is furthermore intended to evoke strong melodramatic emotions in the viewer.

This does not, however, necessarily make the dynamic model less 'real': the rejection of 'realism' and 'naturalism' by aesthetic schools advocating a general criticism and 'deconstruction' of all representations is often motivated by a problematic 'implicit objectivism' (as discussed in Chapter 1).

For Barthes, the 'factualness' of this type of representation immediately evokes the communicative intent of the film-maker or author. They are not genuine 'realist' descriptions, because the 'facts' lose their reference to a non-fictional real world by becoming generic conventions signifying 'reality' (1968; see also Thompson 1987: 197 ff.). Barthes' point makes representations impossible; any representation has to rely on a set of procedures, whether 'natural perception' or cultural codes, and, seen from a point of reception, his description of the reality-effect as coded merely means that the viewer may activate the circumstances of the production of a given fiction as a part of the experience. To some extent a consciousness of the schematic features of representation is an indirect awareness of the schematic basis for a consciousness of the world.

FICTION, GAME, ROLE, AND METAFICTION

At the beginning of this chapter I discussed types of framing and distance that modify empathic identification with the fiction by creating a viewer-persona and mediating supplementary contexts. However, instead of simply modifying the empathic identification, brackets can also be used to make identification conditional. This can be done by creating an awareness in the viewer of participating in a special activity, that of fiction consumption, but the emphasis would now be put on the identification with the protagonist as a special role, a bracketed subset of the full repertoire of the real-life viewer, and carried out according to certain rules. The viewer divides himself into an empirical person anchored in a real-life world, and a 'player'-'persona', who participates in the narrative game. We identify with 'Marilyn Monroe' or 'Humphrey Bogart' but as a result of a clear consciousness of the limited and patterned aspects of the identification.

To play a 'role' is a mediation of the active and passive position. It implies passively the submission to such constraints as a prefixed pattern, a script, or some rules. But it may also imply that the role is isolated, anchored to specific contexts, and that the empirical person can actively manipulate his role and control freely his affective identification with it. In card games, for example, it is easy to see how enjoyment is made possible by isolating roles and relations from real-life contexts and by mixing passive and active positions. The player submits to rules and sometimes to chance, but has certain opportunities for action. 'Games' accentuate experimental and hypothetical behaviour; a person can try out certain behaviour without investing his total personality. The fiction equivalent of game is the blending of explicitly coded narratives and thematic formulas with 'metafictional' markers of distance to roles and patterns. The markers of distance show that the 'obsessional' pattern repetition (and the occasional complete violation of pattern rules) is performed voluntarily (and therefore allows the addressee in a transitional role to consume the fictions 'as a game'). The blend of formula, break of rules, and distance is characteristic of fiction formulas such as parody and pastiche. These narratives are highly encoded and unfree. The viewer is aware of participating in a 'ritualistic' and fully determined repetition that guarantees a high level of signification, although parody often tries to simulate freedom by shock-producing breaks of genre expectations. But, at the same time, the identification with the protagonists is bracketed; the viewer feels free to bale out of the identification at any time. In some recent descriptions of 'metafictional' playfulness, freedom and distance in relation to the patterns are emphasized, for example when Waugh (1984: 41 f.) criticizes Huizinga and Callois for finding the civilizing aspect of learning to follow rules by playing games very important. She emphasizes the 'freedom' of the play as a rebellion against the tyranny of systems, but the metafictional recycling of traditional narrative patterns cannot only be explained by a freedom-producing laying bare of devices, as it is obvious that few people would play card games only to reveal the rules. The metafictional 'playfulness' makes the hypothetical and conditional aspects of rule-following limitations on 'freedom' more obvious, but it presupposes 'acceptance of rules' and evokes pleasures connected with the following of such rules.

The level of signification is often raised dramatically because of the determinism of the narrative and thematic pattern. A leads to B which leads to C, and this isolation produces a high concentration and directedness in the process of signification. The high level of signification by determinism is made possible by the bracketing procedure of voluntarily reducing the active-open world: 'this is only a game', which makes a bale-out from the hypothetical world possible. Seen from this point of view, a parody, for example, not only aims at making fun of a given pattern of fiction and deconstructing the fascination of the parodied texts, but is also a device for magnifying a characteristic pattern and its means of signification and, by that, intensifying its primary affective impact, but embedding this impact by modifying the identification on a secondary level. The viewer is participating as another, and is therefore protected from the full impact of this intensification. The need to embed the roles in modifying frames is relative to the situation of the viewer. Steven Spielberg often embeds his remakes of 'naïve' action films in 'pastiche' frames in order to enable the adult viewer to overcome a blend of 'childish' fascination and adult rejection of the emotions encoded in the fictional pattern, whereas the ambitious 'realist' director would try to put layers of random events and items on top of the narrative pattern, and thus simulate a 'real-world' situation while also having to accept a decrease in sequential directedness.

Metafiction is often described as fiction about fiction, and therefore without meaning except the auto-referential 'I write that I write that I write', 'I see that I see', or 'I play that I play'. But just as 'plain fiction' is a *mise-en-scène* of a wide range of human attitudes and affections, metafiction produces modifications of these patterns by sophistication of the modes of addressee identification with the fictions. The common way of legitimizing metafiction and intertextual fiction is that it is a laying-bare of the devices and therefore part of a critical project, deconstructing the codes (the ideological patterns). Robbe-Grillet's novel *The Voyeur,* for example, lays bare the devices of crime fiction; Babenco's film *Kiss of the Spider Woman* lays bare the implicit fascination of a certain kind of macho-fascist film. However, although this legitimization is true, the metafictions at the same time rely to some extent on encoded fascination to produce their affective charge. The distinction between 'metafiction' and narratives of passion, like melodrama and horror, is related to the viewer's reception preferences. Corman's *The Pit and the Pendulum* uses effects which might be evaluated as metafictional (use of iris-in, iris-out, and explicit use of romantic clichés, like castle, waves, and thunder), and whether the emphasis on the narrative as patterned and as a repetition of fictional schemata is experienced as 'metafictional', as an inducer of a passive viewer-position, or as a metafictional bracket allowing a passive hypothesis, depends on the viewer's choice of reception strategy and preferences of affective tone.

CLICHÉ AS FRAME, STEREOTYPE, AND COMMON DENOMINATOR

In the paragraph above, the effects of identification framing have been mainly described from the point of view of modification of identification. But the reverse side of the modification and bracketing procedure is to circumvent and protect against social restrictions on viewer taste, as in many Spielberg films. The viewer distance to fiction guarantees a free and responsible 'real-world' viewer, irrespective of what takes place in fiction and with which role the viewer identifies. The formulaic and stereotype aspects of the embedded fiction guarantee that the patterns of fiction are common social denominators. By being formulaic, the stereotype fictions establish a 'social contract', a social 'frame' of negotiated acceptability. Social stereotypes like the cliché are a negation of a personalized addresser, and in some aspects come very close to a melodramatic mode by creating an identification with the passive position and a strong sense of playing a role scripted by external enactive principles. A phenomenon like cliché has very negative connotations (for most high-culture partisans) because it lacks individuality, but the negative aspects are closely related to the positive aspects of cliché as a 'common denominator'. The cliché breaks down frames of individuality or 'grown-up-ness' and/or stabilizes systems of socially negotiated affective representations, for example in the sentimental cliché song or the 'evergreen', which seems to say: this is a system of common representations of sentiments with which we can mould our feelings for a moment without being personally 'responsible' for them. The participating 'I' is marked as being only a part of a social 'I', and existing at a distance from the ordinary and responsible real-world 'I', as in Averill's (1980) description of emotions as 'transitory social roles'. In the same way there is no real or responsible addresser: the author/director is 'just' remaking an anonymous common denominator. Like the melodramatic mode, the enactive principle as other governs the affections. The use of the term 'folk' by the romanticists was in some respects just such a 'bracketing' of simple and emotionally charged patterns.[2] The abstraction made by identification with the stereotyped social roles is an isolation, and therefore produces an increased affective charge by cutting off the multiple, concrete, real-world relations of the viewer, who can identify with the state of being 'man', 'woman', 'victim', or 'hero'.

The term cliché has its metaphorical roots in a machine for producing meaning, the printing press, and is differentially defined *vis-à-vis* the 'original' and the 'personal' expressions, and all the individualist connotations clustering around these terms. The effects of cliché are similar to those of social stereotypes found in ritualistic texts; in religious texts unoriginality is a virtue rather than a vice, because these texts are supposed to be transmitters of remote principles, such as God or Tradition, and should repeat and reconstruct common social denominators. Oral poetry, for example, possessed a number of stock formulas; and in medieval literature, to write was to a large extent a noble art of quotation and allusions to other texts. This was repeated in Eliot's (1920) conception of literature: he tried to advocate a balance between the cliché and innovation. The text should be a network of overt or secret allusions and quotation, and yet it should also be an innovative activ-

---

[2] On the emotional impact of cliché see also the analysis of *Casablanca* in Eco (1986).

ity. Cliché is the negatively valorized term for many of the phenomena that are positively valorized in ritual.

It often assumed that what the consumer wants, or should want, is innovation and individualism, for instance receiving a 'personal' message from the addresser. To seek 'common denominators', social mediations, is from this point of view connected with negatively valorized phenomena like 'ideology' or 'abstraction'. If a person chooses to read a crime novel or watch *Dallas* or *Dynasty* in order to lose his individual persona for a moment and participate in common persona-formulas, individualists may see his behaviour as escapism. The metafictional framing of viewing of the cliché patterns of common denominators mediates between the social (cliché) and the individual (the 'free' distance to the clichés); however, from a more fundamental perspective the position of individualism is also a patterned, built-in one.

Pastiche/genre stereotypes allow the viewer to accept an increase in the level of 'signification' of the directedness of fiction because the decrease of 'freedom' in the fiction is offset by the bracketing procedure, underlining the spectator as player. Many pastiche films allow an increase in the level of sex-role signifiers and the level of difference, for instance by a grotesque exaggeration of female weakness and male strength, or by a high-pitched female voice and a low-pitched male one; but, at the same time, pastiche films bracket sex-roles as play (for instance, framed as 'roles of the past' like caveman/woman, or framed in a *film noir* cast of sex roles supposedly from the 1940s). The bracketing-embedding procedure is one of mediation, which attempts to present the pleasures belonging to different levels or spheres (present roles and pleasures versus past roles and pleasures) and claims that they are non-conflictual because of the lack of a common space of interaction. The caveman and modern man are separated by history and mediated, for example, by being aspects of 'the historical variability of human nature'. But bracketing and embedding is also a procedure for allowing the revival of past pleasures: by looking at a self-conscious pastiche of a *film noir* instead of the real thing, the addresser reveals the fascinations, and he can increase the level of signification in the film.

In self-conscious formula fiction there is no longer sheer repetition of a previous formula; the fiction has become an active re-creation of a fascination, as in spaghetti Westerns like *The Good, the Bad and the Ugly* and *Once Upon a Time in the West*, in which the system of characteristic signifiers is melodramatically emphasized and more or less isolated, so that the addresser establishes a complicity of fascinations between himself and the spectator, and seems to say, 'We want to re-enact, relive these signifiers of (past) pleasures. The necessity of their order of display is compatible with our free desire to re-experience them, and they have therefore no bearing on a (present) real-life situation.' The freedom and subjectivity of the viewer is moved from the level of fictional simulation of action to the level of perceptual and affective simulation.

Nostalgia and *retro* films, and television fictions, use history and historical patterns as an embedded space for negotiating social roles and common denominators. Nostalgia is a specific mode of melodrama of the passive position. It blocks enactional identification, highlighting identification with an 'I' as other, as object; and the perceptual identification is directed at images of persons from the past: a memory trace, like recollections of childhood, for example. In order to experience the film sequence, the viewer is supposed to construct a mental model, analogous to those used for memories, in which the experiences of the subject-actant are beyond enactional control, bygone is bygone, and the future is determined. The affective release of nostalgia is caused by the passivity that cues an autonomic response. The emotions are passive experiences, such as actants resembling one's infantile or adolescent 'I'-other. Strong abandonment to the emotions is made possible by embedding the experience in an 'objective' audiovisual form. *La mode rétro* is a more self-conscious version of the nostalgia film. Whereas ordinary nostalgia is caused by an identification with a past 'other' and past experiences, the self-referential film highlights the fact that experience is a patterned social construction. Cinema-goers in the 1920s did not have an open and individual experience when looking at a silent film; style, narrative pattern, and characters provided stereotypical social patterns to which all those living in the period had to mould their mental lives, so that their consciousness was a social construction, just as the way they dressed was an 'unfree' result of the dictates of fashion. The *rétro* film makes the coded character of the systems of consciousness and pleasure explicit. This, in some respects, represents a double system of defence, by having three sets of brackets around the experience: the first bracket consists of putting the experience in a space of pastness, which we can only relive by memory and repetition, not by options to change the fatal course of events; the second bracket consists of a claim that, even in those days, these experiences were patterned, social constructions. A third bracket consists of the explicitness of the patterned, so that present-day viewers know that other viewers also participate in their blend of nostalgic affect and distance, and therefore viewers share not only identification with the fiction but also the voyeuristic viewer-persona. A *film noir* pastiche creates an overdetermined viewer-as-other-persona consisting of a consciousness of pretending to be one of the more unsophisticated viewers of the 1940s, mixed with reminiscences of one's own earlier and more unsophisticated experiences of cinema. The clichés mark the situation as one of sharing experiences with other viewers. These metafictions place the previous pleasures in a position of signified.

An increase in the quantity of metafiction and intertextual fiction is intimately linked with the increased importance of fiction in the socialization of the individual. It begins with the first lullaby, followed by fairy-tales, nursery rhymes, children's television, young people's fiction, and the different levels of grown-up fiction. These fictions not only constitute an important part of representational socialization, but also an important part of affective social-ization. Strings of texts exist with potential affective charge. This socializa-tion is not just a reception of an ever-increasing number of discrete units of fiction. As in other processes of development, a new item will make a new structural situation, in which the previous texts will function as systems of emotionally charged, more or less invisible signifiers for the later texts, that is, as emotionally charged subtexts. Agatha Christie very often uses nursery rhymes or proverbs as affective relays, injecting, for example, an infantile emotional charge into texts. To 'quote' and to embed therefore operates both ways: on the one hand, earlier texts are used as affective relays to the later texts; on the other, the earlier texts will be reframed and re-embedded in the later texts. Dennis Potter's television series *Pennies from Heaven,* and the film version, directed by Herbert Ross, are perfect illustrations of the means by which patterns of fiction function as affective relays in the modelling of every-day life, but also exemplify the way in which the 'self-conscious' frame allows 'sophisticated' viewers to look and listen to earlier and perhaps 'rejected' fascinations. Mahler's use of the theme of a children's song in his First Symphony, or Schönberg's use of 'Ach du lieber Augustin' in *Verklärte Nacht,* are similar examples of 'defamiliarization', but are also affective relays to more popular musical forms.

The growing importance of fiction in the process of socialization increases the importance of reframing and restructuring the individual's whole archive of patterned fascinations, and of making them visible. Metafiction is part of an effort to make fictional patterns visible, but also to 'frame' them in order to protect them, for example, against aesthetic criticism.

MOONLIGHTING: THE DREAM SEQUENCE ALWAYS RINGS TWICE

In 1985 the ABC network introduced a crime series, *Moonlighting,* which in several of its aspects has been regarded as part of what could be called the television avant-garde. Like many experimental series produced in the eight-ies, *Moonlighting* has gender roles as a major issue and narrative device (sim-ilar to *Cagney and Lacey,* for example). The plot-creating gimmick of female boss and male employee was taken from a series *Remington Steele* on the competing network NBC. A major part of the tension in *Moonlighting* is built up around the 'conflict' and ambiguity in gender structure between the social and the sexual role. The woman boss is a representative of the Protestant work ethic and of Victorian morality, while the man has a more working-class, employee-like attitude to work, and is a womanizer. The man in *Remington Steele* is the 'charming British gentleman-crook'; David Addison (Bruce Willis) in *Moonlighting* is a more American and more proletarian, macho Prince Charming.

Furthermore, like many visual fictions of the 1970s and 1980s, *Moonlight-ing* uses metafictional and intertextual devices in its narration and enuncia-tion (see Olsen 1987). These devices, previously more characteristic of high culture, were present in popular fiction mostly in the comic and parodic modes. By metafictional devices, viewers of *Moonlighting* are made aware of being spectators to fiction. The series self-consciously presupposes that the viewer knows that it refers to other 'absent' texts and reconstructs the inter-textual relations. It is thus similar to the nostalgic films in *la mode rétro* that Fredric Jameson (albeit with some problematic conclusions[3]) has analyzed. In pastiche and nostalgia films the viewer is constantly made aware of the his-torical and mental distance between himself and the past textual expressions of emotions. This is explicitly shown in the film *The French Lieutenant's Woman,* in which Victorian and present-day gender and sex roles are con-trasted, and the pleasures and pains of the past roles are thus bracketed (see Grodal 1992).

These two phenomena, the discussion of gender roles and metafiction/inter-textuality, are intimately related in *Moonlighting* because metafictional devices and intertextuality are used in the description of the historicity and relativity of gender and sex-roles. Many of the plot tensions are built up around configurations of active/passive polarizations: on the one hand the 'modern', 'free' variation of being socially active/passive (dominant/ dominated); on the other hand the traditional sexual roles featuring female passivity and male aggression. The detection is not only, as in traditional detective fiction, a quest for dominance over the invisible criminal other, it is also a fight for dominance between the two sexes. The 'constitutional for-mula' of *Moonlighting* prevents sexual intercourse, and the man's active quest for sexual intercourse is deferred *ad infinitum* by the female protagonist because of its implications for the power distribution in the social aspect of her existence. The mediations are then made in embedded levels of significa-tion, as in the episode analyzed below, in which Maddy and David make love, but in a dream and as characters in a *film noir* from the late 1940s. The *film-noir* universe was produced in a social environment in which the welding together of social and sexual roles was already a problem; women's liberation in the 1970s and 1980s made the problems even greater, especially for the large group of well-paid and well-educated younger professional couples ('yup-pies'). Because of their buying-power, this group has become important for advertisers and thus for producers of television. In order to represent social

---

[3] For example, in Jameson (1983). One of Jameson's points is that the nostalgic *rétro* mode is connected with the death of historical consciousness in late capitalism. I believe the contrary to be the case: the modern viewer has a strong historical consciousness and is therefore able to enjoy the play of pastiche using past forms of representation; the viewer puts brackets around the iden-tification with the past in order to sophisticate the historical insight by creating the necessary dis-tance.

and gender roles for this audience, brackets, embeddings, and distance are modes of caution used by producers and a means of mediating between potentially conflicting fascinations for the consumers of fiction.

The title of the episode *The Dream Sequence Always Rings Twice* is an obvious indication of pastiche and *mode rétro*, a remake of the *rétro* remake of *The Postman Always Rings Twice*, which explicitly positions the episode in intertextuality. For several reasons the network thought it wise to put an extra 'frame' around the episode by having Orson Welles, smoking a large cigar and seated in an armchair, introduce it. His introduction indicates that we are about to see a piece of television art, so we must read it in a special way. The television viewer thus receives the information that he must be more patient about discovering the pleasures of this series than those of mainstream television fiction, because, as high art, it could mean extra work in interpretation. The viewer must accept in particular that most of the episode—that is, the two dream sequences—is shot in black and white to attain a genuine *film noir* look. The producers were obviously slightly worried about whether this experiment would be too much for prime-time television. Orson Welles is a representative of the addresser system, but he is also a point of crystallization for the viewer's moulding of his or her attitude toward the fiction, for instance (as in Hitchcock's introductions to half-hour horror) a viewer attitude as distant, semi-sadistic connoisseur. Part of the viewer is supposed to identify playfully with the black-and-white melodrama; part of the viewer can look with sadistic pleasure at people reduced to dummies in a cliché world.

By his recommendation, Orson Welles caters for an audience of middle-aged people; the audience is recommended to confine children and grandparents to another room so as to be able to plunge fully into the pleasures of the episode (thus emphasizing the dreamlike, narcissistic pleasures and immoral sadism in the consumption). This also means that Welles recommends the episode to people who were young during or just after *film-noir*, for whom the *film noir mise-en-scène* of desire was part of the moulding of their adolescent desires, and for whom these encodings of desire exist as subtexts, as non-conscious systems of signifiers below, for example, the pictures and narratives of sexual emancipation in the 1980s.

The main film is about the 1940s and the fascinations of the *film noir*. The *film-noir* system of signifiers is made clear by being magnified in a semi-parodic way and by being explicitly commented upon. In this way the addresser achieves two objectives in one. The level of sex signification is strongly emphasized: dream-David is equipped with an explicitly phallic cornet, dream-Maddie with a (vaginal) bosom-cleavage exposed for the male gaze. This system is however, framed as a historically past system of signification, that of the 1940s.

It is important for the episode self-consciously to highlight the historicity of its style. The historical frame of this system of signification is given in the exposition immediately after the Orson Welles frame. Maddie and David visit a theatre that in the 1940s contained a night club, the Flamingo Club, but in the 1980s has not been used for years. Obviously times and taste have changed, and the theatre is going to be torn down to make way for a commercial building with a more contemporary appeal. It only survives in the 1980s as part of a *rétro*-oriented dream life. Maddie and David are told a story about a man being murdered at the club many years ago, and the subsequent execution of his wife and her lover, although both claimed that they were innocent. Maddie and David argue fiercely about whom they believe to be innocent. After the argument, they both dream their own version of what actually happened at the Flamingo Club.

The dream sequences represent a subjective acting-out of fantasmatic content activated in Maddie's and David's minds by thinking of the former night club. The sequences highlight seduction, the passive pleasures. Both construct their own version of the triangle and the crime. Maddie's sequence shows her as the innocent victim of male aggression and seduction; she is forced to give in to the phallic assault, while David is seduced by the Rita-Hayward-type, active and emancipated *femme fatale* (although the man in both episodes does the actual killing, in his version it is a gallant attempt to protect the woman from her husband). The emancipated woman of the 1980s, Maddie, acts out the passive aspects in the disguise of a historically past period, which might also be the period in which the moulding of the sensuality of the viewer has taken place. This acting-out is also a revelation of the programming of sensuality proceeding from film to person. Similarly David acts out an oedipally-oriented triangle, with its madonna/whore doubling of the woman and the boyish softness of the male intruder, and understands his own role in the oedipal murder situation as that of defender of the madonna aspects *vis-à-vis* the brutality of the man (the 'father').

The acting-out of the episode consists of 'self-conscious' participation in fantasies, in contrast to the unconscious 'seduction' by the imagery of the film. The clichés are highlighted as clichés, as common social stereotypes into which we can plunge (protected by the framing and setting) without being personally responsible for them. Maddie can enjoy exhibiting herself to the male gaze and give in to the passive position as a cliché; the clichés of 'seduction' or 'human nature', for instance, create a social framework (a transitional role) which makes heteronomy acceptable. The legitimation may be that the role does not concern the persons as individuals, but is a special social role they can play. The legitimation of the cliché role may also be 'human biology', understood as a level of otherness in relation to the individual whose mind allows the biological level, the call of nature, to take its course and thus accept a short intermezzo of heteronomy in relation to the biolevel and the dream/fantasy level.

The fiction is thus embedded in four main frames:

Frame 1. Orson Welles: the episode is framed as something extraordinary, art, and at the same time as a world of pleasure which is at the command of the viewer in a combination of participation and sadistic distance.

Frame 2. The historical pastness of the visual, *noir* language of the Flamingo Club.

Frame 3. Cliché and role as non-individual common social denominators that project responsibility from an individual to a social or natural level.

Frame 4. Dream life as a special, bracketed *mise-en-scène* of personal wish-fulfilment, underlined by the difference between the female and the male version of the triangle, and set apart from everyday life.

The episode is, furthermore, set in a post-Freudian and post-feminist environment in which the sexual and sadistic content of detection is laid bare to an audience. The transition from the historical-theatre frame to the dream sequence has as its key word and trigger-mechanism the word 'scrutinize'. The word is contextualized in a way that explicitly associates it with 'screwtinized', and thus makes the phallic implications of detection and research obvious for the very many viewers who have a basic Freudian awareness from college, novels, or psychology sessions. Freudianism is therefore an optional fifth frame for the large minority of viewers who have acquired Freudian mental models.

The episode very consciously intervenes in and tries to mediate the two opposed points of view represented in the two words 'sexist' and 'sexy'. The double viewpoint of the two dream-sequences expresses an effort to cater for both sexes. This gives a split identification: each sex is forced to identify with the point of view of the other, despite the fact that the conclusion states that everybody lives in his/her own fantasy world in which his/her own egocentric viewpoints arrange the facts. Both sexes are also distanced spectators in the game-realization of a biocultural pattern which they themselves control.

The episode advocates fiction as a model for learning to command a broad repertoire of modern social roles and behaviours less tightly tied to each other than was the case for earlier inner-directed personalities (Riesman 1950). The late-nineteenth-century Dr Jekyll–Mr Hyde myth concerning the troubles of multiple personalities is supplanted in *Moonlighting* by a myth relating to relativism of roles. This raises the broad question of the role of film and television fiction in the modernization of the affective and psychological software of mankind.

10

Crime and Horror Fiction

Crime fiction is a subgenre of canonical narratives. As a result of its narrative structure, it has a characteristic strong emphasis on cognitive control, compared with the typical canonical narrative in which cognitive control is more closely integrated with physical acts. The main objective of classic mysteries is to make a valid cognitive representation of a given set of facts, thus solving a mystery, although the solution to problems is often correlated with motivations, like the wish to punish criminals, connected with factual consequences in a non-mental, hypothetical world. It is a subgenre centrally occupied with information-processing and problem-solving; consequently, some social reasons for its rise to fame and glory, in parallel with the increasing importance of professional information processing in society, are self-evident.[1]

Important writers and directors of crime fiction are often also writers or directors of horror fiction (Poe, Doyle, Hitchcock; see Grodal 1984), and this points to the importance of cognitive control in crime fiction and the link between this and 'body control'. Often horror fiction also deals with cognitive control, but, whereas the motivation in detection fiction is primarily cognitive gratification, in horror fiction the effort to gain cognitive control is mostly derived from a motivation to maintain personal body and mind autonomy, which is under severe attack from uncontrollable phenomena. This contrast highlights the aspects of crime fiction which connect cognitive control with mechanisms of distancing: the aloofness of Poe's detective-hero, Dupin, is the contrary to that of his horror 'subjects', who, by being buried alive, for example, have totally lost control of their existence. What distinguishes ordinary detection fiction from the genres of metafiction and distancing dealt with in Chapters 7 and 9, is the degree to which the 'frame of distancing' in crime fiction is a fictional personification, compared to the typical metafiction, in which the frame of distancing is non-fictional personification or a non-personified frame.

Let us consider the way in which classic crime fiction is a special variation of the canonical narrative. We can contrast a mystery fiction and a central

---

[1] Benjamin (1973) further connects crime fiction with the new anonymous interpersonal relations between people in the metropolitan areas of the 19th century with the detective as a *flaneur* comparable to the poet. For a description of the social genesis, cf. also Mandel (1984), Palmer (1978), and Knight (1980).

canonical narrative, like Spielberg's *Raiders of the Lost Ark*. The subject-actant Indiana Jones's structure of motivations and goals exists within a unified diegetic world. Some of the goals and motives are explicit: to retrieve the lost Ark, to 'get even' with adversaries. Some aims are implicit, like Jones's sexual goals in relation to Marion. To achieve his goals, Indiana Jones 'seeks information', and 'performs acts', whereas the 'enablement' is derived from information. Some of his motives are 'higher', for example his wish to serve the United States, the free world, and mankind, but they are directly interwoven with his own motivation. There is thus only one narrative level of which Jones is a full member: his motives and acts may be parallel to or opposed to acts and motives of other actants, but they interact on one common ground. The emotional process of the narrative as simulated by the viewer is consequently a direct function of Jones's goals and motives: these, in turn, are directly linked to possible acts and to consequences of acts performed by Jones or by other actants, but having direct consequences for Jones's preferences. As a result of this, the emotional flow is dominated by tensities or emotivities.

In crime fiction of the classic, detective type (from Poe's *The Murders in the Rue Morgue* to Falk in *Columbo*) the motivational structure is different. There is one narrative level on which we have a subject-actant, the detective, who acts by solving hermeneutic problems as a result of obtaining and processing information. The motivation for solving the hermeneutic problems typically includes the sheer pleasure of processing information and solving riddles; curiosity as to human nature and the enigmatic aspects of society; the desire to be a detective for business reasons; the acquisition of social respect, directly (as in the narcissism of many detectives) or indirectly (by being servants to higher causes like 'justice' or 'the ethics of a small independent businessman', like Marlowe). Then there is another narrative level, made up by the criminals and the victims, and their acts and correlated motives: money and precious objects, power, sexual gratification (normal or deviant), honour, revenge and jealousy, and so on. The emotional flow as simulated by the viewer is therefore a more complex function of the two narrative levels:

Embedded series:	S: Murderer →	O: (Victim) evoking saturated emotions
Link series:	S: Information →	O: (Murderer) Buffer of distanciation
Embedding detection series:	S: Detective →	O: (Information) evoking tensity

The viewer experiences a primary cognitive and empathic identification with the detective. The reconstruction of the embedded series of acts of crime and their motives takes place via the link series of information, which is often nonchronological. We see the dead corpse, for example, but are led by verbal clues into a reconstruction of motives and sequences of acts leading up to the murder. The tensity of the embedding series ensures that their saturated emotions are projected toward the exterior world. In Hitchcock's *Rear Window,* the amateur 'detectives' infer, from the sight of a saw and a knife which the suspect wraps in a newspaper, that the suspect has cut his wife into small pieces in the bathtub. But the gruesome act is performed off-screen, and the saturated emotions evoked by the thoughts of the grim act exist as an embedded activation which creates an emotional background to the tense curiosity of reconstructing the criminal act and establishing the guilt.

The background of crime fiction implies that normally people do not separate a cognitive and an affective representation of the world. To represent the human body with the same lack of emotions with which we would look at any other physical object goes contrary to the normal fusion of cognitive representation and empathy. A rather extreme case of distanciation in Hitchcock's crime-comedy *The Trouble With Harry* indirectly highlights the relation between cognitive and emotional representation in crime fiction. Here the distanciation becomes so great that a dead body does not arouse any interest in the detection and punishment of the criminal, only in its disposal, as if it were any other expendable item. The story takes place during the autumn, in an idyllic rural community. A retired ferry-captain goes hunting in the forest and discovers a body, thinks that he has killed a man by accident, and buries him. However, other gentle souls in the rural community, namely an elderly spinster and a single mother, also think that they have killed the man. The farcical plot unfolds reasons for a continuous re-evaluation of the identity of the killer and for revising decisions as to whether the corpse should be buried in the forest. Soon all join forces to dig up and bury the corpse, and, while so doing, even wash the body in the single mother's bathtub and wash and iron its clothes. Nobody really cares about the fact that a murder has been committed: they only care about minimizing the consequences for their personal well-being. Interwoven with this are two love stories, one between the single mother and an artist and one between the retired captain and the spinster. The love stories are also an attempt to convey a representation of love which, on the surface, is non-passionate: there is no difference in emotional level between the way in which affection is shown and the way in which the weather or a cake is discussed.

Hitchcock's intention is, of course, for the viewer to construct a 'shadow representation' of the way in which these people react emotionally under normal circumstances, so that the unemotional behaviour gives the viewer the comic pleasure of relabelling negative excitement caused by 'guilt', 'embarrassment', and 'spinsterish reactions to sexuality', for example, into a positive excitement. Thus this pleasure is based on the discrepancy between the viewer's 'shadow construction' of the normal reaction and the actual fictional reaction, as in the pornographic use of nuns (the spinster/ captain couple represent a comic variation of the nun–seaman topos). Normally, however, the 'shadow-construction of emotions' in the embedded series of crime fiction is not fully toned down. The detectives will make a professional scrutiny of dead bodies and of blood, will examine people's intimate belongings, and reason dispassionately about the sordid motives of crimes; they will enter striptease establishments without being interested in the naked flesh, or will turn down offers of sex and money, and, by so doing, allow the narrative to evolve against a background of saturated, shadow-constructions of emotions, as in the paragraphs on priming and sequencing in Chapter 3. But—unlike the people in *The Trouble With Harry*—the detectives will, in some situations, show emotions like moral revulsion, empathic fear in identification with threatened clients, or a strong wish for justice. In this way the reader can enjoy many strong emotions integrated within a framework of intellectual, tense, hermeneutic curiosity.

CRIME FICTION AND DEFAMILIARIZATION VERSUS VOYEURISM

In some respects the detective functions as a concrete representation of the viewer in his capacity as distant onlooker, so that crime fiction might appear to be a kind of metafiction, and clearly mysteries have some affinity with metafiction. Our experience of what happens has often to pass the perceptual-cognitive 'frame' of the detective, so that our direct empathic identification is with the detective, not with the other agents. But, contrary to metafiction, the 'frame' is the primary narrative agent, and the distanciation is experienced in a personified mode, as traits characterizing the detective as a subject-actant in the narrative, not as an exterior frame filtering the narrated. Therefore many crime fictions are characterized by the importance given to the cognitive and emotional makeup of the hero-detective, while the 'frame' aspects are experienced as the grandiose 'personality' of the detective, from Holmes via Marlowe to Columbo and Inspector Morse.

The distanciation characteristic of several types of crime fiction has been treated extensively by directors and critics in connection with a Freudian theory of voyeurism. The 'detective', like Jeff in *Rear Window,* or Peter and Jeffrey in thrillers like *Dressed to Kill* or *Blue Velvet,* is a peeping Tom finding satisfaction in looking at other people's emotional behaviour or naked bodies from a safe distance. The word 'private eye' is imbued with voyeurist associations. Now, these three films and many similar ones are heavily influenced by Freudian psychology, so the connection between voyeurism and detectives is a consciously built-in feature. It could be said that these and similar films have two main types of message: the weaker one states that there are such people as 'voyeurs' in the world, and they might even satisfy their desires by becoming detectives. Even films like *Dirty Harry* describe the detective as a voyeur, but add 'so what'? The stronger message states that the detective is just a representative of the viewer (see Douchet 1986) or 'modern man' (both of whom have become voyeurs). This latter message often comes with a moral undertone: voyeurism is a perversion, and is somehow connected with the perversity of modern life,[2] in which seeing is preferred to relating, caring, and doing. The logical ultimate position consequent to this point of view would be to ban visual representations in order to let people live in an 'unmediated world', and to ban all types of restrictions on visual access to phenomena in real life, making voyeurism pointless.

I shall now argue against the moralistic associations often linked to the very broad use of 'voyeurism' in fiction production and fiction criticism. One of the classic examples of crime fiction which plays on the relations between distanciation and full identification is Hitchcock's *Rear Window*. The 'Freudian' director links the distanciation of detection with voyeurism quite explicitly. The 'detective', Jeff, is almost completely immobilized as a result of a broken leg, and his detection is therefore mostly visual: like another peeping Tom, he watches what is going on in the flats opposite, using binoculars and a telephoto lens. His point of observation imposes some restraints on his access to this world, which is only visible through certain 'window' peepholes, while many 'scenes' are masked by the walls. We may assume that Hitchcock intends to convey the Freudian message that Jeff is temporarily 'impotent', and that he is therefore more interested in his 'voyeurism' than in interacting with his lovely girlfriend.

But even for the viewer who does not wholly grasp Hitchcock's Freudian-voyeurist overtones the film makes good sense. It could be argued that many aspects of 'voyeurist' features derive from the fact that visual fiction makes the processes of vision intersubjective. In an age before film and television, people also looked at each other: dress codes, ranging from the dramatic Islamic veiling of the female face to a minimal veiling of the genitals in other cultures, demonstrate a certain cross-cultural interest in looking at the human body and in regulating these acts of viewing. An understanding of other people's behaviour and motives mostly implies an ongoing, 'passive-cognitive' social curiosity by which we process the behaviour of our fellow human beings. Most of what Jeff sees is not strange: the unusual is that the persons looked at do not look back and, furthermore, that Jeff needs special equipment like binoculars and a telephoto lens to establish visual contact. The scenes he sees are mostly quite ordinary everyday events: a young girl dancing or working out in her bikini; a 'Miss Lonely Heart' having trouble finding a boyfriend, whose acts indicate at one point that she is going to commit suicide; a newlywed couple (probably) making love behind the blinds; a composer trying to compose a tune. Jeff further observes an elderly married

---

[2] Stam and Pearson (1986) see the voyeurism in *Rear Window* as connected with film viewing in general, as well as with the McCarthy era and with male behaviour.

couple, and notes that the wife is ill. The couple interacts in a non-spectacular way until the wife disappears, and, using this fact and the husband's seemingly perfectly ordinary behaviour, Jeff enjoys some guesswork which leads him to the conclusion that the husband has murdered his wife. Except for the murder, which is inferred rather than shown, the phenomena viewed are the trivia of everyday life. To observe these phenomena is, except for the binoculars and the one-sidedness of the activity, not 'voyeurism' in any strict sense (which would imply the observation of sexual intercourse, as in *Blue Velvet*).

Instead of seeing the 'voyeurist' elements in *Rear Window* as a realist description of 'the activity of the viewer or modern man' it might be more relevant to describe these elements from a functionalist point of view, as frames which create defamiliarization and tensity by the system of high-order motivation. These high-order systems of motivation are connected with the prominence given to the cognitive and emotional attitude of the detective. In *Raiders of the Lost Ark,* the viewer often shares the hero's reactions quite spontaneously: when we see a huge stone rolling toward Indy, we do not need reaction-shots to establish the hero's reaction, and, if such shots are produced, they are purely for the sake of emphasis. But, in many types of crime fiction, it is the 'reaction' of the detective which constitutes the object, the seen. When Jeff and the viewer see the villain Thorwald packing or carrying a suitcase, it is as a trivial scene which is only imbued with meaning and evokes emotions by the reactions of Jeff/detective, via the non-verbal communication of excitement reflected in facial expressions and the attention shown, and via the schemata expressed verbally, which link the trivial with the non-trivial: murder and its motives. Familiar, trivial phenomena have been made unfamiliar, demanding a new, special explanation. Large parts of the film are actually series of reaction-shots. From this point of view, the 'voyeurist' perspectives are rhetorical devices, used to create salience and emphasis in the viewer's perception of the seen.

The intense interest aroused by the indexing of phenomena by means of camera-work and the facial expressions of the 'detectives' presupposes that we actively construct our emotions and interests in accordance with the mental states of the detective; we are 'on a guided tour' (although we are assisted by a competence constructed from our knowledge of many schemata drawn from crime fiction). Carroll (1988) has given an account of the potential for controlling viewer-attention in the popular narrative film by means of indexing, scaling, and bracketing. This is especially important in many types of crime fiction which deal with the creation of attention to clues and arouse an interest in establishing information about the not yet seen and not yet known. To make the information-processing salient we need the motivational support of the detective's expressions of tense cognitive involvement.

Audiovisual communication makes perceptual, cognitive, and motivational processes intersubjectively transparent by the way in which we can follow the visual and acoustic attention of other people, and this transparency seems to create *malaise* in the critics who propagate the voyeurist theory of modern society. Antonioni's *Blow-Up* and Coppola's *The Conversation* represent two film reactions in which peeping and eavesdropping are condemned, and in which these activities are linked with modern equipment for chemical-electronic recording and recreation of reality. These films express a constructivist nightmare: all the schemata are in the mind of the beholder; the data collected with the camera or tape-recorder do not create a firm basis from which anything can be inferred about the exterior world, but we just project the files of our inner hard disk onto the exterior world. The problems of the perceptual-cognitive processing of data assume an intersubjective, spectacular form by the use of camera, magnifying devices, tape-recorders, or filters, but, as we have seen in previous chapters, human perception relies on sophisticated systems of selective attention, filtering, scaling, top-down hypotheses, and other devices. The use of technical devices to represent these processes in an intersubjective form makes the mental processing visible; the gadgets are real, but they are also an extension of the way normal perception and cognition work, and are therefore mental models of perception and cognition. The exterior form, however, brings about a defamiliarization which isolates the mental processes from modality synthesis and from their normal integration with emotions.

The way in which normal experience integrates different perceptual modalities and emotions into a complex totality is beautifully and negatively demonstrated in the final scene in *Blow-Up*. The hero-photographer watches a tennis game performed by mime actors. There is no visible ball, there are no rackets, the 'players' make no sound; but, nevertheless, they seem tensely occupied with their game, just as the spectators follow the trajectory of the imaginary ball with their eyes. Shortly afterwards, the imaginary ball is 'shot' out of the tennis court and ends near the hero, who is asked to throw it back into the court. He accepts and throws it back, thus accepting the game, and now we only see his eyes, not the game, but, at the same time, the sound of the rackets and the ball hitting the ground is heard. A tennis game consists of a set of schemata, rules, and movements, some visual and acoustic perceptions, and some emotional reactions linked to watching or playing tennis. Antonioni produces a defamiliarization by breaking the game experience up into smaller modules, so that one modality, such as vision, is realized although in an incomplete form (lack of ball and rackets), just as the attentional and motor schemata are activated whereas the sound is absent. Later, the visual presentation is absent, whereas the acoustic representation of the ball is present in combination with a representation of the visual attention and emotional reaction of a spectator. Antonioni's intention is to point to a deeper meaning, whereas, from our perspective, the scene is an experiment which creates an

emotional impact by breaking up a holistic experience. The attentional bracketing of normal holistic experiences is central to the construction of affects in
crime fiction, but, whereas a metafictional crime film like *Blow-Up* draws
attention directly to the procedures of bracketing, normal crime fictions motivate the procedures within the diegetic world.

THRILLERS AND HARD-BOILED CRIME FICTION

Classic detective fiction is often able to enforce a strict distanciation between
the embedded series of vices and crimes and the embedding series of detection
(fictions like *Rear Window* keep the distance until the very last episodes, in
which the watchers, in turn, become the watched, and are even physically
attacked). In hard-boiled American crime fictions this distanciation is weakened, sometimes to the point of a total breakdown of distanciation so that the
two levels merge. The hard-boiled crime fictions are therefore closer to a
clear-cut canonical narrative (unless, as '*noir*-hardboiled' fictions, they take
up melodramatic features). The decrease in distanciation, goes with a toning-
down of the hermeneutic-intellectual element and a greater emphasis on physical action. The tendency to merge the levels of detection and crime is very
obvious in, for instance, *The Maltese Falcon*. The detective Sam Spade falls
in love with his client, who also turns out to be the main villain and killer.
Spade is motivated in his effort of detection by the wish to avenge the death
of his partner Lew Archer, and is himself a suspect because he has had an
affair with Archer's wife. There is a distance to the embedded series: a group
of fortune-hunters have for years pursued the quest for a falcon, and Spade
does not really share their goal or their fascination with the metal bird. But
Spade's distance is more personal, less professional, than Sherlock Holmes's;
his distance is often motivated by 'the cynicism of urban life', rather than
being the intellectual distance of Dupin and Holmes, for whom crimes are
mental puzzles. The same is true of Marlowe in *The Big Sleep*, for instance;
Marlowe starts out as the professional, distant observer, but finally falls
in love with one of the women from the embedded series, just as his in-
fights with the criminals make a physical distance to the level of detection
impossible.

In *The Maltese Falcon*, as in many *noir* crime dramas, the heroine is an
ambiguous *femme fatale* who is both love-object and criminal. This reinforces
the oscillation between enforcing and destroying the separation of the two
series. The attraction toward the woman merges the two series, whereas the
repulsion enforces the distance between the two levels. Not only do the love
story and the revenge drama diminish the distance between the two series, but
the emphasis on physical confrontation also diminishes the aloofness of detection; the life and physical well-being of Spade and other tough detectives are

at stake, so that the viewer's intense projection toward world and hidden enigmas often changes into saturated feelings of fear and empathy with the pain the hero suffers.

Touch of Evil is another example of the way in which the distance between embedding and embedded series breaks down in the tough crime thriller. The hero, Vargas, starts out as a 'detective' who is morally engaged in the enforcement of justice, but not personally interested in the crimes committed. During part of the film the viewer follows the way in which his wife Susan is threatened with sexual harassment and exposed to what looks like rape, whereas Vargas, who knows nothing of this development, carries out a classic detective job. At last, when he discovers this information, the detective throws off the social role of distanciation and behaves, in his own words, 'as a husband', not as a 'cop'.

Touch of Evil demonstrates the way in which tense situations tend to become saturated horror stories because of the overwhelming power of the 'evil' compared to that of the weak protagonist. Or, to put it in another way, if the narrative descriptions tend to focus extensively on the crimes from the point of view of their possible victims, the distanciation and control will evaporate. The very title expresses an implicitly passive position, Subject: Evil, Act: Touch, Object: X. The focus of attention has shifted from mind-control to body-object. In the film the object is (not surprisingly) an innocent, blonde, all-American girl, Susan, trapped in a desert motel and later in a sleazy hotel, whereas the evil forces are dark Mexican males who supposedly enjoy a tacit acceptance of their acts by the overweight and crooked 'cop', Quinlan.

Several features of the horror scene link it to Hitchcock's *Psycho,* which was released two years later. However, the two scenes evoke different emotional responses. The scene in the Welles film plays prominently on the viewer's shadow-construction of tense expectations that now Vargas will smell a rat and arrive as the 'hero on a white horse' to save a damsel in distress, expectations thus dividing the attention between the two parallel sequences (Vargas actively detecting, wife threatened by evil sexuality) and in that way diminishing the horror element. Hitchcock's damsel is totally at the mercy of the evil 'touch', and thrill has become horror.

Vargas is in personal control the whole time, and when he discovers what has happened to his wife while he has been involved in detection he explodes in a new series of acts that finally put him in total control of the situation. So, although the distance between embedding and embedded series closes in, the two continue to be distinct sets of events. This is even more obvious if we look at the relation between *mise-en-scène* and narrative. The background to the detection is often an unfamiliar, night-time world, a run-down border town where the dark oil-derricks and steel constructions, the night clubs, and the hoodlum-ridden streets are frightening, but are, at the same time, fascinating symbols of heteronomy and the surrendering of free will. This is especially expressed by means of the symbolic use of a mechanical piano to indicate an ambivalent fascination for evil forces. The scenery is photographed from odd, often low, angles, with a climax in the subjective shot which shows how the wife wakes up from her drugged condition and sees the weird and bloody head of a murdered man turned upside-down above her. In relation to the embedded series, the *mise-en-scène* strengthens the experience of saturated heteronomy. However, in the detection series, the background only functions as a means of increasing the level of arousal. In the final scenes, Vargas shadows the crooked 'cop' physically and by means of a radio transmitter to another, bugged 'cop', who accompanies Quinlan. Vargas is in control, despite temporary transmitter fall-out and the brief moment in which he is held at gunpoint by Quinlan. The uncanny, dark oil-rigs and bridge pillars serve as backdrops.

In many 'thriller' narratives, the cognitive and enactive distance and control diminish further, so that the subject-actant moves toward a position similar to that of the object in horror fiction. The 'agent' turns into 'patient' in a kind of 'embedding in reverse'. In a Hitchcock thriller like *Notorious,* the narrative structure in some respects has an embedding/embedded structure like *Touch of Evil,* with 'Cary Grant' as a subject-actant but emotionally linked to 'Ingrid Bergman' as an 'agent' turned 'patient'; the viewers are predominantly subjected to saturated feelings by witnessing the way in which the evil forces gain the upper hand, although the viewers also activate optional tensity by expecting the hero to take action. In many typical Hitchcock thrillers, however, like *North by Northwest,* the subject-actant is a 'patient' for prolonged stretches of time, without knowledge or ability to act, sometimes even moved to the verge of entrapment in mentally dissociated interpretations of an opaque world, bereft of cognitive and enactive control, like the intoxicated or persecuted Thornhill.

COGNITIVE CONSISTENCY OR DISSONANCE IN THRILLERS AND HORROR FICTION

Many thrillers and horror fictions have problems of cognitive consistency and of paranoia, as both major elements in the creation of emotion and as means of involving the viewer in a claustrophobic, non-distanced experience. The protagonists are caught between two different models and interpretations of a given set of facts. A given element in the consciousness of a person is often integrated into greater systems representing relatively coherent models of a given aspect of the world. To a certain degree all individuals try to make consistent representations of the world. A consistent system of representations and beliefs is based on cognitive processes, but also on affective phenomena like familiarity and trust. Many of the beliefs and opinions which we think we hold for intellectual reasons are anchored in a general faith which is only substantiated by proof and argument in small fragments: I 'believe' in the 'big bang theory', quarks, genetic codes, the existence of Bolivia, or the historical existence of Julius Caesar, although most of the proofs are beyond my cognitive control. As I have already noted in connection with reality-construction, 'reality' is represented to a considerable extent by means of emotional reactions. Although the extent to which cognitive consistency as a kind of 'drive' has been discussed (see Gross 1987: 278–83), it is reasonable to accept that cognitive dissonance is an arousal state with aversive emotional properties. We act on the basis of our beliefs; to be properly motivated, we have to discard alternative explanations, and, just as individual constructions of status of reality imply an emotional representation, more complex models of reality imply this too.

Some aspects of the anchoring of cognition, action, and a certain feeling of familiarity in more general mental models shared by larger groups of people have often been described under the label 'ideology'. Barthes, for example, implicitly distinguishes between a true, unmediated representation and an ideological, mythological one. But the individual will always base his understanding and acts on systems of models, assumptions, and beliefs, of which he will only be able to 'verify' some of the models and assumptions. Furthermore, even a given society as a whole will not be able to 'verify' all its models, beliefs, and assumptions, partly because of limited scientific knowledge, partly because of the pragmatic and illocutionary-perlocutionary nature of the models and assumptions as part of an ongoing cultural-factual performance. Criticism of the mechanisms of trust, and social pressure for a consensus of models and beliefs, can therefore only be relative criticism.

An important aspect of arousal in horror and thriller fiction is linked to the creation of situations in which one or several people receive experiences which serve as a basis of cognitive dissonance. An example of this is Crichton's horror-thriller *Coma,* in which the conflict centres around a series of cognitive 'dissonances'. The protagonist is a female hospital doctor whose best friend dies during a minor operation (an abortion). This is an emotional loss, but it also represents cognitive dissonance: according to her professional knowledge the probability of a healthy young woman dying during such an operation exists, but it is minimal. Her medical detective-work soon provides her with the outline of an alternative explanation: some patients are being intentionally killed during anaesthesia by the substitution of carbon monoxide for oxygen in ventilation procedures, and later she discovers a motive: the victims' organs are sold at huge profits for transplant purposes. One mental model of the hospital world consists of experiences of complex systems of acts aiming to save the lives of the patients if possible, and all the acts in the hospital acquire an emotional value according to this cognitive model and its built-in ascribed purposes, from the knives and the drugs in the operation room and the diagnoses made to the expressions of paternal authority and other aspects of the personalization of the division of labour. A climax in the film occurs when the villain gives the young doctor a drug which leads to some of the symptoms of appendicitis and which decreases her voluntary control and ability to communicate; he then orders an operation to kill her using carbon monoxide. We therefore have a series of symptoms, diagnosis, operation table, doctor, ventilation machines, and knives which have two opposed functions coupled to the two opposed intentions, to cure and to kill, and with two opposed emotional values connected to the elements of the series. The arousal is further strengthened by correlation with the opposition between voluntary control and autonomic reactions connected with penetration, anaesthesia, and 'coma' blackout.

As the alternative model gains in credibility, the protagonist and the viewer are put in a serious situation of dissociation. All that is familiar, safe, and 'good' in the first model becomes unfamiliar, uncanny, and lethal in the second. The two models are mutually exclusive in the given situation, and, as most people adhere to the first model, they will consider the protagonist as suffering from delusions, hysteria, and paranoia, and any move she makes will be interpreted according to this model. She is accordingly threatened by total expulsion from an intersubjective world and by a totally passive existence, being unable to act within an intersubjectively negotiated set of facts and functions. In order to be 'accepted', she has to delete some of her experiences; in order to stick to her alternative interpretation, she has to maintain strong, aversive reactions.

Now, the viewer of *Coma* and of numerous other thrillers and horror stories has access to the same facts as the subject-actants, and shares the evidence for an alternative model of the facts as well as the aversive arousal caused by cognitive dissonance. In this film the conflict takes place at a medium level of 'models of the world'. Trust in social institutions is important to our daily lives, but we know that institutions may make mistakes or even be used for evil purposes. Our ability to evaluate some of the evidence which we have witnessed personally is controlled by high-level 'mental models of the world' which outline the basic features of the physical and the mental world such as cause and effect, and distinctions between mental and physical objects. We therefore have a basis for planning the way in which the protagonist can 'prove her point', and thus some reason for transforming the arousal into tense projects.

However, in many horror films the cognitive dissonance takes place at the very high level of the fundamental models of the world and mind by displaying evidence of supernatural phenomena, undead, ghosts, or weird causalities and effects, and therefore the emotional reaction is much stronger if the viewer hypothetically accepts the evidence. There is no firm basis for rational inferences and therefore no basis for acts and control, as the phenomena are not linked by normal causality. The acceptance of and faith in a scientific world-view, and the rejection of superstition, are central as high-level models for most viewers of these films and thus for the viewers' mental representation of their ability to control their own existence. The confidence strongly links 'trust in science' and 'trust in society': if 'ghosts' exist, then most institutions are 'frauds'. The supernatural machinery of horror fiction thus activates the emotions linked to the 'incorporation' of the dominant social values by inducing 'dissociation' and aversive reactions. Films of the *Dracula* type, for example, highlight the elements of 'faith' and 'trust' in cognitive processes and substitute a personalized trust in an individual for a general faith in social institutions. No reason is given for the effects of 'garlic', 'wolfsbane', 'cross', or 'pointed stakes through the heart': the 'faith' is substantiated by trust given to van Helsing, and to the effects.

One of the cornerstones of rationality is causality, which in its simplest form is co-variance over time, as exemplified in such conditioning experiments with animals as 'time 1: press lever, time 2: food provided'; or, 'time 1: red light, time 2: electric shock provided'. The conditioning has a cognitive component (the inferred causal link of the two phenomena), and an affective-motivational component (pleasure–pain). The origin of the 'neuronal-mental' model of 'causality' is therefore not primarily its existence as a scientific model, but, on the contrary, that as a basic cognitive-emotional model for animals and humans, by which they can learn, for example, to avoid poisonous substances or creatures, and to predict and approach beneficial phenomena: I eat shrimps for dinner, then I have a stomach ache (store: disgust linked to shrimps); I see a black cat, then I hit my thumb with the hammer (store: pain linked to black cats). The emotional charge of links of causality is central to the functions of learning processes for good motivational reasons, and this emotional charge of causal links is used powerfully in horror films, in which the addressers can stage a controlled 'learning process' by manipulation of the evidence.

Without scientific apparatus to investigate all experienced 'contingencies', many 'false' causal relations must necessarily be established, for instance between black cats and misfortune, but; as Lévi-Strauss has pointed out (1966), what we regard as superstition and myth represent incomplete efforts at scientific descriptions and rational control. The last 200 years have developed an increasingly sophisticated set of high-level models enabling us to supervise the numerous causalities which cannot be evaluated by 'local research'. Testing the causal links established in 'folk wisdom' and 'superstition' requires much research and/or many complicated models of the world. The popular function of 'science' is to provide a model of 'world control', and to criticize and reject false causalities. The function of science in everyday life is thus often 'negative' and 'aversive', and rejects causalities like those found in astrology. Paranoid thrillers and horror fictions often evoke their saturated emotional impact by building a strong case for what is normally regarded as a 'false causality', combining the affect of the fictively established 'causality' and a strongly motivating emotion (fear of death, or loss of body/mind autonomy), and, further, by undermining the 'belief in science'.

The basis of fear in thrillers and horror stories is therefore, in some respects, rational; sometimes horror stories are described as inroads made by forces of the id or the irrational, but, as the facts are presented in most horror fictions, monsters and the undead are locally the most rational hypotheses, and the fear is a rational fear because of the terrible deeds of the monsters. (As noted earlier, it does not seem probable that emotions are archaic or primitive phenomena: reflexes and instinctive acts do not need to separate motivation from cognition, so the strength of emotions and affects does not prove that they are 'archaic' and 'irrational'.) Only if we reject evidence of supernatural phenomena because of a trust in global scientific explanations is fear irrational. Key episodes in many horror films are situations in which the protagonists have a powerful experience of causal links which are rejected by 'science' and situations in which protagonists overlook impending danger, because—unlike the viewer—they have 'restricted' concepts of causality. The conflict is not a conflict between the 'irrational' and the 'rational', because the viewer and possibly the protagonists have the solid, 'rational' evidence of their own eyes and ears regarding the threatened danger; the extreme fear is caused by the lack of normal means to control the monster, often amplified by cognitive dissonance, the helpless horror experienced by confrontation with the inability even to communicate and discuss the danger with other people (many paranoid fictions, like *The Parallax View* and *JFK*, likewise extensively use cognitive dissonance in order to create affect). The horror in *Dracula* consists, among other things, in the 'blindness' of many of the protagonists, their inability to draw the logical inferences and to act accordingly. Their inability to communicate and to imagine possible acts eventually leads to saturated mental fragmentation.

The explicit motivation for horror fiction is therefore—contrary to many types of melodrama, for example—a desire for cognitive and physical control: the problem is choosing the appropriate schemata. This can be illustrated with an example: in the science-fiction thriller-horror film *Them!* the conflict between control and object status is articulated as a variation of the classic opposition between nature and culture. The testing of the first nuclear bomb has created gigantic mutant killer ants in a desert area of the western USA. The fear evoked by the film is based on a fairly widespread aversion to many lower forms of life (insects, reptiles, and so on), as exploited in many other *Arachnophobia*-style horror stories. The extreme effect of alien, nature-based subjectivity on the humans is 'paralysis', lack of flexible human subjectivity, as exemplified at the beginning of the film, which shows a small girl suffering from severe shock (inability to talk, empty, staring eyes, mechanical movements, inability to form emotional attachments). The threat consists in an inability to control possible tactile stimuli or body delimitation. Several of the dreadful confrontations take place during the night or in dark subterraneous places, and are accompanied by diminished visual control. The terror furthermore consists in the isolation of the individual from a group bound together by absolute emotional ties (family relations). Furthermore, there are several scenes of 'cognitive dissonance' in which the evidence of the giant ants is met with disbelief: a sane person is even put into a mental institution because he reports what he has seen.

The antidote has two forms: 'science' and 'uniformed civil servants' (the armed forces, police, and hospital personnel). Although science is personified by an old professor and his attractive doctor-daughter, both experts on ants, they represent a vast set of collective human models and practice enabling world control, although the film is anxious to underline the human-individual aspects of the scientists. The film underlines the ambiguity of the fact that 'poison' and 'ant-i-dote' are similar: the reason for the monstrosity is science, in that nuclear explosions have created mutations. But the antidote also represents science as incarnated in the professor and his daughter. The armed forces and social institutions represent the supra-individual aspects of the individual: their sheer anonymous mass and power when using shells or flame-throwers against the ants is a model of man as 'species'. In a sense, the 'poison' and 'antidote' are also similar; the power of the ants consists in their social organization. Police and hospital staff manifest social, trans-individual 'care', bonding the members of the species together. The individualized care (parent–child) is transformed into 'tribal care' (police–nurse–child). The antidote is the double-sided aversive delimitation of 'us' 'them', and the 'incorporative' affirmation of the intra-species 'grooming' and faith in the superiority of their cognitive-practical control.

PARANOIA AND OBSESSIONAL DOUBT IN THRILLERS AND HORROR FICTION

Much of our understanding is linked to interpretations of motives and intents, as we saw in *Coma*, in which two radically different interpretations and emotional evaluations of 'the same phenomena' were linked to two different hypotheses of intent (and, finally, also of motive). Whether in everyday life we choose one top-down hypothesis or another is dependent on whether we are in a 'trustful-incorporative' or a 'suspicious-aversive' mood, and an important aspect of the art of horror- and thriller-making consists in giving cognitive reasons for a 'suspicious-aversive' mood in protagonists and viewers.

Detection is mostly based on a 'suspicious-aversive' mood: nothing is what it seems to be, neither expressed emotions nor behaviours, and the distanciation characteristic of detection therefore presupposes a 'suspicious-aversive' mood, although the motives and intentions investigated are aimed at a third party, the victim of crime. The detection is, further, exclusively directed at phenomena which are caused by an 'aversive' anthropomorph agent, so that the predominant use of the hermeneutic code in visual fiction *qua* crime fiction is linked to making models of aversive and ill-intending subjects. An increase in cognitively based suspicion and aversion will decrease the possibility of establishing the necessary 'trust' which can lead to a conclusion. In obsessional fictions no fixed frame of reference can be trusted, and the cognition takes place in an 'obsessional' paratelic mode. To draw conclusions, to make a temporary *clôture du texte*, and to perform voluntary acts implies a certain 'trust' and the construction of a fixed goal. It is therefore not surprising that a further increase in 'aversion' often leads to a passive position, paranoia, in which the evil agents have most of the dynamic capabilities, whereas the subject has become a 'patient'.

In *Coma,* the protagonist's 'aversive' detection increasingly leads to situations in which she becomes the object of evil forces. In Conan Doyle's fictions, Holmes's thinking becomes increasingly obsessional and aversive, in parallel to a development in which an arch-antagonist of a 'paranoid' type enters the scene and Doyle starts to write paranoid horror fictions. In Doyle's case, 'trust' reappears as 'credulity', a belief in all types of supernatural causalities (especially in his Professor Challenger fictions).

The lack of distance in paranoid fiction is reflected in its predominant structure of motivations and goals. In ordinary 'distanced' crime fiction, the goals are often aversive: to kill, to commit murder. But in paranoid fictions the goals are 'conjunctive-incorporative': *Dracula* does not want to kill, but to 'share blood' and to incorporate the will of the victims into his own will, while the motive in *The Mummy* is 'love'. In Cronenberg's *Scanners,* the scanners do not have the normal separation of their own minds from the minds and bodies of other people: the many different types of body-snatchers destroy the difference between body-I and otherness. This often goes hand in hand with a breakdown in the correlation between facial expressions and intent, which is even more overt in the 'schizoid' than in the merely paranoid fictions. Films like Polanski's *Rosemary's Baby,* Cronenberg's *The Brood,* Donner's *The Omen,* or Teague's *Cujo* link quite explicitly the horrible phenomena with a breakdown of the correlation between the facial expressions of emotion and the 'inner', 'motivational' structure of the evil forces. This is especially horrifying because a breakdown of the cognitive ability to interpret facial expressions also takes place between people with strong emotional ties, like wives, husbands, children, and, in the case of *Cujo,* domestic pets. The collapse of the normal cognitive framework for establishing emotional relations based on unambiguous intentions makes only strong, saturated emotions possible.

Freud linked the problems of obsessional doubt, paranoia, and the ambiguity of facial expressions respectively with the rejection of female castration, homosexuality, and an infantile interpretation of parental intercourse as a painful fight. I have argued against the general validity of the concept of 'castration'; as to the validity of a connection between homosexuality and paranoia and the infantile interpretation of parental intercourse, Freud's explanations point to the role played by mental models in the interpretation of motives and the hedonic value of signs of passion. As I described in Chapter 4, according to the theory of emotional reversals, the hedonic value of a high state of arousal is dependent on a cognitive evaluation, which can either be positive, in which case a further increase in arousal is experienced as positive, or negative, in which case only a decrease in arousal is pleasurable. The second ambiguity is connected with the interpretation of signs of passion. Whether another person is suffering from severe pain or experiencing great pleasure is often difficult to determine, except by means of contextual clues and mental models of human motives and preferences. If we look at scenes like the murder of Grandi in *Touch of Evil* or the shower scene in *Psycho* we see women in situations of great pain in both, but both in contexts that would normally be associated with pleasure (bed, the shower). In *Touch of Evil* the nightmarish convulsions are further visually connected with the strangulation and death-struggle of a man. The connecting link between passion and pain is, of course, that both are results of a very strong arousal which supersedes voluntary control, and the difference consists in their different causes and different cognitive-hedonic evaluations. Without being masochists or sadists it is difficult for viewers not to have an ambiguous interpretation of the seen in situations which, by 'bracketed' contextual clues like 'bed' and 'shower', are indicated as possibly erotic scenes, an arousal that is primarily labelled as pain, but which is visually expressed by many of the signs normally interpreted as pleasure.[3] In a true sado-masochist scene like the one in *Blue Velvet*, the interpretive problem for the protagonist, Jeffrey, may be said to derive from his/the viewer's difficulties in deciding whether the usual signs of normal non-sado-masochist sexual intercourse indicate a pleasurable or a painful experience.

Explicit sado-masochism highlights the erroneous, but possible, interpretation of normal sexual intercourse, which, although rejected, is activated as an associative background in many horror films and thrillers. In many other films horror has little or no sexual content.

From the point of view of emotion-engineering in visual fiction, fear and terror caused by cognitive dissociation and/or violence have the morally dubious advantage of creating high levels of arousal and strengthening the viewers' wish for emotional autonomy and control by aversion, unless 'trust' is established by credulity, a situation that most viewers only accept as a game.

---

[3] Possible pleasures from this are clearly 'perverse', but to generalize from the existence of perverse scenes in film to general statements, like film and cinema being institutions of perversion, cf. Bellour (1979: 310), would be to suppress the majority of the meanings and emotions in film.

11

Melodrama, Lyrics, and Autonomic Response

In this chapter, I shall analyze aspects of the melodrama, emphasizing especially its nature as a conflict between active and passive reactions. I shall also examine the problems connected with the mental and interior aspects of melodrama, on its procedures for labelling arousal, and on the relation between lyrical and melodramatic structures. My analytical point of departure will be the films *Gone With the Wind* and *Vertigo,* which in many respects are central prototypes of the melodrama genre.

MELODRAMA

Melodrama is a genre that is characterized by large issues, such as time, space, causality, life, death, sexuality, and emotions. Dealing with large issues has not always conferred respect on the genre. The word 'melodramatic' has mostly been used pejoratively by intellectual critics as meaning 'too much'. A film or a novel is called melodramatic when the themes are 'too huge', when the means of expression are too exaggerated, and when the emotions they evoke in the spectators are too strong. Recently many critics, starting with Elsaesser and Brooks,[1] have tried to reverse this evaluation, and some have seen subversive and radical elements in melodramatic excesses. They have, for instance, seen excess as an actual or potential transgression of bourgeois or patriarchal order and restriction.[2] These re-evaluations have led to some perceptive conceptions of melodrama and have created analytical tools for dealing with the genre.

There are certain problems in understanding melodrama in terms such as those of transgression and excess. The term excess easily becomes associated with passion in the traditional and problematic, romantic dualism of reason and passion (as discussed in the Introduction, above).[3] Melodrama is intensely

[1] Cf. e.g. Elsaesser (1972), Brooks (1985), Gledhill (1987), and Bondebjerg (1989).

[2] In Bordwell, Staiger, and Thompson (1985: 71). Bordwell has objected that the unexpected and the excess represent a generic convention and that the subversiveness is therefore conventionalized.

[3] An example of excess as passion as opposed to 'reason' is given in Lang (1989: 27) and describes the way in which the feminine is allied with the pre-oedipal, the imaginary which

concerned with the depiction of passion, and it is not by chance that passion has close connections with the word 'passive', while, as we have seen in Chapter 2, autonomic emotional response is an alternative to non-expressive, voluntary, motor response. Traditionally melodrama has been described as a conservative genre because it very often portrays the protagonists as passive victims of fate and destiny, or as passive participants in natural or social events. To make melodrama politically legitimate several critics have described it as active intervention, as a protest by its excess and transgression. This is still unnecessarily normative and renders an acceptance of the passive elements of life suspicious, as if melodrama were only a shrewd way of mobilizing the viewers into action and not also a representation of passive and passionate experiences which are valuable in their own right. Melodrama provides mental software for the conscious control of the relations between voluntary and involuntary mental reactions, and for experiencing the passive aspects of life.

WIND, FIRE, AND PASSIONATE HETERONOMY IN *GONE WITH THE WIND*

Let us return to the large issues, to time, space, causality, passion, and mental life, and consider *Gone With the Wind*. Like many melodramas, this film is a mixture of romantic and naturalistic features. We follow part of the life of Scarlett O'Hara, with a focus on periods of transition: we meet her as a flirtatious adolescent and child of a wealthy Southern plantation owner; soon she marries a man whom she does not love, because she cannot have the man whom she does love, the weak Ashley; her husband is subsequently killed in the American Civil War. War and widowhood make her independent, and soon she has to be the head of the family, to try to save mansion and plantation and to provide for her sisters and her mentally confused father. She marries a second time, for money, and is transformed into a shrewd businesswoman, but her second husband also dies quite soon. Finally she marries the rich, strong, and handsome Rhett Butler, but their marriage ends in divorce.

Scarlett's personal development is set against a background of the Civil War and its aftermath, and the transition from 'feudalism' to capitalism and individualism. The word 'background' might be misleading, because the film clearly intends to tell a story in which we see individual fate as part of a 'big picture', a whole society driven toward a common tragedy. As in many melodramas, we find a coupling of history and individual fate. In *Gone With the Wind* the historic events have already taken place, as emphasized by the old-fashioned, chronicle-like texts which often mark the narrative transitions, fix the chronology, and explain the development of the Civil War. The addresser

'contradicts what the Symbolic stands for. It is towards bliss, the shattering of boundaries, the subversion of the Symbolic, in music, all moments of excess, nonsense, perhaps all emotion itself.'

positions the viewer at a historical distance from the narrative. The historical development is not open: not only, has it already taken place, but it has been written down and given an authoritative form. The viewer is not able to construct the events as matters that can be changed by voluntary acts, and this in itself evokes emotional reactions. As early as the beginning of the film the text tells us that the outcome of the historic events even at that historical time was determined by objective causes, such as the industrial superiority of the Yankees. The film is therefore told by an almost omniscient addresser, who underlines the concept that not only did history happen as shown, but also that its course was inevitable.

Scarlett therefore is incapable of performing acts that, in any decisive way, influence the basic factors in the 'grand narrative' and the 'great picture': events are already decided. She can adjust to the circumstances, the war and the poverty of the postwar period, or she can be crushed by the developments. The spectators feel that they are passive participants in events that cannot be altered by hypothetical expectations and simulations of acts that would alter the grand narrative. This passive, melodramatic feeling in the viewers is evoked by a special narrative strategy: the telling of a well-known story, such as a historical event. The outcome will be known beforehand, and the time represented will be a passive one in which the human beings are objects of major forces. This produces a feeling of heteronomy, of being carried away by sublime exterior forces, inputs that can only be processed by non-motor-simulating, affective reactions. Such a feeling of heteronomy (experienced in the viewer by empathic identification) is clearly visible in the many scenes in which people are transformed from individuals to parts of a mass: several scenes depict crowds, consisting of soldiers or civilians, running away from the advancing Federal troops. Some scenes further show the difficulties for the individual (Scarlett, for example) of moving in the opposite direction to or across, this human tide. Sometimes the defeated soldiers are shown only as shadowy creatures; other scenes show people turned into a rebellious, plundering, and lust-inflamed mob, and we witness the difficulties for the individual of preserving independence and free will.

Time tends to be ruled by 'historical laws' which, within the framework of the representation, appear almost as natural laws with an inflexible connection between causes and effects. The mental model used to construct the human masses is not very different from those used to understand the concept of 'mass' as we know it in physics. The title of the film, *Gone With the Wind,* uses a metaphor from the world of meteorology as a mental model for the laws ruling the narrative. There are no explicit human subjects or objects in the title, only a subject-actant of nature, the Wind, which, we must assume, has carried something somewhere. The title suggests a dynamic, causality-ruled, linear, and anonymous time-space: something carries something in a certain direction in time.

From the title, we might hypothesize by negative inference that, before the change indicated in the film, there existed another type of time-space. Such a hypothesis could receive certain confirmation from the title-sequence. In this we see fragments of a time-space which looks as if it is ruled by cyclical time, and in which there is no real linear and teleological time. The fragments are cut out from a harmonious rural world, in which men are fused with nature in cyclical time composed of eternal repetition, and questions of cause and effect are not relevant. Day and work are followed by night and rest in a pattern which we connect with eternal repetition, and spring and blossom are followed by harvest, so that 'life' and 'death' are parts of one harmonious cycle. Within the narrative, the title sequence is a prehistory, a glimpse of ways of existence preceding the beginning of history as represented in the narrative proper.

Soon, however, the winds of history begin to blow through this rural, prelapsarian paradise. This is most salient in the figurative description of fire and in the depiction of time-space. In the cyclical time-space, the agent of fire represents the life-giving and difference-negating sun. In a key scene we have a traditional filmic description of sunset. The whole space glows, air-space almost acquires the same tangible quality as the red soil of Tara, and daughter Scarlett is shown united with her father by ideas of blood, soil, and generation: the O'Haras will succeed each other on the soil of Tara in a cyclical repetition of the same pattern. Later, after the beginning of the 'real', linear time, fire is figuratively connected with destruction. Fire, for instance, destroys the houses of Atlanta. When Scarlett and Rhett try to escape from the burning Atlanta in a horse-drawn carriage, they become—as in the sunset scene—surrounded by an almost tangible, glowing space. Now the individuals are objects of destructive forces that undermine their ability to act freely. Symbolically, Rhett is forced to blindfold the horse with Scarlett's handkerchief, so that the horse can overcome its fear of flames and destruction. Blind and passive, the horse is led through the flames. A little later, Scarlett and Rhett are united for a few seconds by a kiss—one which does not unite individuals, but socio-biological, anonymous entities. The dialogue expressly states that Rhett understands the kiss as given by a woman to a man and soldier before he departs to war and death. Scarlett abandons herself to an anonymous-collective role of being just the socio-biological entity of 'woman', driven by the mechanisms of biology and history; but soon she returns to her existence as an individualized person and woman, and to a marginal possession of autonomy and free will.

Her autonomy *is* marginal: after the tangible, glowing space that threatens to swallow her up, comes another, not less 'tangible' space, consisting of thunder, lightning, and rain. She can resist being touched by Rhett, but she cannot resist being touched by rain and by the water of a river into which she has to flee. Very much later in the film, a third kind of 'tangible' space is represented, filled with fog which makes it impossible to control the space using sight, and which therefore limits the potential of the characters to perform voluntary acts.

The weather and catastrophes of nature represent a common condition for all. Like melodrama, weather forecasts and natural catastrophes reported on the radio and television often have an important role as mental models for the way in which man is in the grip of causal laws, common conditions that are outside the influence of man and society. Melodrama employs the type of weather, the type of time-space, which emphasizes the way in which human beings live at the mercy of nature. Whereas the action-oriented Western often employs a fully lit and 'transparent' space, perfect for action, the melodrama employs weather-types which block the remote control of space by sight, and/or activate the contact-senses. This means weather-types like darkness and fog, which block the act-supporting remote sensation, and strong thunder, wind, and rain, which activate the contact-senses. For this reason, 'romantic' weather-types have also been (ab)used in music videos, to block enaction and to simulate and evoke strong sensations of contact.

We might imagine that melodrama, of the type represented by *Gone With the Wind* and many other romantic or naturalistic melodramas, would communicate an experience for the viewer marked by objectivism, if we consider solely the weight given to historical or natural determinism. But the emphasis on deterministic features in a given narrative is quite a different experience, characterized by an extreme subjectivism and emotionalism. One explanation for this is that quite 'excessive' melodramatic representations, such as thunder, rain, storm, sunset, and fire, as represented in film melodrama, seem to be larger than life (that is, prototypical life); and, if experienced as something beyond a rule-bound everyday existence, the prototype for realism, the representations must be subjective. A complementary explanation is based on considerations of the way in which causality is prototypically modelled mentally. Determinism is only experienced as something objective and rational if we can hypothetically identify with the subject or agent of the causalities. The experience of objectivism and reality is linked to the ability to experience a real or hypothetical simulation and to influence the phenomena by actions. Using the explanations of professors of physics or meteorologists, we can mentally simulate the 'acts of nature' and understand 'where they will lead' and, by means of hypothetical examples, transform causal laws into 'teleological acts'. Causality is always mentally modelled by hypothetical extrapolations in time. But if we are transformed into a passive object for the objective laws, the hypothetical-enactive identification is weakened or blocked, and the experience loses its character of being rational and exterior-objective, and, by negative inference, is experienced as a mental event. In the great melodramatic moments in *Gone With the Wind*, the agents lose their full ability to act in the world, which is therefore only experienced as sensation, as input, and so remains a mental phenomenon.

'In itself', the visual medium exists in an eternal third person. But, as shown in Chapters 4 and 5, we are normally able to make cognitive and empathic identifications and simulate enactive experiences in the first person. There are many scenes in *Gone With the Wind* in which such an identification is blocked. This happens, for instance, in the long melodramatic episode dealing with the burning of Atlanta. Here the photographer makes extensive use of *backlight* and *silhouetting*.[4] The light comes from a source behind people, from the gigantic flames of the fire, and we are not able to see Scarlett and Rhett clearly; their dark figures are seen against the background of burning space; we see the characters as enigmatic blackboards, whom the viewers have to interpret and 'describe' for themselves. We cannot fully guess from the expression on the characters' faces, which we can barely see, what is taking place in their consciousnesses; we can only guess by using contextual clues, the background, the environment, as circumstantial evidence. We might think that Scarlett and Rhett, seen from our point of view, are reduced to reflexes of their environment by our having to infer their mood from what we see as the situation causing their experience. When the world is on fire, their minds and bodies also become fire. But we experience this a little differently, and with an extra dimension. The episode is experienced as symbolic and mental, not just as a representation of people who are reflexes of their environmental conditions. The symbolic-mental quality of the experience may be caused by a primitive technique—the flames look somewhat unrealistic, more like backdrops—but it also results from our feeling that such an excess can only represent images of mental life. As soon as the viewer receives a perceptual overload by the combination of strong images and inactive protagonists who cannot abreact the input, he reacts by cognitively and affectively labelling the situation as an image of mental life. (This is also the case when the overload is caused by fatigue, as we know from the experience of unreality caused by the perception of white road-markings during a long and tiring drive, or the impressions resulting from perceptual overload during high-speed flying.) This further implies that we experience the typical romantic confusion of relations between causes and effects in the relation between mental and exterior reality. In romantic melodrama, nature is often only a screen for the expressive projection of scenes from mental life. When the hero or heroine becomes passionate, nature begins to produce thunder and lightning or gales. Passion may be caused by nature, but it might also be the case that thunder and lightning are, in turn, caused by passion.

Many aspects of our mental life exist at the limit of or beyond our conscious and voluntary control. Certain types of thoughts and images are experienced as being under voluntary control; but many of our ideas, imaginations, and moods emerge suddenly in our consciousness from an invis-

---

[4] The subjective use of lighting is analyzed in Place and Peterson (1976).

ible 'hard disk'. Even if we have some general ideas of what we want to say, the concrete realizations, illustrations, and jokes are produced by non-conscious functions and in non-conscious areas of the brain. There is a parallelism between the passive position by which consciousness registers pure sensations of the exterior world, and that by which it registers many aspects of mental life. The exterior world is constantly projected onto our senses, and, although we often try to keep pace with these projections by active constructions and the ordering of input, we sometimes become aware of the passive aspects of sensation. Melodrama makes the passive aspects of sensation and mental life visible by showing people being carried away by their emotions.

Backlight-technique and silhouetting are often used on film as a means of expressing inner passions.[5] In *Gone With the Wind* people are, for instance, positioned in front of windows. Outside it might be raining, and the plants and trees in motion indicate that a wind is blowing, as when Rhett Butler has a passionate conversation with Melanie. Here the silhouetting is only hinted, manifested for a few moments when the scene fades out. But outside the window it may also be foggy, as in the last quarrel between Scarlett and Rhett. Every time this combination of silhouetting and backlight is shown on the screen, the effect is highly melodramatic. The protagonists' mental life does not seem to be under voluntary control, because we can only reconstruct it if we assume that it is isomorphic with the natural world outside the windows.

The most spectacular and symbolic use of backlight, silhouetting, and nature are found in the three symbolic scenes that mark the beginning, the turning-point, and the conclusion of the film. In the first symbolic scene Scarlett and her father are seen, and in the second and third Scarlett is seen alone. In all three scenes the characters are shown in silhouette on a hill near Tara, with red sky as a background. The scenes begin as full shots, then the camera tracks backward into long shots, leaves Scarlett, and reduces her size so that her black silhouette fuses with the vast space. In the first and the third scenes the sky and Scarlett are framed by an old tree in the foreground, and the expanding–receding space has a vanishing-point in the solid mansion of Tara. All three scenes perform the same transformation: the viewer loses access to a format of visual information that enables him to identify with Scarlett as an individual person in a space of action, and is compensated by seeing a mental landscape outside time and action. The spectator is moved, because he does not have an enactive possibility of abreacting the impact of the scenery and the visual adieu of the backtracking.

Peter Brooks (1985) has characterized melodrama by the term 'muteness', which indicates that an interior life which cannot be fully verbalized is expressed by excess, stylization, and gesture. The observation of a connection

---

[5] Cf. e.g. Sirk's *All That Heaven Allows*.

between a certain non-communication and melodramatic excess and stylization seems to be valid. But perhaps Brooks' description of the link is putting the carriage before the horse; the problem is not that the interior phenomena are weird and strange and therefore not communicable, but that melodrama blocks their verbalization and enaction *in order to evoke saturation.* None of the visual elements in the three symbolic scenes in *Gone With the Wind,* or the implied meanings of the scenes, is particularly complicated or strange. They attain their symbolic mental power by isolating Scarlett from a world of action by means of visual forms of representation which tend toward abstraction and distance. What is inexpressible and unutterable is not the meaning, but the interior emotional salience of the experience. Body tensions and mental intensities and saturations can be represented in exterior space, but are by definition something felt in the body and the brain, and they can be represented in exterior space not by analogous, but only by indexical means. The melodrama uses a set of techniques to build up strong emotional (in)tensities so that the spectator can empathically simulate these feelings and emotions. This is an adequate way of communicating these phenomena. If we want to communicate a referential meaning, we can point to objects or pictures; if we want to communicate emotions, we can simulate the emotion-producing situations. As verbalization often has a very low qualitative definition compared with a picture of the verbalized item, so a verbal representation of emotions often has a low quantitative definition compared with the felt emotions which trigger autonomic reactions like crying and hysterical laughter. A full 'understanding' of these phenomena (for example, of their motivational and hedonic qualities) often demands an addressee simulation of the reactions.

From what I have said so far, it might appear that Scarlett is a very passive woman, who abandons herself to history and the course of nature. The case is quite the opposite. She is depicted as being individualistic and determined to have her own way. Her dominant conceptions of love consist in ideas of active possession, including possessing the attention and admiration of everybody. When the feudal South suffers a defeat, she quickly converts to the new system, becomes a hard-boiled capitalist, and soon leaves the 'feudal' plantation in order to live a bourgeois life in Atlanta, although she partly preserves a 'feudal' motivation for her capitalist activities: all the money will be used to save Tara and the family. One of the most selfish acts she commits, according to the implicit norms of the film, is that she denies motherhood. When she gives birth to a baby she is so dismayed at her enlarged waist that she decides this will be her first and last child. She denies Rhett access to her bedroom, and leaves him to have full parental responsibility for the child. It is because of this activity and independence that Scarlett is torn between the forces of autonomy and heteronomy, and thus the film can amplify the conflict between action and passion to the limit.

The opposition between autonomy and heteronomy in the film has three main fields of articulation: the opposition between capitalism and feudalism/patriarchalism; between society and the individual; and between different sexual roles. The opposition between culture and nature serves as a kind of mental metamodel for the other domains. These three fields interact in many different ways.

In 'feudal' and patriarchal society, as described in the film, the individual has commitments to his family and slaves which set limits on the individual pursuit of happiness. Dependence and heteronomy are just as important and valued as independence. Scarlett is dependent on her father, who is only a servant of the soil, of Tara, and of divine principles. By serving a higher master and a higher cause than ourselves, we win esteem and personal value. But for Scarlett as a capitalist, and for Rhett in his early capitalist period, honour and servitude are empty words, restraining the individual. There are only two ways in which we can relate to other people: either we do business with them, exchanging objects and services which are mutually beneficial, or we exploit and control them.

War is the great symbol of the opposition between the individual and society. The Civil War reduces young men to mere social beings: they do not die in the battlefield as individuals, but as anonymous quantities of the category 'male Confederates'. Tara is plundered not because of any individual act by the O'Hara family, but because of their social identity as Southerners and Confederates. Individualism and personal acts are therefore only valid under certain conditions and within certain limits. Beyond these limits, the destiny of the individual is tied to a social or biological identity, whether sexual or racial. Scarlett's confrontation with the endless masses of wounded and dying soldiers at the hospital, the transformation of Atlanta to a place of mob rule, and the burning-down of a whole local community, give her a violent shock, which, as we have seen, almost leads her to abandon herself to Rhett and to a traditional gender role.

The most complicated opposition between autonomy and heteronomy is connected with the field of sexual roles. On the surface there are two clear-cut pairs of oppositions: a female and a male variation of the Madonna–whore opposition. The female Madonna is Melanie, for whom mothering is an ideal and a model of altruistic heteronomy, existing for the other, the man, the child, the neighbour. She is married to a male Madonna, the idealistic Ashley. The 'whores' are Scarlett, Rhett, and the real prostitute, Belle. They claim personal autonomy and use their sexuality mainly for personal gratification, whether this means a sexual or a financial advantage. But prostitution consists of active and passive components. It means emitting sexual signals actively and trying to earn money or other material advantages. It also means accepting personal heteronomy passively—possibly to be bought and treated as an object—and accepting a socio-biological identity as just man or just woman, and in that way being at the disposal of the anonymous other. Prostitution is conceived as a way of preserving autonomy by impersonalizing the sexual relation and bringing it under commercial control. However, both Rhett and Scarlett refuse to accept the other side of the bargain: Rhett refuses Scarlett's offer of prostitution because she is using him as an object which she can exploit, and Scarlett refuses to offer herself without conditions: if she did this it would not be prostitution any more.

The film states that individualism is not fully satisfying, because it isolates the individual from the social community and from a full fusion with a person of the opposite sex. Nevertheless, giving up independence is not fully satisfying either. The film is, to a certain extent, committed to the emancipation of women. Traditional womanhood *à la* Melanie is not presented as being particularly attractive, although it has some positive qualities. *Gone With the Wind* solves the problem by showing Scarlett's autonomy as threatened by every possible external force of nature or history, but it further stages an act which is a symbol of ultimate heteronomy: rape. Rhett loses control because of jealousy and frustration, and takes his wife by force. This gratifies her, and she falls completely in love with Rhett until he apologizes for the rape. This in turn disappoints her deeply, because she wants to be carried away, and not compelled to admit her love. The rape is therefore a parallel to the wind, the thunder, the war, and the fire, in being a compromise between autonomy and heteronomy. Scarlett is carried away despite her wish for independence, just as Rhett is carried away by his emotions in committing the act. Historically, the melodrama came into existence in its modern form at a time when active mental control took a qualitative step forward at the end of the eighteenth century and the beginning of the nineteenth (see Elias 1994). Melodrama might be seen as an expression of a compromise or a mental technology by which we consciously and actively stage the passive position and its emotions, just as Margaret Mitchell, the author of the novel *Gone With the Wind*, actively staged the passive position and its winds as counterpoints to Scarlett's conscious acts and calculations. Melodrama provides mental software for the conscious manipulation of the relations between voluntary and involuntary mental systems.

The rape makes it clear that Scarlett's consciousness exists in a physical body in space, and that her body can be treated as an object among other objects, independently of her will. Just before the rape, Rhett exclaims that he would tear Scarlett to pieces with his hands if this would tear Ashley from her mind. The whole scene establishes models that can mediate between physical and mental reality. Present-day viewers might find it difficult to accept that an author or director can offer a positive description of rape to illustrate the problematic relationship between body and mind and to simulate the experience of heteronomy, although the scene plays a prominent part in the fascination the film holds for many viewers (see Taylor 1989). In the same way, many will consider it unacceptable to stage scenes of terror, or war, or other types of violence to provide viewers with intense feelings of being physical objects which can be treated as things by other agents. Strong and emotionally charged descriptions of the passive position and the limits of the free will are often characterized by terms like 'speculation'. Many might further find it morally objectionable that Scarlett is not only a victim, but also enjoys being one. On the other hand, the film does not allow rape to solve any problems, and the result of the rape is a miscarriage. The film ends with no clear solution in sight. Furthermore, even if it is correct that we are conscious, intentional beings, it is also correct that we are a biomass in space, and that our sensibility is partly linked to this fact. This can be represented by a distancing which eliminates empathic identification, as in many schizoid forms of fiction; but the object-status can also be represented by means of an identification with the passive position, as happens in the melodrama.

The attitude of the film in relation to action and passion seems to be dualistic: they are two equally important, but antagonistic, forms of behaviour. If the viewer feels that *Gone With the Wind,* like most other melodramas, favours a passive and deterministic view of the world, the reason for this may partly be that an active and voluntaristic *Weltanschauung* has become the dominant narrative norm. Deterministic films like the *film noir,* which are positively evaluated by intellectual critics, partly acquire this positive evaluation because their deterministic outlook is bracketed as expressive-hypothetical, as a special and exotic mental attitude, or because of excessive stylistics marked as a special theatrical way of creating effect.

Seen in a greater perspective, the question of free will versus determinism is linked more to the question of level of description, of narrative strategy, of scaling and format, than to the question of degree of realism. Our brains, mental models, and emotional life are linked to certain formats. If we shoot a film of the growth of plants and flowers at normal speed, the growth will probably be experienced as a long and boring exemplification of biological causality. Plants just grow according to their conditions. But if we shoot the film by taking only a few frames per period of time of the same phenomenon and then show the film at high speed, the plants and flowers will suddenly appear as if they had intentions and free will: they will grow toward a source of light, and quickly grow in other directions if the source of light is moved. The abbreviation of time provides our experience of the plants with an intentional and teleological quality. Our conceptions of passivity versus activity and goal-directedness are therefore partly a question of the speed and plasticity of reactions to input from the exterior world. A 'slowed-down' version of an action-genre like the Western becomes a melodrama, as we see in 'spaghetti Westerns' like *Once Upon a Time in the West.*

If we make a fictive representation of aspects of an individual's life, we can represent that life in connection with 'the big picture', history, life, and death, as in the naturalistic novel or film, or the melodramatic film. Or we can represent them as action and free will in a 'small picture' by showing aspects of the individual's life. We can choose between a long shot, a close-up, or an ultra-close, detail shot: they would all be 'realistic' in an objective sense, but would probably have quite different emotional impacts, because our mental and emotional life is linked to certain formats.

The 'big picture' is a mental abstraction, and its categories, where of man, woman, child, love, passion, life, death, time, space, or causality, are abstractions and 'clichés', mental models, and prototypes. Emotions are somehow connected with abstraction and the suspension of individualism and concretion. Melodrama achieves its emotional effects by abstraction—by representations of prototypes—and by representations of passive experiences, situations which make voluntary response impossible and evoke autonomic response.

TENSIONS OF FABULA AND PLOT IN *VERTIGO*

Vertigo, like *Gone With the Wind,* obviously represents an effort to describe intense passion, although the passion is located in a mental interior, in contrast to the 'objectivisms' of wind and fire. Despite *Vertigo*'s partly modern setting, its thematic universe has strong roots in the Gothic novel, like Hitchcock's Gothic film *Rebecca*. From the beginning, the film exhibits non-narrative, lyrical features. *Vertigo* is supposed to be a film about mental life; its title indicates that it is about a state of consciousness, which sets it apart from the mainstream of narrative films but links it with *Psycho,* the film that Hitchcock made two years later, which deals with deviating mental states. Even the credit-sequence signals a discourse to come in which time and space are tampered with in order to create a metaphoric narrative. Another crucial sequence in which photography is supplemented with graphics—the dream sequence that make a caesura between the first and the second part of the film—is explicitly associative in its structure. Although in some respects the sequences include action and motion, the motion is abstract and metaphorical, different variations of the 'same'. It is reasonable to suppose that many of the formal experiments in the film are made in an effort to visualize Freud's descriptions of the dreamwork and its chains and clusters of associations, and, with *Psycho* and *Marnie,* *Vertigo* is the culmination of Hitchcock's Freudian inspiration that started with *Spellbound*. All Hitchcock films are strongly psychologically motivated, but, in some films, the depiction of deviating mental states is more the main issue than mere narrative motivation.

There are many stylistic and thematic indications that *Vertigo* is a film dealing with phenomena beyond the exterior and visible world. The 'vertigo' of the title, dizziness caused by the fear of heights, and the traumatic incident as described in the film, provide us with the addresser's own suggested hypothesis of interpretation: the film is about people who have lost normal voluntary control of their acts, who perform traumatic, autonomic, and repetitive acts, and who suffer from an inability to see objectively (expressed in vertigo-induced dizziness) combined with high arousal. The main characters are more or less 'bewitched', like the protagonist in Hitchcock's previous film *Spellbound;* besides blocking free will, the traumatic past interferes with the processing of perceptual input, and sometimes the old, traumatic memories replace the present experience in a hallucinatory way.

In the psycho-thriller, affective reaction is often the main signifier of meaning, contrary to its role in standard detective fiction. In canonical detective fiction the detective has a problem, a crime has been committed, and he has some preliminary hypotheses: for instance, a cigarette-butt might give a clue to the identity of the murderer. The percepts, the clues, acquire cognitive salience by the viewers' sharing of a dispassionate hypothesis and perhaps a less dispassionate, camera 'indexing' (see Carroll 1988: 199 ff.). But, in the psycho-thriller, the main signifier of meaning is 'violent emotional reaction' pointing to past perceptions. In *Marnie,* a trivial thing like the colour red acquires a strong but hidden meaning as a result of Marnie's violent reactions; in *Spellbound,* dark stripes on a white ground evoke strong, signifying reactions; in *Vertigo* it is the vertical dimension. The emotional affect (represented by facial expressions, perceptual distortions, and obsessive acts) will then eventually bring about a reconstruction of those perceptions of episodes in the past that have caused the traumatic effect. Therefore, whereas the normal fictions of detection have a progressive sequence of acts and cognitions revealing past acts and motives, the psycho-thriller's progressive sequence uses an affective reaction as clues to a reconstruction of past subjective experiences.

The psycho-thriller starts midway, with an emotional reaction lacking any obvious perceptual reason, thus blocking enaction and creating saturations or autonomic response. It often makes an 'enactive' framework for the viewer by providing a subject-actant, the 'investigator' (psychologist or detective), for whom 'guessing' the reasons of the perceived emotions is a mental act within a canonical framework. In *Spellbound* 'Gregory Peck' evokes saturated feelings in the viewer by empathic means, whereas 'Ingrid Bergman', at least to some extent, activates canonical schemata in the viewer. However, most of the film cues an activation of emotional affects tied to unconscious or conscious memories, to scenes for which enactive control has passed. The investigator's active attention in some respects increases the viewer's experience of the saturated aspects of the cobweb of traumatic memories.

The plot in *Vertigo* follows a progressive–retrogressive time pattern. The plot seems to progress by future-directed acts, but elements of the past surface continually, so that a cyclical-circular oscillation between progressive and retrogressive movements is produced. The plot is as follows. A policeman, Scottie (James Stewart), pursues a crook over the rooftops and stumbles. A colleague is killed while trying to help him. Scottie survives, but with a trauma, fear of heights, and has to leave the police force. An old friend, Elster, hires him to tail his wife, Madeleine, who is supposed to be mentally ill. Scottie finds out that she is obsessed with her grandmother's mother, Carlotta. Madeleine seeks places and things which have a connection with Carlotta, and imitates her hairstyle and clothes. Scottie saves Madeleine from an attempt to commit suicide, and they become acquainted and fall in love. Scottie guesses that the traumatic location of Madeleine's obsession is a mission station, and, to cure the trauma, they drive down to the mission; however, Madeleine now becomes totally obsessed, runs up the bell-tower, throws herself off, and dies. Scottie's vertigo makes him unable to follow and stop her. At the inquest, he is severely rebuked for his failure, and he becomes seriously ill (shown by a nightmare sequence which marks the transition from first to second act in the film) and is hospitalized. Scottie slowly recovers, but still seeks the dead Madeleine, and perpetually, but mistakenly, thinks that he can see her. Finally he spots a saleswoman, Judy, who looks very much like Madeleine; he persuades her to meet him. Now it is revealed to the audience that Judy is the same person as Madeleine, hired by Elster to act as his wife in order to let his murder of her look like suicide to Scottie. But Scottie does not know any of this, and slowly forces Judy to dress and arrange her hair exactly as Madeleine did. He thus repeats Elster's 'directorial' job, but for him the motive is not money but a 'fetishist' craving for a complete repetition of the signifiers of emotion and desire. Finally, when Judy wears Madeleine's necklace, he understands everything, takes her down to the mission, and forces her to go up to the scene of the crime and confess. The repetition has cured him of vertigo. When a nun arrives at the bell-tower, Judy is frightened, tries to get away, and dies by falling from the tower in an exact repetition of the death of Elster's wife, the true Madeleine. The cured Scottie can look down into the 'abyss'.

On the surface of the story-iceberg, the fabula and plot overlap completely in a progressive narrative time. This begins with Scottie developing vertigo, and, through mediating actions, ends when he is cured. But beneath this high level there are multiple themes and plot-elements with a much stronger, Janus-like orientation, looking forward as well as backward into different prehistories. Scottie is hired as a very private eye in order to observe a woman who desperately tries to be united with someone from the past, a retrogressive quest. The quest to reveal Madeleine's secrets also becomes an investigation into her past and that of a long-dead woman. By Scottie's pursuit of a woman trying to find an identity in the past, his quest also becomes retrogressive on several levels, because the dead woman and her destiny represent a symbolic mental model of old-fashioned, passionate womanhood, contrasting with modern women like Scottie's friend Midge. That the union of Scottie and Madeleine is a fusion with the past and a rescaling of temporal dimensions is explicitly indicated by the setting of the beginning of their romance among the thousand-year-old sequoia trees, and by remarks on the brevity of human life compared with that of the trees.

The introduction of a supernatural theme, that is, Madeleine's conviction that she is the reincarnation of a dead woman, itself leads to a blocking of forward-directed acts. That something is supernatural implies that it cannot be the object of ordinary acts. The extensive use of supernatural phenomena in Gothic fiction serves the purpose of suspending cognitive and motor reactions in order to produce arousal and moods of timelessness. In *Vertigo,* the viewer is given reasons to believe that Madeleine exists in a supernatural timelessness, out of reach of Scottie's earthly endeavours.

There are also indications that Scottie's personal quest is retrogressive. In the second part of the film, his project is explicitly nostalgic and consists of reviving and repeating the past. When Scottie forces Judy to imitate Madeleine in dress and hairstyle, the present becomes a symbol of the past; his acts and emotions are not directed toward a person of flesh and blood, but become signs indicating the past, and timeless memories. The viewers' experience of time is furthermore complicated by the fact that they know about Judy's double identity, and therefore have forward-directed expectations of a future revelation of Judy's identity and, at the same time, have to model Scottie's retrogressive *recherche d'un temps perdu*. In his interview with Truffaut Hitchcock indicated two aspects of the film, a thematic-motivational and a narrative one. He was very interested in Stewart's impossible desire to recreate the image of and sleep with a dead woman, and he was occupied with his choice of revealing Judy's identity as Madeleine in the middle of the film to evoke suspense instead of surprise. The viewer would then ask the questions: Scottie doesn't know this, does he? and what will he do when he finds out about it? (see Truffaut 1984). The narrative will generate 'active' expectations, but they will exist in combination with a strong activation of Scottie's retrogressive associations. The tensity will therefore take place within a framework of saturation.

The temporal confusion could be made complete if the viewer did not accept the traumatic rooftop experience at its face value as the traumatizing incident, but made hypotheses about Scottie having an extradiegetic trauma. An understanding and interpretation of a given narrative consists of constructing what is seen with a set of mental models and schemata stored in the viewer. A viewer who had already seen *Marnie* and *Psycho* might have noticed that both have as their traumatizing scene a textbook Freudian 'primal scene' of a child watching the intercourse of grown-ups, and that this is mixed with another textbook Freudian motive, of incestuous jealousy leading to murder. Without voting for or against the truth of the Freudian textbook descriptions, the viewer-interpreter might take the triangular primal scene (man doing something violently to a woman, third party watching in a state of affect) and the triangular incest-figure of attraction–aversion as widespread cultural schemata of representations of traumatic episodes, which have been used by the director in several films and therefore might describe aspects of the construction of *Vertigo*. This film has three 'traumatic' incidents in which people participate in or suffer a fall, the middle one brought about by voluntary intentions similar to the infantile interpretation of intercourse in *Marnie,* the two others caused by involuntary fatal circumstances. The stylistic equivalent of the primal scene in *Marnie* is the dream version of the inquest scene in *Vertigo,* in which there is also a triangle of people: Elster, Carlotta, and Scottie. The dream-sequence proceeds by visual associations which take their point of departure in an ultra-close-up of red, oval-shaped gems in a painted portrait of Carlotta (the colour being repeated by glimpses of red light during the rest of the dream-sequence). Scottie is seen approaching Madeleine's open, dark, and demonic grave. Fall and vertigo are then hinted at by a sequence in which Scottie's head moves through a cobweb-like structure, and finally the dream closes with a remake of the bell-tower fall, but with a male figure as the falling person.

An interpretation according to hypothetical Freudian schemata would blur the causal and chronological order of the narrative development: it would be uncertain whether the inquest-dream of a fall were a remake of traumatic infantile experiences prior to the rooftop scene, or just a consequence of the second traumatic experience.[6] A viewing according to more widespread mental schemata would blur the chronological order by experiencing the dream-sequence as consisting of primitive, 'early' ways of structuring the world. Most interpretations would end up noting that some of the elements of the narrative are beyond voluntary control, such as the perceptual structure and effect of the vertigo experiences and the nightmare.

A typical viewing response would then be one of confusion because of the ambiguous temporal and causal relations, the many representations of non-objective mental states (such as dreams, and thoughts of transtemporal identifications), and the strong indications of associational levels of meaning. The response would be one of arousal, because of the many dramatic episodes of danger, death, and love. The description of non-voluntary and autonomic reactions (falling, dreaming, or vertigo) would make probable the triggering of an autonomic affective response in the viewer.

---

[6] Wood (1991: 385 *et passim*) emphasizes the incestuous-tender aspects of *Vertigo;* Modleski (1988: 95 f.) sees Scottie as not only in love with, but identifying with, 'the lost object' .

In the following I shall look at the way in which the lyrical-melodramatic effect of *Vertigo,* which has already been described according to the tensions between plot and fabula construction, is correlated with the stylistic level, which relies on networks of associations and repetitions creating 'achronicity' or rhythm.

The film is characterized by its mixture of filmic and graphic elements, both in the title-sequence at the beginning of the film, and in the caesura-dream dividing the first part of the film from the second. These two sequences are strong markers of a meaning outside normal phenomenological reality. Closely linked to these are the two 'vertigo' shots, producing a strong subjective distortion of normal reality, plus, to a certain extent, the scene describing the night-time chase over the roofs that establishes Scottie's trauma. The film draws powerfully on metaphoric similarity within the narrated. The basis for strings of similarities is established in the museum sequence, in which, for example, the 'whirlpool' of Madeleine's hair is isolated by close-up and shown to be nearly identical to that of Carlotta Valdes. The space is fragmented, and some details are isolated from their metonymic relations and shown as linked to phenomena with another type of reality-status: for example, picture/Madeleine. This isolation, plus associations of similarity, produce affective concentration: some parts of the frame have a very strong 'connectionist' significance, and the affective charge of the whole frame is concentrated in the supercharged significant detail, sometimes shown blown up to full-frame. When Hitchcock, in films like *Notorious,* isolates a significant detail like the key, the charge of meaning and affect is part of a tightly controlled narrative structure. But, although Madeleine's hair-'maelstrom' indicates that she is imitating Carlotta, the isolation is somehow not fully motivated by the narrative in the same tight, metonymic way as is the key in *Notorious:* the metaphoric qualities of the 'maelstrom' are also linked with the whirlpool of the credit sequence, and give the viewer a feeling of a not-fully-comprehended, saturated network of associations.

Later, in the dream-sequence especially, a fully developed network of metaphoric similarities is shown, consisting of hair-whirlpool, posy, and necklace with ruby-red stones. This breaks down the metonymic, action-oriented, forward-directed time. Like Herrmann's music, many networks of supercharged metaphoric similarities and isolated frames are only partially integrated as clues in the forward-directed narrative, and, contrary to the network of red colour-phenomena in *Marnie,* which can be fully transformed into meaning, many of the associations in *Vertigo* remain on a premeaning level of perceptual resemblance.

Many cuts in the film are perceived as discontinuities, and this impression is produced by cuts between ultra-close-ups or between scenes with no obvious narrative connections. The isolation and discontinuity of the shots may be seen as metaphorically connected with the eye-glance mechanism. The field of vision is not continuously present for the viewer, but is discontinuously scanned, although built-in mechanisms normalize the discontinuities and fill in the blanks so that at best the discontinuity is felt subliminally. Directors who want to represent this phenomenon may use projections of stills. Glance-of-eye and mechanical shift-of-slides are both part of a subhuman, unintentional subjectivity, characterized by fragmentation, repetition, and causality, in opposition to a human 'teleology' based on continuity and the ability to act according to free will. Hitchcock establishes this association in the credit sequence, in which a close-up of an eye hints at the twitch and start of a blink and shows the involuntary pupillary motion of accommodation. Furthermore, the film uses rhythmic oscillations of light several times to depict subconscious and involuntary processes.

Vertigo makes widespread use of parallelism and repetition. The film has two acts that in some respects are repetitions of each other, and in other respects are a counterpoint-like repetition in reverse. Each act culminates in a tower sequence consisting of a character mounting a tower and falling, just as the narrative begins with a fall from a height. There is repetition of place, as when the atmosphere of the church and Carlotta's grave is repeated in that of the mission station. Between the vertical, repetitive culminations are repetitions of horizontal motion, for instance when Scottie is tailing Madeleine by car or on foot. Not only are the sequences of tailing by car repeated (for instance, Scottie waiting in a car, Madeleine coming down and driving away, Scottie following), but also within the individual sequence the repetitive structure is underlined by sequences such as a shot from Scottie's point of view of Madeleine's car turning left, then an anchoring shot of Scottie and his reaction, then Madeleine's car turning right, then again a reaction shot, then again Madeleine's car turning left; these scenes are all located in the city. Another type of horizontal motion consists of sequences in which Scottie and Madeleine go out driving, such as the 'purposeless' trip when they wander around among sequoia trees, their visit to the beach, and their two trips to the mission station. These trips go from city/present to country/past.

The systems of repetition in the sequences of shots and acts sometimes come close to producing a rhythmic effect, transforming the viewer's telic, narrative expectations into paratelic-rhythmic ones. The ritualistic, rhythmic, and repetitive patterns serve as relays for involuntary mechanisms of melodramatic lyrical motion. Even in details repetitions are used, as when Madeleine's closing of a window is repeated in Judy's closing of a window. The discourse therefore appears to consist of an endless mass of *déja-vu* experiences, so that the real signifying episodes seem to exist in a previous time, and the present is felt with a strange 'familiarity' as indexing previous episodes. The prospective elements are thus counterbalanced by retrospective ones, and the result is a decrease in projection and tensity and an increase in saturation, intensity, and timelessness, by means of an activation of the viewer's memory of the previous parts of the film (as in the description in Chapter 2 of the function of a feeling of familiarity in memory, and in Chapter 6 of activating timelessness by activating networks of associations).

The film very often uses dissolves instead of a clean cut, in order to link jumps in time and space. This can be seen as an old-fashioned way of establishing continuity within the narrative abbreviation, especially because the absence of dialogue and the frequent prominence of music may be associated with the silent film. However, dissolves point either to an agency of enunciation or to an interior world or consciousness, for which two perceptions such as two different times and two different spaces can exist at the same time. As contextualized in the film, the dissolves create a melodramatic, durative timelessness and a rhythmic-interior-subjective dynamic. In the context of the film, the dissolves are linked to the erotic situation so that they support experiences of a dynamic, symbiotic fusion of the two sexes.

Whereas dissolves perceptually associate different points in time–space to create durative lyrical motion, Hitchcock moves in the opposite direction several times during the film when he creates static, lyrical perceptions by isolating specific points in time–space. The film very often juxtaposes shots with little motion, and the shots thus converge into stills. The phenomenological reaction to the montage of the different semi-frozen shots is one of static perception, 'contemplation'. This is clearly demonstrated in the graveyard sequence and in the creation of forest mysticism, in which a play on the presence/disappearance of Madeleine is made by fragmentation of visual access to the scene. Whereas the dissolves of the drive create a 'moved' symbiosis, the still-effect creates distance by disconnecting enaction from perception, as in a photograph.

The use of reaction-shots is central in the film. All the characters exist, to a great extent, in a third-person or phenomenological otherness, and the spectator is permanently confronted with the task of guessing their emotional interior from their facial expression rather than from verbal communication or actions. Music plays a prominent role in the film. There is an overall scarcity of dialogue; very often the film consists of long silent episodes, in which the viewer is confronted with two levels of signification: a visual narrative (objectivity), and music (subjectivity), with the music providing the subjectivity and emotional drive. The social middle ground of verbal communication is omitted, and visual objectivity and musical subjectivity are fused without social mediation.

SPACE DIMENSIONS, AUTONOMIC RESPONSE,
AND THE RELABELLING OF AROUSAL

The space in *Vertigo* is divided into two subdimensions with quite different symbolic meanings: the vertical and the horizontal. Most of the film takes place in the horizontal dimension. As mentioned above, the first part in particular has many sequences built around horizontal motion, mostly car-driving, whether as an element of spying and pursuit or as an aspect of wandering, driving without a specific purpose and as a purely subjective expression. But Scottie and Madeleine also walk together in the forest and at the seaside, and the ultimate point of pursuing and wandering is union, fusion, and stasis, as when they kiss and embrace by the sea. The horizontal dimension is the dimension in which symbiotic tenderness and strong, time-less emotions are expressed. The protagonists live in a positive achrony out-side time and space, symbolized by the seaside episode against a background of the eternal, repetitive motion of the waves. Normally, in canonical narra-tives, the horizontal dimension is the scene for quest of object control; but, in *Vertigo*, the voluntary sequences are counterbalanced by sequences of paratelic enaction and of perceptual fusion and tender (e)motion.

The vertical dimension is used much less; but, on the other hand, the episodes taking place in the vertical dimension are highly charged and signif-icant, as a result of their position within the narrative and their visual appear-ance and content. In the real action, there are five vertical situations: the 'all-male' rooftop episode; the 'male' stepladder episode; Madeleine jumping into the Bay and Scottie following and rescuing her and later undressing her in his bed; the two episodes, linked with the bell-tower, in which a man pur-sues or forces a woman; plus an additional 'male' vertical situation in the dream-sequence in which Scottie jumps into the grave and down from the bell-tower. The credit sequence, with its abstract graphics and its predomi-nantly rotating motion, seems to be connected to the vertical/vertiginous dimension. The all-male situation has only a forced involuntary 'fall', a down-ward movement, while Madeleine's jump into the bay is supposed to be caused by an unconscious compulsion, and has a downward movement fol-lowed by the upward movement of the rescue operation leading to the 'sym-biotic' situation in Scottie's flat; he is clearly in conscious control of the situation, and there are no signs of vertigo.

Vertigo seems to be connected to the process of ascending as implying a subsequent fall. In this context, it is tempting to explain the stairwell ascen-sion and the subsequent fall as a classic symbolic representation of sexual intercourse, with the descent as the orgasm, especially if we bear in mind the symbolic 'coupling' of ascent and descent with a climax and turning-point in the belfry, actualizing the traditional bell/clapper symbolism of sexual organs.

In the first bell-tower episode Scottie tries to follow and pursue Madeleine up the stairs, but is unable to continue to the top because he looks down and is overwhelmed by vertigo. None the less, many viewers will see the scenes and experience the strong psychosomatic reactions evoked by, for example, the famous vertigo shots, without thinking of sexual intercourse. An explanation of the emotional impact of the scenes must therefore be founded on psychosomatic models with a broader range of application than sexuality as such.

In order to understand the structure of this fear and its phenomenology, I shall examine more closely these vertigo shots, and the reasons that they evoke such strong emotional reactions. They consist of a shot of the vertical dimension, supposedly seen by a man suffering from vertigo looking down a stairwell. The shot has been made by counterpointing zooming and tracking. At the beginning the stairwell is seen with a relatively small perception of depth, because the camera is zoomed in. Then the camera starts to track forwards (down), and at the same time zooms out, increasingly creating a depth of perception without changing the size of the picture because of the simultaneous tracking.[7] The change in the perceived is therefore a function of a change in perception, without any simulation of action, whereas a zoom-out would simulate 'moving a subject away from the perceived' and a track-in 'moving a subject toward the perceived'.

If the perceived is a function of perception, then projection is blocked; there is not an object-world to charge affectively and modify by actions, and the variations in the perceived will be regulated by invisible fluctuations within the apparatus of perception. An example of this is dizziness induced by intoxication, when perception fluctuates irrespective of, for example, an unchanging object-world, and is correlated with a breakdown of motor control, as illustrated in Hitchcock's next film, *North by Northwest,* in the drunken-driving episode. Dizziness, vertigo, and so on are therefore caused by the breakdown of a subject–object schema; the subject no longer has any ability to influence the perceived by acts of motor control, by modifying the objects, or by escape. This also means a breakdown of the distancing and voluntary inhibition mechanisms that seem to be closely related to the voluntary motor

---

[7] There is some confusion in descriptions of what actually takes place. For example, Bordwell and Thompson (1990: 187), Spoto (1983: 429) and Wood (1991: 379) describe the shot as a track-out, zoom-in, following Hitchcock's own acceptance of Truffaut's guess as to how it was made (Truffaut: *Le Cinéma Selon Hitchcock,* Paris 1966: 188 f.) Monaco (1977: 63), however, describes the shot as a track-in, zoom-out. Bordwell *et al.*'s description implies that the depth will decrease over time as a consequence of increasing the focal length of the lens, ending with a shallow image, whereas Monaco's description would increase the depth (which would not be completely offset by the tracking). Inspection of the frames indicates an increase in depth, and consequently I have described the shots as a track-in-zoom-out, which is also consistent with the intuitive experience of the increasing perceptual 'weirdness' of the shot (the weirdness of shallowness would typically be connected to motion, for instance a mismatch between the speed and the progress made by a moving object). Hitchcock might merely have remembered that tracking and zooming worked in opposite directions, but forgotten the details.

system, placing a perceiving subject *vis-à-vis* a perceived object world, mediated by actual or optional motor mediations. In vertigo and other similar experiences of (possibly) fascinated terror and a feeling of being spellbound, there is often a strong fear of losing control and wishing to do such things as throw oneself into the abyss, or touch the poisonous snake. It is as if the voluntary autonomy disappears as a result of high levels of arousal connected with lack of models of active defence/arousal reduction, and therefore the brain accepts even life-damaging arousal-reducing impulses: instead of having a tense alertness, something wants the subject to give in, to relax. Besides the high level of arousal the short-circuit might be caused because, mentally, the abyss is no longer modelled 'out there', but representationally modelled 'in here'. In Scottie's case, he experiences high arousal and paralysis even before he reaches dangerous heights.

The common denominator between strong arousal by fear and high sexual arousal is the arousal itself and the possibility of an autonomic response of relaxation, although in normal conditions they have different evaluations (death-producing as opposed to pleasure-producing). Most viewers would experience a high level of arousal in the vertigo-tower-scene because of the fear element explicitly stated and represented in the perceptual deviations (parallel to the temporary fallout of object and projection in orgasm). If the viewers have fear of falling as their only understanding of the situation they will cling to an urge for voluntary control, although the high level of arousal would activate thoughts of an autonomic bale-out reaction. However, if they also have a conscious or semi-conscious erotic model of the situation, they will be able to relabel and positively re-evaluate an autonomic response. If, like Hitchcock perhaps, they have problems with a positive evaluation of high levels of sexual arousal (see Spoto 1983), they could relabel the arousal as fear and then make a voluntary model for dealing with this fear by removing the fear-creating object. Scottie is cured of his vertigo when he discovers a reason for fearing the murderer-accomplice Judy, and so acquires a reason to act violently and remove a possibly arousal-evoking object.

To interpret the vertigo scenes in a strictly Freudian manner would be a misleading description of the typical viewer's cognitive experience of those episodes (although probably in accordance with Hitchcock's intentions). Nevertheless, it is reasonable to suggest that such scenes of fear and suggestions of autonomic response would evoke arousal and response-patterns similar to erotic experiences, and therefore have a similar attraction for the viewer. In some aspects, these representations of fear are more able to simulate orgasm-like mechanisms than pornography is, because pornography moulds an enactive response directed at the object-world and therefore supports voluntary experiences, whereas narratives of fear activate states of paralysis and autonomic reactions.

THE SUBLIME, THE PASSIONATE, AND THE MODERN

Normally the human consciousness works at a certain level and on a certain scale determined by the size of humans and their mental software. Whole human bodies or human faces are central to the pre-set format of attention, whereas atoms or galaxies are outside the dimensions for which the human perception and consciousness have been constructed by evolution, just as the representation of fragments of the human body or of isolated representations of organ or muscle reactions falls outside the holistic mental models of representation (as discussed in Chapter 5). Deviations from the norm produce not only cognitive effects, but also affective ones. Hitchcock films mainly use representations within the level of a prototypical 'human format', but, in the credit sequence particularly, he works consciously at showing formats of representation which deviate from the norm in order to use them with an affect-evoking purpose. The representational inspiration comes to a great extent from modern science, and its model descriptions of anonymous systems and forces in the cosmos and the atom-world which are incompatible with a 'human', teleological model of reality.

The title-sequence of *Vertigo* begins with a detail-shot of a female face, and the picture-frame cuts out half of a red mouth, half of the nose, and half of a cheek. Then it pans to a focus on red lips, which have muscular twitches; and tilts to a focus on the eyes, which follow an invisible object by movements from side to side; and then pans to a focus on the left eye (as seen by the viewer). We have been shown a human face, but it has been fragmented by detail shots, so that the human parts have been isolated, perhaps in an 'inhuman way', from a whole person capable of voluntary acts. We see small twitches around the eye and the start of a blink and then pupillary accommodation, followed by a wide opening of the eye as in sudden surprise. The detail-shot of the eye is changed via graphics, which come out of the eye, into a world of graphic rotation, oscillation, and gradual change, emphasized by the cyclical pulsation of the visual network and tissue-structure.

In a Freudian reading of the film, it is obvious that the oval lips may be seen as having a metaphoric association with the vagina. Some of the changes of form in the graphics consist of making a continuum between circle (eye, pupilla, 'sun', 'perception'-consciousness) and ellipsis (mouth, vagina, galaxy, cosmic maelstrom), as a possible association-field activated in a low-definition, parallel processing in association areas. With a single brief exception, the oscillations between elliptic and circular forms arise from counterclockwise rotation. The circular rotations of graphics have some manifestations of circular expansion and contraction, which are linked to the involuntary eye-movements (pupillary accommodation and twitches), while, *qua* their involuntary nature, orgasm-contractions are a further field of association which might be activated with low definition in the viewer.

Several aspects of the credit sequence can be seen as indications that we are about to watch something hyper-modern (from a 1958 point of view). The abstract, graphical elements would suggest associations with modernity; the soundless rotation of the graphic structure would possibly be associated with sublime cosmic forces and scales beyond prototypical humanness, as in Kubrick's later pure cultivation of the grandiose aesthetics of space in *2001— A Space Odyssey,* in which the absence of the acoustic modality except as music plays an important role for the experience of reality-status. The grandiose forces of space are mental models of phenomena beyond an enactive human control, and they evoke pure perception and contemplation.

The fragmented detail shots of the human face in the title-sequence are more ambiguous. The analytic distance which is a presupposition for such a dissection of the face evokes associations with a futuristic modernity, cut off from emotional life, like the modernity presupposed in the discussion between Scottie and Midge about aircraft-engineer-designed bras. In a broader context, the face-dissection and the eye-metaphors might be linked with voyeurism as a symbol of the widespread belief in a modern emancipation from saturated, tender feelings, as in *Rear Window*'s depiction of the voyeurism supposedly typical of modern life. But, at the same time, it is as if the detail-shots 'emancipate' a humanness which is below the level of the whole person controlled by voluntary processes and which lays bare the lower levels of involuntary processes. The organs become isolated from their integration in a whole (associated with moral irresponsibility, as in the distinction between premeditated and impulse-driven, unpremeditated behaviour), and the organic processes only obey their local, autonomic tendencies, as in the pupillary accommodation or the twitches of the eyes.

Around 1960, Hitchcock's films were an important part of the representation of modernity in popular culture, especially his depictions of the obsessional instinct-and-trauma-controlled person and of ritualized behaviour associated with pre-modern man; this was linked with a modern setting and modern forms of representation, meaning that the modern world represented a new primitivism. An example *par excellence* is the shower-scene in *Psycho,* with its use of 'modern' fragmentation to represent ritualism and evoke strong effects; similarly, Hitchcock's representations of a 'modern' or 'voyeuristic' separation of human, interpersonal visual perception and virtual or optional interpersonal interaction, eyes isolated from interaction by touch and acts— as in *Rear Window* and the title-sequence in *Vertigo*—all contributed to a popular-culture representation of modernity.

In some respects it is as if Hitchcock's myth, or mental model, of modernity consists of a representation of an archaic culture, which resembles industrial rationalism by the depiction of individuals in whom biological and psychological laws rule just as severely and impersonally in their mental life as the laws of physics do in nature. The romantic parts of *Vertigo* (represented by music in the credit sequence) in many ways express a *Zeitgeist* which is very different from the modernity of the credit sequence, but is closely connected with romanticism and the world of the Gothic novel. However, the Gothic love story in *Vertigo* is a fiction which Elster directs as a cover-up for murder.

The credit-sequence is based on fluctuations of similarities with no temporal structure except that of the audiovisual track, and it therefore depicts timelessness. Its microcosm, eye and pupilla, resemble macrocosm, the rotating, galaxy-associating graphics. The affective correlation to the macrocosm is the sublime perception; to the microcosm, the affective correlation is the autonomic, affect-charged abreaction. The narrative that follows may be seen as an effort to construct a prototypical, human-scale level, but the result of the constructions and puzzle-unravelling is not—as in *Marnie*—the establishing of a fairy tale, 'and they lived happily ever after'. The film ends in *stasis*, and with saturated melancholia.

Recapitulation and Conclusion

The aim of this book has been to show the way in which cognitions and emotions in the experience of viewing visual fiction are part of a holistic framework. This holism has its origin in the way that fictions are experienced by the viewer. Central elements in the book can be summed up by some key concepts:

Holism

I have shown that it is imperative to describe the relations between body, mind, and world as an interacting whole in order to understand the way in which visual fiction cues a simulation of body–mind states.

Ecological conventions

It is possible to steer a middle course between realism and formalism by describing the way in which aspects of the human mind have been formatted by evolution. This provides us with an understanding of the hardwired basis of the effects produced by representational and stylistic deviations. It further provides some clues to the ecological and functional benefits of our emotional makeup, such as the role of bonding and identification or the 'physical', direct transmission of emotions by facial expressions and tone of voice. To know what is hardwired also makes it possible to determine what is historical and what belongs to specific cultural layers such as ethnic group, gender, age-group, or individual experiences.

Innate mental models acquire a special visibility in visual fiction, because audiovisual media are the most sophisticated yet invented by man for simulating and manipulating the many different aspects of the ways in which we perceive, feel, think, act, memorize, associate, and socialize.

Reality-simulation

I have shown the means by which the aesthetic, narrative simulations of different types and dimensions of reality use the same cognitive and affective mechanisms that we use in our real-life experiences and in our mental representations of them. Higher mental life relies on the ability to execute hypothetical, fictitious imaginations. However, as our minds have no 'direct' contact with the world, they have to rely on cognitive-emotional evaluations of the reality-status of a given image-configuration, such as perceptual salience, type of intent, or sensory holism, like feelings of irreality made by 'sound-of', 'image of', 'tactile qualities of' (ghosts), or status in relation to possible acts. As the feeling of reality is made up of many different types of evaluations and standard procedures, it is easy to short-circuit these evaluations by all kinds of ambiguities and representational paradoxes (for example, *mise en abyme*) in order to create aesthetic effect. I have demonstrated the way in which redefinition of reality-status plays a central role in comic fictions, and the reason that theories based on textual features like 'paradox' fail to explain many comic fictions. A number of different phenomena, such as empathy, mental overload, surprise, 'robotism', lack of voluntary control, and stereotypes, may be redefined into a mental hypothesis by a reaction of laughter.

Aesthetic flow

I have made a model of the aesthetic-narrative experiential flow, based on the way in which experiences activate both different psychosomatic dimensions (perception, cognition, memory, affect, and enaction), and also different mental forms (the associative and the sequential). I have shown that mental flow is directed from perception to enaction, that is, 'downstream', but also that one may cue a direction 'upstream' or make short-circuits in order to evoke aesthetic effects. The linear forms of canonical narratives are not caused by abstract logic, but by real-world constraints on the sequencing of events and by the 'downstream' relations between motives, cognitions, and acts. Associative forms therefore lead to different 'upstream' emotional tones.

The book has discussed the use of cognitive-labelling theories in film and media studies, and has illustrated the way in which the 'narrative scene' in a canonical narrative will be the typical mental format for the interaction of cognitions, emotions, preferences, and enactive potentials.

Intensity, saturation, tensity, and emotivity

I have described these four prototypical aesthetic tones, correlated with both the type of psychosomatic dimension activated, and the (cued) mental or physical strategy required for handling a situation.

Focus

The book has explained that we have only have a limited conscious capacity and that, therefore, a given audiovisual experience represents a mental hierarchy in which some phenomena, often linked to tense enactive interests, are at the focus of attention, whereas others are activated as a non-conscious associative network enriching the experience, or active as a macro-frame, a set of propositions determining the nature of the attended focus.

Subjective toning

A special-focus function indicates whether a phenomenon is experienced as proximal focus, as an aspect of the experiencer, or as object-centred, an aspect of the experienced. The book has demonstrated that subjectivity is linked to constraints on voluntary acts. It has further shown that temporal experience is part of the subjective toning of experience, and that it is cued both by several levels of mental models representing chains of events and by the emotional strength, perceptual salience, modal form, and reality-status of a given visual fiction. Of special importance for film aesthetics is that time is experienced differently when it is represented by modifications of perceptual sequences (for example, slow/fast) and by modifications of sequences of act schemata (by insertions or ellipsis), and that time-experiences may be linked to the temporal domain of the represented (for instance, 'eternity', or durative phenomena, like 'the summer').

Visuo-motor models

Based on, among others, Kosslyn's, Johnson's, and Johnson-Laird's descriptions of mental models, I have shown that image schemata are used as software and relay in the structuration of input as well as output. This book has delineated the way in which narrative film takes place on a certain 'categorical level' and at a certain focus of attention, cued by the given type of enaction. This level will typically have elements such as house, door, road, entry, fight, or embrace, but will not have, for instance, elements of texture. Deviations from the prototypical level, the mid-sized world, and the prototypical 'downstream' direction, will often cue special effects.

Identification and empathy

Fiction films are about human concerns, and it follows that identification with and simulation of the cognitive, motivational-affective, and enactive processes of the protagonists are central activities in film-viewing. By using frames and filters—such as 'realism', 'fiction', or 'generic convention'—some fictions may diminish or block such empathic simulation; and by using a comic redefinition of reality-status fictions may even evoke reactions contrary to empathic identification.

Models of humans

I have shown that central to our cognitive-emotional experience of visual fictions are general and holistic models of humans: we experience the general formation of the protagonist's body in space, and the importance of hedonic tone (pleasure or pain) as motivators of the body–mind configuration, and we analyze the degree to which a given being is 'human' according to whether it shows flexibility, empathy and emotions, consciousness, and intentional, goal-directed behaviour. These functions are based on innate brain-circuitry, and serve as basic models for the way in which we orient ourselves in the physical and social world; their presence or absence infuses feelings of familiarity or unfamiliarity in the viewer.

Important for our experience of behaviours and scenarios are whether they relate to non-conscious, autonomic types of reactions (themselves related to early, rhythmic-repetitive mechanisms and to passive bale-out mechanisms), or to conscious, voluntary, goal-directed, telic behaviours (related to late, neo-cortical functions). Songs and some emotional behaviours relate to autonomic reactions, whereas canonical narratives mostly relate to telic behaviours. A blend of telic and autonomic features will be found in behaviours like dancing, or those in which means and processes are more important than ends, and I have called this type paratelic, a term that also indicates the functions which attempt to increase the level of activation, as opposed to telic functions, which attempt to reduce activation by reaching a certain goal.

Genre typology

The central genres will often be strongly determined by their relation to a mental function: lyrical genres to autonomic or paratelic forms, canonical narratives to telic forms, horror fiction to autonomic responses, and so on. Genres of visual fiction will further be determined by whether the fiction cues an unmediated simulation of the fiction from the point of view of a protagonist, whether some emotional filters mediate the relation to the protagonists (as in metafictions), or whether some other mechanisms take place, like comic reactions in comic fictions, or dissociation of holistic experiences as in schizoid fictions.

I have suggested that eight genre-types are central prototypes: associative lyricism; canonical narratives of action; obsessional fictions of paratelic cognition and enaction; melodramas of the passive position; fictions of horror; schizoid fictions; comic fictions; and metafictions. My hypothesis has been that many viewers of visual fiction have emotional impact as an important parameter when they choose the film they wish to see. Producers of visual fiction therefore tend to produce visual fictions which rely on optimizing their emotional impact. This does not mean that we have an innate genre system, only that we have innate emotional functions and schemata which may or may not be used as a basis for creating an overall emotional tone by those producing visual fiction. My typology is meant as a guideline for understanding some of the parameters determining the prototypical emotional effect of dominant genre-patterns, and for understanding the way in which changes of certain parameters (for example, a change from a telic to a paratelic pattern) will influence the experience of emotional tone, and the reason for this. The prototypical patterns can be mixed in many ways; for example, the cueing of comic reactions or the production of metaframes can also be applied to any other genre.

Formalist, structuralist, and semiotic narratology have described narrative structure by means of verbal, 'logical', and 'causal' models: the narrative pattern is a device, a logic, or an ideological pattern. However, as I have shown in this book, such descriptions do not explain why the 'logic' is fabricated using these specifications, and they do not account for the emotional effects of rearranging phenomena (for instance, temporal rearrangements) or the experienced difference between active and passive narrative forms. I have chosen to generalize these approaches by demonstrating that what formalists, structuralists, and semioticians describe as 'forms' and 'narrative logics' may be described within the larger framework of 'psychosomatic superschemata'.

I have not felt the need in this book to make a total shift of framework when moving from a cognitive explanation to an affective one. We need not leave out our conscious phenomenological experience of emotions (for example, experiences of our ecological heritage as manifested in our autonomic reactions, or experience of voluntary acts). The subject-model used in film studies based on psychoanalysis and psychosemiotics is simplistic in its reliance on the one main function of unconscious sexual desire. Mental models and image-schemata can provide more general descriptions of the cognitive and emotional role of the human body than can Lacanian descriptions of mirror-identification. Our acts and feelings are mediated by image-schemata serving as relays between perceptions, emotions, and acts. These image-schemata are neither imaginary, in a Lacanian sense, nor images of something else; some aspects of our perceptions are used as mental models, and their non-metaphoricity is linked to their functional role as 'software'. Mental models, like canonical narrative schemata or 'a holistic image of self as object in space', are therefore not ideological constructions or misrecognitions.

What we see is what we get. The beauty and fascination of visual fictions is that they activate all our central faculties and aspirations, our perceptions, cognitions, emotions, and enactions. My own aspiration has been to provide holistic explanations for what we all know about visual fictions, not to claim that what we get is the opposite of what we see. I hope that I have provided the outline of a holistic framework which can be used to describe and explain the relations between cognition and emotion in visual fiction.

Glossary of Terms

Autonomic: Processes based on non-voluntary mechanisms (supported by the autonomic nervous system) like laughter, crying, orgasm, shiver.

Canonical narrative: A narrative which cues the experience of sequences of acts, emotions, and perceptions of living beings. The events are represented by a straightforward temporal progression, and the living beings are able to perform voluntary mental or physical acts.

Comic: An autonomic (parasympathetic) reaction of reception on a high level of arousal, based on a redefinition of the reality-status of the arousing phenomenon into 'hypothetical-playful'.

Distal: Perception experienced as located in the perceived object.

Emotivities: The emotional modality connected to the activation of autonomic response.

Empathic identification: The viewer's cued activation of emotions by means of a hypothetical simulation of being an actant in the diegetic world.

Frame: A set of propositions or an analogue structure controlling focus of attention (by exclusion, salience, or guiding top-down processes).

Genre: A prototypical set of narrative schemata.

Intensities: The 'emotional' tones connected to the activation of perceptual processes.

Introjection: Redirecting the attention from a distal to a proximal focus.

Lyrical: The reception experience linked to intense perceptions or saturated networks of associations.

Melodrama: A narrative which follows the emotions and perceptions of living beings. The beings have a reduced ability to perform voluntary, telic mental or physical acts: they are passively acted upon. The enactive deficit leads to paratelic or autonomic response, either positive (as, for instance, in musicals) or negative.

Modality: 1. A sensory system, such as vision or touch. 2. The way in which a given experience is modified by the structure, location, type, and format of the cued mental activation.

Mood: The local emotional tone of a sequence in a given fiction as opposed to its global emotional tone (linked to genre schemata).

Paratelic: The experience of directedness towards the future as a process, that is, linked to a positive evaluation of arousal (as opposed to directedness as telic, linked to goals and activating arousal-reduction).

Priming: The activation of associations at a non-conscious level, or at the periphery of the focus of conscious attention.

Projection: Redirecting the attention from a proximal to a distal focus.

Proximal: Perception experienced as located in the perceiving subject. The term is used in a broader sense than in experimental psychology, in which it indicates the perceptual stimulus.

Reality-status: The evaluation of the mode of existence of a given phenomenon, such as online perceptual existence, hallucination, memory, 'real act' versus act with expressive, communicative, or hypothetical intent; the evaluations have cognitive as well as affective representations in consciousness.

Saturations: The emotional modality connected to the activation of networks of associations which in turn are connected to affect-charged phenomena in relative isolation from act-schemata.

Telic: The experience of voluntary, goal-directed (motor) schemata linked to arousal-reduction.

Tensities: The emotional modality connected to the activation of telic, enactive response.

Tone: General term indicating the way in which feelings, affects, and emotions are continuously experienced as aspects of conscious processes.

List of References

Altman, R. (1985), 'The Evolution of Sound Technology', in E. Weiss and J. Belton (eds.), *Film Sound: Theory and Practice* (New York: Columbia University Press), 44–53.

—— (1987), *The American Film Musical* (Bloomington, Ind.: Indiana University Press).

—— (1992), 'Reading Positions, the Cow Bell Effect, and the Sound of Silent Film', (unpublished paper).

Anderson, J. R. (1990*a*), *Cognitive Psychology and Its Implications* (3rd edn, New York: W. H. Freeman).

—— (1990*b*), *The Adaptive Character of Thought* (Hillsdale, NJ: Lawrence Erlbaum Associates).

Andrew, J. D. (1976), *The Major Film Theories* (New York: Oxford University Press).

—— (1984), *Concepts in Film Theory* (Oxford: Oxford University Press).

—— (1985; first publ. 1978), 'The Neglected Tradition of Phenomenology in Film Theory', in B. Nichols (ed.), *Movies and Methods*, ii (Berkeley: University of California Press), 625–32.

Apter, M. J. (1982), *The Experience of Motivation: The Theory of Psychological Reversals* (London: Academic Press).

Arnheim, R. (1957), *Film as Art* (Berkeley: University of California Press).

—— (1969), *Visual Thinking* (Berkeley and Los Angeles: University of California Press).

—— (1974; first publ. 1954), *Art and Visual Perception: A Psychology of the Creative Eye* (Berkeley: University of California Press).

Aumont, J., Bergala, A., Marie, M., and Vernet, M. (1992; first publ. 1983), *Aesthetics of Film* (Austin, Tex.: University of Texas Press).

Averill, J. R. (1980), 'A Constructivist View of Emotion', in R. Plutchik and H. Kellerman (eds.), *Emotion: Theory, Research, and Experience, i: Theories of Emotion* (New York: Academic Press), 305–39.

Baars, B. J. (1988), *A Cognitive Theory of Consciousness* (Cambridge: Cambridge University Press).

Bakhtin, M. (1968), *Rabelais and His World* (Cambridge, Mass.: MIT Press).

Balázs, B. (1970), *Theory of the Film: Character and Growth of a New Art* (first publ. 1945; New York: Dover Publications).

Barthes, R. (1968), 'L'effet de réel', *Communications*, 11: 84–9.

—— (1972*a*; first publ. 1957), *Mythologies* (New York: Hill and Wang).

—— (1972*b*; first publ. 1970), *S/Z* (New York: Hill and Wang).

—— (1977*a*; first publ. 1970), 'The Third Meaning', in *Image, Music, Text* (London: Fontana), 52–8.

—— (1977*b*; first publ. 1966), 'Introduction to the Structural Analysis of Narratives', in *Image, Music, Text* (London: Fontana), 79–124.

Barthes, R. (1981; first publ. 1980), *Camera Lucida: Reflections on Photography* (New York: Hill and Wang).

Bateson, G. (1985; first publ. 1955), 'A Theory of Play and Fantasy', repr. in R. E. Innis (ed.), *Semiotics: An Introductory Anthology* (Bloomington, Ind.: Indiana University Press), 129–44.

Baudrillard, J. (1994; first publ. 1981), *Simulacra and Simulation* (Ann Arbor: University of Michigan Press).

Baudry, J.-L. (1988; first publ. 1975), 'The Apparatus: Metapsychological Approaches to the Impression of Reality in the Cinema', in P. Rosen (ed.), *Narrative, Apparatus, Ideology* (New York: Columbia University Press), 299–318.

Bazin, A. (1967, 1972), *What is Cinema?* i and ii (Berkeley: University of California Press).

Beardsley, M. C. (1958), *Aesthetics: Problems in the Philosophy of Criticism* (New York: Harcourt, Brace).

Bellour, R. (1979), *L'analyse du Film* (Paris: Albatros).

Benjamin, W. (1973; first publ. 1963), *Charles Baudelaire: A Lyric Poet in the Era of High Capitalism* (London: NLB).

—— (1977; first publ. 1955), 'The Work of Art in the Age of Mechanical Reproduction', in *Mass Communication and Society*, ed. J. Curran, M. Gurevitch, and J. Wollacott (London: Edward Arnold), 384–408.

Benveniste, É. (1971; first publ. 1966), *Problems in General Linguistics* (Coral Gables, Fla.: University of Miami Press).

Bergson, H. (1911), *Laughter: An Essay on the Meaning of the Comic* (New York: Macmillan).

Blakemore, C. (1990), 'Understanding Images in the Brain', in H. Barlow, C. Blakemore, and C. Weston-Smith (eds.), *Images and Understanding* (New York: Cambridge University Press), 257–83.

Bondebjerg, I. (1990), 'Popular Fiction, Narrative and the Melodramatic Epic of American Television', in M. Skovmand (ed.), *Media Fictions* (Aarhus: Seklos/Aarhus University Press), 35–51.

Booth, W. C. (1965; first publ. 1961), *The Rhetoric of Fiction* (Chicago: Chicago University Press).

Bordwell, D. (1980), *French Impressionist Cinema* (New York: Arno Press).

—— (1986; first publ. 1985), *Narration in the Fiction Film* (London: University Paperbacks, Methuen).

—— (1989a), 'A Case for Cognitivism', *Iris*, 9: 11–40.

—— (1989b), *Making Meaning: Inference and Rhetoric in the Interpretation of Cinema* (Cambridge, Mass.: Harvard University Press).

—— and Thompson, K. (1990), *Film Art: An Introduction* (3rd edn., New York: McGraw-Hill).

——, Staiger, J., and Thompson, K. (1985), *The Classical Hollywood Cinema: Film Style and Mode of Production to 1960* (London: Routledge).

Bower, G. H., and Morrow, D. G. (1990), 'Mental Models in Narrative Comprehension', *Science*, 247: 44–8.

Branigan, E. (1984), *Point of View in the Cinema* (Berlin: Mouton).

—— (1992), *Narrative Comprehension and Film* (London: Routledge).

Brecht, B. (1963), *Schriften zum Theater*, iii (Frankfurt: Suhrkamp).

Bremond, C. (1966), 'La Logique des possibles narratifs', *Communications*, 8: 60–76.

Brooks, P. (1984), *Reading for the Plot: Design and Intention in Narrative* (New York: A. A. Knopf).

—— (1985; first publ. 1976), *The Melodramatic Imagination: Balzac, Henry James, Melodrama, and the Mode of Excess* (New York: Columbia University Press).

Browne, N. (1982), *The Rhetoric of Filmic Narration* (Ann Arbor: Michigan, UMI Research Press).

Bryant, J., and Zillmann, D. (eds.) (1991), *Responding to the Screen: Reception and Reaction Processes* (Hillsdale, NJ: Lawrence Erlbaum Associates).

Burch, N. (1981; first publ. 1969), *Theory of Film Practice* (Princeton: Princeton University Press).

—— (1990), *Life to those Shadows* (Los Angeles and Berkeley: University of California Press).

Burgoon, J. K., Buller, D. B., and Woodall. W. G. (1989), *Nonverbal Communication: The Unspoken Dialogue* (NewYork: Harper and Row).

Cannon, W. B. (1970; first publ. 1929), *Bodily Changes in Pain, Hunger, Fear and Rage* (2nd edn., New York: Appleton).

Carroll, N. (1984), 'Toward a Theory of Film Suspense', *Persistence of Vision*, 1: 68–89.

—— (1988), *Mystifying Movies: Fads and Fallacies in Contemporary Film Theory* (New York: Columbia University Press).

—— (1990), *The Philosophy of Horror, or Paradoxes of the Heart* (London: Routledge).

—— (1991), 'Notes on the Sight Gag', in A. Horton (ed.), *Comedy/Film/Theory* (Berkeley: University of California Press), 25–42.

—— (1993), 'Toward a Theory of Point of View Editing: Communication, Emotion, and the Movies', *Poetics Today*, 14/1: 123–41.

Casetti, F. (1990; first publ. 1986), *D'un regard l'autre* (Lyon: Presses Universitaires de Lyon).

—— (1995), 'Face to Face', in W. Buckland (ed.), *The Film Spectator: From Sign to Mind* (Amsterdam: Amsterdam University Press), 118–39.

Cassirer, E. (1953–7; first publ. 1923–9), *The Philosophy of Symbolic Forms*, i–iii (New Haven: Yale University Press).

—— (1962; first publ. 1944), *An Essay on Man* (New Haven: Yale University Press).

Cavallero, C., and Foulkes, D. (1993), *Dreaming as Cognition* (New York: Harvester Wheatsheaf).

Cawelti, J. G. (1976), *Adventure, Mystery and Romance* (Chicago: University of Chicago Press).

Chatman, S. (1978), *Story and Discourse: Narrative Structure in Fiction and Film* (Ithaca, NY: Cornell University Press).

Chevalier-Skolnikoff, S. (1973), 'Facial Expression of Emotion in Nonhuman Primates', in Ekman (1973), 11–89.

Churchland, P. M. (1988; first publ. 1984), *Matter and Consciousness* (Cambridge, Mass.: MIT Press).

Churchland, P. S. (1986), *Neurophilosophy: Towards a Unified Science of the Mind/Brain* (Cambridge, Mass.: MIT Press).

Corballis, M. C. (1991), *The Lopsided Ape: Evolution of the Generative Mind* (New York: Oxford University Press).

Culler, J. (1975), *Structuralist Poetics: Structuralism, Linguistics and the Study of Literature* (London: Routledge and Kegan Paul).

Culler, J. (1983), *On Deconstruction: Theory and Criticism after Structuralism* (Ithaca, NY: Cornell University Press).

Damasio, A. R. (1994), *Descartes' Error: Emotion, Reason, and the Human Brain* (New York: Grosset/Putnam).

—— and Damasio, H. (1993), 'Brain and Language', in *Mind and Brain: Readings from Scientific American* (New York: W. H. Freeman), 54–65.

Davidoff, J. (1991), *Cognition through Color* (Cambridge, Mass.: MIT Press).

Dayan, D. (1976), 'The Tutor-Code of Classical Cinema', in B. Nichols (ed.), *Movies and Methods*, i (Berkeley: University of California Press), 438–51.

Deleuze, G. (1991; first publ. 1985), *Cinema 2: The Time Image* (Minneapolis: University of Minnesota Press).

Dember,W. N., and Warm, J. S. (1979), *Psychology of Perception* (2nd edn., New York: Holt, Rinehard and Winston).

Dennett, D. C. (1990), 'Quining Qualia', in Lycan (1990), 519–47.

Doane, M. A. (1987), *The Desire to Desire: The Woman's Film of the 1940s* (Bloomington, Ind.: Indiana University Press).

Douchet, J. (1986; first publ. 1960), 'Hitch and His Public'; repr. in M. Deutelbaum and L. Poage, *A Hitchcock Reader* (Ames, Ia.: Iowa State University Press), 7–15.

Dretske, F. (1988), *Explaining Behavior: Reasons in a World of Causes* (Cambridge, Mass.: MIT Press).

Ducrot, O., and Todorov, T. (1979; first publ. 1972), *Encyclopedic Dictionary of the Sciences of Language* (Baltimore: John Hopkins University Press).

Durgnat, R. (1967), *Films and Feelings* (London: Faber).

Eco, U. (1970), 'Sémiologie des messages visuel', *Communications*, 15: 11–51.

—— (1979), *A Theory of Semiotics* (Bloomington, Ind.: Indiana University Press).

—— (1984; first publ. 1980), *The Role of the Reader: Explorations in the Semiotics of Texts* (Bloomington, Ind.: Indiana University Press).

—— (1986), *Faith in Fakes* (London: Secker and Warburg).

—— (1989), *The Open Work* (Cambridge, Mass.: Harvard University Press; chs. 1–6 translated from *La struttura assente*, Milano, 1962).

Eisenstein, S. (1949), *Film Form: Essays in Film Theory* (New York: Harcourt Brace Jovanovich).

—— (1968; first publ. 1943), *The Film Sense* (London: Harcourt Brace Jovanovich).

Eisner, L. (1973; first publ. 1969), *The Haunted Screen: Expressionism in the German Cinema and the Influence of Max Reinhardt* (Berkeley: University of California Press).

Eitzen, D. (1994), 'Attending to the Fiction: A Cognitive Account of Cinematic Illusion', *Post Script*, 13/1: 43–66.

Ekman, P. (ed.) (1973), *Darwin and Facial Expression* (New York: Academic Press).

—— and Friesen, W. V. (1975), *Unmasking the Face: A Guide to Recognizing Emotions from Facial Clues* (Englewood Cliffs, NJ: Prentice Hall).

Elias, N. (2nd edn., 1994; first publ. 1969), *The Civilization Process* (Cambridge, Mass.: Blackwell).

Eliot, T. S. (1920), *The Sacred Wood* (London: Methuen).

Ellis, A. W., and Young, A. M. (1988), *Human Cognitive Neuropsychology* (Hove: Lawrence Earlbaum Associates).

Elsaesser, T. (1972), 'Tales of Sound and Fury', *Monogram*, 4: 2–15.

Esslin, M. (1961), *Brecht: The Man and His Work* (Garden City, NY: Anchor Books).

Evans, P. (1989), *Motivation and Emotion* (London: Routledge).

Eysenck, M. W., and Keane, M. T. (1990), *Cognitive Psychology* (Hove: Lawrence Erlbaum Associates).

Finke, R. M. (1989), *Principles of Mental Imagery* (Cambridge, Mass.: MIT Press).

Fiske, J. (1990), *Introduction to Communication Studies* (2nd edn., London: Routledge).

Fiske, S. T., and Taylor, S. E. (1991), *Social Cognition* (2nd edn., New York: McGraw-Hill).

Freud, S. (1953; first publ. 1900–1), *The Interpretation of Dreams*, iv–v (London: Hogarth Press).

—— (1955; first publ. 1920), *Beyond the Pleasure Principle*, xviii (London: Hogarth Press).

—— (1960; first publ. 1904), *Jokes and their Relation to the Unconscious*, viii (London: Hogarth Press).

Friedman, W. (1990), *About Time: Inventing the Fourth Dimension* (Cambridge, Mass: MIT Press).

Frijda, N. H. (1986), *The Emotions* (Cambridge: Cambridge University Press).

Frye, N. (1957), *Anatomy of Criticism* (Princeton: Princeton University Press).

Genette, G. (1980), *Narrative Discourse* (Ithaca, NY: Cornell University Press).

Gibson, J. J. (1986), *The Ecological Approach to Visual Perception* (Hillsdale, NJ: Lawrence Erlbaum Associates).

Gledhill, C. (ed.) (1987), *Home is Where the Heart is: Studies in Melodrama and the Woman's Film* (London: British Film Institute).

Goffman, E. (1986; first publ. 1974), *Frame Analysis: An Essay on the Organization of Experience* (Boston: Northeastern University Press).

Gorbman, C. (1987), *Unheard Melodies: Narrative Film Music* (Bloomington, Ind.: Indiana University Press).

Gombrich, E. H. (1968), *Art and Illusion* (3rd edn., London: Phaidon).

—— (1982), 'Image and Code: Scope and Limits of Conventionalism in Pictorial Representation', in *The Image and the Eye: Further Studies in the Psychology of Pictorial Representation* (London: Phaidon), 278–97.

Goodman, N. (1969; first publ. 1968)), *Languages of Art: An Approach to a Theory of Symbols* (London: Oxford University Press).

Grant, B. K. (ed.). (1986), *Film Genre Reader* (Austin, Tex.: University of Texas Press).

Gray, J. A. (1994), 'Three Fundamental Emotion Systems', in P. Ekman and R. J. Davidson (eds.), *The Nature of Emotion* (New York: Oxford University Press), 243–7.

Greenfield, P. M. (1984), *Mind and Media: The Effects of Television, Computers and Video Games* (Cambridge, Mass.: Harvard University Press).

Gregory, R. L. (1990), *Eye and Brain: The Psychology of Seeing* (4th edn., Princeton: Princeton University Press).

Gregory, R. L. (1970), *The Intelligent Eye* (London: Weidenfeld and Nicolson).

Greimas, A. J. (1970), *Du sens: Essays semiotique* (Paris: Seuil).

—— (1983; first publ. 1966), *Structural Semantics: An Attempt at a Method* (Lincoln: University of Nebraska Press).

Grixti, J. (1989), *Terrors of Uncertainty: The Cultural Contexts of Horror Fiction* (London: Routledge).

Grodal, T. K. (1984), 'Sherlock Holmes: En professionel voyeur', in J. Holmgaard and B. T. Michaelis (eds.), *Lystmord* (Copenhagen: Medusa), 113–79.

—— (1990), 'Potency of Melancholia', in M. Skovmand (ed.), *Media Fictions* (Aarhus: Seklos/Aarhus University Press), 52–75.

—— (1992), 'Romanticism, Postmodernism and Irrationalism', in *Postmodernism and the Visual Media (Sekvens Special Issue)* (Copenhagen: Dept. of Film and Media Studies), 9–27.

—— and Madsen, P. (1974), *Tekststrukturer* (Copenhagen: Borgen).

Gross, R. D. (1987), *Psychology: The Science of Mind and Behaviour* (London: Arnold).

Hamburger, K. (2nd edn., 1973; first publ. 1968), *The Logic of Literature* (Bloomington, Ind.: Indiana University Press).

Hamilton, V. (1988), 'A Unifying Information Processing System: Affect and Motivation as Problem-Solving Processes', in V. Hamilton, G. H. Bower, and N. Frijda (eds.), *Cognitive Perspectives on Emotion and Motivation* (Dordrecht: Cluver), 423–41.

Harries, M., Mistlin, A. J., and Chitty, A. J. (1990), 'Three Stages in the Classification of Body Movements by Visual Neurons', in H. Barlow, C. Blakemore, and M. Weston-Smith (eds.), *Images and Understanding* (Cambridge: Cambridge University Press), 94–107.

Havelock, E. A. (1963), *Preface to Plato* (Oxford: Basil Blackwell).

Hayward, P. (1988), 'The Moonlighting Story', *Mediamatic*, 2/4.

Heath, R. G. (1986), 'The Neural Substrate for Emotion', in R. Plutchik (ed.), *Emotion: Theory, Research and Experience*, iii (New York: Academic Press), 3–35.

Heath, S. (1981), *Questions of Cinema* (Bloomington, Ind.: Indiana University Press).

—— (1985; first publ. 1976), '*Jaws*, Ideology and Film Theory', in T. Bennett, S. Boyd-Bowman, C. Mercer, and J. Wollacott (eds.), *Popular Television and Film* (London: British Film Institute), 200–5.

Henry, J. P. (1986), 'Neuroendochrine Patterns of Emotional Response', in R. Plutchik and H. Kellerman (eds.), *Emotion: Theory, Research and Experience*, iii (New York: Academic Press), 37–60.

Hobson, J. A. (1988), *The Dreaming Brain* (New York: Basic Books).

Hochberg, J. E. (2nd edn., 1978), *Perception* (Englewood Cliffs, NJ: Prentice Hall).

Hogan, D. (1986), *Dark Romance: Sex and Death in the Horror Film* (Jefferson, NC: McFarland).

Holenstein, E. (1995), 'Human Equality and Intra- as well as Intercultural Diversity', *The Monist*, 78/1 (La Salle, Ill.: Hegler Institute), 65–78.

Holub, R. C. (1984), *Reception Theory: A Critical Introduction* (New York: Methuen).

Horowitz, M. J. (1978; first publ. 1970), *Image Formation and Cognition* (New York: Appleton-Century-Crofts).

Horton, A. S. (ed.) (1991), *Comedy/Cinema/Theory* (Berkeley: University of California Press).

Humphreys, G. W., and Bruce, V. (1989), *Visual Cognition: Computational, Experimental and Neuropsychological Perspectives* (Hove: Lawrence Erlbaum Associates).

Izard, C. E. (1991), *The Psychology of Emotions* (New York: Plenum Press).

Iser, W. (1978; first publ. 1976), *The Act of Reading: A Theory of Aesthetic Response* (Baltimore: John Hopkins University Press).

Jackendoff, R. (1987), *Consciousness and the Computational Mind* (Cambridge, Mass.: MIT Press).

Jakobson, R. (1956), 'Two Aspects of Language and Two Types of Aphasic Disturbances', in R. Jakobson and M. Halle, *Fundamentals of Language* (The Hague: Mouton), 55–82.

—— (1960), 'Linguistics and Poetics', in T. Sebeok (ed.), *Style in Language* (Cambridge, Mass.: MIT Press), 350–77.

Jameson, F. (1983), 'Postmodernism and Consumer Culture', in H. Foster (ed.), *The Anti-Aesthetic: Essays on Postmodern Culture* (Port Townsend: Bay Press), 111–25.

Jauss, H. R. (1982), *Aesthetic Experience and Literary Hermeneutics* (Minneapolis: University of Minnesota Press).

Johnson, M. (1987), *The Body in the Mind: The Bodily Basis of Meaning, Imagination and Reason* (Chicago: University of Chicago Press).

Johnson-Laird, P. (1988), *The Computer and the Mind: An Introduction to Cognitive Science* (Glasgow: Fontana Press).

Kant, I. (1987; first publ. 1790), *Critique of Judgement* (Indianapolis: Indiana Hackett).

Kaufmann, G. (1990), 'Imagery Effects on Problem Solving', in P. J. Hampson, D. F. Marks, and J. T. E. Richardson (eds.), *Imagery: Current Developments* (London: Routledge), 169–96.

Kazanskij, B. (1981), 'The Nature of Cinema', in H. Eagle, *Russian Formalist Film Theory* (Ann Arbor: University of Michigan Press), 101–29.

Keane, M. E. (1986), 'A Closer Look at Scopophilia: Mulvey, Hitchcock, and *Vertigo*', in M. Deutelbaum and L. Poage (eds.), *A Hitchcock Reader* (Ames, Ia.: Iowa State University Press), 231–48.

Kentridge, R. W., and Aggleton, J. W. (1990), 'Emotion: Sensory Representation, Reinforcement and The Temporal Lobe', in A. Gray (ed.), *Psychobiological Aspects of Relationships Between Emotion and Cognition* (Hove: Lawrence Erlbaum Associates), 191–208.

Kern, S. (1983), *The Culture of Time and Space 1880–1918* (Cambridge, Mass.: Harvard University Press).

Knight, S. (1980), *Form and Ideology in Crime Fiction* (London: Macmillan).

Kolb, B., and Whishaw, I. O. (1990), *Fundamentals of Human Neuropsychology* (New York: W. H. Freeman).

Kosslyn, S. M. (1980), *Image and Mind* (Cambridge, Mass.: Harvard University Press).

—— (1983), *Ghosts in the Mind's Machine* (New York: Norton).

—— (1994), *Image and Brain: The Resolution of the Imagery Debate* (Cambridge, Mass.: MIT Press).

Kozloff, S. (1988), *Invisible Storytellers: Voice-over Narration in American Fiction Film* (Berkeley, Los Angeles: University of California Press).

Kracauer, S. (1961; first publ. 1960), *The Nature of Film: The Redemption of Physical Reality* (London: Oxford University Press).

—— (1971; first publ. 1947), *From Caligari to Hitler: A Psychological History of the German Film* (Princeton: Princeton University Press).

Krutnik, F. (1991), *In a Lonely Street: Film Noir, Genre, Masculinity* (London: Routledge).

Kuleshov, L. (1974), *Kuleshov on Film: Writings by Lev Kuleshov*, ed. R. Levaco (Berkeley: University of California Press).

Lacan, J. (1977), *Ecrits: A Selection* (New York: W. C. Norton; first pub. as *Écrits*, Paris 1966).

Lakoff, G. (1987), *Women, Fire and Dangerous Things: What Categories Reveal about the Mind* (Chicago: University of Chicago Press).

—— and Johnson, M. (1980), *Metaphors We Live By* (Chicago: University of Chicago Press).

Lämmert, E. (1965), *Bauformen des erzählens* (Stuttgart: Metzler).

Lang, R. (1987), *American Film Melodrama: Griffith, Vidor, Minelli* (Princeton Princeton University Press).

Larsen, P. (1990), 'Beyond the Narrative: Rock Videos and Modern Visual Fictions', in M. Skovmand (ed.), *Media Fictions* (Aarhus: Seklos/Aarhus University Press), 21–34.

de Lauretis, T. (1984), *Alice Doesn't: Feminism, Semiotics, Cinema* (Bloomington, Ind.: Indiana University Press).

Lévi-Strauss, C. (1967), *Structural Anthropology* (Garden City, NY: Doubleday).

—— (1966), *The Savage Mind* (Chicago: University of Chicago Press).

Lazarus, R. S. (1991), *Emotion and Adaptation* (Oxford: Oxford University Press).

Lycan, W. G. (ed.) (1990), *Mind and Cognition: A Reader* (Cambridge, Mass.: Basil Blackwell).

Loewe, D. M. (1982), *History of Bourgeois Perception* (Chicago: University of Chicago Press).

MacLean, P. D. (1986), 'Ictal Symptoms Relating to the Nature of Affects and Their Cerebral Substrate', in R. Plutchik and H. Kellerman (eds.), *Emotion: Theory, Research, and Experience*, iii (New York: Academic Press), 61–90.

Malmo, R. B. (1975), *On Emotions, Needs and Our Archaic Brain* (New York: Holt, Rinehart and Winston).

Mandel, E. (1984), *Delightful Murder: A Social History of the Crime Story* (London: Pluto Press).

Mandler, J. M. (1984), *Stories, Scripts and Scenes: Aspects of Schema Theory* (Hillsdale, NJ : Lawrence Erlbaum Associates).

Marr, D. (1982), *Vision: A Computational Investigation into the Human Representation and Processing of Visual Information* (San Fransisco: W. H. Freeman).

Mast, G. (1979), *The Comic Mind: Comedy and the Movies* (2nd edn., Chicago: University of Chicago Press).

Mayer, R. E. (1983), *Thinking, Problem Solving, Cognition* (New York: W. H. Freeman).

Merleau-Ponty, M. (1962; first publ. 1945), *Phenomenology of Perception*, trans. Colin Smith (London: Routledge and Kegan Paul).

Messaris, P. (1994), *Visual Literacy: Image, Mind, and Reality* (Boulder, Colo: Westview Press).

Metz, C. (1966), 'La Grande Syntagmatique du film narratif', in *Communications*, 8 (Paris): 120–4.

—— (1972), *Essais sur la signification au cinéma*, ii (Paris: Kliencksieck).

—— (1974*a*; first publ. 1968), *Film Language: A Semiotics of the Cinema* (New York: Oxford University Press).

—— (1974*b*), *Language and Cinema* (The Hague: Mouton).

—— (1982; first publ. 1977), *The Imaginary Signifier* (Bloomington: Indiana University Press).

—— (1986), *Essais sur la signification au cinéma*, ii (Paris: Kliencksieck).

—— (1991), *L'Énonciation impersonelle ou le site du film* (Paris: Klienksieck).

Miller G. A. (1956), 'The Magical Number Seven, Plus or Minus Two: Some Limits on our Capacity for Processing Information', *Psychological Review*, 63: 81–97.

Minsky, M. (1988; first publ. 1985), *The Society of Mind* (New York: Simon and Schuster).

Mitry, J. (1963, 1965), *Esthétique et psychologie du cinéma*, i–ii (Paris: Presses Universitaires).

—— (1987), *La Sémiologie en question* (Paris: Editions Universitaires).

—— (1990), *Esthétique et psychologie du cinéma* (Paris: Editions Universitaires).

Modleski, T. (1988), *The Women Who Knew Too Much: Hitchcock and Feminist Theory* (New York: Routledge).

Monaco, J. (1977), *How to Read a Film: The Technology, Language, History and Theory of Film and Media* (New York: Oxford University Press).

Morin, E. (1985; first publ. 1956), *Le Cinéma ou l'homme imaginaire: essai d'anthropologie* (Paris: Éditions de Minuit).

Morley, D., and Silverstone, R. (1991), 'Communication and Context: Ethnographic Perspectives on the Media Audience', in K. B. Jensen and N. W. Jankowski (eds.), *A Handbook of Qualitative Methodologies for Mass Communication Research* (London: Routledge), 149–62.

Motley, M. T. (1993), 'Facial Affect and Verbal Context in Conversation', *Human Communication Research*, 20/1: 3–40.

Movshon, A. (1990), 'Visual Processing of Moving Images', in H. Barlow, C. Blakemore, and M. Weston-Smith (eds.), *Images and Understanding* (Cambridge: Cambridge University Press), 122–39.

Mulvey, L. (1975), 'Visual Pleasure and Narrative Cinema', *Screen*, 16/3; repr. in L. Mulvey (1989), *Visual and Other Pleasures* (Bloomington, Ind.: Indiana University Press), 14–26.

Münsterberg, H. (1970; first publ. 1916), *The Film: A Psychological Study* (New York: Dover).

Neale, S. (1980), *Genre* (London: British Film Institute).

—— (1990), 'Questions of Genre', *Screen*, 31/1 (Spring): 45–66.

—— and Krutnik, F. (1990), *Popular Film and Television Comedy* (London: Routledge).

Nichols, B. (1981), *Ideology and the Image: Social Representation in the Cinema and Other Media* (Bloomington, Ind.: Indiana University Press).

Norman, D. A. (1976), *Memory and Attention: An Introduction to Human Information Processing* (New York: Wiley).

Nowell-Smith, G. (1977), 'Minelli and Melodrama', *Screen*, 18/2; repr. in Gledhill (1987), 70–4.

Olsen, R. S. (1987), 'Meta-Television: Popular Postmodernism', *Critical Studies in Mass Communication*, 4: 284–300.

Olson, E. (1968), *The Theory of Comedy* (Bloomington, Ind.: Indiana University Press).

Ong, W. (1982), *Orality and Literacy* (London: Methuen).

Ornstein, R. E. (1972), *The Psychology of Consciousness* (San Fransisco.: W. H. Freeman).

Ortony, A., Clore, G. L., and Collins, A. (1990; first publ. 1988), *The Cognitive Structure of Emotions* (Cambridge: Cambridge University Press).

Paivio, A. (1966), *Mental Representations* (Oxford: Oxford University Press).

Palmer, J. (1978), *Thrillers: Genesis and Structure of a Popular Genre* (London: Edward Arnold).

—— (1987), *The Logic of the Absurd: On Film and Television Comedy* (London: British Film Institute).

Panofsky, E. (1955), *Meaning in the Visual Arts* (Garden City, NY: Doubleday).

Perkins, V. F. (1974; first publ. 1972), *Film as Film: Understanding and Judging Movies* (Harmondsworth: Penguin Books).

Perret, D., Harries, M., Mistlin, A. J., and Chitty, A. J. (1990), 'Three Stages in the Classification of Body Movements by Visual Neurons', in H. Barlow, C. Blakemore, and M. Weston-Smith (eds.), *Images and Understanding* (Cambridge: Cambridge University Press).

Peterson, J. (1994), *Dreams of Chaos, Visions of Order: Understanding the American Avant-Garde Cinema* (Detroit: Wayne State University Press).

Petric, V. (ed.) (1981), *Film and Dreams: An Approach to Bergman* (South Salem, NY: Redgrave).

Place, J. A., and Peterson, L. S. (1976), 'Some Visual Motives in *Film Noir*', in B. Nichols (ed.), *Movies and Methods* (Berkeley: University of California Press), 325–38.

Plantinga, C. (1994), 'Affect, Cognition, and the Power of Movies', *Post Script*, 13/1: 10–29.

Plutchnik, R. (1980), 'A General Psychoevolutionary Theory of Emotion', in R. Plutchnik and H. Kellerman (eds.), *Emotion: Theory, Research and Experience*, iii–xxxi (New York: Academic Press).

Pribram, K. (1982), 'Brain Mechanism in Music', in Clynes, M. (ed.), *Music, Mind and Brain: The Neuropsychology of Music* (New York: Plenum Press), 21–35.

Propp, V. (1968), *Morphology of the Folktale* (Austin, Tex.: University of Texas Press).

Pudovkin, V. I. (1970; first publ. 1949), *Film Technique and Film Acting* (New York: Grove Press).

Punter, D. (1980), *The Literature of Terror: A History of Gothic Fictions from 1765 to the Present Day* (London: Longman).

Reisz, K., and Millar, G. (1968), *The Technique of Film Editing* (2nd edn., London: Focal Press).

Richoeur, P. (1981), 'Narrative Time', in W. J. T. Mitchell (ed.), *On Narrative* (Chicago: University of Chicago Press), 165–86.

Riesman, D. (1950), *The Lonely Crowd* (New Haven: Yale University Press).

Rimmon-Kenan, S. (1987; first publ. 1983), *Narrative Fiction: Contemporary Poetics* (London: Methuen).

Schachter, S. (1971), *Emotion, Obesity and Crime* (New York: Academic Press).

Schank, R. C. (1990), *Tell Me a Story: A New Look at Real and Artificial Memory* (New York: Scribner).

—— and Abelson, R. (1977), *Scripts, Plans, Goals and Understanding: An Inquiry into Human Knowledge Structures* (Hillsdale, NJ: Lawrence Erlbaum Associates).

Schatz, T. (1981), *Hollywood Genres: Formulas, Filmmaking, and the Studio System* (Philadelphia: Temple University Press).

Scherer, K. R. (1994), 'Emotion Serves to Decouple Stimulus and Response', in P. Ekman and R. J. Davidson (eds.), *The Nature of Emotion* (New York: Oxford University Press).

Searle, J. (1969), *Speech Acts: An Essay in the Philosophy of Language* (Cambridge: Cambridge University Press).

—— (1984), *Minds, Brains and Science* (Cambridge, Mass.: Harvard University Press).

Shallice, T. (1988), *From Neuropsychology to Mental Structure* (Cambridge: Cambridge University Press).

Silverman, K. (1983), *The Subject of Semiotics* (Oxford: Oxford University Press).

Sklovskij, V. (2nd edn., 1965; first publ. 1929), *Theorie der Prosa* (Frankfurt am Main: S. Fischer).

Sobshack, V. (1992), *The Address of the Eye: A Phenomenology of Film Experience* (Princeton: Princeton University Press).

Spelke, E. S. (1990), 'Origins of Visual Knowledge', in D. N. Osherson, S. M. Kosslyn, and J. M. Hollerbach (eds.), *Visual Cognition and Action* (Cambridge, Mass.: MIT Press), 99–127.

Spoto, D. (1983), *The Dark Side of Genius: The Life of Alfred Hitchcock* (Boston: Little, Brown).

Stam, R., and Pearson, R. (1983), 'Hitchcock's *Rear Window*: Reflexivity and the Critique of Voyeurism; repr. in M. Deutelbaum and L. Poage (1986), *A Hitchcock Reader* (Ames, Ia.: Iowa State University Press).

Stam, R., Burgoyne, R., and Flitterman-Lewis, S. (1992), *New Vocabularies in Film Semiotics: Structuralism, Post-Structuralism and Beyond* (London: Routledge).

Stanzel, F. (1955), *Die Typischen Erzählsituationen im Roman* (Vienna and Stuttgart: Wilhelm Braumüller).

Steinweg, R. (1972), *Das Lehrstück Brechts: Theorie einer politisch-ästhetischen Erziehung* (Stuttgart: J. B. Metzler).

Sundberg, J. (1982), 'Speech, Song, and Emotions', in M. Clynes (ed.), *Music, Mind, and Brain: The Neuropsychology of Music* (New York: Plenum Press), 137–49.

Taylor, H. (1989), *Gone With the Wind and Its Female Fans* (New Brunswick, NJ: Rutgers University Press).

Thompson, K. (1988), *Breaking the Glass Armor* (Princeton: Princeton University Press).

Todorov, T. (ed.) (1965), *Théorie de la littérature* (Paris: Edition du Seuil).

—— (1966), 'Les catégories du récit littéraire', *Communications*, 8 (Paris).

—— (1975; first publ. 1970), *The Fantastic: A Structural Approach to a Literary Genre* (Ithaca, NY: Cornell University Press).

Tomachevski, B. (1925), 'Thematique', in Todorov (1965).

Truffaut, F. (1984; first publ. 1966), *Hitchcock* (New York: Simon and Schuster).

Twitchell, J. B. (1985), *Dreadful Pleasures: An Anatomy of Modern Horror* (New York: Oxford University Press).

Van Dijk, T. A. (1980), *Macrostructures: An Interdisciplinary Study of Global Structures in Discourse, Interaction, and Cognition* (Hillsdale, NJ: Lawrence Erlbaum Associates).

—— and Kintsch, W. (1983), *Strategies of Discourse Comprehension* (New York: Academic Press).

Vincent, J.-D. (1990; first publ. 1986), *The Biology of Emotions* (Oxford: Blackwell).

Vygotsky, L. (1986), *Thought and Language* (Cambridge, Mass.: MIT Press).

Waugh, P. (1984), *Metafiction: The Theory and Practice of Self-Conscious Fiction* (London: Methuen).

Weisstein, N., and Wong, E. (1987), 'Figure-Ground Organization Affects the Early Visual Processing of Information, in M. A. Arbib and A. R. Hanson, *Vision, Brain and Cooperative Computation* (Cambridge, Mass.: MIT Press), 209–30.

Wellek, R. (1955), *A History of Modern Criticism (1750–1950)* (New Haven: Yale University Press).

Wendorff, R. (1980), *Zeit und Kultur* (Wiesbaden: Westdeutscher Verlag).

Willats, I. (1990), 'The Draughtsman's Contract: How an Artist Creates an Image', in H. Barlow, C. Blakemore, and M. Weston-Smith (eds.), *Images and Understanding* (Cambridge: Cambridge University Press), 235–54.

Wimsatt, W. K. (1949), 'The Affective Fallacy', *Sewanee Review*, 57 (Winter); repr. in *The Verbal Icon* (1966; New York: Noonday Press), 21–39.

Winnicott, D. W. (1971), *Playing and Reality* (London: Tavistock).

Winograd, T., and Flores, F. (1986), *Understanding Computers and Cognition* (Norwood, NJ: Ablex).

Wollen, P. (1972), *Signs and Meaning in the Cinema* (Bloomington, Ind.: Indiana University Press).

—— (1986), 'Godard and Counter-Cinema: *Vent d'Est*', *Afterimage*, 4 (1972); repr. in P. Rosen (ed.), *Narrative, Apparatus, Ideology: A Film Theory Reader* (New York: Columbia University Press), 120–9.

Wood, R. (1986), *Hollywood from Vietnam to Reagan* (New York: Columbia University Press).

—— (1991; first publ. 1989), *Hitchcock's Films Revisited* (London: Columbia University Press).

Woody, C. D. (1982), *Memory, Learning and Higher Function: A Cellular View* (New York: Springer Verlag).

Zeki, S. (1993), *A Vision of the Brain* (London: Blackwell).

Zillmann, D. (1991), 'Empathy: Affect From Bearing Witness to the Emotions of Others', in Bryant and Zillmann (1991), 135–67.

Index